SOVIET ECONOMY AND SOCIETY

DAVID LANE

Soviet Economy and Society

NEW YORK UNIVERSITY PRESS
WASHINGTON SQUARE, NEW YORK

© David Lane, 1985

First published in 1985 in the USA by
New York University Press,
Washington Square, New York, N.Y. 10003

Library of Congress Cataloging in Publication Data

Lane, David Stuart.
  Soviet economy and society
  Includes index.
  1. Soviet Union—Economic conditions—1918—
  2. Soviet Union—Social conditions—Social conditions—
  1917—
  I. Title
  HC336.L29 1984   306'.0947   84-16523
  ISBN 0-8147-5015-X
  ISBN 0-8147-5016-8 (pbk.)

Printed in Great Britain by T.J. Press Ltd., Padstow

CONTENTS

LIST OF TABLES

LIST OF DIAGRAMS AND MAPS

PREFACE

This book has grown out of an earlier work, *Politics and Society in the USSR*, published fourteen years ago. Reflecting the more open nature of Soviet society and the greater availability of information, there are now two books instead of one. Each book is self-contained. The present volume is in two parts: the first on the economy and the second on the social structure. It is intended for students of sociology, economics, social studies and Soviet society. The companion volume, *State and Politics in the USSR*, deals principally with recent history, Marxist-Leninist ideology, political institutions and processes and is intended primarily for students reading politics, political sociology, history and Soviet studies. Both volumes, however, are written in a style which should be accessible to non-specialist readers who wish to be acquainted with modern Soviet society, its history and contemporary structure.

Among the most crucial problems of writing a book about the USSR are those of selection and emphasis. Here the Soviet Union is depicted as a modernizing industrial society, and those past events and policies have been selected which elucidate the present and, hopefully, point to the future. I have attempted to describe the Soviet Union both in terms of its own theory and in accounts of Western writing on the subject. It is hoped that the book will enhance a more comparative approach to the study of society: not only to bring home to Soviet 'area specialists' the fact that Soviet society is in many ways like other industrial societies, but also to awaken the interests of sociologists and others to the problems of 'directed' social change and to the structure of a command or state socialist society.

The book has the following plan. In Chapter 1 are outlined the structure of the economy, the bodies involved in planning, the nature of management and trade unions, the role of the party in industry and the problem of control. In Chapter 2, the performance of the economy, the rate of economic growth and the levels of living standards are discussed and various approaches to economic reforms are outlined. In the final chapter on the economy, contemporary Western Marxist critiques of economy and society are considered in addition to the Soviet notion of 'developed socialism'.

In Part 2, the subject of inquiry is the social system. In Chapter 4 is outlined the changing pattern of population and the family. In Chapter 5 I focus on social classes and strata (including gender divisions). There follow individual chapters on nationalities and ethnic relations, the Christian religion, and the structure and functioning of educational institutions. In all these chapters, an historical introduction shows how such aspects of Soviet life have changed since the October Revolution under the impact of Marxist ideology. An attempt is made to distinguish between social phenomena which might be shaped by ideology, those of a 'traditional' kind and processes which may be called into being by the exigencies of an industrial society. It is my contention that many of the practices and institutions of the contemporary USSR have antecedents in traditional Russian culture.

I have appended population statistics and a number of documents which illustrate discussion made in the text. Wherever possible, I have referred to English language sources so that the widest possible range of readers may use them. The bibliographies at the end of each part are intended to systematize references given in the text and may be used for more detailed study. I am indebted to many people for helping me to complete this book: some are mentioned in footnotes to specific chapters, my thanks also to June Brough and Diane Davies who did most of the typing.

David Lane

THE UNION OF SOVIET SOCIALIST REPUBLICS

ICELAND

SCOTLAND

ARCTIC OCEAN

WRANGEL I.

Kamchatka Peninsula

SAKHALIN

JAPAN

Vladivostok

SEA OF JAPAN

Okhotsk

Khabarovsk

CHINA

NEW SIBERIAN IS.

SEVERNAYA ZEMLYA

Verkhoyansk

Yakutsk

Y A K U T S K   A. S. S. R.

Vilyuisk

R.

S.

F.

S.

BURYAT A.S.S.R.

Ulan-Ude

Lake Baikal

Irkutsk

TUVIN A.S.S.R.

MONGOLIA

Igarka

Krasnoyarsk

Tomsk

Novosibirsk

NOVAYA ZEMLYA

Salekhard

Tobolsk

Omsk

Karaganda

CHINA

FINLAND

KARELIA A.S.S.R.

Archangel

White Sea

Onega

Ladoga

Volga

KOMI A.S.S.R.

Syktyvkar

R.

S.

Lake Balkash

Alma Ata

KHIRGIZ S.S.R.

AFGHANISTAN

Leningrad

MOSCOW

R.

Gorky

10

Kazan

Ufa

9

Perm

Sverdlovsk

K A Z A K H S T A N

Karsakpai

S. S. R.

ARAL SEA

Tashkent

UZBEKISTAN S.S.R.

KARA-KALPAK A.S.S.R.

Riga

POLAND

Minsk

BYELORUSSIA S.S.R.

6

5

Kuibyshev

Volgograd

Guryev

20

Astrakhan

TURKMENISTAN S.S.R.

Ashkabad

Kiev

UKRAINE S.S.R.

Kharkov

Rostov

CASPIAN SEA

Baku

Odessa

BLACK SEA

11

15

13

Tbilisi

16

17

19

18

Batumi

12

ROMANIA

TURKEY

PERSIA

0   500

Miles

1   Lithuania S.S.R.
2   Latvia S.S.R.
3   Estonia S.S.R.
4   Moldavia S.S.R.
5   Mordvinia A.S.S.R.
6   Chuvash A.S.S.R.
7   Mari A.S.S.R.
8   Tatar A.S.S.R.
9   Udmurt A.S.S.R.
10 Bashkir A.S.S.R.

11 Abkhaz A.S.S.R.
12 Adzhar A.S.S.R.
13 Kabardin A.S.S.R.
14 North Osetia A.S.S.R.
15 Georgia S.S.R.
16 Dagestan A.S.S.R.
17 Armenia S.S.R.
18 Nakhicheva A.S.S.R.
19 Azerbaidzhan S.S.R.
20 Kalmyt A.S.S.R.

Part I
ECONOMY

1

PLANNING AND ADMINISTERING THE ECONOMIC SYSTEM

The economy of a society has a pivotal position for all social scientists. For Marxists, not only is the economy a font of wealth but its character defines the mode of production. In this chapter we shall consider the major structural features of the Soviet economy and in the next we shall turn to its performance and to proposals for reform. At the outset we may distinguish between a 'capitalist' and a 'communist' economic order. The economy under capitalism has the following features: capital-intensive production, private ownership, competition between firms, production for the market (for exchange), wage labour and the extraction of surplus value or profit. Save for a very high level of capital-intensive production, an ideal communist economy would have none of these features. It would be characterized by collective ownership, a rational system of production and exchange, and the production of use values meeting people's needs; there would be an abundance of goods, and money would not be necessary; individuals would work 'according to their ability' and receive 'according to their needs'. No one would claim that the Soviet economy is a communist one in this sense. It is variously called by its own theorists and supporters 'transitional', 'socialist', 'developed socialist', 'command', 'planned' and 'collectivist'. Some critical commentators even dub the Soviet Union 'state capitalist' or 'bureaucratic collectivist'. We shall turn in chapter 3 below to discuss some of these concepts.

The label adopted in this book is that of 'state socialist'. It is 'socialist' in the narrow sense that capitalist ownership has been abolished through the nationalization of property. Social ownership of the means of production rests with the Soviet state (party and government), which seeks to direct the economy. Under state socialism, ministries and local authorities manage production enterprises. Prices and output of individual firms are largely determined by central or regional boards. Industries and their sub-units (enterprises) operate like ministries in Western countries. Profits and losses accrue to the state exchequer. It is preferable to call such a system 'state socialism' and reserve the term 'state capitalism' for societies in which industry is privately owned but state controlled (such as in Britain or Germany during the Second World War). This conforms to the generally accepted distinction between capitalism being based on private ownership and socialism on public, or state, ownership.[1]

The Soviet economy is an 'administered' or 'command' economy in which the influence of individual consumers and producers is replaced by administrative bodies, which make decisions for the whole economy. These determine what and how much is to be produced and the price at which things must be sold. This entails decisions by the central planners about which goods are to be produced. In industry, all prices (of goods and labour) are fixed by the planners. The state monopoly of production, distribution and exchange replaces the market, and, as a result, the consumer is less powerful in the USSR than his counterpart in the West. Such a stark model is modified in practice. We shall see that, though the Soviet economy is predominantly of the 'command' type, market elements exist.

The fundamental distinction between a capitalist 'market' economy and a Soviet 'command' one is that in the former, in theory, individual interests are dominant, the state providing mechanisms to promote them; in the latter case, collective or state interest is dominant, the government acting to prevent the sovereignty of individual interests. In a 'free economy' property is privately owned, and the state intervenes to protect the consumer and worker against exploitation. In a 'command' or state socialist economy, property is communally owned, and the state directly controls the economy. As Galbraith[2] has pointed out, this is not to say that contemporary Western societies are composed of small competing private businesses: many large American corporations are closely geared to the demands of the government. But Western societies contain a large number of private businesses, small manufacturers, retail shops, garages, farms, which depend on the market and give consumer demand a power unknown in Soviet society. The large Western manufacturer also produces for the market with the objective of sale for profit.

After the October Revolution in 1917, government control in the USSR was ensured by the nationalization of industry and the land. It is now illegal for one person to employ another for trade or production. Ownership is vested in the state, and control in government ministries. There are, however, important areas of economic activity which are outside direct government control. There is a 'co-operative' sector and a small private sector, and various types of markets exist through which resources are allocated. The collective farm (*kolkhoz*) is technically a form of co-operative production governed by its members, but working within the confines of the economic plan. There are also private plots of land, which are leased to farmers and from which produce is freely traded on the market for prices determined by supply and demand. Some of the produce from collective farms is also sold in this way. There is a small co-operative industrial sector, which is based on the group activity of a number of workers who own and market their produce. Individual craftsmen (cobblers, watch repairers) and some professional specialists (dentists, doctors) can still give private services – provided that they are registered. Secretaries and domestic helps may be hired privately. In addition, there is the illegal and semi-legal production and provision of services; the so-called 'second economy'. This is economic activity which is unplanned and unregulated by the state. It ranges from workers utilizing government materials to do repairs 'on the side', to black markets in illegally imported foreign goods.

The System of Planning and Economic Administration

Centralized planning, however, directly affects industrial enterprises and 'state' farms (not 'collective' farms). The government decides what shall be produced and what proportion of output is devoted to consumption and investment; it is responsible for fixing the price of inputs (raw materials and basic wage rates) and outputs (finished and semi-finished products). The enormous task involved in central planning may be illustrated by the fact that from eight to nine million prices have to be fixed by the many price control organs located in the various planning departments.[3] It has been estimated by Soviet researchers that in the mid-1960s, the Soviet apparatus performed some ten thousand fewer operations than were needed for efficient managment.[4] Soviet planning is sometimes called 'directive planning', indicating that plans are obligatory on management, unlike the 'indicative planning' adopted by Western governments, which aims to influence the economy indirectly. The forces of supply and demand also operate in the Soviet economy. The work force is recruited by the enterprises, and workers can usually change their place of work at will. (This does not apply to collective farmers, and residence in most cities is controlled.) Most of the retail trade operates on market principles in that, though prices are fixed, consumers may allocate their money to satisfy their own preferences.

The Soviet centrally planned economy is organized around four concepts: planning, administration, juridical regulation and control.[5] The planning departments devise the form that economic activity should take in the production enterprises, e.g. the rate of growth, the price and amounts of inputs and outputs. But such organs do not actually run enterprises. The administration is composed of an apparatus which guides productive and distributive units. The methods used are not simply coercive; rather, enterprises are put in a position in which it is 'in their interest' to execute the plan. The courts, guided by legislation, regulate the relationships between enterprises and administrative bodies. Lastly, control refers to the political organizations (such as the party, people's control units and unions) which seek to ensure that the economy is regulated in keeping with the political goals articulated by the Soviet state.

It is the Soviet government that directs the economy. Under the government are numerous committees which do the planning and there are ministries which see that plans are carried out. In addition the Communist Party exercises leadership and control. Let us consider these institutions in turn: first, planning; second, execution of plans; third, the role of the party.

Policy is elaborated by the various committees on all aspects of the economy – foreign economic relations, prices, construction, supplies, labour. There are in all twenty-three committees, the most important of which are shown on Diagram 1.1. Gosplan, the state planning committee, is responsible for co-ordinating the preparation of various types of plans, both short- and long-term. The 1976–1990 plan, for example, attempted to take account of developments in the countries of Comecon (Council for Mutual Economic Assistance: including the countries of Bulgaria, Cuba, Czechoslovakia, German Democratic Republic, Hungary, Mongolia, Poland, Romania, Vietnam and USSR). Forecasts of trends in consumption and investments and plans for scientific-technical developments for the USSR in relation to its economic allies are also made here.

The most comprehensive detailed planning is embodied in the Five-Year Plans. The Eleventh Five-Year Plan covers the year 1981 to 1985. It defines targets for growth of various aspects of the economy, and has sections on agriculture, industry, communications, geographical areas, foreign economic relations and living standards. The plan is concocted after the working out of problems by the various committees and discussion in the party and government apparatuses. The Five-Year Plans include detailed projections for economic enterprise, with targets or 'control figures' for developments during the five-year period with breakdowns by year. These cover production and sales, investment, wages and labour, profit, incentives, technical developments and productivity, and a financial plan. The details are worked out in consultations between the various committees, the bank and the ministries to which the enterprise is subordinate.

In addition, operational plans are worked out on a one-year basis. Ministries and enterprises work to detailed targets covering inputs of

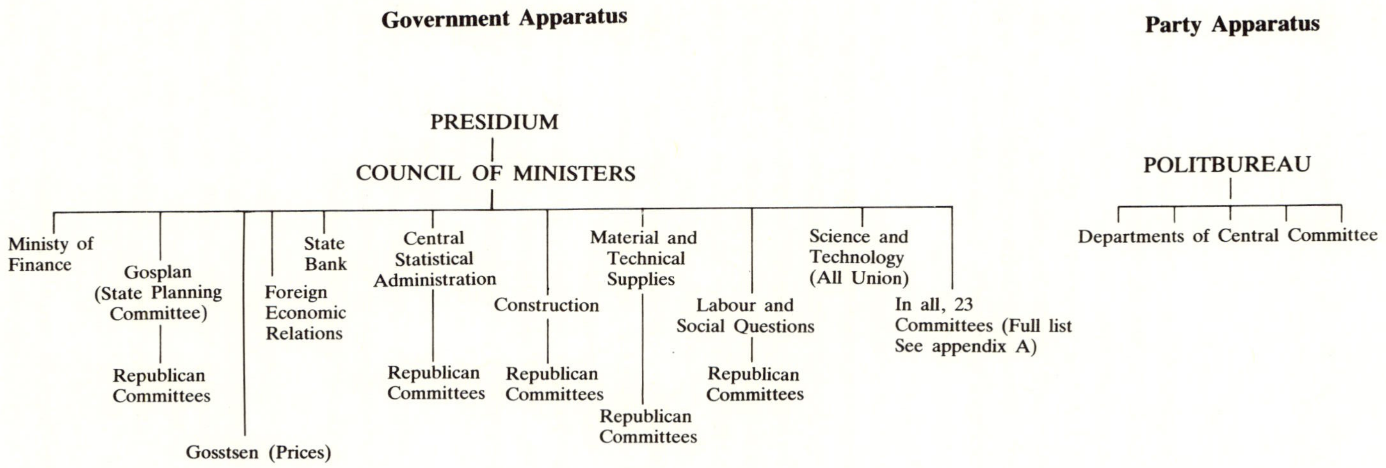

Government Apparatus

Party Apparatus

PRESIDIUM

POLITBUREAU

COUNCIL OF MINISTERS

Departments of Central Committee

Ministry of Finance

Gosplan (State Planning Committee)

State Bank

Foreign Economic Relations

Central Statistical Administration

Material and Technical Supplies

Labour and Social Questions

Science and Technology (All Union)

Construction

Republican Committees

Republican Committees

Republican Committees

Republican Committees

Republican Committees

Gosstsen (Prices)

In all, 23 Committees (Full list See appendix A)

DIAGRAM 1.1: CHIEF ECONOMIC PLANNING AGENCIES

materials, a wages fund, and the specification of outputs. The annual plans are again divided with targets for each quarter and month.

The Execution of Plans

The organizations responsible for the execution of plans are ministries. There are two principles on which the administration of the economy is organized: sectoral and territorial. The sectoral principle has as its criterion a particular branch of the economy – coal, steel, textiles, aviation, argiculture – each of which is the responsibility of one of the ministries. Betweeen 1928 and 1957, the Soviet economy was organized on this principle, with All-Union ministries headquartered in Moscow running affairs throughout the whole of the USSR (hence 'All-Union'). By contrast, the territorial principle has as its frame of reference a given geographical area and administration pertains to a mixture of economic activities in that area. Between 1957 and 1965 many of the activities previously carried out by All-Union ministries were handed over to the Sovnarkhozy, or Regional Economic Councils. The country was divided into 104 geographical units, each having such a council. Their role was to co-ordinate industrial activity and to prevent wasteful transfers between areas. Excluded from the Councils' orbit were agriculture, much of capital construction and industries concerned with defence. In 1965, the Councils were abolished and replaced by a two-tier arrangement of ministries, based on the sectoral or branch principle.

The 1965 reforms established two types of ministry: All-Union and Union-Republican. An All-Union ministry directly controls all the activity with which it is concerned in all the relevant republics of the USSR. The Union-Republican ministries are located in the various republics and are subordinate both to headquarters in Moscow and to the Council of Ministers of the republic. Outside this network and subordinate to the republican and local government authorities are republican industrial ministries. These include local building and transport, some food and local handicraft factories.

In 1984, All-Union ministries were 39 in number and included: the chemical industry, oil and gas, defence industry, electronics, heavy and transport machine building, machine tools, railways and shipbuilding. There are 46 Union-Republican ministries including: agriculture, coal mining, construction materials, ferrous metallurgy, fisheries, food, industrial construction and light industry. (The numbers mentioned above also include non-economic industries. For a full list, see Appendix A.) In 1981, the share of total production from enterprises controlled by All-Union ministries was 54 per cent; and from those controlled by Union-Republican and Republican ministries, 46 per cent.[6]

All enterprises (in their production, distribution and exchange functions) are subordinate to a ministry (exceptionally, some are under a state committee, such as television and international tourism). Once plans have been drawn up by Gosplan after consultation with the ministry, ministries in turn discuss projected plans with the directors of production enterprises. Enterprises' plans stipulate specific quantitative inputs and outputs, and the enterprise is legally obliged to fulfil these directives. That is, with so much resources of materials and labour[8], so many units of cars or tables must be produced. All the prices of inputs and outputs are defined by the plan. The administrative framework for state-planning in the USSR is shown in diagram 1.2. On the left of the diagram are the executive organs of government, in the middle the planning apparatus and to the right the party which is *not* part of the government.

Not all aspects of economic activity, however, are 'planned' by the government agencies. Minimum wages are fixed, but labour is not controlled: enterprises must recruit and retain their labour force; workers may change their job and their place of work, and frequently do so. The consumption of consumer goods is not 'planned': prices are fixed, but individuals are paid with money and can choose, as in the West, between the assortment of goods available. Moreover, since 1973, an attempt has been made to strengthen the initiative of enterprises and to reduce excessive central control by introducing various forms of 'horizontal' associations. Such 'trusts' handle sales and supply, and liaise with the higher organs like Gosplan. In addition, many industrial 'associations' (*ob'edinenie*) have been formed by merging many smaller enterprises into larger units.[7] (Soviet industrial establishments are large, even huge, by Western standards. In the USA, the average number of employees in industry (with the exception of power stations) is 48 per enterprise: in the USSR, it is 565; for machinery and metalworking enterprises the respective figures are 74 and 2,608.)[8] The various forms of devolution which have been practised in the USSR since the death of Stalin have weakened the ministries but have not seriously undermined their powers.

The economic ministries are important political entities. Almost the sole criterion for their success is fulfilment (or, preferably, overfulfilment) of their plans. At all levels, success and promotion follow 'plan fulfilment'. The ministries are, therefore, in a strong position *vis-à-vis* party organizations and groups which are supposed to exercise political leadership. Not only do they possess crucial organizational experience and 'know-how' in relation to certain areas of economic production, but they are legally responsible for carrying out the plans.

The threat posed by the economic ministries to 'political' groups located in the party is obvious. Confronted by the well-organized opposition of bureaucrats with the material means of the economic ministries at their

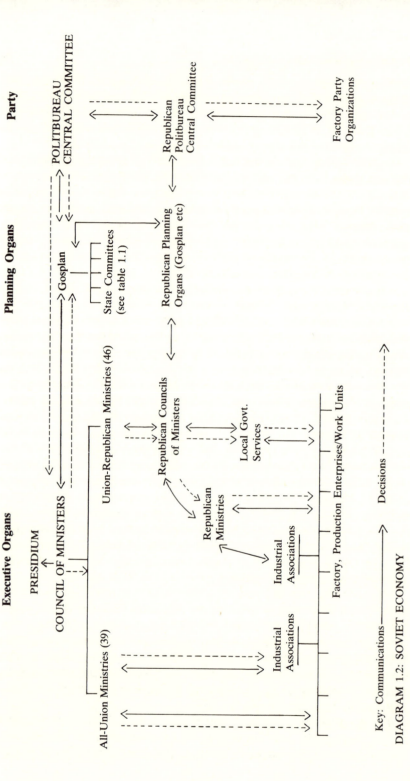

Executive Organs　　　**Planning Organs**　　　**Party**

PRESIDIUM

COUNCIL OF MINISTERS

POLITBUREAU
CENTRAL COMMITTEE

Gosplan

State Committees
(see table 1.1)

Union-Republican Ministries (46)

Republican Planning
Organs (Gosplan etc)

Republican
Politbureau
Central Committee

All-Union Ministries (39)

Republican Councils
of Ministers

Republican
Ministries

Local Govt.
Services

Industrial
Associations

Industrial
Associations

Factory, Production Enterprises/Work Units

Factory Party
Organizations

Key: Communications ———————>

Decisions – – – – – – – >

DIAGRAM 1.2: SOVIET ECONOMY

disposal, the party functionaries may lack not only technical expertise but also the specialized information to exercise control over the economy. It is unrealistic to argue that party control of only a few 'key' decisions is necessary. Decision-making involves competence, knowledge and the ability to pose alternatives, which only specialists possess.

As Max Weber has pointed out, bureaucracy is a 'power instrument of the first order – for the one who controls the bureaucratic apparatus . . . And where the bureaucratization of administration has been completely carried through, a form of power relation is established that is practically unshatterable.'[9] He concludes that 'the "political master" finds himself in the position of the "dilettante" who stands opposite the "expert", facing the trained official who stands within the management of administration.'[10]

If Weber is correct, this would suggest that ministries in the Soviet state are all-powerful, for they have control of financial means and are staffed by experts. Nevertheless, though it must be conceded that, within an economic ministry, the leading bureaucrats have much power, it would be wrong to categorize the USSR as one giant bureaucracy. The individual ministries have specific responsibilities. Their scope of interest is narrowly focused, and some general direction is still needed to balance the demands of one ministry against another. Even the extent of their internal unity is a matter for empirical investigation and should not be assumed *a priori*.

Under Stalin, the final aggregation of ministerial interests was performed to a large extent by the master himself. When the industrial apparatus was set up in the 1930s, the economy was relatively simple, but since that time the industrial labour force has risen from some four million (in 1928) to over thirty-seven million (in 1982), when the total employed work force was 115.2 million.[11] Even under Stalin, control of the system was difficult, and police powers had to be utilized. In the modern period, the greater complexity of the economy, the entrenchment of the ministerial bureaucracies and the expansion of the administrative and executive personnel have made political control – through the party and planning agencies – even more problematic.

Agriculture: State and Collective Farms

While industrial production is organized by government ministries and by factories run by appointed managers, which are similar in structure to their Western counterparts, Soviet agriculture has units of production unknown to farming in the West, in particular, the collective farm, or *kolkhoz*. The collective farm is one of three distinct economic units of the agricultural sector: the state farms (*sovkhozy*), the collective farms and private plots. At one end of the scale are the state farms, where, as in industry, the 'command' principle operates; at the other end, we find the private plots which are completely outside government control and are in many ways similar to Western agricultural smallholdings.

The Soviet *sovkhoz* has the same legal status and organizational subordination as a Soviet industrial enterprise. The management is appointed by the Ministry of Agriculture and its organization, internal order and budget are the concern of the Ministry. As the produce of the farm is state property, the state farm agricultural workers receive a wage from state funds related to their skill in the same way as factory workers, and have similar rights as factory workers to welfare services. The management, technical and clerical staff are classified as non-manual workers, as in industry; agricultural labourers and other workers engaged full-time on the *sovkhoz* are classified as 'workers'. While individual private agricultural production on a large scale was abolished with the development of the collective farms, individuals were allowed to keep a small number of animals and a private plot. (At present, plots average 1½ acres of ground per household.) Thus, farmers may not only be employed on the collective and state farms, but may also become smallholders in their own right. Such plots are worked with primitive methods (sickle and hoe are the main tools) and, although animals are sometimes used for ploughing, manual labour is the chief source of power. The produce from the plots, together with any surpluses from the collective farm, may be freely sold at the collective farm markets set up in the urban areas.

The bulk of Soviet agricultural production is provided by the collective and state farms. The numbers of state farms have risen over the last twenty-five years and those of the collective farms have fallen significantly (see table 1.1), so that their numbers are now roughly equal. The state farms are far larger units, covering 793.4 million hectares, while the collective farms utilize 250.4 million. Collective farm plots account for another 4.1 million, and private plots utilized by workers and employees for 0.38 million.[12] The *area* of land used by various types of agricultural unit, however, may be misleading, since the intensity of cultivation affects yields. In 1980, private plots, which together represented about one

TABLE 1.1: NUMBERS OF STATE AND COLLECTIVE FARMS

	*1940**	*1950**	*1960**	*1970**	*1981**
No. of state farms	4,159	4,988	7,375	15,000	21,600
No. of collective farms	235,500	121,400	44,000	33,000	25,900

Source: Narodnoe khozyaystvo SSSR (Narkhoz) 1922–1982 (1982), p. 25.
*31 December.

five-hundredth of total cultivated area, contributed the following percentages of marketed output: 49 per cent of the potatoes, 15 per cent of the vegetables, 14 per cent of the meat, 6 per cent of milk and 6 per cent of all eggs.[13] Industrial agricultural commodities (flax, cotton) were wholly produced on state and collective farms. It is sometimes argued that the collective farmer neglects 'collective' work in favour of activity on his own plot. Soviet research suggests that female labour is primarily expended on the plots; over a third of all female agricultural labour time in the RSFSR (Russian Federation) was spent this way, compared with only 9 per cent of the male.[14]

The *collective farm* or *kolkhoz* is a form of co-operative rather than a unit run directly by the government. In 1917, after the revolution, the land was nationalized, but given to the peasantry to use with their own tools, seeds and livestock. Collectivization changed the basis of production from an individual to a co-operative one. The land remained state-owned, but the tools (excepting large-scale agricultural machinery), seeds and produce were the property of the collective. In an industrial enterprise, of course, the state owns the tools and the produce.

The supreme body is the collective farm meeting, which meets at least four times a year and is composed of all working members over sixteen years of age. It elects a managing committee and chairman, who are responsible for the work of the collective, and an auditing commission. The managing executive committee and chairman appoint charge-hands responsible for various aspects of farm work, who in turn control the work of different sections or work gangs and maintain discipline. Certain decisions are reserved for the general meeting of the farm: the admittance or expulsion of members as well as permission to leave the farm, the adoption of the farm's charter, the election or demotion of the chairman and criticism of the management committee, the adoption of the farm's annual plan and changes in boundaries of the farm.[15] In addition, it allocates the earnings of the collective to various funds: insurance, capital and cultural funds and the wages fund are the most important recipients. The collective farms have to find money for investments out of their own revenue (and from loans), whereas in the state farms (as in industrial enterprises) it is allocated by the government.

It would not, however, be correct to see the collective farm as an independent self-governing unit; it is guided by the government economic administration. Its decisions must conform with the Soviet Constitution, with the laws and economic plans. A collective farm general meeting cannot unilaterally decide the content of the annual production plan: this must be agreed by the state planning authorities, to which it is subject. It must also hand over to the state procurement bodies the quotas defined by them and is paid by the government for such deliveries. Moreover, the farm chairman is subject to strong influence from government and party bodies, which are also able to reject uncooperative or inefficient chairmen. While the Ministry of Agriculture is for the collective farm sector the equivalent of the industrial ministries, it does not directly organize production. The district Soviet passes target figures to the farms, and gives technical advice through its agricultural specialists on rotation, produce and methods.

Since 1958, the Soviet authorities have attempted to improve incentives for the collective farmers and to reduce authoritarian controls, with the aim of bringing the conditions of the collective farmers into line with those on the state farm. Since 1965, minimum targets for various types of produce have been given to the farms; prices for produce have been fixed regionally and are intended to cover costs and a reasonable profit for the farms. Sales in excess of the minimum have been at a premium. As in industry, the strategy has been to make it in the farm's interest to produce more.

In recent years, with the growth of collective farm party membership, the control of leading personnel can be managed by the party group, rather than externally. While the district Soviet can, and often does, interfere with planning and planting, the collective farm has considerably more control over finance, general operations and investment than has the management of an industrial enterprise.

Until 1958, most collective farmers were paid according to the *trudo-den'* or 'work-day' system, under which the wage fund was divided among the collective farmers according to the number of 'work-days' performed by the individual farmer. Since 1958, payment has been introduced at similar rates for the job as in state farms, and a regular wage is now paid to the collective farmer. Collective farmers have also been brought under the national social security programme (for health, medical care and pensions). They are able to join a trade union and, as members of the farms come of age, they are issued with an internal passport: these measures are intended to give them a status in line with urban workers and employees.

In the past, the machine-tractor stations (MTs) were another important instrument of control by the government over the collective farm. These were units under government management which carried out all machine work on the farms, and facilitated intensive use of scarce machines. They, too, were abolished in 1958, and now the farms own their machinery. Since 1965, collective farms have also been allowed to develop non-agricultural activities, and collective and state farms are able to form joint enterprises (*mezhkhozyaystvennye predpriyatiya*) for irrigation, building, and the processing of products. The numbers of such units has risen from 3,400 in 1965 to 9,767 in 1982.[16] Experiments have also been conducted with 'team assignments' (the *zveno*). Here the idea is to give a team (say 10 people) the responsibility for a given job from start to finish and to pay them on the basis of their results. All these measures have strengthened the collectives and helped to improve the status and conditions of the farmers.

Control of the Economy

The system of central control and planning which has developed in the USSR deals with two different types of problems. First is that of ensuring efficiency; and second, that of political control. The overcentralization of the Stalinist system has itself led to the misuse of resources, and the centre has been overwhelmed in the process by the complexity of the planning process. Since the 1960s, various kinds of decentralization have been introduced with the aim of increasing efficiency.

The 'Kosygin reforms', instituted since 1965, are among these, and, within the framework of a ministerial system, greater initiative has passed to enterprises. To prevent waste and to encourage efficient use of materials, a larger part of the surplus is now retained in the enterprise and various types of incentive have been introduced, including the work 'Brigade' methods, which will be discussed below. After meeting its costs (including a planned surplus, which is paid to the government) any 'excess' profits may be kept by the enterprise. Such profit may be used either as direct financial reward to employees, or for welfare services – the provision of factory creches or housing – or for capital investment. In 1981, of total profits, 42 per cent remained for distribution within the enterprise: 4 per cent went on capital investment, 17 per cent was used for incentives and 21 per cent was to be utilized for other purposes including the finance of circulating capital and the repayment of bank loans.[17] Wage scales are still determined centrally, but differentials may now be increased through various types of bonuses from profits.

The reforms have affected several other aspects of the running of an enterprise. Before 1965, plan completion was measured in quantities of output produced (e.g. 5 million tons of cement, 1,000 iron bedsteads), but this did not always ensure the correct allocation of sizes. For example, to take hypothetical cases, too many large nails may have been produced because output was measured in weight, too few large hats because materials could be economized on small sizes, and consumer goods were often distasteful or old-fashioned. Since 1965, output has only been credited to an enterprise after it has been accepted by a purchasing unit. The aim of this measure was to strengthen the influence of factor, or consumer, demand. In fact, purchasing units may still have to accept unsatisfactory commodities because of the lack of alternatives.

The Kosygin reforms, described above, retain the framework of the traditional physical planning system, but graft on to it elements of a market type: particularly, the 'stimulus' of demand and more emphasis on economic 'calculation'. In practice, however, by the early 1980s these proposals had not been fully implemented, and in the late 1970s the 'overwhelming bulk of turnover in materials is still allocated rather than traded'.[18] (Reforms of the 1980s are discussed below in chapter 2.)

The Party in the Economy

The second problem facing the Soviet economic order is that of political control. The very essence of a socialist system is that economic interests do not dominate society and production and exchange are organized on a 'rational' basis to fulfil human needs: i.e. to satisfy people's wants, for work, consumption, leisure, health and education. The objection made by socialists and Marxists to the operation of capitalist economies is that 'economic efficiency', measured in terms of the profitability of capitalist firms, cannot be equated with the social good, which includes other criteria. The Communist Party of the Soviet Union is widely considered as playing the leading role in defining the political objectives of economic planning. As Alec Nove has pointed out, 'Underlying all (the) elaborate government structure is the Communist Party of the Soviet Union, the "directing nucleus"... of all state organs and social organisations. In a very real sense, the government at all levels exists to carry out the policies of the party.'[19] As indicated a little earlier, however, this is a problematic rather than a statement of fact.

All political parties attempt to influence, in some respects, the operation of the economy. Their role in the economy of a liberal society is mainly to unify and co-ordinate. To this end, parties formulate general economic programmes for public approval. Under normal circumstances, they aggregate demands to maintain a political equilibrium. In the aggregation process some groups will be favoured relative to others, though, to be sure, party statements will attempt to show, perhaps disingenuously, how all groups will benefit. In the West, party policies often proclaim targets of economic growth for a given period and define the distribution of resources between different headings – such as, for example, investment and consumption, social services and defence.

In the Soviet Union, the Communist Party has a comprehensive economic programme. As noted above, this programme is translated into practical plans and economic activity through the ministerial apparatus. The party itself does not directly organize the economy: it has no economic establishments under its command, since all these are legally and organizationally under government ministries. Party organizations must *not* 'act in place of Soviet, trade union, co-operative or other public organizations... they must not allow either the merging of the functions of the party and other bodies or undue parallelism in work' (*Party Rules*, Article 42). In theory, then, the party does not aspire to administer, but 'to guide' or to bring influence to bear on industrial organizations controlled by the government. Between 1940 and 1953 under Stalin, and from 1958 to 1964 under Khrushchev, the leadership of the party and the government was unified; one man held both the top jobs. But even then the existence of separate party and government organizations may have lead to dualism and conflict.

The degree of responsibility and the extent of public control over industry are of crucial importance in a socialist system, where industry is a government responsibility. For without it ministries, if dominated by factory directors and executives, could come to form a new ruling stratum. In such a case, party control might be too weak to assert its own values over the ministerial elites or, alternatively, the party leadership might be corrupted and act in its own interest and not for the popular good. Though having no ownership rights over industry, such groups could secure a commanding or controlling position. Indeed, some critics of Soviet society have suggested that this is the predominant characteristic of the USSR – bureaucrats forming tight social groups based on self-interest.[20] It is also true that popular control of the executive by the legislature is ineffective in the USSR. Deputies are part-time and the Soviets meet infrequently; ministerial industrial enterprises are outside local government control and All-Union factories are answerable to headquarters in Moscow. The role of the party is to act as a guardian of the revolution and the class its triumph is said to represent. In some ways, it may be considered as providing a form of public control similar to that of elected bodies (councils) in Britain and the USA. In industry, the party is sometimes seen as safeguarding the interests of the dominant class under socialism in the same way as shareholders are seen in Marxist theory to be the dominant class in capitalist society. David Granick has argued that 'in one basic sense, both groups (i.e. capitalist shareholders and the Russian Communist Party) play the same role in their respective societies. Each represents legitimacy of power.'[21]

Khrushchev and Brezhnev both strengthened the role of the party, and the party programme and statements by its General Secretary now serve to reinforce the ideological control it exerts. Party influence on economic policy has also increased through the inclusion of more 'party men' in the Politbureau and the greater role given to party control over the administration and the enterprise in recent years.

The Industrial Enterprise

While the industrial ministry is legally vested with the ownership and control of the Soviet enterprise, the factory director and the management are in *de facto* control. The question which poses itself is whether a shift of control from ministry to management has taken place in the USSR resulting in something like a 'managerial revolution'.

In the early days of industrial capitalism the entrepreneur combined the role of owner and manager of an enterprise. In the twentieth century, the joint stock company vests ownership in its shareholders who generally play no direct part in the operation of the enterprise, and control in the directors, who often own only a small proportion of the shares. James Burnham[22] has argued that effective control now lies with the managers and is based on their technical skill and competence. Thus, it is said that a divorce has taken place between ownership and control. The interest of the 'controllers', it is argued by the managerial revolutionaries, is contrary to that of the owners: the controllers seek, for example, expansion of the firm and re-investment, rather than profit distribution. This analysis, if true, would seriously undermine a Marxist critique of society, for its postulates a managerial, bureaucratic stratum controlling the means of production, rather than an owning class. Paradoxically, this argument is often applied by Western Marxist critics to the Soviet enterprise.

Before considering this problem in relation to the USSR, it will be as well to consider the structure of the typical production unit in each society: the capitalist firm and the socialist enterprise. Their structure is summarized in diagram 1.3.

Under conditions of modern capitalism, the ownership of the means of production of the typical corporation or firm is vested in a joint stock company. Shareholders contribute capital to the company, they elect its officers and receive a share of its produce (profits, interest), but they do not individually contribute to its activity. At the company's general meeting they elect a board which runs the company primarily to secure a profit for the shareholders. The legal unit of production is the firm (or company). The economic production unit is the factory or plant producing and marketing a product. A firm such as ICI may embrace a whole variety of products in separate independent production units.

The Western Firm

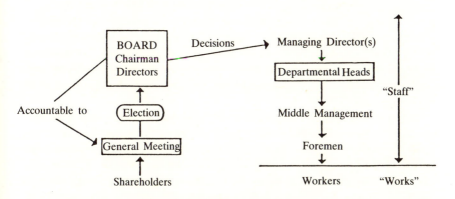

PROCEEDS OF PRODUCTION   PRODUCTION FUNCTIONS
OWNERS   NON-OWNERS

BOARD — Chairman — Directors — Decisions → Managing Director(s) → Departmental Heads → Middle Management → Foremen → Workers

Accountable to — Election — General Meeting — Shareholders

"Staff" — "Works"

The Soviet Production Enterprise

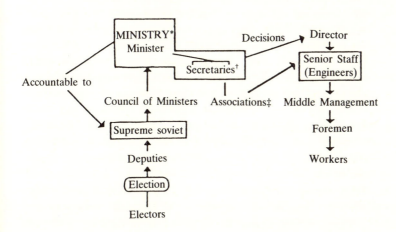

PROCEEDS OF PRODUCTION   PRODUCTION FUNCTIONS

MINISTRY* — Minister — Secretaries† — Decisions → Director → Senior Staff (Engineers) → Middle Management → Foremen → Workers

Accountable to — Council of Ministers — Associations‡ — Supreme soviet — Deputies — Election — Electors

DIAGRAM 1.3: THE WESTERN FIRM AND THE SOVIET PRODUCTION ENTER-
PRISE

Notes: *Here I have considered an All-Union Ministry. For "Republican" industries and local ones,
subordination is to the Republican and local Soviet, respectively.
†"Secretaries" are senior permanent high-ranking officials, similar to "administrative" class civil
servants in Britain. They are in Russian terminology heads (*nachal'niki*) of branches (*glavki*).
‡Since 1973, groupings of enterprises into *obedinenie* and *glavki* have taken place. This has
weakened the power of individual factory directors.

In the Soviet Union there are no 'firms' in the Western sense of the word. (The Soviet *firma* is a grouping of enterprises.) Ownership and control are vested in government ministries, as defined above. The minister, aided by secretaries (*nachal'niki*), is responsible to the Council of Ministers for the organization of an industry. He appoints directors who are in charge of 'enterprises', or production units which are analogous to factories and plants in capitalist states. The Soviet 'enterprise', therefore, has the standing of a subsidiary or branch. As a production unit, however, it is similar in function to the capitalist firm, save that less distinction is made between 'staff' and workers. (There are, however, official and technical groups – 'leading personnel', 'engineering-technical staff', and 'workers'.)

The greatest similarity between the two production units is in the production functions. Both the Soviet enterprise and the Western firm have in common a managing director solely responsible for the operation of the factory; beneath the managing director is a hierarchy with the industrial worker at the bottom. In the West, the firm or company is a private venture; the board is not responsible, or answerable to society at large – though, of course, business is subject to government intervention. In the USSR, it is important to remember that it is the ministerial bureaucrats at the centre who have the power and organization to run the economy; the industrial manager is a subordinate.[23]

Another major point of difference is the criterion for success of the two types of enterprise. The Western joint stock company's *raison d'être* is to make a profit for its shareholders. The activities of the firm are geared to this: if it continuously makes a loss and it cannot meet creditors, then it is declared bankrupt and the employees lose their jobs and the shareholders their money. In the Soviet Union, by contrast, there is no profit maximization as a *general principle* of industrial administration. The Soviet enterprise is geared to complete the plan given it by the ministry, and management has a strong incentive to fulfil the plan, for which it is paid a bonus or premium.

In spite of this, the Soviet industrial enterprise has some autonomy from ministerial control. Even before the reforms of 1965, the enterprise had financial autonomy. Rather like a British nationalized industry, each unit had to work within the plan and cover its costs from revenue, but managers also had detailed inputs and outputs imposed on them. Output was specified in quantitative terms and selling prices were also fixed. Producers had captive markets: the customers were also earmarked for their products. Costs were controlled and payments were only made by the State Bank for items specified in the plan. The wages fund determined how much could be paid out; and bonuses were calculated for extra above-plan production. Raw materials to be used were also detailed in the plan. There was little room here for managerial initiative, let alone the rise of a new 'managerial class'.

Since 1965, the powers of managers have increased somewhat, but they are still fairly closely controlled. In the 1976–80 period, the rules for drawing up plans mentioned the following indicators which were binding on managers: (i) a certain amount of output must be sold (i.e. accepted by a consumer, rather than being merely produced); (ii) the output of certain types of products is defined in physical terms; (iii) the proportion of this 'top category' output to total output is given; (iv) target growth of labour productivity is defined; (v) the total wages fund is specified; (vi) the (minimum) profit is established; and (vii) the profitability is given (i.e. ratio of profit to total capital investment).[24] Since the 1960s, planning has given the managers some discretion and initiative. The details of product mix, for example, have been left to negotiation between producers and their customers (e.g. the sizes of screws or shoes and the amounts for each size). In addition, the system of planning now attempts to encourage initiative and reward efficiency by giving the enterprise a share in the profits. As noted above, after fulfilling the 'planned profit', some 40 per cent of excess profits may be utilized by the director for the enterprise's benefit; all proceeds from the use of 'waste materials' are at the disposal of the director (see below, chapter 2, for other proposals). However, the use of such profits is circumscribed by the ministry: the Bank and the ministry accountants, as well as the party organization and troubleshooters from the People's Control Commission, cannot see everything, but they prevent widescale misappropriation of resources.

The power of Soviet managers arises from their knowledge of and day-to-day control of the enterprise. In the planning process, for instance, information and proposals are submitted by the enterprise to the ministry and to the planners. As one East European has expressed it: 'The commands are written by the recipients.'[25] Inputs to the enterprise are often not forthcoming and management is dependent on an array of informal and often illegitimate channels to ensure supplies (see chapter 2).

It has been argued that the introduction of the 'profit motive' in the USSR has led to the growth of capitalism, but this cannot, to my mind, be substantiated. While it must be conceded that directors have been given more power, in the context of Soviet industrial organization, it is clear that this is not yet equivalent to that of a Western company chairperson with an effective voting majority on the board. Managerial power is limited in three ways. First, a Soviet director cannot produce or market new products: he cannot shift production from radios to space-invaders to meet an unfulfilled demand. Such entrepreneurship, which is a characteristic of the Western firm, does not exist at the enterprise level in the USSR. Second, the director has detailed orders given by the ministry, which also hires and fires. Third, the enterprise director works in an economic-political milieu alongside party and union organizations.

What the recent changes do signify is the enhanced importance of monetary or utilitarian incentives in the operation of the plant and in the motivation to work. In this context, it is particularly important to bear in mind that labour policy in the USSR is planned, and that the basic philosophy of the planners is that of a low-wage, full-employment economy. As a result management cannot 'shed labour' (i.e. create unemployment). The strategy that lies behind the recent economic reforms is to replace administrative measures of control over economic enterprises with financial incentives, thereby making it in the interest of the enterprise to overfulfil the plan. A major problem of this approach has been to reconcile enterprise initiative with the political interest of the state. As we shall discuss below, many critics argue that the reforms do not go far enough and that political priorities overrule economic efficiency.

The Soviet manager, then, may be said to have control over the process of production, but he has little power over its proceeds. Probably the best description of him is, in Kerr's terms, that of a 'constitutional manager', whose authority is circumscribed by government, party and unions.[26]

At this stage, it may be useful to draw up an organizational scheme of a 'typical' Soviet factory. The factory manager is responsible to the ministry, by which he is appointed. Under him are production departments headed by assistant managers, and production shops, by foremen. The production aspects of Soviet factories are generally similar to those of factories in Western countries, but with some differences: quality control and inspection are usually organized under production, rather than in separate independent departments. Is also notable that, unlike in Western firms, sales departments are generally very small and have little, if any, influence over production. But the most striking differences lie in the parallel chains of command that extend through the factory, and into the political hierarchy. We may distinguish between three separate organizations associated with three kinds of activity: production (the ministry), politics (the party), social and welfare matters (the trade union). These are shown in diagram 1.4.

The director is solely responsible to the ministry for the operation of the plant. This is responsible to the Council of Ministers (in which the minister in charge of the industry will have a place), and this, in turn, is answerable to the Supreme Soviet – at least in principle. Running parallel with the ministerial chain of command are the party and union hierarchies. These are shown on diagram 1.4, to the left and right of the ministerial hierarchy.

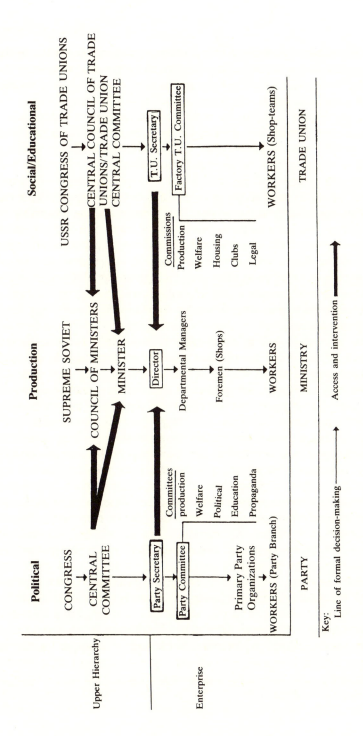

DIAGRAM 1.4: PARTY, MINISTERIAL AND TRADE UNION HIERARCHIES

The party committee is charged with a general political supervision of the plant, and the union is particularly responsible for workers' welfare. In theory, the three groups work in harmony. In Soviet parlance, they have to 'speak the same language'.

To the Western student, the ministerial and trade union hierarchies are not too foreign, particularly if comparison is made with a nationalized industry. But the role of the party has no parallel in the West. The growing dependence of enterprises on 'market forces' (in practice, their ability to determine the precise details of output and the amount of labour employed, as well as their ability to keep and distribute a proportion of the earnings of the enterprise) has made the enterprise less amenable to central control and increased the possibility of fraud and embezzlement and the utilization of the plant for private ends. As a party secretary has pointed out, the duty of party factory committees 'is to restrain too ardent businessmen and to see that in the search for high profitability preference is not given to the most lucrative type of production to the detriment of state interest'.[27] The party and other voluntary bodies in the factory may serve as useful constraints.

The party organization in the factory is also useful in securing the compliance of workers in the changes required by technological advance and the changing needs of the economy. In addition, together with the union (see below), it carries out much of the welfare work required in a large industrial enterprise. But its role as a 'controller' may decline in future with government departments strengthening their own checks over factories. The regulations defining party commissions make it clear that the management remains responsible for managing: the commissions are auxiliaries having no legal powers over the enterprise. Recent policy on the role of party primary organizations and their rights of control over the administration puts an emphasis on the 'assistance' given by these groups to the enterprise administration, which is still legally responsible for its performance.* This stands in marked contrast to the situation in Yugoslavia, where the workers' committees have more power and can even remove factory directors.

The party, however, is a powerful political organization at the national level, and its conception of communism entails party control. Moreover, in recent years it has reiterated its prerogative of overseeing the administration, even though economic efficiency was conceived of in terms of utilitarian stimuli. Thus, the position of the factory manager cannot be

---

*The relationship between party and government has been discussed in detail in *State and Politics in the USSR*, chapter 7.

described as hegemonic in the USSR. Though one of the most important social forces outside the political leadership in Soviet society, the factory director is constrained by the party and, to a lesser extent, by the union. These groups give him (directors are usually men) help, they provide him with information, they mobilize the work force, they suggest how improvements may be made, they facilitate links in other geographical areas and with different industries.

Trade Unions

One of the most widely accepted definitions of a trade union is that of the Webbs: 'A trade union ... is a continuous association of wage earners for the purpose of maintaining or improving the conditions of their working lives.' Trade unions are composed of workers, organized either by trade or industry. Their main object, especially in Western societies, is to increase wages, and this may be classified as an 'industrial' objective. Wider political goals are pursued and include parliamentary representation to ensure favourable labour legislation. In the West, however, such activity is secondary to industrial activity, and unions work within the structure of society rather than in opposition to it. The final sanction a union can use against the employer is the withdrawal of labour, the strike. Unions are enduring institutions with a membership usually, but not always, voluntary in character and with full-time salaried officials elected by the membership.

In Western societies, the improvement of workers' conditions, particularly wages, is paramount, and the right to enforce sanctions against the employers by withdrawing labour is considered a fundamental right of unions and even a necessary condition for their existence. In liberal-democratic states, the separate and conflicting interests of employers and employed is institutionalized through collective bargaining between both sides. In addition, the roles of union and management are highly distinct: the management is primarily concerned with production and associated problems (product design and quality, trade training, hiring and firing) and the union with the improvement of workers' conditions. One of the conditions for a 'pluralist' society is that various groups of persons may form associations to pursue their common interests. All contemporary liberal theorists view the existence or otherwise of separate workers' and employers' associations as one of the most important distinctions between a totalitarian and democratic society. However, under capitalism unions are rarely confrontational with employers, so that many Western writers point to the integrative aspect of union activity: they regulate conflict and discontent and they have a negligible effect on the allocation of capital either within the economy or at the level of the firm.[28] The betterment of wages and conditions at the place of work remains the overwhelming objective of organized unionism.

Under state socialism, as it prevails in the USSR, rather than a number of separate and conflicting interests, one common interest is assumed, and the notion of the representation of separate workers' and employers' interests is, therefore, alien to the dominant Soviet ideology. It is argued that unions are formed in Western states to protect the worker from the oppression of capital. But in a society like the USSR, where the means of production are nationalized, and controlled by the state, and where the state, in the last analysis, articulates the public interest, it follows, say Soviet writers, that confrontation should not occur between workers and management.

In the early days of the Soviet regime, there was much controversy concerning the role to be played by the unions. One group saw the existing unions as 'cells of the coming socialist social order' and another referred to them as 'living corpses'.[29] The former view, later shared by the Workers' Opposition led by Shlyapnikov, was that the unions should strengthen their structure and should dominate over the state apparatus and its economic administration. Control of the enterprise, they argued, should rest with the union committee, but that of the economy with the trade unions. This was essentially a syndicalist position. The other group, led by Trotsky, wanted the 'stratification' of the unions. He argued that a workers' state was organized under the party for the well-being of the working class as a whole. Thus, the unions should be seen as part of the economic administration and perform a management function. Lenin's position was between these two extremes: the unions should stand between party and government, albeit performing a rather limited number of functions.[30] The power of the unions as independent units defending the interests of specific groups of workers was broken following the Eighth Trade Union Congress in 1929. And, during the First Five-Year Plan (1928–32), the central planning agencies asserted full control over labour. A trade union structure remained, however, and to it were left many aspects of worker welfare.

In theory, at the present time the Soviet unions act in harmony with the Soviet government in the general interests of the economy; they enhance the material and spiritual position of labour in the building of communism.

> The trade unions ... play a major part in implementing measures to improve working conditions and, as mass organisations with extensive rights, collaborate with the state authorities on the most important questions relating to labour and remuneration. They encourage workers' initiative in developing new forms of work – socialist emulation, the shock-worker movement, the Communist labour

brigades and enterprises – and help workers to acquire experience in dealing with production, state and community matters. As society has developed and its material level has risen, the unions have taken over functions previously performed by the state. They at present participate directly in public administration in fields closely related to workers' needs such as social insurance, the running of sanatoria and rest homes, physical culture and sports.[31]

Unions in the USSR, unlike their Western counterparts, have a dual function: a management role, essentially to increase productivity and to fulfil the factory's plan, and a defensive role, to safeguard the workers' interests against malpractice and possible forms of exploitation by the management. While 'official' Soviet writers see no contradiction between these ends, many Western commentators[32] point to a conflict between priorities or at least to a duality in the roles of the trade unions. In understanding Soviet unions it is imperative to bear in mind that they function within an economic system which is planned. Unions under capitalism operate in a quite different economic context: competitive capitalism calls for economistic market-type bargaining by unions. The absence of such bargaining is to be expected in a planned system where wage funds are determined centrally and where full employment is ensured under the plan.

The argument that Soviet unions are illegitimate because they do not function like American or British unions is as fallacious as saying that American unions are illegitimate because they lack a political wing, like the British Labour Party, and do not function like British unions. In all industrial societies there is a correspondence between union structure and activity, on the one hand, and historical experience and the type of political economy, on the other.

In the Soviet Union, however, the union organization may influence priorities at a higher level in the hierarchy of decision-making and may have an impact on the allocation process, as well as on the operational aspects of the economy. Greater dependence on 'the market' involving redundancy and unemployment seem to have been blocked in the USSR – perhaps as a consequence of party and union power. Shalaev, the chairman of the trade union organization, has pointed out in an article in *Pravda* that, unlike unions in the West, Soviet unions have an influence on the distribution of the social product, especially for social services and consumption goods.[33] In the late 1970s and early 1980s the unions have been strengthened in their role as defenders of labour.[34] Soviet writers claim that the Central Council of Trade Unions must be consulted by the Soviet government on all matters concerning labour, and the union's executive has the right to initiate legislation in the Supreme Soviet.[35] The council, in conjunction with appropriate government departments, issues 'rules and standards on occupational safety and health', and centrally the unions act as advisory bodies on labour problems and also as government agencies.

One of the most important tasks of the unions is to administer some of the social insurance schemes. These include sickness, maternity, industrial injury, and family allowances, as well as old-age, disability and dependants' pensions. Unions supervise the collection of premiums and help determine the level of benefits.[36] Health and safety regulations are supervised by the unions. The work of health and safety inspectors is administered by them, and local union officials are responsible for ensuring that labour legislation is enforced. Social services are also administered by the unions, and numerous rest homes and sanitoria come under their jurisdiction. Lastly, under the union organizations come many types of leisure activity, including the prominent and famous ice hockey and soccer teams.

Union Organization

The membership of trade unions in the USSR is open to all workers. Though collective farmers are not classified as 'workers', present policy is to encourage them to join the Agricultural Workers' Union. Membership is voluntary and workers are required to pay a subscription. This is one per cent of their earnings and entitles them to welfare benefits at an enhanced rate, plus access to the sporting and tourist facilities of the union. (Union dues are reduced somewhat for the most lowly paid categories of workers.) In 1983, total membership was 132 million,[37] and accounted for more than 98 per cent of manual and non-manual workers in paid employment. Of a total of 13.2 collective farmers, in 1982, 11.9 million were in a trade union, and another 9.1 million students and pupils in vocational schools were union members.[38]

As in some capitalist countries, such as Germany and the USA, workers are organized by industry. In the USSR, *all* workers from clerks to engineers employed in a given industry will belong to the same union. Thus, an electrician will be attached to the coal mining union if he works in a coal mine, or to the railway union if he works on the railways. No divisions of the work force by skill or position are reflected in union structure. In a given factory, its director, the administrative and technical personnel and the unskilled workers all belong to the same union. An exception, however, is made for medical employees, who, wherever they work, are members of the Health Workers' Union. Employees of factory clinics are employed by the Ministry of Health – not by the enterprise. Obviously, the union structure helps promote unity and solidarity and weakens the stratification by profession and grade from which Western (and especially British) unions suffer. There is, however, another side to this. The industrial unions make it relatively easier for the planning authorities to alter or maintain differentials between trades and occupations since there are no organized union groups to defend particular interests; by the same token, craft monopoly of skills to ensure high wages by certain groups of workers (printers, medical practitioners) is precluded.

Unions cover the whole of the USSR. In 1982 there were thirty-one unions, including: the Agricultural Workers' Union; Aircraft and Defence Industry; Aviation; Communications and Road Transport; Education and Scientific Institutions; Geological Prospecting; Co-operative and Government Trade; Government Employees; Railways; Cultural Workers; Timber, Paper and Woodworking; Engineering; Metallurgical; Sea and River Transport; Health Workers; Local Industry and Municipal Enterprises; Oil and Chemical; Food and Food Industry; Agricultural and Government Purchasing; Construction and Building Materials; Textile and Light Industries; Coal Mining; Power and Electrical.

The unions have an organizational structure similar in pattern to that of the Communist Party. Unions are 'constructed on the basis of democratic centralism according to the production principle'. The structure of Soviet unions is shown in diagram 1.5. At the bottom is the primary union group formed at the place of work. This is at least 15 strong. The factory committee is usually elected directly (sometimes on a workshop basis, depending on the size of the factory). But it is sometimes elected indirectly by deputies chosen by union members. Factory committees nominate delegates both to industrial regional conferences (i.e. the regional conference of members of *one* union) and to regional inter-union conferences. These is turn elect to the trade unions' own congress and to the Republican inter-union conference. Finally, delegates are chosen for the All-Union (Federal) Congress of Trade Unions. At the Seventeenth Congress in March 1982, 5,024 delegates (52.4 per cent of whom were manual workers or collective farmers) were elected to the Congress.[39] The pyramid of membership in the executive bodies is illustrated in table 1.2.

The union structure, therefore, ensures considerable overlap between unions and (as some two-thirds of the delegates to the Federal Trade Union Congress are elected by the regional inter-union conferences) gives the central authority considerable control over the lower organs. Furthermore, the 'centralism' of the union structure demands the subordination of lower units to the higher ones and means that the implementation of centrally made decisions is mainly the responsibility of the executive organs. The lower executive bodies are dually responsible to the higher executive organs (linked by broken lines). In Britain, by contrast, the unions are strongly organized on a trade basis, and inter-union

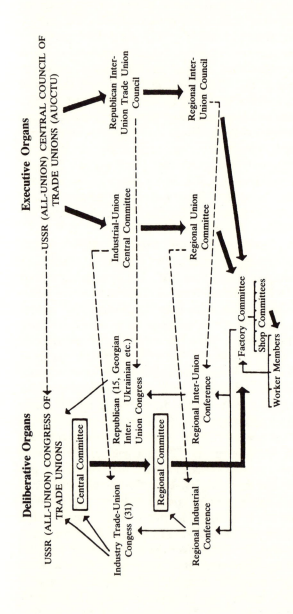

DIAGRAM 1.5: TRADE UNION STRUCTURE IN THE USSR

Sources: Diagram constructed on the basis of information given in: 'Ustav professional'nykh soyuzov SSSR' in *Materialy XVI s"ezda professional'nykh soyuzov SSSR.* (M. 1977), pp. 138–54 E.C. Brown, *Soviet Trade Unions and Labour Relations* (Harvard, 1966), p. 67.

TABLE 1.2: TRADE UNION MEMBERSHIP

	Membership	Women %
All-Union Central Council of Trade Union and Central auditing commission	590	35.8
Central Committees of trade unions and audit commissions	5,537	43.5
Republican, Area (*kraevye*), and Regional (*oblastnye*) TU Councils and auditing commissions	23,245	47.4
Republican, Area, Regional, Railway District (*dorozhnye*), Coal Field (*basseynovye*), and Territorial (*territorial'nye*) TU Committees and audit commissions	196,460	51.3
District and town committees of trade unions and audit commissions	688,178	61.5
Trade union committees, audit commissions and union organizers	7,044,395	65.5
Members	132,000,000[1]	—

Sources: S. Shalaev, 'Sovetskie profsozuzy v obshchestve razvitogo sotsializma', *Pravda*, 12, Oct. 1983.
    Narkhoz 1922–1982 (1982), p. 50.
[1]The rank and file members are organized in 753,000 primary trade union organizations, more than three million union groups, and half a million shop-floor committees.

co-operation is minimal; the Trade Union Congress has no power (though it does have influence) over the individual unions which make up its membership. The two national union structures reflect the pluralist and unitary theories on which the politics of each society are based.

The Central Council, elected by the Congress, plays a leading role in the union movement. Among its activities are: to determine the immediate tasks of unions generally, to participate in the elaboration of national economic plans, to submit to legislative organs draft laws and decrees, to carry out the direction of the state social insurance system, to approve the budget of the trade unions and the state social insurance budget, to define the general structure of trade unions and their staffs, and to represent Soviet trade unions in the international trade union movement.[40] It has staff throughout the lower echelons of the union administration. Thus, while the Republican Inter-Union Trade Union Council is elected by the Republican Union Congress, the full-time officials have a responsibility to the secretariat in Moscow. The power of this central body contrasts with the weak control which Western union secretariats have over individual unions. For example, during the decentralization of industrial management, the number of unions was halved by order of the All-Union Central Committee of Trade Unions (AUCCTU). Each union, however, elects its own central committee, both at a federal and at a regional level. Work peculiar to that union is carried out by the secretariat of the union.[41]

In the West, Soviet unions are regarded by many commentators as mere 'puppets' of the central authorities. Indeed, there can be no doubt that they are not workers' organizations divorced from management of the kind found in Great Britain. But this does not mean that 'management' and 'unions' are equally intermeshed at all levels of the Soviet economy. Mary McAuley has argued that at the regional level and above the unions' organizations are 'more closely tied in with the administrative apparatus – both in terms of personnel and functions – than at the enterprise'.[42] At the higher levels, the promotion of the more sectional interest can be pursued without any loss to either side; also an industrial union and ministry (or a branch of it) may combine to promote their common interest against competitors. At the enterprise level, however, the process of production gives workers and management different roles, which may result in strife.

Since 1957, the role of unions in supporting workers' interests has been strengthened. Factory trade union committees have the right to veto dismissals, union members serve on 'production conferences' and the TU committee has been encouraged to take initiatives over the 'collective agreement' (i.e. the yearly plan, in which work norms and wage rates are specified, see below). The status of leading TU officials has risen and they have become more prominent in the party.[43] Under Brezhnev, unions were implored to strive to improve living and working conditions.[44] They have been encouraged to check 'bureaucratic' tendencies and to 'curb the actions of plant managers who neglect the needs of the working people'. Inefficiency and incompetence were to be exposed. In 1980, it was reported that, at the insistence of the unions, 3,093 industrial managers had been disciplined and 200 removed from their posts.[45] In 1982, 'requests from trade unions in connexion with violations of the norms for occupational safety and health led to the suspension of operations at 180 enterprises and 3,000 shops and to the dismissal of 9,800 managers'.[46]

Trade Union Activity in the Factory

The main difference between Western unions and the Soviet kind may be illustrated by considering the kind of activities performed by the unions at the place of production.

The Soviet factory or farm union committee has the following responsibilities:

(a) the mobilization of all workers, collective farmers and employees in the enterprise, building site, collective farm, institution, state farm or establishment for the fulfilment and over-fulfilment of the state plan, the strengthening of labour discipline and the development of socialist emulation and the movement for communist labour;

(b) the elaboration and putting into effect of practical measures aimed at steadily raising labour productivity, the maximum utilization of internal production reserves, the improvement of quality and the lowering of production costs;

(c) enlisting workers, collective farmers and employees into active participation in questions of the activity of the enterprise, farm or establishment and in the administration of production and social matters;

(d) organizing the popularization of advanced experience, the latest achievements of science and technology, the development of the mass movement of rationalizers and inventors; raising the level of general education and the technical knowledge of the working people;

(e) daily concern for the improvement of labour protection, the improvement of the material position and everyday conditions of workers and employees; carrying out among working people and their families mass cultural, physical education and sports activity, as well as the development of tourism,

(f) fostering in workers, collective farmers, and employees a high political consciousness, dedication to the public interest and love of the socialist homeland, friendship between nations, observation of Soviet laws, honesty and truthfulness, high moral qualities;

(g) fulfilling obligations taken under the collective agreement;

(h) implementing decisions of higher trade union organs and resolutions of general meetings;

(i) enlisting all workers, collective farmers, and employees into membership of the trade union;

(j) the development of criticism and self-criticism, the education of trade union members in a spirit of intolerance to shortcomings, to manifestations of bureaucracy and to the issuing of false returns, to mismanagement and waste and negligent attitudes to public property.[47]

As we saw earlier, Soviet unions play an important role in the production process, unlike their Western counterparts who have no such duties. A second difference is in membership, where in the Soviet case management can and does participate in union affairs. The factory director or other supervisory staff might well be members of the factory union committee. McAuley, for instance, says that, of 25 members of the Skorokhod factory committee, five were full-time union officials; seven were specialists – the chairman had been the former chief engineer, and the vice-chairman was an official from the production department.[48] But at another plant, the Moscow Watch Factory No. 2, Ruble reports that, of a 35-member committee, 80 per cent were manual workers.[49]

The range of union activities also includes many aspects of production problems (for example, wages, output). The union has a specific duty to increase output, to encourage more effective use of labour, to root out practices which restrict production, to encourage workers to improve their qualifications and to devise more efficient production methods. 'Socialist emulation', or comradely co-operation and mutual assistance in the labour process, is to be encouraged at the point of production – not only to improve output but to develop a co-operative spirit towards work.[50] In the factory, a number of commissions are organized under the union committee (see diagram 1.6). In addition, under the factory union committee come the shop committees, which are mainly concerned with

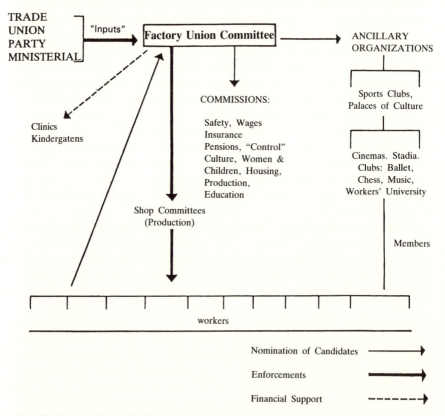

DIAGRAM 1.6: FACTORY UNION COMMITTEE AND SUB-UNITS

production and act, at the point of production, as liaison units between the factory director and the worker.

The 'commissions' of the union are charged with specific duties, often defined by the USSR Central Council of Trade Unions. For example, one commission will have particular responsibilities concerning insurance and will administer the housing constructed for factory personnel. Another group will be responsible for encouraging invention and rationalizing production. In the Moscow Watch Factory No. 2, Ruble reports that thirteen commissions come under the trade union committee: production (15 members), organizational (15), pension (15), labour protection (13), cultural (13–15), family and school (15), youth (15), housing (15), election (7), labour disputes (13), consumer services (15), women's concerns (15). In all these groups voluntary workers participated, and each was chaired by a member of the factory committee.[51] Such activity includes work which would be carried out in the West by the social services departments of the local authority, and some of the union's activity comes under what Western firms would call 'personnel' work. In addition, union committees are required to deal with workers' personal problems and to issue holiday and sanitoria vouchers, besides dealing with grievances and disputes. In the factory studied by Ruble, the factory union committee administered a budget of 1.5 million rubles.[52] The improvement of levels of skill and production is also furthered by union activity. In 1983, the All-Union Society of Inventors and Rationalizers (VOIR) and the Scientific Organization of Labour (NTO) had 24 million members. Under NTO were organized 62 'complex, scientific-technical and social-economic programmes'.[53] The Scottish TUC delegation to the USSR in 1982 was told that in 1981 36 million unionists participated in different kinds of production conferences; 1,500,000 proposals on production and social issues were considered.[54]

To the right of the diagram are 'ancillary organizations' run by the local union committee. 'Palaces of culture' are the equivalent of the English working-man's club. The larger factories have premises (often literally former palaces) where artistic (painting, sculpture) and general leisure activities can take place. Sports clubs and stadia, cinemas and theatres often form part of the Palace of Culture complex. Such well-known teams as Moscow Spartak and Riga Vef are among the voluntary societies coming under the unions. The sports clubs embrace a wide variety of sports: in 1979 there were 33 million participants in union sports societies.[55] In 1977, some 22,000 clubs, 49,300 cinemas and 23,000 libraries with 306 million books and 25 million readers were organized under the unions. The 33 voluntary sports societies had 30 million members in 1977. Educational activities (rather like the British Workers' Educational Association) also come under the unions: 7,225 people's universities were organized in 1977 with 948,800 participants.[56] These ancillary organizations are administered by a director and a committee responsible to the factory committee. The finances of the Palaces are the concern of the union: income from dances, cinema shows and football matches accrues to the union. In 1982, 71.8 per cent of union income derived from members' subscriptions and 5.7 per cent from fees received from cultural and sporting activities; 39.1 per cent of expenditure was used for 'cultural and mass work' and 25 per cent went on physical culture and sport.[57]

On the left of diagram 1.6 joined by a dashed line, are the institutions which come under the administration of separate government departments but which may be sponsored by the local factory committee. A district polyclinic located in the factory's catchment area might receive financial help to buy special equipment, and a local kindergarten might be helped to provide toys and apparatus for the children.

Locally, at the level of the enterprise, the unions participate in the drawing up of the collective agreement (*koldogovor*), which defines the level of output and the division of bonus between workers and its utilization for collective provision (e.g. new housing). In 1976, 143,100 collective agreements were concluded.[58] The workers themselves, of course, participate in meetings to discuss aspects of the agreement, and this discussion may be an important means of reducing stress in industrial relations. The fact that the workers may keep a certain proportion of profits for their own use helps to strengthen collective responsibility. As a trade union pamphlet puts it: 'The agreement has a great influence on the most diverse aspects of the factory's life. The better the collective works, the more profit it receives, which it may use at its own discretion.'[59] Ruble describes the process of drawing up the plan at Moscow Watch Factory No. 2 as follows.

Union and administration begin consultation at Moscow Watch Factory No. 2 in October for the next year's collective agreement. A joint union-management commission assesses the performance of factory officials in meeting the previous agreement and invites the recommendations of individual workers, trade union groups, and shop brigades. The commission reviews each proposal until January, when it prepares a draft agreement. For the next few weeks, union representations present the draft to enterprise employees, and then, in early February, a factory conference convenes to discuss the agreement. If approved by a majority of those present, the new agreement goes into effect immediately. Quarter-annual factory conferences convene to evaluate compliance to the agreement.[60]

The extent to which the unions and the rank and file workers participate in drawing up the collective agreement has not been thoroughly studied. In McAuley's study of six Leningrad factories, the contentious points were not very important. Extra holidays, the opening of a new cafeteria and the shortage of children's creches were the most important areas of dispute between management and union.[61]

Local union committees participate with management in the elaboration of the economic plan and its execution. They must help the management promote efficiency and maintain discipline, and they encourage workers to improve their qualifications and to suggest improvements in productive capacity. Workers, management and the government in theory have a common interest – to increase production. This view of industrial relations is not unlike that of progressive German and Japanese firms, which have introduced profit-sharing and other forms of 'workers' participation' schemes in order to bring management and workers closer together. The factory operates in a paternalistic way, providing not only work, but a whole network of welfare support and leisure activities. Guaranteed income and permanence of employment have the effect of 'incorporating the worker'.[62] In this respect the Soviet enterprise has much in common with the Japanese. The attempt of the British government and unions in recent years to relate wage increases to increases in productivity and to secure the workers' agreement to this is a policy similar to that adopted in the USSR. The falling rate of economic growth in the USSR in the 1980s (see below chapter 2) has led Soviet leaders to place more emphasis on the importance of productivity, and to link increases in the standard of living with increases in production, as well as with the quality of work.[63] Union leaders for many years have publicly called on union organizations actively to defend workers' interests against management. In *Pravda* in March 1982, the first secretary of Tula oblast' party committee complained that 'it is still no rarity to find factories where trade union organs become in effect adjuncts of management, with no character of their own.'[64]

Disputes

There is, however, evidence of conflict between the various interests. On the one hand, factory management and the factory union committee share a common interest in securing as large a wage fund as possible from the higher industrial administration. On the other, conflict takes place between the union and the factory administration on the grading of jobs. Here is how a British study comments on wage scales.

At the Leningrad enterprises, it seemed usual for all decisions or suggestions to come from management. The *fabkom* (factory TU committee) saw its task to be that of checking a proposed list of changes and making the occasional query or objection to a particular point. But if, subsequently, a change brought protests from the workers involved, the *fabkom* then felt entitled to take the matter up and take a decision on it ... The *fabkom* acted ... as a body for resolving disputes.[65]

It is also interesting to find that, as the management's bonus partly came from economies on the factory wages fund, this caused opposition from the workers, who wanted, of course, to overspend this fund.[66] It seems most probable that considerable bargaining goes on about the wage structure of the enterprise and that the union committee plays an important part in resolving conflicts of interest. Here it acts more like the personnel department of a Western firm.

The existence of disputes is recognized by Soviet commentators, who explain them as being due to 'inadequate knowledge of labour legislation on the part of individual management representatives or workers, or through its faulty application'. There are three channels for the resolution of conflict: the labour disputes board (made up of equal numbers of members of the trade union and management), the local trade union committee and the people's courts. The disputes board is the most important medium and deals with cases which have been passed to it after preliminary investigation by the trade union committee.

The procedure of the labour disputes board is quite informal. After an aggrieved worker hands in his complaint, if it cannot be resolved by the management, the board must meet within five days. The number of disputes per annum brought before these boards, according to McAuley's study, represents three to ten per cent of the labour force.[67] As far as cases in the 138 enterprises studied were concerned, nearly twice as many decisions went in favour of the worker as against him.[68] The disputes referred to these boards were on the following topics (in order of frequency): holidays, wages, dismissals, subtraction from pay, bonus, transfer to other work, disciplinary procedure (based on 32 Urals factories).[69] The employees may appeal, if dissatisfied, to the trade union committee and from there to the people's court; the management, if it considers the trade union committee's decision illegal, may also appeal. Ruble cites the case of the Donets region where the regional procuracy initiated the following actions against factory management: 490 protests, 453 representations, 108 disciplinary proceedings, 14 criminal proceedings, and 23 civil actions.[70]

A Soviet researcher surveyed, between 1975 and 1980, 1,220 workers at a Gorky diesel factory. He found 38 per cent of his respondents had had a disagreement with the administration concerning allegedly poor levels of work organization and production (most of this group were manual workers or engineering/technical male employees). Another large group of complaints about amenities at the factory came mainly from women workers: in all 28 per cent of respondents had been involved in such conflicts. Other forms of disagreement were over premiums for the introduction of new technology (18.5 per cent), the employment of engineering/technical personnel on lower qualified and lower paid work (16%), the non-recognition of safety regulations (15.9%), the distribution of housing (17.1%), the 'style of leadership' (15.2%), insufficiencies in the union's defence of workers' rights (9.8%), and suppression of criticism (5.4%).[71]

The importance of the unions in improving production encourages criticism of the management. While there is no 'workers' control' in the USSR, the unions are sometimes effective critics of management and may work independently or with the party branch to remove management staff. The Scottish TUC delegation was informed that in 1981 '6,000 business managers who neglected workers' interests were called to administrative account at the trade unions' request. More than 150 of them were relieved of their posts'.[72] (See above p. 32).

In sharp contrast to the practice in Western countries, the local union in the USSR has to agree with the management before a worker may be dismissed. The case may then be referred to the people's court and yet again an appeal may be made to a higher court. Soviet labour relations are characterized more by judicial procedures than they are in Great Britain. How far union committees ensure that workers' rights are respected is extremely difficult to estimate. The union newspaper *Trud* often complains that unions do not protect workers' rights. McAuley's study shows that about half of the requests made for the dismissal of workers were agreed to by the unions. In such cases, workers had either been previously threatened with dismissal or frequently reprimanded. Requests for dismissals were dealt with as follows:

It was usual to call the worker before the *fabkom*. This meant that discussion of management's request could be turned into a discussion of the worker's behaviour in his presence. At Karl Marx (factory), workers who did not bother to attend were more likely to find themselves dismissed.

At Mikoyan, where the requests were not frequent and where the *fabkom* laid great stress upon educational measures, one worker who refused to listen to the *fabkom's* discussion of his behaviour and became extremely rude was, as a consequence, dismissed.[73]

Workers receive free legal help through their union in order to defend their legal rights, and may appeal to the court against the decision. In McAuley's study, only one case went to court. 'The worker had been dismissed for repeated infractions of labour discipline; he claimed before the court that he should have been dismissed for 'unsuitability at the job' because his health was poor and he could not manage his work. The court granted the claim and ordered the enterprise to make the corresponding change in his work-book.'[74] Claims for reinstatement dominate court proceedings, followed by claims over wages. Soviet courts in the late 1970s have emphasized 'the inviolability of the work contract and maintained that management may dismiss workers only with the approval of a majority of the factory union committee . . . .' Studies have shown that workers who do bring cases for wrongful dismissal to the courts have a good chance of being reinstated by them.[75] Back pay is also reimbursed.

While the factory TU committee seems to have had some effect in preventing dismissals, it takes a rather different view of workers who want to leave; in this case it seems to interpret its role as a defender of the plan and management. As skilled labour is scarce, workers who leave may seriously disrupt the plan – and the wages of other workers. The trade union committee, therefore, assumes that it has a responsibility to reduce labour turnover. At one factory a TU commission was established to investigate turnover, and those who had given in their notice were referred to it. This body could bring pressure to bear on workers who wanted to leave by saying that they first had to investigate the case.[76] (On penalties for the infringement of labour discipline, see also the following chapter.)

The explicit role of the union in engendering a 'collective consciousness' would seem to operate to strengthen the worker's attachment to his or her present place of work. Management and TU branches sometimes unite against the central authorities and may also share a common interest in opposing the wishes of the worker who sees better opportunities elsewhere. The local interest, therefore, can on occasions come before the national interest.

Strikes and Discord

Strikes are not specifically prohibited by law in the USSR, though there are laws covering acts which undermine or weaken the Soviet state, and these could possibly be used against strikers. However, strong sanctions are used against strikers and strikes are effectively proscribed in the USSR. Strikes in fact do occur, and workers sometimes go slow or walk out because of poor conditions. Most demands are 'economistic' – for better conditions and more pay – though there are rare instances known of mass protest. (Such labour unrest has been documented by Teague, Pravda and Gidwitz.)[77] These writers bring out the fact that Soviet labour disturbances are mainly due to economic rather than political causes. In Sverdlovsk in 1956, a riot was reported over 'poor living conditions'. In Novocherkassk in 1962, riots occurred following price rises and an increase in work norms: it was also reported that some people were killed following confrontation with the police. In 1963, 'disturbances' were recorded in Ryazan, Baku, Omsk, Kryvy Rih, and in Odessa dockers are said to have refused to load a ship bound for Cuba. In 1969, workers went on strike at the Kiev power station (in protest at housing conditions) and there was an eight-day pay rise strike in Lvov. In the 1970s, protests and strikes were reported to have occurred at Kiev, Vitebsk, Vladim, Sverdlovsk, Chelyabinsk, Baku, Dnepopetrovsk, Kamyanets-Podil'sky, Kaunus, Riga and Tol'yatti. In the 1980s, strikes have been reported in Tol'yatti and Gorky. In the former, the factory stopped work allegedly because of inadequate meat and dairy supplies. At the Kama truck factory Western journalists have reported a strike over food shortages in 1980.[78] Soviet officials deny such stoppages. In 1981, a strike was reported in the Kiev motorcycle enterprise. This was caused by cuts in piece-work rates. In response, the authorities relented and made good the rates.

Attempts to call out the workers for political causes have failed: a call by Estonian dissidents for a half-hour general strike against Soviet policy in Afghanistan and Poland and against food shortages went unheeded in 1981.[79] There is little support in the Soviet Union for Polish-type 'Solidarity' political action. Interviews conducted with Soviet citizens travelling abroad found that, in September 1980 to February 1982, 24 per cent 'supported liberalization' in Poland, 32 per cent had no opinion, and 44 per cent opposed liberalization; in December 1981 to May 1982 only 15 per cent were in support, 13 per cent had no opinion and 71 per cent were opposed.[80]

In 1981, 'scattered demonstrations' were said to have occurred in Sverdlovsk, Tobolsk, Odessa and Krasnodar.[81] The sources of such reports are unclear: many are based on the testimony of émigrés and may originate in rumour. If all are true, and even allowing for underreporting of other events, such accounts would indicate very little in the way of worker unrest. There is nothing comparable either in days lost or number of strikes to the experience of capitalist countries: in Britain in 1972, for example, nearly 24 million days were lost as a result of 2,500 industrial stoppages. (Despite folklore to the contrary, the number of industrial stoppages in Britain, is not particularly high – Australia, Canada, Finland, Ireland, Italy, and the USA had higher rates in the 10-year period, 1966–1975.[82]) Pravda, after a detailed study of the sources and multiplying the known industrial action to give 'a figure approaching the true total', concludes that the occurrence of strikes in the USSR is 'no more than a few dozen per year, even during what appears to be a peak period in the early 1960s'.[83]

Dissatisfaction may show itself in other ways. Workers may work poorly, they may 'lack discipline' at work, they may change their jobs,[84] though it may be argued that such activities are not forms of protest; they may legitimately be attributed to poor management or seen as an artefact of urbanization or insufficient and poor training. Many infringements of labour discipline are committed by workers with low educational levels who also have poorer levels of productivity.[85] A study of letters to the press (to the trade-union paper, *Trud*) has shown that employees do voice discontent about factory conditions (25 per cent of letters 1972–76), labour organizations (26 per cent), income and living standards (20 per cent), management and performance (16.5 per cent), trade union performance (6.6. per cent).[86] It is also conceded that safety regulations are often violated.[87] The Soviet film, *The Train Has Stopped* (1982), portrays a crash caused by multiple 'labour indiscipline' (a faulty speedometer, excessive speed of a train; and only half the number of brake shoes being fitted to trucks on an inclined siding). The film shows the public supporting the villains, who point out that, if safety regulations were enforced, nothing would ever get done. In all work organizations including those in Western states there are violations of regulations for similar reasons. Under Andropov and Chernenko the authorities have attempted to 'clamp down' on infractions of labour discipline.

Unions in Comparative Perspective

One must bear in mind that industrial conflicts of one kind or another (indiscipline, sabotage, strikes) are to be expected in any advanced industrial economy. The forms that such conflict take and its incidence vary from one society to another. In the Soviet Union, there are many formal and informal methods of resolving industrial disputes. There is no earlier (pre-revolutionary) tradition of unions organizing strikes to improve wages or conditions. The participation of management in union activities in the factory is comparable to that of Japanese unions – as is the paternalism of the economic enterprise. The activity of Soviet unions in 'management' functions and their identification with the production goals of the enterprise is something which Western capitalist countries seek to achieve. In the Soviet Union, the macro system of planning incorporates wage bargaining within the process of the 'collective agreement'. (The 'collective agreement' also has historical roots in pre-revolutionary Russia; one was concluded between workers and management in the Caucasus in 1904.)[88] Soviet industrial relations, therefore, should not be regarded as the 'bottling down' of legitimate workers' grievances by the trade unions as they are sometimes characterized in the West. Rather, Soviet unions have successfully helped to reduce stress in the factory and have played a most important part in encouraging the workers to increase production. Nevertheless, by so doing, the unions have often ignored the legitimate grievances of their members. This led in the early 1980s to calls for greater vigilance on the part of unions in support of workers' interests against management and also the beginning of the 'independent' groupings.*

Soviet trade unions cannot be seen as 'equivalents' to their Western namesakes. The 'bargaining' role of unions, expressed through wage negotiation procedures, backed by strike action (or the threat of such action) is a major difference compared with Western unions. The process of industrial relations is conditioned by the structure of the economy, by planning and by a full-employment labour policy. The range and extent of the Soviet unions' social and welfare activity far surpasses anything known in Western states. Unions in the USSR are organized on the basis that society is politically homogeneous, and that sectionist trade groups as such can have no interest above or separate from that of society as a whole, which is represented by the government. But in practice there are conflicts of interest: between union branch and management; between the enterprise and the central administration; between individual enterprises – who want to keep their own skilled workers and entice others from competitors. Rather than articulating a 'workers' interest' against other parties and aggregating a workers' interest as a whole, the unions seek to resolve disputes, and to cooperate with management to improve production – indirectly benefiting members. In Western societies, by contrast, it is held that group relations are essentially conflicting: an equilibrium is maintained through competition between sectional interests, an important one of which is the trade union which articulates and aggregates a specific workers' interest. It is essential, however, to remember that Western unions operate in quite a different context – one in which profit maximization is the goal and control of the allocative process is the right of business firms. Governments contrive to help businesses to achieve these ends and the operation of the market leads to economic crises and to unemployment.

Some Conclusions

In the fifty or so years of Soviet rule, the Soviet authorities have been faced with different kinds of economic problems. In the Stalin era, to ensure economic growth, the movement of the peasantry from village to town and to maintain labour discipline, the use of normative or ideological means were replaced by administrative control of labour and by a greater emphasis on monetary or utilitarian stimuli. The economy was a 'command' one and the ministerial apparatus was dominant. After Stalin,

---

* The 'free trade union' movement has been discussed in the companion volume in the chapter on dissent, *State and Politics in the USSR* (1984) chapter 9.

Khrushchev sought to strengthen normative sanctions and the power of the Communist Party. To this end his decentralization schemes were related. To combat the negative aspects of the government bureaucracy (localism, a tendency to inertia), Khrushchev tried to revive the party as an administrative unit of control, and, at the same time, he strengthened the lay control of administration ('control' and innovation commissions). Here the problem was not primarily one of inducing rapid economic change, but of efficiently managing a complex economy. The Brezhnev–Andropov–Chernenko leadership relied more on utilitarian means, 'economic stimulation'. Brezhnev restored the ministerial system, and Andropov and Chernenko have increased somewhat enterprise competition along market lines.

The Soviet ideology of management has consistently emphasized the unity of interest between party, state and worker. Unions promote this 'general interest', Compared with factories organized on a competitive capitalist model, there is probably greater homogeneity of interest and co-operation between worker and manager. Party and union help mobilize the worker and they provide management with information about morale and about factory problems; they help to integrate the worker into the enterprise.

The controversy over economic planning has probably weakened belief in this theoretical unity. There is also in some respects a conflict of wills between ministries, between ministry and party, between management and ministry, between management and party, between union, management and party, between enterprises and between the worker and authority.

There are also important structural differences between Soviet and Western societies. While the *process* of production is becoming more alike (more technocratic), the *proceeds* of production are quite differently apportioned. In the USA, as Galbraith has pointed out: 'no grant of feudal privilege has ever equalled, for effortless return, that of the grandparent who bought and endowed his descendants with a thousand shares of General Motors or General Electric. The beneficiaries of this foresight have become and remain rich by no exercise of effort or intelligence beyond the decision to do nothing ...'[89] There is no such apportionment in the USSR and this socially and politically gives each society unique features.

In the discussion of the performance of the economy which follows, we shall see that planning has been generally effective: it has ensured growth, full employment, basic levels of social security, a rising standard of living and a very low rate of price inflation. Generally, 'fulfilling the plan' entails the fulfilment of social needs. This is why the view that the Soviet economy is 'unstable and unviable' should be rejected (see below, chapter 3). The development of a new form of capitalism dominated by industrial managers is also an unrealistic proposition: even with the move to greater decentralization of control in the 1980s, large-scale investment still needs the approval of the Council of Ministers on the recommendation of Gosplan.[90] But the Soviet economy does face many problems. The rise of a more mature economy requires greater attention to economic calculation, and more sophisticated consumers seek higher-grade production.

NOTES

1 See: P. Wiles, *The Political Economy of Communism* (1964); M. Ellman, *Socialist Planning* (1979); M. Lavigne, *The Socialist Economies of the Soviet Union and Europe* (1974); A. Nove, *The Economics of Feasible Socialism.* (1983).
2 J.K. Galbraith, *The New Industrial State* (1967), chapter 35.
3 R. Belousov (ed.), *Sovremennaya praktika tsenobrazovaniya* (1965).
4 I.G. Petrov, *Predmet i metody sotsiologicheskikh issledovanii* (1965); English extract in *The Anglo-Soviet Journal* (London), vol. 26, no. 1/2 (1965), p. 23.
5 M. Lavigne, *The Socialist Economies...*, pp. 25–6.
6 *Narodnoe khozyaystvo SSSR 1922–82* (1982), p. 151.
7 See further details in A. Nove, *The Soviet Economic System* (1977), pp. 79–84.
8 *Ibid.*, p. 84.
9 H.H. Gerth and C.W. Mills, *From Max Weber* (1948), p. 228.
10 Ibid.
11 *SSSR v tsifrakh v 1982g* (1983), p. 163.
12 *Narodnoe khozyaystvo SSSR v 1979g.* (1980), p. 237. Henceforth abbreviated to *Narkhoz v 19..g.*
13 *Narkhoz 1922–82* (1982), p. 232. Actual production would be higher than these figures, much production not being marketed.
14 M. Makeenko, 'Ekonomicheskaya rol' lichnogo podsobnogo khozyaystva', *Voprosy ekonomiki,* no. 10 (1966), p. 63.
15 'Text of the Model Collective Farm Charter'. *Current Digest of the Soviet Press,* vol. 21, no. 50, p. 14. A. Vucinich, *Soviet Economic Institutions* (1952).
16 *Narkhoz 1922–82*, p. 225 *Narkhoz v 1982g* (1983), p. 274.
17 *Narkhoz 1922–82* (1982), p. 550.
18 M. Ellman, 'Seven Theses on Kosyginism', *De Economist* (Leiden) vol. 125, no. 1 (1977), p. 29.
19 *The Soviet Economic System,* p. 21.
20 Max Schachtman, *The Bureaucratic Revolution* (1962), p. 50, see also below, chapter 3.
21· *The Red Executive* (1960), p. 188.
22 *The Managerial Revolution* (1945).
23 See discussion on managers as a pressure group, D. Lane, *State and Politics in the USSR,* chapter 4.
24 This list from *Ekonomicheskaya gazeta,* no. 3 (1975), is cited by Alec Nove, *The Soviet Economic System,* pp. 118–9.
25 I. Vajda, cited by A. Nove, *The Soviet Economic System,* p. 92.

26 C. Kerr et al., *Industrialisation and Industrial Man* (1960), pp. 156–7.
27 M. Sergeev, 'Khozyaystvennaya reforma-vazhny rychag pod 'ema ekonomika', *Partiynaya zhizn'*, no. 12 (1966), p. 28.
28 See S. Hill, *Competition and Control at Work* (1981).
29 E.H. Carr, *The Bolshevik Revolution 1917–1923* (1952), vol.2, pp. 106–7.
30 The history of trade unionism in the USSR is discussed in detail by I. Deutscher, *Soviet Trade Unions* (1950). For early history see also Frederick I. Kaplan, *Bolshevik Ideology and the Ethics of Soviet Labor* (1968).
31 A. Piatakov, 'Labour Administration by the State and Trade Unions in the USSR', *International Labour Review*, vol. 85 (June 1962), pp. 558–9.
32 For example R. Conquest, *Industrial Workers in the USSR* (1967).
33 *Pravda*, 12 October 1983.
34 See B.A. Ruble, 'Soviet Trade Unions and Labor Relations after "Solidarity"', in *Soviet Economy in the 1980's: Problems and Prospects*, Part 2 (1982), pp. 349–55.
35 See B.Q. Madison, 'Trade Unions and Social Welfare', in A. Kahan and B.A. Ruble (eds), *Industrial Labor in the USSR* (1979), p. 86.
36 For details of scales of payment, which vary according to the kind of labor and the duration of work and average earnings, see *Gosudarstvennoe sotsial'noe strakhovanie* (1965). For a description of unions' role in social welfare see: B.Q. Madison, *ibid.*, esp. pp. 94–6. This article also discusses the social welfare provision.
37 S. Shalaev, 'Sovetskie profsoyuzy v obshchestve razvitogo sotsializma', *Pravda*, 12 Oct. 1983.
38 *Narkhoz 1922–82*, pp. 50, 315.
39 *Pravda*, 18 March 1982.
40 See Article 29, *Ustav professional'nykh soyuzov SSSR*. Printed in *Materialy XVI s"ezda professional'nykh soyuzov SSSR* (1977), pp. 142–3.
41 The duties of the respective organs are defined in the Statutes of the Trade Unions, *Ustav professional'nykh soyuzov SSSR, ibid.*
42 Mary McAuley, *Labour Disputes in Soviet Russia 1957–1965* (1969), p. 72.
43 See Discussion in B.A. Ruble, *Soviet Trade Unions* (1981), pp. 34–46.
44 Ibid., p. 35.
45 BBC (London) summary of world broadcasts SU/6920/B/2, 6 Jan. 1982.
46 E. Kuzmin. *Pravda*. 23 Dec. 1983 CDSP vol. 35, no. 51 (18 ga. 1984), p. 13.
47 *Ustav professional'nykh soyuzov SSSR*, paragraph 47 (1977).
48 Mary McAuley, *Labour Disputes in Soviet Russia 1957–65* (1969), pp. 76–7.
49 Ruble, *Soviet Trade Unions*, p. 49.
50 A. Shibaev, 'Samaya massovaya organizatsiya trudyashchikhsya', *Kommunist*, no. 4 (1981), pp. 72–83. Shibaev, then chairman of the union organization, defines union activity.
51 Ruble, *Soviet Trade Unions*, p. 49.
52 Ibid., p. 50
53 Shalaev, 'Sovetskie profsoyuzy ...'.
54 'Scottish TUC Delegation in USSR', *Soviet News* (London), 11 August 1982.
55 *Komsomol'skaya Pravda*, 6 February 1979.

56 'Profsoyuzy SSSR v tsifrakh i faktakh', *Sovetskie profsoyuzy,* no. 6 (1977), p. 4.
57 *Trud,* 13 March 1982.
58 'Profsoyuzy ... ', p. 4.
59 I. Vladychenko, *Uchastie rabochikh i sluzhashchikh v upravlenii proizvodstva* (1967), p. 36.
60 Ruble, *Soviet Trade Unions,* pp. 57–8.
61 McAuley, *Labour Disputes ... ,* p. 80.
62 See D. Lane and F. O'Dell, *The Soviet Industrial Worker* (1978), Chapter 3.
63 See Shalaev, 'Sovetskie profsoyuzy ... '.
64 Ivan Yunak, *Pravda,* 9 March 1982. Cited by E. Teague, 'On the Eve of the Soviet Trade Union Congress', RL 121/82. These views, she points out, echo those of Shelepin in 1966 and 1968.
65 McAuley, *Labour Disputes ... ,* p. 97.
66 Ibid., p. 101.
67 Ibid., p. 154. That is, in a factory employing 300 men, there would be from 9 to 30 disputes per annum brought before the boards.
68 Ibid., p. 156.
69 Ibid., p. 160
70 Ibid., p. 67.
71 V.I. Sin'kov, 'Konflikty v trudovom kolletive', *Sotsiologicheskie issledovaniya,* no. 2 (1982), p. 171.
72 *Soviet News,* 11 August 1982.
73 McAuley, *Labour Disputes ... ,* p. 124.
74 Ibid., pp. 124–5.
75 Ruble, *Soviet Trade Unions,* pp. 68–9.
76 McAuley, *Labour Disputes ... ,* pp. 126–7.
77 M. Holubenko, 'The Soviet Working Class', *Critique* (Glasgow), no. 4 (1975), pp. 14, 16; A. Boiter, 'When the Kettle Boils over ... ', *Problems of Communism* (Jan./Feb. 1964); E. Teague, 'Workers' Protests in the Soviet Union', RL 474/82 (1982); A. Pravda, 'Spontaneous Workers' Activities in the Soviet Union', in A. Kahan and B. Ruble, *Industrial Labor,* in the USSR (1979); B. Gidwitz, 'Labor Unrest in the Soviet Union', *Problems of Communism,* vol. 31, no. 6 (Nov./Dec. 1982), pp. 25–42.
78 Teague, *ibid.,* Gidwitz, ibid., pp. 32–5.
79 Teague, *ibid.,* p. 8.
80 Data cited by E. Teague, 'Workers' Protests in the Soviet Union', RL 474/82, p. 15. V. Zaslavsky's 'unofficial survey' conducted in the Soviet Union confirms these findings with respect to the reform movement in Czechoslovakia. *The Stalinist State* (1982), pp. 22–43.
81 Cited by Teague, ibid., p. 8.
82 C.T.B. Smith et al., *Strikes in Britain.* Department of Employment, London, Manpower Paper no. 15 (1978), p. 93.
83 'Spontaneous Workers' Activities' ... , p. 349.
84 These aspects are described by Alex Pravda, 'Spontaneous Workers' Activities ... ', pp. 333–42. D. Lane and F. O'Dell, *The Soviet Industrial Worker* (1978), pp. 70–73.

85 See Lane and O'Dell, ibid., pp. 70–1.
86 Pravda, *'Spontaneous Workers' Activities...'*, p. 344.
87 Ruble cites the RSFSR Ministry of Education reporting 30,000 labour safety violations in 1978 and 1979 in its establishments. 'Soviet Trade Unions and Labor Relations...', p. 360.
88 See D. Lane, *The Roots of Russian Communism* (1975), p. 86.
89 J.K. Galbraith, *The New Industrial State* (1967), p. 394.
90 M. Kaser, 'The Economy: A General Assessment', in A. Brown and M. Kaser (eds.), *The Soviet Union Since the Fall of Khrushchev* (1975), p. 210.

2
ECONOMIC PERFORMANCE AND REFORM

Assessing the current economic performance of a country is fraught with difficulties of measurement and comparison. In the ideological battle between the USA and the USSR, comparative rates of growth are more than indicators of national income and wealth; they are symbols of the efficiency, vigour and effectiveness of capitalism and socialism respectively.

In analysing the performance of any economy one may distinguish between three types of economic activity: regular, shadow (or alternative) and social. The regular economy is one which is subject to formal legislation and control: transactions are recorded in the books of the enterprise. A social economy, which will not concern us in this book, involves activities being performed in kind and having no exchange of money. A 'shadow' or alternative economy is one in which money transactions take place but are not recorded; they do not figure in formal legislative requirements – in Western societies they are not subject to tax, and in planned ones they do not figure in returns of goods produced or sold under the plan. The alternative or shadow economy exists because of inadequacies in the official one: under capitalism tax rates may be a disincentive for effort, fixed rates of remuneration (for solicitors, electricians) may be too high for consumers, and unemployment may induce workers to provide services 'on the side'. Governments may define certain activities as illicit (making, selling and consuming drugs, selling sex). Every country has its particular configuration of regular, shadow and social economic activities. They are created by the cultural norms and the legislative control of economic activity. The predominant role in modern economies is played by the regular economy. It has been estimated that the alternative economy in Britain generated the equivalent of 7½ per cent of gross national product in 1980 (or 16 per unit of gross domestic product in 1982) the American 10 per cent and the Italian as much as 30 per cent.[1] (It has been estimated that the Soviet alternative economy accounts for 10 per cent. See below.)

In this chapter we shall describe first the performance of the regular economy. Second we shall examine some of its problems (inflation, planning inadequacies) and the operation of the 'shadow' economy. Third we shall discuss various proposals for reform.

The Composition and Growth of the Gross National Product

Herbert Block has constructed an informative table comparing the gross national product per capita of the USA and Russia/USSR from 1860 to 1975. His data are reproduced in table 2.1. In addition, I have added an official Soviet comparison for the years 1950 to 1981. The figures show, despite revolution and wars, a constant rise in Russian GNP from 1913 to 1975. The gap between Soviet and American living standards has closed by nearly a half between these two dates; the Soviet data show a larger decrease to 65 per cent in 1970 and 67 per cent in 1981. However, in quantitative terms, in 1975 US dollars, the USSR had a per capita GNP of $3,088 compared to a total of $6,972 in the USA. Such data, it must be reiterated, are only rough approximations. Biases are due to relative

TABLE 2.1: LONG-TERM COMPARISON OF RUSSIAN/SOVIET AND UNITED STATES GNP

Year	Population (millions)		GNP per capita (1975 dollars)		Soviet-USA ratio (per cent)	Official Soviet calculation of Soviet– USA ratio (per cent)
	Russia*/ USSR	USA	Russia/ USSR	USA		
1913	157.9	97.2	600	2,500	24	—
1928	151.1	120.5	629	2,931	21	—
1940	195.1	132.1	904	3,182	28	—
1950	180.1	152.3	1,213	4,315	28	31
1960	214.3	180.7	1,838	4,993	37	58
1965	230.9	194.3	2,182	5,882	37	59
1970	242.8	204.9	2,722	6,523	42	>65
1975	254.5	213.6	3,088	6,972	44	—
1977	—	—	—	—	60	—
1982	—	—	—	—	—	67

Note: *Population: 1913: boundaries of Imperial Russia; for 1928, those of the inter-war USSR; from 1940, post-war boundaries.
Sources: Herbert Block, 'Soviet Economic Growth – Achievements under Handicaps', Soviet Economy in a New Perspective, Joint Economic Committee of the United States Congress, Washington (1976), p. 268. Narkhoz 1922–1982 (1982), p. 91, Narkhoz v 1982g (1983) p. 56.
Imogene Edwards et al., 'US and USSR: Comparisons of GNP'. Soviet Economy in a Time of Change, vol. 1. Joint Economic Committee of Congress, Washington DC (1979), p. 370.

levels of prices (transport, rent, electricity and health are lowly priced in the USSR, but expensive in the USA), to the bundles of goods available for consumption in the different countries, and also to theoretical differences in the compilation of material product.[2] Taking indexes of output of various commodities, which may be measured in quantitative (rather than price) terms, the USSR by 1981 was the second most powerful economy in the world. Industrial production was 80 per cent of American in 1981 (30 per cent in 1950), electrical power was 53 per cent (22 per cent in 1950), oil 145 per cent (14 per cent in 1950), steel 133 per cent (30 per cent in 1950), cement 167 per cent (26 per cent in 1950) and textiles 179 per cent (32 per cent in 1950). In 1982, the USSR claimed to be the world's leading producer of iron, steel, oil, cement, woollen goods; from being the fourth major producer of industrial goods in 1913, it now claims to be the first.[3]

While the Soviet Union has effectively reached a high level of material production as measured by many economic indicators, the performance of the Soviet economy is criticized in the West on two counts. First, it is held to be inefficient, and second, it is said to be suffering declining growth rates since the 1950s.

As far as growth is concerned, Western (especially American) estimates tend to be lower than Soviet ones. Table 2.2 shows CIA calculations and Soviet ones for selected periods from 1951 to 1980.

TABLE 2.2: AVERAGE ANNUAL PERCENTAGE GROWTH OF SOVIET GNP

	CIA Estimate	Soviet Estimate
1951–1980 GNP	4.7	7.4
Industrial product	6.8	8.7
Agricultural production	2.8	3.1
Per capita consumption	3.5	5.0

	CIA Estimate
1951–55	5.5
1956–60	5.6
1961–65	5.9
1971–75	3.7
1976–80	2.7

Source: USSR: Measures of Economic Growth and Development, 1950–80, Joint Economic Committee, US Congress, Washington DC (1982), pp. VIII, 15, 26.

These figures undoubtedly show a long-term drop in growth rates. Two points must be borne in mind in evaluating these trends. First, other industrial countries experienced decline in these years. OECD countries experienced an average growth rate of gross domestic product of 5.2 per cent 1961–65 and only 4.0 per cent 1976–79; the USA had comparable rates of 4.6 per cent and 4.4 per cent for the respective dates.[4] Clement has calculated comparative average annual rates of growth of produced national income per capita of the population for the period 1976–1980. On this index the USSR had a growth rate of 3.4 per cent, the EEC countries averaged 2.8 per cent (W. Germany 3.7 and Great Britain 1.6).[5] Second, countries have different factor endowments (i.e. level of technology and labour skills) and are at different stages of development. As economies reach an advanced industrial state, it becomes increasingly difficult to increase levels of productivity and labour. Falling growth *rates* do not necessarily entail an absolute decline in gross or per capita national product. For instance, the average American would be better off following a 1 per cent increase in American GNP than would the average Russian or Briton consequent on a 2 per cent rise in GNP of the Soviet or British economies. Since the late 1950s, the Soviet Union has had declining levels of capital productivity and labour productivity. Such trends are shown in table 2.3. In comparative and in absolute terms, productivity is lower in the USSR than in the USA and other advanced European capitalist countries.

On the basis of comparing the market value of output with the utilized input (labour and capital), many writers have argued that the historical experience of the USSR demonstrates the economic superiority of capitalism over socialism.[6] However, and as Ellman has pointed out, this is an unsound way of comparing economic systems. Czechoslovakia is more efficient than India in this respect, but this hardly 'proves' the superiority of socialism over capitalism. The fallacy of this line of argument is that it

TABLE 2.3: COMPARATIVE TRENDS IN LABOUR AND CAPITAL PRODUCT-
IVITY (PERCENTAGE GROWTH)

| | Labour Productivity | | Capital Productivity | |
	1960–73	1974–78	1960–73	1974–78
USSR	3.7	2.3	−3.2	−4.5
USA	3.1	1.4	0.3	−0.7
United Kingdom	3.8	2.0	−1.0	−2.9
Japan	9.9	3.6	−1.4	−3.4

Source: Stanley H. Cohn, 'Sources of Low Productivity in Soviet Capital Investment', *Soviet Economy in the 1980's: Problems and Prospects.* Joint Economic Committee, US Congress, Washington DC (1982), p. 173.

does not take account of the stage of development of the economic system and it ignores other measures of economic and social well-being. Economic 'efficiency' is not synonymous with social welfare. One might have an extremely cost efficient Coca-Cola plant located in a poverty-ridden, mass unemployment underdeveloped society. Even so, Soviet Marxists would concede that the USA is superior in terms of capital and labour productivity.[7]

The Marxist criteria of economic welfare focus on the 'available inputs and the social utility of output'.[8] This takes into account the level of technology and cultural differences (a mobile, 'ambitious' work force in the USA, a traditional peasantry in the USSR). The inefficient utilization of resources as a whole is also considered in a Marxist comparison: i.e. high levels of unemployment of the labour force, idle capacity of capital. Under-utilization of industrial capital in the United States in the 1970s was approximately 20 per cent, and registered unemployment was around 8 per cent (the actual level was higher than this[9]); in the early 1980s registered unemployment was over 8 million in the USA, with another 5 million on short time (under 14 hours per week); in Britain registered unemployment reached 3.3 million, 13 per cent of the work force. Moreover, notice should be taken of the kinds of commodities produced and the distribution of goods and services. Armaments production, income of parasite groups (rentiers), advertising, built-in obsolescence, pollution, crime, and poverty have to come into the reckoning in the appraisal of an economic system. The criteria invoked by defendants of the economic systems of capitalism and state socialism entail ideological and moral judgments of values.

Distribution of Gross National Product by Origin and End Use

Gross national product may be considered from the point of view of its sector of origin – what gives rise to national income, and its form of distribution – how national income is distributed.

The development of the Soviet economy has led to a decline in the share of GNP attributable to agriculture and a rise in that of industry. Agriculture accounted for 31 per cent of GNP in 1950 and only 14 per cent in 1980; the relative share of industry rose from 20 per cent to 37 per cent.[10]

Since the early 1950s, Soviet agricultural production has shown a steady increase.[11] The total agricultural output has increased fairly constantly since 1950, though grain output has fluctuated. Taking 1960 as a base (100), gross agricultural production, according to official figures, rose to 146 in 1972–74 (using a 3 year average). There have, however, been severe fluctuations: in 1972, 1974 and 1975 there were *negative* growth levels of

4.1 per cent, 2.7 per cent and 6.0 per cent.[12] For the period from 1970 to 1978–80, the average annual rate of growth was 1.2 per cent.[13] From 1950 to 1980 agricultural output grew at a rate of 3 per cent per annum. While these statistics show respectable, though fluctuating, rates of growth, they are generally conceded, even by Soviet writers, to be inadequate to meet demand.

Part of the problem is pricing policy. Prices have been held constant since 1950 and, given the rising standard of living, demand is not fulfilled. A consequence is the absence of goods in the shops, particularly better quality food goods, such as meat, poultry and fruits. Consumption of meat, for instance, has doubled since 1950,[14] and the price of meat in the collective farm (or 'free' market) is double that of official prices. To meet the shortfall the Soviet authorities have attempted to increase domestic production. Plans, however, have not been achieved: the 1976–80 plan was only 94.3 per cent fulfilled for grain, 97.4 per cent for meat and 82.4 per cent for potatoes.[15] Food and feedstuffs have been imported, notably from the USA. Severe fluctuations in output occur in the USSR. Ostensibly this is due to climatic conditions, but lack of reserves and storage facilities are equally important. The USSR has bought its way out of agricultural shortages by using the world market.

The major change in end use of Soviet GNP since 1950 has been an increase in total investment and defence expenditure. Investment climbed from 14 per cent in 1950 to 33 per cent in 1980. The *growth* rate for investment, however, has declined: it was 11.5 per cent per year in the 1950s and only 5.8 per cent per year since 1960.

Defence Expenditure

Attempts to quantify the 'defence effort' of the superpowers are even more fraught with difficulties than estimating the economic performance. Soviet writers rely on budget allocations for defence: they say that between 1971 and 1980, the proportion of the Soviet budget for defence declined. In the years 1971–75, it averaged 9.5 per cent of outgoings; in 1976–80, it fell to 6.6 per cent, in 1982 the figure was 5.3 per cent.[16] In the late 1960s, the Institute of Strategic Studies estimated that Soviet arms expenditure in total was only half that of the USA. A revised basis of estimation provided by the CIA has changed the picture considerably in the 1970s. Basing their estimates on the costs of the defence effort and including other items in the budget (such as investment and research), defence expenditure has been estimated at 11 to 13 per cent of GNP in 1970. According to the CIA, it has increased at an average annual rate of 4 to 5 per cent per year since 1965.[17]

TABLE 2.4: DEFENCE EXPENDITURE, UK, USA, USSR.

	Defence expenditure (million US $) 1968	1982	As a % of GNP 1968	1982	As a % of total central government expenditure 1982	Per capita $ 1968	1982
Britain	5,450	24,200	5.3	5.1	11.9	98	432
USA	79,576	215.900	9.2	7.2	29.2	136	938
USSR	39,780	267.000*	9.3	10–20†	N.A.	169	N.A.‡

Sources: Institute of Strategic Studies. *The Military Balance 1968/69* (1968), pp. 55–6. *The Military Balance 1983/84* (1983), pp. 13–14, 125–6.

Note: *1981

　　†Range of Western estimates, Soviet calculation 4.8 per cent.

　　‡1978 estimate was US $574 when the comparative American figure was US $782. *The Military Balance 1982/83* (1982), p. 124.

By 1982, it was estimated at 13 per cent of GNP, and projected to rise to 14 per cent by 1985.[18] As we see from table 2.4, Soviet defence expenditure in 1982 is considered to be more than that of the USA. As GNP in the Soviet Union is much smaller, the 'defence burden' is that much greater.

The effects of Soviet defence expenditure have been deleterious to the Soviet economy. Allocation of resources to defence has been at the cost of investment which might have offset the decline in capital productivity. Military procurement is given priority for supplies, and this probably makes worse materials shortages and bottlenecks for the rest of the economy.[19] It has not only reduced investment levels, as noted above, but has diverted machinery output from consumer to military production.

Consumption

Consumption as a proportion of GNP has fallen from 60 per cent in 1950 to 54 per cent in 1980. But the consumption of goods has risen at an annual rate of 4.3 per cent per year since 1950, and services at 4.2 per cent. Food as a percentage of GNP has dropped to 23 per cent in 1980, from 32 per cent in 1950. Soviet per capita consumption grew at 2.9 per cent per annum from 1950 to 1970, but between 1970 and 1980, it dropped to 2.2 per cent per annum.[20] In 1981, it was less than 2 per cent and fell to some 1 per cent in 1982.[21] The rates of growth for different kinds of goods and services since 1966 are shown in table 2.5.

Economic performances may be more concretely studied by consideration of the levels of pay and typical forms of consumption in the Soviet Union compared to other states.

TABLE 2.5: AVERAGE RATES OF GROWTH IN CONSUMPTION PER CAPITA IN USSR (PER CENT PER ANNUM)

	1966–70	1971–75	1976–80	1981
Total Consumption	5.1	2.8	2.4	1.9
Goods	5.4	2.8	2.3	2.0
Food	4.3	1.6	1.3	0.7
Soft goods	7.1	3.0	3.1	2.4
Durables	9.1	10.0	5.4	6.4
Services	4.3	3.0	2.4	1.8
Personal	5.8	4.6	3.4	2.1
Education	2.9	1.4	1.6	0.6
Health	3.2	1.4	1.1	0.1

Source: Gertrude E. Shroeder, 'Soviet Living Standards: Achievements and Prospects', in *Soviet Economy in the 1980's: Problems and Prospects* (Part 2). Joint Economic Committee, US Congress, Washington DC (1982), p. 370.

The standard of living in the USSR is lower than that in the advanced countries of the West. Just how much lower and how it should be calculated is a bone of contention between economists. Western analysts have compared, 'earned incomes' per capita in different countries. In 1981, it has been calculated that for industrial workers average net take-home pay (i.e. after deductions of tax and additions of family allowances) in the USSR was 171 rubles per month. This comes to US$238, compared to a monthly take-home pay of $984 in the USA, and $738 in the United Kingdom at the 1981 official exchange rates.[22] These figures cannot be assumed to measure purchasing power: first, the ruble rate of exchange may be artificial; second, the level of employment is higher in the USSR and the number of wage-earners per family is larger (usually wives are in full-time jobs); third, the structure of prices varies; fourth, 'income in kind' is a higher share of consumption in the Soviet Union than in capitalist countries (e.g. low 'uneconomic' rents, free social services, subsidized meals). Even if one were to compensate Soviet wage levels to take account of the first two of these qualifications, Soviet earned income would still be less than half the American figure.

Soviet citizens are faced with a different pattern of prices compared with those in capitalist countries. Many services are provided at no charge by the government and others do not reflect their scarcity value. One estimate is that necessaries (shelter, medical care, transport, insurance) account for some 15 per cent of Soviet money income, whereas they come to about 50 per cent of the American family's. In the USSR rent, heating and light are provided very cheaply, other services, (medical, dental, child care) are

TABLE 2.6: CONSUMPTION OF CONSUMER GOODS AND FOOD IN USSR

Durable Consumer Goods	Per 100 families		
	1965	1975	1982
Watches	319	455	520
Radios	59	79	90
Televisions	24	74	92
Cameras	24	27	32
Refrigerators	11	61	89
Washing machines	21	65	70
Motor cycles and scooters	6	8	13
Sewing machines	52	61	65

Food Products	Per capita (kg.)			
	1913	1950	1975	1982
Bread products	200	172	141	137
Potatoes	—	241	120	110
Vegetables and pulses	40	51	89	101
Sugar	8.1	1.6	40.9	44.5
Vegetable oils	—	2.7	7.6	9.3
Meat and meat products	27	26	57	57
Milk and dairy products	154	172	316	295
Fish and fish products	6.7	7.0	16.8	18.4
Eggs	48*	60*	216*	249*

Note: *Eggs, per capita
Sources: Narkhoz v 1978g. (1979), p. 412; Narkhoz 1922–82 (1982), pp. 447, 448. SSSR v tsifrakh v 1982 g
(1983), pp. 197, 199.

highly subsidized. Rent payable for housing and repair of property has remained unchanged since 1928.[23] Philip Hanson has estimated Soviet average expenditure and British 'low income expenditure', in which he shows that the Soviets spend five per cent of their income on housing, fuel, light and power whereas the British spend twenty-seven per cent.[24] The Soviet family has more for discretionary purchasing after shelter has been paid for.

Production of consumer goods has increased regularly in the Soviet Union in the past twenty years, and food products, with some exceptions, have also improved in quantity. The absolute consumption per head (for food products) from 1913 to 1982 and per family (for consumer durable goods) from 1965 to 1982 is shown in table 2.6. The calorific food value is roughly equal to that of the American per capita though the Soviet consumer's diet contains more bread and less meat and milk. The Soviet citizen is at a comparable level with Western societies as far as radios, fridges and washing machines are concerned – though these are often of inferior quality. One notable absence in the tables is the motor car which is not a mass consumption commodity in the USSR. In most consumer fields the USSR lags behind the USA and UK. In the mid-1970s ownership per thousand of the population of various goods was as follows[25]:

	USSR	USA	UK
Radios	211	1965	340
Television sets	182	474	305
Telephones	53	627	314
Cars	12	448	234

An American estimate is that total consumption has increased by 36 per cent from 1970 to 1979. For various goods the percentage increase was: food, 23; soft goods, 41; durables, 113; consumer services, 39; repair and personal care, 76; leisure, 42; education, 24; health, 23.[26]

A study of consumer needs by the Lenkoran City Party Committee's Sociological Research Council illustrates the present levels of consumer satisfaction and also aspirations for different goods by different social classes. Some of the results are shown in table 2.7.

Bush has overcome the problem of index number comparisons by ingeniously calculating purchasing power in terms of working time. Some of his data are shown in table 2.8. Apart from public transport and rent, all consumer goods require more labour time to earn in the USSR than in the USA or UK. Of a comprehensive list of goods and services, only the

TABLE 2.7: PRESENT AND DESIRED OWNERSHIP OF VARIOUS ARTICLES IN THE USSR

	State Farm Workers		Industrial and Building Workers		Intelligentsia and Office Workers	
	Own	Want to Acquire	Own	Want to Acquire	Own	Want to Acquire
Washing machine	16.5	63.9	25.3	33.7	37.0	40.7
Vacuum cleaner	0.8	33.9	16.8	25.3	29.7	34.0
Black/white TV	87.8	5.2	83.1	4.8	84.5	6.7
Colour TV	1.6	2.6	7.2	14.4	10.0	34.5
Car	4.4	18.3	12.0	28.9	11.5	41.0
Cow	53.9	20.0	19.2	9.6	20.0	4.0
Household plot	76.5	2.6	53.0	9.6	50.7	6.2

Sources: Adapted from Ch. A. Mansimov, 'Izmeneniya v zhiznennom uklade semey lenkoranskogo rayona', *Sotsiologicheskie issledovaniya*, no. 3 (1981), p. 105.

TABLE 2.8: LABOUR TIME PURCHASING POWER FOR SELECTED COMMODITIES, USSR, USA AND UK

Minutes of Work Time Necessary to Purchase 1 kg	USSR (Moscow) 1971	1982	USA (Washington) 1971	1982	UK (London) 1971	1982
White bread	23	17	8	16	25	25
Beef	168	123	52	69	115	115
Potatoes	8	7	3	7	7	3
Butter	295	222	39	55	79	50
Vodka (0.7 litre)		452		61		131
Petrol (10 litres)	82	185	21	32	92	85
Bus fare (3 km)	4	3	6	7	6	11
Hours of Work Time						
Apartment rent month (hours)		12		51		28
Colour TV	1169	701	165	65	498	132
Months of Work Time						
Small car		53		5		11

Sources: K. Bush, 'Soviet Living Standards', *Aspects of Daily Life in the USSR* (Brussels: NATO, 1975), pp. 5, 11.
K. Bush and A. Tenson, 'Indicators of Living Standards in the USSR and Eastern Europe', *Radio Liberty Research*, RL 101/77 (May 1977), p. 12.
K. Bush, 'Retail Prices in Moscow and Four Western Cities in March 1982', RFE/RL (June 1982).
Note: Data are based on average net income of industrial workers.

following on Bush's calculations were cheaper in Moscow than in Washington: veal, cod, beetroot, cotton wool, subway fare, cinema (also theatre, I would add), hotel room, electricity, gas, local telephone call, telegram, men's haircut, women's manicure.

Social Benefits

Soviet writers would retort that these figures reflect only one part of consumption and that other factors have to be taken into account. As noted earlier, in capitalist countries registered unemployment is often in excess of 10 per cent of the work force, leaving literally millions of workers unemployed. Even if one were to concede that Soviet writers ignore their own frictional unemployment (people changing jobs), Soviet citizens in this regard are better off; they also do not experience the uncertainty about keeping a job. Full employment is ensured by the centrally organized economy. The costing of labour has a different value from the point of view of the capitalist enterprise and that of the socialist economy.[27] Under capitalism a firm is concerned only with making a profit and will employ labour only to the point where marginal product equals wage (i.e. if wages are $500 per week and the output attributed to an extra worker is $490, he will not be employed). Unemployed workers, however, are social costs to society. Not only is there an 'opportunity cost' involved in their not working (skills and labour time wasted), but the government has to pay social security benefits to keep the worker and his family alive. In a planned economy, however, the government can take account of the cost to society as a whole of people being unemployed. Not only is there a benefit in terms of individual well-being and social status to employment, but in economic terms it makes sense to employ workers as long as the loss to production is less than the social security benefits saved. In the case above, for instance, if unemployment benefit came to $310 per week, it would make more economic sense to keep the person in work and pay the employer $10 per week: the government would save $300 and the worker would contribute $490 in output. Hence the 'inefficiency' of Soviet labour observed by many Western commentators (i.e. low output and a surplus of workers) has to be balanced against the high work rate of the *employed* Western work force, plus the army of unemployed on social security and a largely dependent female unpaid domestic labour force. The Soviet Union has secured full employment as a social policy: over 95 per cent of the male population of employable age are at work and the figure falls only to 82 per cent for women. Frictional unemployment (people changing jobs) is about 2 per cent and time lost in such movement is under half that of the USA.[28]

A low-wage, full-employment policy, however, brings in its train other problems. First, the existence of a reserve army of unemployed in the West acts as a form of discipline over labour. It discourages industrial militancy and allows the employer choice over the hiring and firing of personnel. Second, a low-wage policy reduces the incentive of workers to extend themselves to greater effort. Hence if growth of national product is dependent on increases in labour productivity, the lack of wage differentials (economic stimulus) and an inadequate assortment of quality consumer goods gives the worker little 'economic' incentive to work harder. Managers are unable to 'shed labour' because of the political and social reasons mentioned above. A vicious circle develops of low pay, lax work attitudes, poor morale and declining efficiency. Alternatives suggested (see below) are greater reliance on 'the market' (financial incentives, 'shedding' labour) and more draconian labour laws.

In addition to security of employment, the Soviet worker is guaranteed a minimum wage (currently 70 rubles per month; 80 rubles is planned in the current Five-Year Plan), provided that he or she works efficiently. Men, on reaching 60 years (having worked 20 years), have guaranteed pensions ranging from 50 to 55 per cent of their pay: in 1980 the average pension (including those of collective farmers) was 45.4 rubles per month; for those receiving pensions from state insurance funds, it was 60.1 rubles.[29] In 1980 the average wage for manual and non-manual workers was 168.9 rubles per month). (Women workers have a pension entitlement at 55 years of age.)

Maternity leave for one year is granted to women who interrupt their work: payment ranges from 35 rubles to 50 rubles per month and is thus much lower than full rates of pay. A non-recurrent maternity grant of 50 rubles is payable for the first child and 100 rubles for the second and third child and a monthly family allowance is paid for the fourth and every subsequent child (for the first five years only). Single mothers receive 20 rubles per month from the government for each child. These social service payments are now fairly common in European countries and levels are even better in welfare states such as Denmark and Sweden. The Soviet Union has enhanced the provision of education: in the USSR there were 197 students per 10,000 of the population in 1981–82; in Britain 98; in West Germany 106 (1979–80); the United States was at the top of the league with 261. Medical care in the USSR is provided free by the government (though a charge is made for prescriptions); the number of doctors in the USSR comes to 38.5 per 10,000 of the population; comparative figures are 22.6 for the USA, 18.3 for Great Britain, 26.7 for West Germany and 15.3 for France.[30] Life expectancy is comparable to Western states: in 1980 it was 70 years in the USSR (71 in the USA and 72 in the UK). The infant mortality rate was somewhat greater: 230 (per 10,000 live births) in the USSR, 192 in the USA and 178 in the UK.[31] (See discussion below p. 117). But social provision is not of a uniformly high standard. In 1977, the average person had only 12 square metres of house space. In 1981, 20 per cent of urban families still lived in communal flats.[32] There are still serious pockets of poverty: McAuley has estimated that in the late 1960s, 40 per cent of the Soviet population were below a poverty line of 50 rubles per month.[33] The raising of the minimum wage, the improvement of the earnings of collective farmers and the rise in child allowances have reduced the size of this group in the 1980s. Distribution of income is much more equal in the USSR than in the advanced capitalist countries.[34] Critics would argue that the greater the scale of social provision, the less important becomes the instrumental use of money for consumption and hence the incentive to work is diminished.

Inflation

Another major difference between capitalist and state socialist economies is the absence of price inflation in the latter. Prices are fixed by the government. Between 1955 and 1974, the official index of prices rose only 1.2 per cent.[35] Such figures give too low a weight to the prices of new products and, of course, ignore completely the price structure in the markets for collective farm produce. Even so, all Western commentators would concede that price levels have been held down and that price inflation in the USSR is not the problem that it is in the West. Price inflation, according to reliable Western studies, has been 'mild', averaging in the 1960s and 1970s from 0.8 to 1.2 per cent per annum.[36] However, there are other kinds of inflation besides price inflation. One of the most important is that of suppressed inflation. Here the demand for goods exceeds the supply of goods at the ruling price. Goods vanish when they are put on the market, services are oversubscribed – e.g. queues form for goods in short supply at the fixed price. We noted above that the supply of commodities and levels of consumption have increased in the USSR. This does not mean that the shops are full of goods. Many Soviet writers complain about the *defitsit* (shortage) of certain goods. The Western press contains many accounts of food and other shortages in the USSR. A study of 782 Soviet travellers in Europe in 1981 reported that they said that only 3 out of 19 foodstuffs (sugar, bread, vodka) were regularly available in shops in 80 per cent of 102 cities.[37] While no hard and fast data are available, there is much evidence of shortages and the lack of sufficient supply to meet demand.

There are three reasons for this state of affairs. First is price inflexibility: prices are fixed by the planners either on a cost plus profitability margin (for most wholesale goods) or a cost plus estimated market demand, or on the basis of political considerations. The last criteria apply to utilities such as gas and house rents and to essential commodities such as meat and butter. These have been held constant for many years. The prices of other consumer goods (taxi fares, some consumer durables) have increased in recent years. Prices, however, tend to lag behind demand. Second, there are regional and temporal shortages of certain goods. These are created by transport bottlenecks or shortfalls in production of certain goods (e.g. potatoes at times of drought). Unlike in capitalist market societies, prices do not rise to equate demand and supply. Third, there has been an increase in purchasing power: the amount of money in circulation has increased, driving up demand.[38]

The negative consequences of suppressed inflation are similar to those of price inflation. Unless supply can respond to meet demand – the response favoured by the Soviet government – money loses its value. Administrative means (seniority), corruption (under-the-counter deals), bribery (paying over the odds) replace the market. The effective role of material incentives at the place of work declines. Consumers lack confidence and when goods are available they are hoarded, creating greater supply difficulties, which exacerbates the problem.

Just as some goods are priced too low in relation to demand, others are too expensive. Goods are produced in quantities and styles which suit the producers 'plan maximization' rather than consumer needs. Output is often valued by weight of materials and consequently Soviet goods are often too heavy as a result. Producers also sometimes try to maximize their total sales by inflating the costs of their products or services. Restaurants 'encourage' the consumption of bread and the taking of drinks with meals. The following example is reported in *Izvestiya*:

About two years ago, garment manufacturers . . . began sewing mink collars on women's winter coats costing 150 rubles each. The price jumped all the way to 500 rubles . . . [The planners] had good reason to rejoice: the fulfilment of the plan for deliveries of expensive articles (in retail prices) has a direct effect on the formation of the bonus fund.

But then the goods entered the trade network . . . . 'As of 1 February 1983 [said the director of the Moscow Clothing Stores Association] our stores alone still had 10 million rubles worth of these items in stock . . . .'

The women's winter coats hanging in the stores are made of an unattractive, faded material that doesn't match the buttons or trim, and the luxuriant mink collars look completely out of place on them.[39]

The inadequacies of the planning mechanism and distortions in production and exchange have led to the formation of the 'shadow' or alternative economy as defined above.

The Alternative Economy

Under capitalism an alternative economy accounts for some 10 per cent of GNP of advanced industrial societies (see above). It is a response to distortions of market conditions created by governments. Transactions take place in cash rather than through credit or bank debits. The regular economy based on large-scale production provides materials and commodities for the shadow one: the latter is dependent on the former.

While the official market with controlled prices covers the great bulk of transactions in the USSR, there are other markets in which the owners of commodities effectively fix their own price in relation to demand. There are secondhand shops and 'flea' markets in most major towns (not Moscow). The collective farm market deals in produce from private agricultural plots. This is the most important in quantitative terms (there are about 8,000 of such units in the USSR). In addition, there are semi-legal and illegal markets. These markets fill the gaps left by the state system and reflect the unfulfilled demand side of the inadequacies of economic calculation mentioned above. Katsenelinboigen[40] has classified such forms of exchange as grey, brown and black markets. The 'grey' market deals in transactions which are not officially recorded and are untaxed. These include renting flats and houses (owners simply let their premises to anyone prepared to pay the asking price), private tuition, in the form of coaching for exams, and individual payment for a doctor's or dentist's private services.

Provision of craftsmen's services for the repair of houses and cars are other examples. The authorized and forbidden areas of artisans' activities are defined in Appendix D. Tailoring is a major activity. This breaches the boundaries of legality when materials are diverted from the regular economy. According to Grossman, construction teams (*stroitel'nye arteli*) who work mainly in the summer months for high wages (a year's pay for 8–12 weeks' work) often use materials obtained illegally.[41] Illegal distilleries are another source of private production and trade.

Private agricultural production and sale is one of the more important forms of 'unplanned' activity. It is perfectly legal. In 1980, for instance, some 49 per cent of potatoes sold where from the private sector; vegetables accounted for 15 per cent.[42] About a quarter of the gross value of agricultural production and some 3 per cent of meat production comes from this source.[43] This represents a decline of production from 31½ per cent in 1965. Prices are much higher than in the government shops; for a given range of goods in 1970, prices were 55 per cent greater on the collective farm market. This figure soared to 76 per cent in 1975.[44] Such activity, it should be reiterated, is only marginally part of the second economy.

A more recognized area of a 'shadow economy' is the practice of doing private work in company time. Radio sets are said to be produced on this basis and then sold privately. Private illegal manufacture is also carried out. Grossman cites the case of the 'lipstick king' who contracted out lipstick manufacture but marketed them from a house in Moscow.[45]

Production enterprises sometimes barter their excess products for materials in which they are short; hence, a kind of unofficial redistribution of production takes place. The 'brown market' is one where there is an excess of demand for a commodity at its official price; such commodities vanish when they come into the shops: examples are fashionable clothes, furniture, cars, fruit at certain times, building materials. This results in an illegal market in which commodities sell at above-market prices and often leads to the corruption of sales staff. Products made abroad and imported by Russians or foreign tourists, or bought in foreign currency shops, also lead to speculative sales. The 'black market' is an extension of the 'brown market' and involves speculation on a wider scale. Such trade includes imported commodities and those with limited sale (such as vodka); stolen goods from enterprises and those which are 'sub-standard' are important sources here. 'Illegal goods', such as foreign currency, gold, certain gramophone records, drugs, and prostitutes' services, also come into this category.

A crucial dimension of the shadow economy is its scale. Does it undermine the basis of planning and provide a different order of distribution? The evidence is extremely unreliable respecting the extent of the shadow economy. Grossman is unable to come to a quantitative conclusion: he says that its 'effect on nominal personal incomes is not negligible'.[46] In his 1983 work he asserts that 'the weight of circumstantial evidence suggests that the shadow economy is growing relative to the national economy as a whole.'[47] However, he provides insufficient data to come to this conclusion. Ofer and Vinokur,[48] on the basis of interviews with 1,000 urban Soviet Jewish émigrés to Israel, conclude that 10 to 12 per cent of their total income came from private sources; they estimate that the shadow economy represents an addition of 3–4 per cent of GNP. It is open to question whether 1,000 Jewish urban ex-Soviet immigrants to Israel are representative of the Soviet population as a whole. Shakharov has guessed the figure of '10 per cent or more'.[49] These estimates, however, would suggest a shadow economy smaller in size that those of industrial Western societies.

The alternative economy is an informal economy. It is restricted to personal contacts and to direct exchange of products or service for money. Mars and Altman have shown how the alternative economy is supported by the folk culture of the Georgian republic (or at least the Jewish Georgian culture). They argue that, rather than there being a universalistic achievement-orientated social system, relationships are specific, patronage and kin relations predominate, cheating is widespread and conspicuous consumption is a trait of high status. The 'second economy', they argue, is a part of the 'core values' of Georgian society.[50] 'Georgian men not only benefit economically from "screwing the system" – their very honour as men demands that they should screw it excessively.'[51] Whether these are values for Georgian *society* may be questioned, as most of their observations are derived from life among recently arrived immigrants to Israel from Georgia. Mars and Altman, however, do make the very good point that traditional culture (or, as I would prefer, sub-cultures) does sustain the alternative economy on the basis of personal social networks.

Control and ownership of large-scale production is firmly in the hands of the state, and the alternative economy in the Soviet Union is likely to be a relatively small part of gross national product; it may become more visible as affluence grows and semi-legal or illegal markets respond to consumer demands. The alternative economy has some positive effects. It overcomes the inflexibility of the price system in the planned economy, and it provides an added incentive to labour. It also has negative elements: it is a form of redistribution which undermines the wage structure, it rewards only those people with marketable skills, it does not encourage the planners to improve their work by providing what people want, it militates against a socialist ethic of distribution.[52] It is perhaps too easy to become moralistic about a second market. Its existence is probably inevitable in any society, and governments attempt suppression at their own peril. Under socialism, the 'alternative economy' is compatible with planning if it complements rather than undermines central planning. How to ensure a better mix of planning and market forces is the concern of economic reform.

ECONOMIC REFORM

The economic problems we have discussed have led to the call for economic reform in the USSR. There are two approaches to reform. The first prognosis is that there are profound faults and inadequacies in the present system of planning. Some Soviet writers even suggest that the present form of the control of the means of production is no longer compatible with the relations to the means of production. A major change in the productive relations of state socialism is necessary. As Ellman has put it, a reform analogous to the transition from War Communism to the New Economic Policy is required.[53] The second approach concedes that changes are necessary to bring planning into line with the more advanced economy, but insists that the existing structure of ownership, control and exchange be maintained. Reform is limited to improving the forms of administration of the economy within the existing context of central planning. Such reforms are referred to in the USSR as changes in the 'economic mechanism'.[54]

The more radical solution is of two kinds. First is the call for the development of market relations in the context of a socialist market economy. Second is the view that the Soviet Union can only move towards socialism following a revolutionary change in the nature of power relationships. Proponents of the 'revolutionary' solution, which involve a critique of both the 'market' solution and the 'conservative' one, will be discussed in the next chapter.

The Reform of Administrative Procedures and the Apparatus

Reforms of the 'economic mechanism' are limited in scope. The following structural features of planning are to remain: the definition of economic goals by the political leadership and their execution by the government planning agencies; central planning of the activities of economic enterprises; the maintenance of full employment; the relatively not too unequal distribution of incomes; plan fulfilment continues to be the major criterion for the 'success' of enterprises; consumer demands and enterprise activity expressed through market relationships stay severely curtailed. Improvements in the form of administrative management take many forms. These have included the formation of 'production associations'; this process may be conceived of as something akin to takeovers in capitalist states. The grouping together of enterprises, it is thought, leads to economies of scale, more efficient distribution and saving on overheads, such as research and administration. The planning process may be improved through the wider use of modern data processing equipment to ensure more accurate economic calculations.

The kinds of economic reforms likely in the 1980s may be anticipated by the 1979 decree of the CPSU Central Committee and USSR Council of Ministers: 'On the Improvement of Planning and the Strengthening of the Action of the Economic Mechanism on the Raising of Effectiveness of Production and the Quality of Work'. Four main modifications to the planning process were suggested.[55] First, 'normative net output' is used as a measure of output in manufacture; this replaces the previous index of gross output or sales. Second, a system of 'counter-planning' is favoured; this entails enterprises having stable five-year plans with annual targets and improving on these yearly targets gives enhanced levels of bonuses. Third, plan fulfilment is assessed on a yearly basis rather than quarterly; this enables enterprises a longer time span for alterations and improvements. Bonuses are paid to enterprises on the basis of labour productivity, fulfilment of contracts and 'quality mix' – by quality is meant the extent to which the product is 'up-to-date' and comparable to products on the world market. Fourth, ministries and enterprises are to finance operations from internal funds and bank credits.

Bonuses for enterprises are important incentives. The 1979 decree indicated that bonus would be payable when 98 per cent of the delivery contracts were fulfilled, the size of bonus being determined by improvements in labour productivity and the 'quality mix' of output. The aim here is to encourage labour productivity and to discourage substituting the output of one commodity for another. New and better quality products are to be priced at higher levels, thereby rewarding innovation.

Following the 1979 decree, wholesale prices were revised. The objective was to bring prices into line with costs – particularly the rising costs of raw materials, wages and research. The new prices, it was hoped, would give incentives to produce high quality goods, which were to be given higher profit margins. Regional differentials were also introduced for fuel to encourage the efficient use of materials.

By 1981, progress had been made with self-financing of ministries out of their earned profits. In that year, for instance, the Ministry of Heavy and Transport Machinery kept 76 per cent of its profits (the remainder going to the state budget). The figure for the Ministry of Power Machinery was 80.7 per cent, for the Electrical Equipment Industry 76.6 per cent, for the Ministry of Instruments, Automative Equipment and Control Systems 48.6 per cent and for the Ministry of Tractors and Farm Machinery 68.9 per cent.[56]

A decree of the Central Committee of the CPSU and the USSR Council of Ministers ('On Additional Measures for Expanding the Rights of Industrial Production Associations (Enterprises) – Planning and Economic Activity and for Strengthening their Responsibility for the Results of Their Work') in July 1983 endorsed the proposals of the 1979 decree and proposed its operation as described above, for five ministries from 1 January 1984.[57]

Labour is a particularly arduous commodity to plan. The Soviet leaders seek the maintenance of full employment and the securing of progressive increases in productivity. Policies have included encouraging enterprises to 'shed labour', introducing team or brigade methods to stimulate productivity, and instituting penalties for indiscipline. These topics will be discussed in turn.

The 'Shchekino' Method

The Shchekino method (or experiment) illustrates one of the ways that the economic leadership has tried to encourage enterprises to cut back on the number of workers. Shchekino is the name of a chemical combine in Tula. The objective of the Shchekino 'economic method' has been expressed by the aphorism: 'Fewer personnel – more output'.[58]

The combine was given a (rising) production plan for a five-year period and a stable wages fund: that is, the combine was unable to take on more workers, as it was given no money to pay for them. Output was to be considerably increased in the given period. The advantage to the employees was that savings on labour (i.e. a reduction in the numbers of workers) can be used for extra pay and social benefits. The combine 'shed' 1,324 jobs. With the finance so released, wages rose by 45 per cent. Over a ten-year period, chemical output rose by 170 per cent and labour productivity by 240 per cent. Wage outlays fell from 13.9 kopecks to 5 kopecks per ruble of commodity output. Social amenities were also improved: housing and rest homes were constructed out of savings.

Other enterprises have adopted the Shchekino method. In the period of the Ninth Five-Year Plan, about 1,000 enterprises utilized the method including 150 plants and associations in the chemical industry; 45,500 manual workers and 10,600 non-manuals were 'freed' for other work. Greater success is claimed in the Tenth Five-Year Plan: 968,000 people were 'freed' in 11,710 enterprises. Between 1980 and 1982 labour productivity in such enterprises improved by 3.4 per cent, compared with 'non-Shchekino' plants average of 1.5 per cent. Such measures led to further labour savings of 216,100 jobs.[59]

Workers displaced were found other jobs, usually in the same industry, though sometimes in other enterprises. Many workers were retrained in a second skill. A thorough search of the Soviet press has revealed no evidence of unemployment of such displaced workers. An article by G. Popov in *Pravda* pleaded, rather in the vein of Mrs Margaret Thatcher, that management was not tough enough and tolerated surplus labour. He argued that wages should be cut to increase incentives; redundant workers, he said, should be paid a minimum wage of 80 rubles and could be employed in street weeping or farm work.[60] (There is at present no unemployment benefit in the USSR, as there is no registered unemployment.)

The Shchekino scheme has met with resistance. As a *Pravda* article put it: '... every innovation encounters psychological barriers of negation, doubt and attachment to the old ways.' To counter the increased work load and transfer to another plan, 'For a full six months prior to the first release of production workers, hundreds of Communists conducted explanatory work in the collective.'[61] Resistance to the methods also came from management. A letter in *Sovetskaya Rossiya* (22 July 1981) complained that: 'It is more advantageous to an enterprise to have a surplus rather than a shortage of labour. The enterprise's grade is determined by the number of people it employs. The more people there are, the bigger the wage fund and the bonus resources.' Payment to the factory administration is also linked to numbers employed. Reserves of labour are useful when 'storming' methods have to be used. They are also necessary for ancillary type work, such as housebuilding, even picking vegetables in a collective farm coming under the enterprise's patronage. The proportion of manual labour employed in Soviet factories is much higher than that in the West, and despite the admonitions of the State Committee on Labour and Social Questions, its size declines very slowly.[62] Leaders of production units also have good reason to resist increasing productivity – because plan targets are revised upwards, thereby making life harder. An article in *Pravda* emphasized the role of the party in combating both such localism and indolent administrators in the ministerial *apparat*.[63] The resolution, cited above, of the Central Committee and the Council of Ministers in July 1983, extended the opportunities of enterprises to make savings in the wage fund, and to pay over the basic wage scales for skill, output and combining jobs. Bigger bonuses were allowed for saving materials and for fulfilment of delivery commitments.

The Brigade Contract

The brigade contract is another innovation which seeks to increase labour productivity. The 'brigade contract' involves payment to a group of organized workers on the completion of a job of work. The 1979 decree on the economic mechanism called for 'an extensive development of the brigade form of the organization of labour and incentives'. Brigades were given the right through the brigade council (*sovet*) to allocate rewards among the members according to their effort. The aims of the brigade system are (a) to encourage maximum effort by individual members, (b) to provide an incentive to economize on labour employed and (c) to stabilize labour mobility and enhance labour discipline.[64] Prior to the introduction of this method, individual rates of remuneration were negotiated between worker and administration. Workers maximized their earnings by securing a higher rate for the job than was strictly necessary (i.e. by working slowly when tested): in such a way, labour productivity was kept low. By working as a member of a group, a worker has an incentive to increase his productivity – not only should this enlarge output and wages, but the brigade will pressurize him/her to work as efficiently as possible. As the brigade council decides the distribution of the wage fund, 'holding back' effort will be recognized and penalized in the pay packet. The brigade system, it is hoped, would also encourage workers to participate actively in the management of production. They would of necessity be involved in the production process and would understand the need for higher productivity to increase output. The growing fragmentation of the labour process under modern production, Soviet specialists recognize, has led to monotonous repetitive tasks. The brigade system gives every member an identifiable goal and enables him or her to see how his/her own contribution fits into the overall production plan.[65]

Soviet writers claim many successes for the new methods. On the basis of interviews with workers, managers and party members, Kogan and Merenkov point to considerable improvements in labour productivity, work discipline, reductions in loss of labour time, and to minor advances in the strengthening of personal relationships and in improving the 'moral and psychological climate'.[66] In empirical terms, it has been reported that, in shipbuilding enterprises, labour productivity rose by 20 to 30 per cent, while wages increased by 10 to 12 per cent. The duration of equipment being out of order has been reduced by 30 to 35 per cent.[67]

Despite these improvements, the brigade method has not yet solved the problem of low productivity and labour indiscipline. Shapiro in *Planovoe khozyaystvo* has pointed out that, though in 1981–82 60 per cent of all workers at industrial enterprises worked in brigades, productivity of labour rose by 1.7 per cent in 1981 and 1.8 per cent 1982, instead of 2.8 per cent per year.[68] Other reports in the Soviet press refer to the obstacles the new methods encounter. V. Parfenov, in *Pravda*, has complained that the brigade contract method is becoming adapted to 'the old way of organizing labour'.[69] He pointed out that master-craftsmen were reluctant to join brigades because they feared becoming 'less prominent in the collective'. Another obstacle was that brigades were often 'organized mechanically', 'from above', and 'with no preparation and without the active participation of the workers themselves'. Insufficient incentive, he claims, is given to workers, and in half the brigades 'pay does not depend on final results.'[70] There is underlying resistance to the brigade system from management. The effects of greater productivity are that the factory's plan will be raised to higher levels, together with a cut in the wages fund. As two writers to *Literaturnaya gazeta* put it: 'Knowing this, many directors dread not only collective forms [of labour] but any kind of innovation that sharply raises an enterprise's potential. Hence the reserves hidden away, the lackadaisical manner of working, and the lazy, undisciplined life style of the collective ...'[71]

Strengthening Labour Discipline

In addition to economic incentives, the Soviet political leadership has resorted to strengthening labour discipline by administrative means. In 1983, it has been reported that spot checks have been carried out in large cities to detect workers who have been illegitimately absent from work. This process carried out mainly by *druzhiniki* (volunteer police) followed TV programmes showing workers complaining about lateness and drunkenness at work of other employees.[72] Changes in the laws instituted in August 1983 made it possible to deduct days from holiday entitlement from workers who were absent from work without good cause (subject to workers having a minimum of 12 days holiday).[73] Similarly, a day's attendance will be lost if a worker is absent for more than three hours. Workers who are idle or drunk on the job may be demoted to a lower job. Workers dismissed for such infractions of discipline are to receive only half of the normal bonus for the first few months in their next job. Workers may be required to pay compensation of up to a third of average monthly salary for materials wasted – though in some cases workers may have to pay more than this. The cost of damage caused by drunks is subject to being repaid in full by such miscreants, who are liable to instant dismissal (subject to trade union approval). In 1979 notice of leaving a job was lengthened from two weeks to one month and in 1983 the period of notice required was extended to two months (unless there is a good reason – such as change of residence by spouse, illness, or an appeal for volunteers). A person's 'uninterrupted work record' (which is used to calculate various social welfare benefits, such as pensions) is maintained only if a worker voluntarily leaving a job is employed within three weeks. In my view, such measures may be difficult to enforce, are not comparable in importance to the Shchekino and brigade methods and are likely to have a negligible effect on worker behaviour.

The various policies and procedures described above are indicative of the ways that the Soviet leadership is trying to improve the economic mechanism without changing the essentials of the traditional structure. Western analysts, and some Soviet ones, argue that such tinkering will not suffice. Two main drawbacks are often cited: first, centralized planning does not find it possible to process sufficient information to draw up an accurate plan. Not only is the available information often faulty and sometimes out of date, but also it requires the simultaneous solution of extremely complicated equations to ensure that demand, output and price are equilibriated. Second, the present system is supplier-dominated. Insufficient economic power is given to consumers of output. Hence the *raison d'être* of production – to satisfy demand – is replaced by producers fulfilling their own interests. More radical solutions, critics argue, are necessary not only to exploit the full potentialities of the Soviet economy, but also to move to socialism.

Market Socialism

There are many variants of 'market socialism'.[74] The essence of the model is a combination of some features of the traditional Soviet economic structure and processes of exchange which determine prices and output mix. As Berliner has aptly expressed it, market socialism involves 'central planning without assignment of directive targets to enterprises'.[75] The 'socialist' aspects usually refer to: nationalization of the means of production, the political hegemony of the Communist Party, the control of central planners over money supply, the banks, major investments and some of the major industries. Market elements take the form of enterprises determining their output plans in relation to demand from consumers; prices are to reflect consumers' preferences, and supply and demand are equilibriated; profits are used for further investment and payment of bonus, and some is returned to the central exchequer; 'economic calculation' in general is refined through the operation of supply and demand. The bureaucratic hypertrophy associated with central control is replaced – the advocates of market socialism would argue – by the instantaneous decisions of the market. As an ideal, market socialism is said to combine the best of state socialism and capitalism: the equity of state ownership and planning of the former, and the economic efficiency of the latter.

Various forms of market relationships have been introduced in Yugoslavia, Hungary and China, and have been advocated by reformist economists such as Sik and Brus.[76] In more concrete terms, the market mechanism takes the place of obligatory targets placed on enterprises by the central planners. The government monopoly of foreign trade is relaxed. Profit earned by enterprises is the criteria for 'success' rather than plan fulfilled. Finance and fiscal policy – indirect economic control – replaces bureaucratic control. An important variant in some of the proposals is a form of workers' participation in the strategic decisions of the industrial enterprise.

Some of these ideas have been articulated in the Soviet Union. Following the 1979 reforms, cited above, Volkonsky has advocated the introduction of something similar to 'market equilibrium prices', the 'devolution of price-setting powers to ... associations, who would negotiate quantities and prices with suppliers and customers, complete freedom for enterprises and production associations to choose their own suppliers and customers ... Competition and customer power are credited with a greater capacity to prevent "unjustified" price increases and maintain and improve product quality than is possessed by central administrators.'[77]

A more general critique has been formulated by T. Zaslavskaya, in what has become known as the 'Novosibirsk paper'.[78] The writer complains of 'the top-heavy character of planning, the inhibition of market forces, the centralised regulation of all forms of material incentive for labour ... the limitation of all kinds of unformalised economic activity by the population in the sphere of production, service and distribution'.[79] Like the Western writers discussed above, the paper complains that the 'complexity of the economic structure has long overstepped the threshold of its efficient regulation from a united centre.'[80] The author of the paper calls for greater reliance on 'regulators connected to market relations, which would "automatically" balance production ... To solve [the current economic problems] will require ... abandoning administrative methods of management ... in favour of a transition to truly economic methods of management.' Apart from a general theoretical and philosophical position in favour of decentralization and reliance on the market, there is no discussion of the detailed arrangements of such a system.

Berliner has outlined what such a model based on Yugoslav and Hungarian experience might look like if applied to Soviet circumstances. First, investment would be controlled centrally. Second, selective price regulation would also be the prerogative of the government. Third, there would be no form of 'workers' control' : the party would remain a dominant political force. Fourth, taxation would be the chief means of regulating income distribution.[81]

Such proposals, whilst being initially attractive, have their own ambiguities and contradictions. Objection is often made that central planning will effectively cease if directive targets to enterprises are no longer at the behest of the planners: the supply of materials will be undermined. If profit maximization becomes the criterion of management in determining output, the economic system will come to work like capitalist ones. Regional, incomes and welfare policy will be shaped by forces of the market and may lead to greater inequality. If employment policy is left to market forces, the large surpluses of labour said to be 'hoarded' by enterprises will be put on the market, or in other words will become unemployed. Market regional development would increase the gap between the Slavic European areas and the periphery. The task of developing Siberia would become harder. Present levels of repressed inflation would become open: prices would rise. The transfer of effective decision-making from the centre would undoubtedly reduce 'bureaucratic' power, but in its place the power of lower level economic functionaries (factory, and trust directors) would also become greater.[82] This in turn has led to the accusation that capitalism has been reinstated in the USSR. (This theme will be examined in the last chapter.)

The risks of such a reform for the political leadership are very great. First, short-term economic setbacks might weaken the country's defence capacity: the USSR is a world super-power, and even a temporary weakening of its position would be of great concern to its leaders – this contingency does not apply in other smaller Eastern European countries, which are prepared to take greater risks. Second, while some groups of the population might be better off financially, other constituencies (the unemployed, pensioners, marginal regional groups) would suffer and social and political discontent would occur. Third, and most important of all, the political power of the present incumbents of power – particularly in the government planning and ministerial realms – and the economic security of a large number of people would be put at risk. As long as the economy continues to grow (even slowly), it is likely that the political leadership will continue with a policy of attempting to improve the existing system.

Conclusions

The major achievements of the Soviet government are in the field of maintaining economic growth over a fairly long period of time with full employment and the absence of price inflation. In terms of economic efficiency as measured by the market value of output with given utilized inputs, the American system is superior to the Soviet. (The American is also superior to the British and other capitalist states.) The USSR is still at a relatively early stage of industrialization. Its *per capita* output is much lower than that of its major Western rival, the USA. Its social provisions, given its level of economic development, compare fairly well. In evaluating the lower level of consumption by Soviet citizens, attention must be drawn to the higher defence burden.

Has the Soviet Union succeeded in eliminating waste? Is it less wasteful than the capitalist economy? The answer is ambiguous. Central planning has ensured a low-wage full-employment economy: the waste of structural unemployment has been eliminated. But labour power and capital are inefficiently used. Both the USA and USSR produce wasteful and even harmful goods: nerve gas, hydrogen bombs, cigarettes and hard spirits; the USSR has wasteful occupations – police, 'controllers', censors – though less so than the armies of salesmen, insurance officials, tax accountants and stockbrokers endemic to advanced capitalism. The USSR produces many goods that people do not want, as Western capitalism often produces gluts of products that people want, but are destroyed because their market price would be too low to ensure a profit. Both systems give rise to pollution, waste and pockets of poverty. Though economic levels are below those of the advanced West, standards are rising and so are consumer demands. The USSR is experiencing a heightening of expectations on the part of the population.

Soviet central planning has been more successful in pioneering methods of economic planning in a relatively simple economy than in a complex large-scale industrial order. Problems are in the field of raising the quality of goods and in the provision of sufficient commodities and services to meet demand. Policy does not respond to demand push, and official prices do not always reflect scarcity: this leads to suppressed inflation and to distortions in allocation which give rise to minor but significant grey and black markets. Labour productivity is much lower than in advanced capitalist states and its improvement is a key to future economic growth. The present concern is to develop methods and a structure which can cope with the very large number of economic variables generated by a modern economy.

We have considered the performance and reform of the economy chiefly from an economic point of view. Some writers would argue that the economy must be considered in a wider context in terms of the Marxist category of the mode of production. This will be one of the subjects of the next chapter.

NOTES

1 See *New Society* (London), 3 November 1983. Data for 1982, K. Mathews, *Journal of Economic Affairs.* vol. 3, no. 4, July 1983.

2 For a detailed discussion of the latter see: John Pitzer, 'Gross National Product of the USSR, 1950–80', in Joint Economic Committee US Congress, *USSR: Measures of Economic Growth and Development, 1950–80* (1982), pp. 11–14.

3 *Narkhoz 1922–82* (1982), pp. 91–2. *Narkhoz v 1982g* (1983), p. 59.

4 Pitzer, *USSR: Measures of Economic Growth* . . . , p. 20.

5 Hermann Clement, 'CMEA Economic Performance in the 1970's', in *The CMEA Five-Year Plans (1981–85),* (1983), p. 38.

6 See particularly the discussion in A. Bergson, *Planning and Productivity under Soviet Socialism* (1968), and the trenchant analysis of such views in M. Ellman, *Socialist Planning* (1979), esp. chapter 10.

7 See V.M. Kudrov, in *Mirovaya ekonomika i mezhdunarodnye otnosheniya,* cited by Ellman, ibid., pp. 253–4, no. 10 (1972).

8 Ellman, ibid., p. 251.

9 Imogene Edwards et al., 'US and USSR: Comparisons of GNP', in Joint Economic Committee US Congress, *Soviet Economy in a Time of Change,* vol. 1 (1979), p. 376.

10 CIA estimates. Data cited by John Pitzer, 'Gross National Product of the USSR, 1950–80', pp. 16–17.

11 D.B. Diamond, 'Trends in Output, Inputs and Factor Productivity in Soviet Agriculture', in Joint Economic Committee US Congress, *New Directions in the Soviet Economy* (1966), p. 346.

12 R.V. Greenslade, 'The Real Gross National Product of the USSR, 1950–1975', in Joint Economic Committee US Congress, *Soviet Economy in a New Perspective* (1976), p. 272.

13 David M. Schoonover, 'Agriculture and the Grain Trade', *Soviet Economy in the 1980's: Problems and Prospects,* Part 2 (1982), p. 8.

14 Ibid., p. 9.

15 Ibid., p. 11.

16 *Gosudarstvenny byudzhet SSSR i byudzhety soyuznykh respublik 1976–1980g.* (1982), p. 6. See G. Spiridonov, 'USSR's Budget Priorities for 1982', *Soviet News,* 1 Dec. 1981.

17 J. Pitzer, 'Gross National Product of the USSR . . . '.

18 Gregory G. Hindebrandt, 'The Dynamic Burden of Soviet Defense Spending', in Joint Economic Committee US Congress, *Soviet Economy in the 1980's:*

Problems and Prospects, Part 1 (1982), p. 331. For a review of CIA estimates see: Donald F. Burton 'Estimating Soviet Defense Spending', *Problems of Communism,* vol. 32, no. 2 (March–April 1983), pp. 85–93. M. Kaser has an informative discussion of defence estimates, 'Economic Policy', in A. Brown and M. Kaser, *Soviet Policy for the 1980's* (1982), pp. 204–207.

19 Abraham S. Becker, 'Military Allocations and Burden', in *Soviet Economy in the 1980's: Problems and Prospects,* Part 1 (1982), pp. 289–9. See also Myron Rush, 'The Soviet Policy Favoring Arms Over Investment Since 1975', in *Soviet Economy in the 1980's: Problems and Prospects,* Part I (1982), pp. 319–330.

20 CIA estimates. Joint Economic Committee, *USSR: Measures of Economic Growth . . . ,* pp. 18–19.

21 Gertrude E. Schroeder, 'Soviet Living Standards: Achievements and Prospects', in *Soviet Economy in the 1980's: Problems and Prospects* (1982), p. 368.

22 K. Bush, 'Retail Prices in Moscow and Four Western Cities in March, 1982', REF-RL (June, 1982), p. 32.

23 For details, see K. Bush, 'Rents and the Social Contract in the USSR', RFE-RL 410/82 (1982).

24 Philip Hanson, *The Consumer in the Soviet Economy* (1968), p. 73.

25 K. Bush, 'Soviet Living Standards', *Aspects of Daily Life in the USSR* (1975).

26 G.E. Schroeder and M.E. Denton, 'An Index of Consumption in the USSR', in *USSR: Measures of Economic Growth . . . ,* pp. 359–61.

27 See M.J. Ellman, *Full Employment: Lessons from State Socialism* (1979).

28 Ibid., p. 8.

29 Further statistics on pension payments may be consulted in A. McAuley, 'Social Policy', in A. Brown and M. Kaser (eds), *Soviet Policy for the 1980's* (1982), pp. 159–61.

30 *Narkhoz 1922–82* (1982), pp. 116–8.

31 A.S. Milovidov, *Gody zhizni i gody truda* (1983), p. 15. There has been an increase in the death rate, particularly for males, in the late 1970's and early 1980's. This has been caused partly by the higher proportion of the population in the older age brackets. See A. Helgeson, 'Demographic Policy', in Brown and Kaser, *Soviet Policy . . . ,* pp. 124–6. My thanks to A. Helgeson for reference to Milovidov.

32 *Narkhoz 1922–1982,* p. 431.

33 A. McAuley, 'The Distribution of Earnings and Incomes in the Soviet Union', *Soviet Studies,* vol. 29, no. 2, 1977, p. 234.

34 See below chapter 5, and P. Wiles, *Distribution of Income: East and West* (1974), p. 25. Discussion in M. Ellman, *Socialist Planning* (1979), pp. 188–9.

35 Cited in Ellman, ibid., p. 183.

36 David H. Howard, 'A Note on Hidden Inflation in the Soviet Union', *Soviet Studies,* vol. 28, no. 4 (Oct. 1976), p. 606.

37 Data cited by G. Grossman, 'A Note on Soviet Inflation', *Soviet Economy in the 1980's,* Part 1, p. 267.

38 See Grossman, ibid., pp. 269–84.

39 Report by special correspondent in *Izvestiya,* 16 March 1983. Excerpts in

CDSP, vol. 35, no. 11 (13 April 1983), p. 7. On 18 April 1983, *Pravda* announced that the USSR State Prices Committee had approved new price lists effective on 25 April 1983 ... 'Karakul collars [are reduced by] 35 per cent, retail prices of women's winter coats with mink collars [are dropped by] 21 per cent ... certain types of silk bedspreads and pillow cases by an average of 40 per cent.' Text in *CDSP,* vol. 35, no. 16 (18 May 1983), p. 22.

40 A. Katsenelinboigen, 'Coloured Markets in the Soviet Union', *Soviet Studies,* vol. 29, no. 1 (1977).

41 Gregory Grossman, 'The "Shadow Economy" in the Socialist Sector of the USSR', in *The CMEA Five-Year Plans (1981–1985) in a New Perspective* (1983), pp. 102–3. See also his: 'Notes on the Illegal Private Economy and Corruption', in *Soviet Economy in a Time of Change,* vol. 1 (1979).

42 *Narkhoz 1922–82,* p. 232.

43 Ann Lane, 'USSR: Private Agriculture on Center Stage', in *Soviet Economy in the 1980's* Part 2 (1982), p. 23.

44 V. Rutgaizer, *Pravda,* 16 Nov. 1981, see abstract *CDSP,* vol. 33, no. 46, 16 Dec. 1981, p. 18.

45 Grossman, 'Notes on the Illegal ... ', pp. 838, 839.

46 'Notes on the Illegal ... ', p. 851.

47 'The "Shadow Economy" ... ', p. 11.

48 G. Ofer and A. Vinokur, *Private Sources of Income of the Soviet Urban Household* (1980).

49 Cited by H. Smith, *The Russians* (1976), p. 114.

50 G. Mars and Y. Altman, 'The Cultural Bases of Soviet Georgia's Second Economy', *Soviet Studies,* vol. 35, no. 4 (Oct. 1983), p. 557.

51 Ibid., p. 559.

52 D. O'Hearn, 'The Consumer Second Economy: Size and Effects', *Soviet Studies,* vol. 32, no. 2 (April 1980), pp. 218–34.

53 M. Ellman, *Planning Problems in the USSR* (1973), p. 134.

54 For general discussions of reform see: Joseph S. Berliner, 'Managing the USSR Economy: Alternative Models', *Problems of Communism,* vol. 32, no. 1 (Jan.–Feb. 1983), pp. 40–56; Abram Bergson and Herbert S. Levine (eds), *The Soviet Economy: Towards the Year 2000* (1983); Holland Hunter, 'Soviet Economic Problems and Alternative Policy Responses', in Joint Economic Committee US Congress, *Soviet Economy in a Time of Change* (1979), vol. 1, pp. 23–37; Alec Nove, *The Soviet Economic System* (1977), esp. chapter 11; Gertrude E. Schroeder, 'Soviet Economic "Reform" Decrees: More Steps on the Treadmill', in *Soviet Economy in the 1980's ...,* Part I (1982), pp. 65–88.

55 See discussion in: G.E. Schroeder, ibid.; P. Hanson, 'Success Indicators Revisited: The July 1979 Soviet Decree on Planning and Management', *Soviet Studies,* vol. 35, no. 1 (Jan. 1983), pp. 1–13. This paragraph and the following draw on the analysis in Hanson's article. The decree was printed on 29 August in *Pravda* and translated in *CDSP,* vol. 31, no. 30 (1979).

56 G. Bazarova, *Ekonomicheskaya Gazeta,* no. 9 (February 1983). Abstract in

CDSP, vol. 35, no. 11 (13 April 1983), p. 14.

57 Resolution published 26 July 1983; summarized in *CDSP,* no. 30, vol. 35 (24 Aug. 1983), p. 3.

58 'Shchekino Experiment is Ten Years Old', *Pravda,* 28 March 1977; summarized in *CDSP,* vol. 29, no. 13 (1977), pp. 14–15.

59 R. Batkaev and S. Semin, 'Shchekinski metod v usloviyakh sovershenstvovaniya khozyaystvennogo mekhanizma', *Sotsialisticheski trud,* no. 1 (1983), p. 44.

60 *Pravda,* 27, December 1980. Abstract in *CDSP,* vol. 32, no. 52 (1980), pp. 7–11.

61 *Pravda,* 28 March 1977.

62 See L. Kostin, in *Pravda,* 9 Sept. 1983. Abstract in *CDSP,* vol. 35, no. 36 (1983), pp. 19–20.

63 G. Grotseskul, 'Ostaetsya v deistvii', *Pravda,* 18 Oct. 1983, p. 2.

64 L.N. Kogan and A.V. Merenkov, 'Kompleksnye brigady: mneniya, otsenki, opyt vnedreniya', *Sotsiologicheskie issledovaniya,* no. 1 (1983), p. 86.

65 See discussion of results of brigade activity at *Promsvyaz* enterprise, *Ekonomika i organizatsiya proizvodstva,* no. 3 (1978), p. 50.

66 Kogan and Merenkov, 'Kompleksnye brigady...' p. 90.

67 *Ekonomicheskaya gazeta,* no. 45. Extract in *CDSP,* vol. 32, no. 46 (Dec. 1980), pp. 6–8.

68 I. Shapiro, 'Razvitie brigadnoy formy organizatsii i stimulirovaniya truda', *Planovoe khozyaystvo,* no. 7 (July 1983), pp. 99, 100.

69 Vasily Parfenov, *Pravda,* 27 June 1983. Extract in *CDSP,* vol. 35, no. 26 (1983), p. 8.

70 Ibid., p. 9.

71 D. Kaidalov and E. Suimenko, *Literaturnaya gazeta,* no. 11 (1982), p. 8. Cited by A. Tenson, 'Payment by Results Shows Promise but Faces Obstacles in Soviet Economy', RL 189/82 (4 May 1982), p. 3.

72 See account in Jonathan Steele and Eric Abraham, *Andropov in Power* (1983), p. 160.

73 See discussion in *Izvestiya,* 12 Aug. 1983; summarized in *CDSP,* no. 33, vol. 35 (14 Sept. 1983), p. 7.

74 See further discussion in A. Nove, *The Soviet Economic System* (1977), chapter 11.

75 Ibid., p. 47.

76 O. Sik, *Plan and Market under Socialism,* (1967); W. Brus, *The Economics and Politics of Socialism* (1973).

77 Cited in Hanson, 'Success Indicators Revisited...', pp. 10–11.

78 This is a 'leaked' paper, and authorship has been attributed to T. Zaslavskaya by Western analysts. See P. Hanson, 'Discussion of Economic Reform in the USSR: the "Novosibirsk Paper"', RL 356/83 (1983), and P. Hanson, 'The Novosibirsk Report: Comment', *Survey.* vol. 28. no 1. (1984), pp. 83–108. A full English translation of the Report is appended to this article.

79 'Novosibirsk paper', pp. 1–2.

80 Ibid., p. 3.
81 'Managing the USSR Economy...', p. 47.
82 For a more optimistic view of a mixed type of economy see Alec Nove, *The Economics of Feasible Socialism* (1983).

3

COUNTERPOINTS: THE POLITICAL ECONOMY OF THE USSR

Mode of Production or Social Formation?

In attempting to generalize about socialist systems in general and the Soviet system in particular, many Marxists in the West have sought to provide their own distinctive position in opposition to that of the Soviet standpoint. While the Soviet model of 'developed socialism' has many deficiencies, it is argued here that these contesting schools fail to explain the structure of the Soviet Union. Finally, I turn to my own position: that the Soviet Union is best labelled as a social formation distinct from the capitalist and communist mode of production but containing elements drawn from both. It is suggested that contradictions are located in the relationships between the state and the economy as well as in the cultural and social processes of the superstructure.

Critical Marxism takes as its point of departure the more traditional view that the Soviet Union has transcended capitalism as a mode of production and has entered into the first stages of communism. The Soviet ideology of socialism has four basic components:

1 that the class *relations* to the means of production have been socialized following the seizure of power by the Bolsheviks and the nationalization of the means of production;
2 that state planning has replaced the bourgeois market as a method of coordination of the economy and allocation of resources; competition between capitals has been superseded and labour has lost its character as a commodity;
3 that, following the major socialist industrialization process (during the first Five-Year Plan in Russia) the *level* of productive forces was sufficient to define the economy as being at the socialist stage;
4 that, given the hegemony of the Communist Party and its control of the major institutional systems (ideology, science, education), the super-structure is socialist and the remaining incongruities or 'left-overs'

(religious views, personality cults, petty crime) from other modes of production will gradually disappear with the maturation of Soviet society.

The current Soviet notion of developed socialism (*razvitoy* or *zrely sotsializm*) enlarges on these points somewhat. Soviet theorists argue that their society has to be analysed dynamically and in terms of 'non-antagonistic contradictions'. Such non-antagonistic contradictions are being resolved and lead to a greater social homogeneity, to the growth of what Semenov calls 'a new historical community of people'.[1] Such distinctions as between town and country, manual and non-manual are becoming of less significance with the development of the productive forces. Rather than to *inter*-class differences (between collective farmers and manual workers), which it is asserted are declining, attention is turned to the greater significance of *intra*-class distinctions, based on the division of labour. But greater social unity is achieved through the modernization of diverse areas of Soviet society – by improvements in educational and cultural provision expressed in reduced income differentials and in the greater participation of the masses in public affairs. The actual developments and improvements in the Soviet Union, such writers would argue, should not be obscured by their difficulties and imcompleteness. Soviet writers believe that under developed socialism the working class will have a higher political consciousness[2] and will participate in 'party, state, parliamentary (*sovetskoy*), trade-union and controlling (*inspektsionnoy*) work'.[3]

'Critical Marxism', on the other hand, holds that some, or all, of these points are false. In common they share the view that exploitation and conflict of one form or another continue in Soviet-type states and that the revolution has not ushered in a new socialist type of society. While on these general points they are agreed, there is much dissent as to how such conflict or exploitation should be generalized in a Marxist paradigm of society.

Western critical Marxist accounts of Soviet-type societies may be analysed into four different types.[4] First are those who argue that such societies have not transcended the capitalist mode, but are merely a special type of capitalist society. Second, and the one which has had most influence in the West as a critique, is the theory, derived from Trotsky's views, of the transitional society of a workers' state – albeit a degenerate one. Soviet-type societies have the theoretical status, not of a socialist mode of production, but of a social formation transitional to socialism. Third are theorists who argue that these societies are neither capitalist nor socialist, but a new mode of production derived from the Asiatic mode of production. A fourth school, associated with Hillel Ticktin and the journal *Critique,* also conceptualizes state socialism as a social formation but, and distinct from the Trotskyists, denies its dynamic or progressive tendencies: for them state socialism is a hybrid but in a 'moribund historical cul-de-sac'.

The State Capitalist Thesis

The thesis of 'state capitalism' (or bureaucratic state capitalism) as applied to the Soviet Union has an ancestry which may be traced to the social-democratic opponents of Bolshevism, even before the October Revolution, though these writers did not develop the idea of state capitalism. Originally, the Menshevik line of argument stressed the inadequacy of the level of productive forces, either as a legitimation for the seizure of power for the proletariat or as a necessary condition of the creation of a socialist society. It was thought that socialism could not be built at that time in such countries as Russia because the highest level of productive forces (and in advance of capitalism) had not been achieved. The October Revolution was politically opportunistic, because the working class (as the ascendant class) was not in a majority and because it lacked sufficient political consciousness. Political organization or hegemony by the party could not compensate for this inadequacy in the level of productive forces. Contemporary advocates of the 'state capitalism' thesis modify this view somewhat by pointing out that the October Revolution could be justified on a world scale, if it was to be 'the prelude to a series of new revolutions which would break out immediately or after a certain interval'.[5] As revolutions did not break out in the advanced capitalist states, the revolution did not have the world impact intended by its leaders. Under these circumstances,

In Russia the revolution got rid of the impediments to the development of the productive forces, put an end to the remnants of feudalism, built up a monopoly of foreign trade which protects the development of the productive forces of the country from the devastating pressure of world capitalism, and also gave a tremendous lever to the development of the productive forces in the form of state ownership of the means of production. Under such conditions all impediments to the historical mission of capitalism ... are abolished ... *Post-October Russia stood before the fulfilment of the historical mission of the bourgeoisie* ... The fulfilment of the bourgeois tasks was the *central* problem in post-October Russia with its low level of national income ... [After the First Five-Year Plan] the bureaucracy sought to realise the historical mission of the bourgeoisie as quickly as possible ... The bureaucracy which became necessary in the process of capital accumulation ... became the oppressor of the workers ... [and made] use of its social superiority in the relations of production in order to gain an advantage for itself in the relations of distribution.[6]

The bureaucracy, however, not only became an 'oppressor' of the workers, but became a ruling class analogous to that of the capital class under traditional capitalism. Cliff points out: 'The state bureaucracy ... possesses the state as private property. In a state which is the repository of the means of production the state bureaucracy – the ruling class – has forms of passing on its privileges ... '.[7] Whilst this school does not accept the traditional Menshevik analysis which denies *a priori* that a revolutionary seizure of power by the party of the working class is justifiable in anything but an advanced capitalist country, the Menshevik position none the less is adopted when such a revolution does not spread to the advanced capitalist world.

The characterization made so far may readily be seen to emanate from the political sociology of the October Revolution and the Stalinist order; state capitalist theory, however, has also developed a political economy. State capitalist theorists concede that in Soviet-type societies there is no competition between enterprises.[8] There is then no competition of capitals (which is the economic dynamic of capitalism) and production for exchange, for the realization of exchange values does not occur. Cliff concedes that the economy produces mainly use values, not exchange values.[9] An ingenious argument is put forward, however, to explain the tendency of the ruling class to further capitalist accumulation – the economy is subject to the forces of the world economy, to 'world competition'. As international trade enters into but an insignificant part of Soviet gross national product, Cliff argues that 'international competition takes mainly a military form'. The 'Russian state is in a similar position to the owner of a single capitalist enterprise competing with other enterprises'. This has the effect of creating 'a bourgeoisie' which acts as the 'personification of capital and is itself driven by what appear to it as "external coercive laws"'.[10] The Soviet system then is 'a totalitarian tyranny devoted to maximising capital accumulation at all costs ... '.[11] State capitalist theorists regard the course of events in Soviet-type societies as part of the development of capitalism on a world scale and point to the changes occurring in Western capitalism. 'State capitalism is *not* an analysis of Eastern Europe but an analysis of capitalism in general of which these societies are a part.'[12] Binns and Haynes point to the decline of the market and to the rise of the state as producer and coordinator of the economy.[13] This is a theory which shares much of the analysis of modern bourgeois sociologists such as Dahrendorf, Bell, Brzezinski and Gouldner – an emphasis on control rather than ownership, on authority rather than class, with little attention paid to the definition of class boundaries and class consciousness.

Tony Cliff and the state capitalist school put forward a consistent (though as we shall see later an erroneous) model: in terms of the level of productive forces, the relations to the means of production, and the superstructural social relations, Soviet-type societies are 'capitalist', merely different versions of Western capitalism. (Some Chinese communists in the 1970s came to similar conclusions, though by a different route, and stressed the importance of changes in relations to the means of production.)[14]

A number of theoretical and empirical criticisms may be made of the state capitalist perspective. Firstly, its political economy does not make out a good case for convergence to the system of Western capitalism. If it is conceded that there is no competition of capitals and that production is of use rather than exchange values, then something more than military competition and arms expenditure is necessary to make the economic system 'capitalist'. There is nothing peculiarly 'capitalist' about a society devoting resources to defence, particularly if, as some 'state capitalist' theorists would agree, these needs are dictated by aggressive external interests. These decisions are taken in the same way as others concerning the use of surplus product. This again is not evidence, in itself, of class exploitation, Marx himself explicitly recognized that all, except the most primitive, forms of social production need to extract a surplus. Even under ideal communist conditions the extraction of surplus would be necessary for the expansion of the process of reproduction, for the renewal of capital as well as for the maintenance of non-productive labour (e.g. pensioners, children).[15] Under capitalism the extraction of surplus labour 'assumes an antagonistic form and is supplemented by the complete idleness of a stratum of society'.[16]

Second, the above cited phrase of Marx points to the political sociology of class under capitalism. However much the Western capitalist world has changed, it has abolished neither private ownership of the means of production nor the private appropriation of profit. State capitalist theorists assume that 'control' is tantamount to ownership and hence they have to conceive of state capitalism without capitalists. The supposed 'capitalist class' is left with no proprietary rights, and the class boundaries of this group are unclear. However much 'control' managers and administrators have over Soviet production enterprises, they cannot dispose of their assets for their private good; nor have their children any exclusive rights to nationalized property. The attempt by Sweezy and Bettelheim[17] to locate the capitalist class among the captains of industry, in the 'control of enterprises in the enterprises themselves, (in) coordination through the market, and (in) reliance on material incentives', is erroneous because investment, production and personnel of enterprises are firmly controlled by industrial ministers and the possibilities for extracting and distributing an economic surplus at the factory level are severely limited. The political leadership has resisted devolution of economic power. At higher levels of the power structure it is assumed that party and government apparatuses are fused and thus the differentiation which takes place between these groupings is ignored. Members of the 'state apparatus', it is said, include a wide range of institutional groupings (police, industrial, party, scientific, welfare, educational) but it needs to be shown that the incumbents of top positions share a common class interest antagonistic to the masses. Unlike under Western capitalism there is no identifiable group of persons who enjoy a source of income derived from the ownership of property. It may be conceded that a political elite operates within the political system, but a Marxist analysis must specify elite interests within the context of class structure. The attendant area of class consciousness is also weakly linked to Marxist theory by the state capitalist writers. The ruling elite has no ideology which justifies any form of expropriation of surplus to itself, and there appears to be no consciousness by an 'ascendant class' of its own class interest justifying revolutionary change. The Soviet 'ruling class' also is a category of paid labour, dependent on occupation, whereas a capitalist class (which in fact may not rule directly) draws a dividend which is a surplus left after wage labour is paid. Writers such as Binns and Hallas tend to conflate the ruling stratum, the ruling class, and the state into one category of 'the bureaucracy'.

The Social Formation of a Transitional Society

Accepting many of these criticisms are the theorists of Fourth International who have followed and developed Trotsky's analysis. The classical statement of this school may be found in *The Revolution Betrayed* (1945) in which it was argued that Soviet society was fundamentally different from capitalism: 'It is a contradictory society, halfway between capitalism and socialism.'

Trotsky accepted Marx's definition of classes as being 'characterized by their position in the social system of economy and primarily by their relation to the means of production'. He agreed that the class character of the Soviet Union was 'proletarian' – in so far as this had been guaranteed by 'the nationalization of the land, the means of industrial production, transport and exchange, together with the monopoly of foreign trade . . . ' He held that under capitalism the bureaucrats who run the government and the capitalist corporations play a subservient role to the ruling property-owning classes. But in Soviet society the working class, which was 'hardly, emerging from destitution and darkness, [had] no tradition of domination or command', and therefore such a bureaucratic group was able to manipulate its position to become 'the sole privileged and commanding stratum in Soviet society'. Although the polarization of socialist society was between this group and the working class, the dominant exploiting stratum was not a class in the Marxist sense for it had 'neither stocks nor bonds. It is recruited, supplemented and renewed in the manner of an administrative hierarchy, independently of any special property relations of its own and the individual bureaucrat cannot transmit to his heirs his rights in the exploitation of the state apparatus.' For Trotsky the Soviet Union was transitional: it was a society between capitalism and socialism. It had a dual character being 'socialistic, in so far as it defends social property in the means of production, bourgeois, in so far as the distribution of life's goods is carried out with a capitalistic measure of value and all the consequences ensuing therefrom'.[18]

Trotsky was mainly concerned with the political and social aspects of Soviet society under Stalin, and his standpoint has been refined and expanded by Ernest Mandel as the theory of the transition.[19] Mandel points out that the 'decisive difference' between a mode of production and a transitional society 'lies in the different degree of *structural* stability, or fixity, of the existing relations of production'. The new higher mode of production is not 'economically safeguarded', it is only 'politically and socially facilitated'.[20] The transitional society is not a combination of two modes but a specific social formation. Existing transitional societies (from the USSR to China and Cuba) are characterized by 'socio-economic underdevelopment' and by forms of 'bureaucratic deformation'.[21]

For Mandel, the 'conscious distribution of economic resources through the plan is now the *decisive* characteristic of the new production relations.'[22] Consumer goods though have the 'form' of commodities – through a purchase and sale. There are then two 'antagonistic logics', that of the plan and that of the market; of 'non-capitalist economic planning' on the one hand, and 'elements of commodity production . . . which arise from the basically still bourgeois distribution relations' on the other. As the Soviet Union is not part of the capitalist mode of production, and as it has no ruling capitalist class, the state cannot be bourgeois; it is a 'deformed workers' state'. The bureaucracy which rules is not a new ruling class because it 'cannot use the control over [the] means of production, which it monopolises, for the acquisition of private property, nor for any other specific economic purpose outside the consumptive sphere'.[23] It is not, however, ' . . . any form of socialism, or any "combination" of capitalism and socialism'. A transitional society, according to Mandel, may 'grow into a socialist society' with the simultaneous operation of six factors: the growth of productive forces; the institution of workers' self-management;

political democracy; withering away of the commodity – money relationship; a continuous revolution in daily habits, morals, ideology and
culture; and 'international development of the revolution, which
alone ... is capable of creating the necessary preconditions for a successful
conclusion to the process of constructing a socialist society ...'[24]

The main difficulty with the theory of Mandel and his followers is to
determine what is essentially *socialist* about Soviet-type societies and, if
they are 'transitional', whether or not they must evolve away from
bourgeois or capitalist tendencies towards socialist ones.[25] This problem
may be discussed in the context of the third approach, that of the *Critique*
school.

By not making clear the socialist character (rather than a tendency to
socialism) of Soviet-type societies, and by pointing to 'deformations' of the
workers' state, an ambiguity is built into the Trotskyist position. It is not
clear when these deformations, or the political Thermidor, cause the
society to revert to the capitalist mode.

The Social Formation of an Historical Cul-de-Sac

One of the major concerns of the writers gathered around the journal
Critique is to provide an alternative analysis to that of Ernest Mandel. The
gist of Ticktin's and Meikle's 'critique' is that the 'distortions' or
'deformations' of Soviet-type societies make them 'deviant transitional
societies'.[26] They are a 'new form of hybrid ... the product of a transitional
epoch between modes of production, the product of conflict between the
laws of the declining mode and those of the social relations of the invading
mode, but which is [in an] historical blind alley thrown up by the conflict
without itself having any tendency of motion towards the new mode of
production'.[27] As Ticktin puts it: 'The USSR is not a society in which,
socialist elements are dominant, or becoming dominant.'[28]

This political tendency does not regard Soviet societies to be analogous
to capitalist states for reasons already outlined: goods produced do not
'function as commodities' because there is no production of exchange
values and no market; there is no commodity production and no
commodity fetishism.[29] It is not like the capitalist mode of production in
this sense. In the political sociology of Soviet society too, Ticktin
recognizes that the 'members of the elite' have no individual control over
economic enterprises. 'Neither individually nor collectively can [the elite]
dispose of state property either to themselves or to the West for their own
immediate gain. Going beyond the legal form of property, the competitive
individuals in the elite do not, *as individuals,* have any means of control
over the surplus product.'[30]

Whilst the system is not capitalist, it is *not* moving towards socialism. At the heart of the matter for Ticktin is the absence of 'planning' in Soviet-type societies. 'Instead of a law of planning we can talk of a law of organization which expresses the requirement of the elite that their occupations and privileges be maintained through the functioning of the economy.'[31] Socialist planning cannot exist because the 'direct producers are not involved ... so calculation and information are impossible, while the imposing of targets is simply negated by those who either do not agree with the targets or are not interested in their fulfilment.' Soviet-type societies have 'administration and organization' rather than planning.[32] The working class, rather than being a political community controlling the economy, is atomized politically – and this ensures not only its subordination to 'the elite', but also major distortions in the operation of the economy.

For the *Critique* school, the lack of participation in planning by the worker in Soviet-type societies leads to wastefulness – of material resources and of labour. Indeed, Ticktin has gone as far as saying that 'the central economic feature of the USSR today is its enormous wastefulness.'[33] This wastefulness is the equivalent of Marx's idea of 'the operation of fetters on the forces of production'[34] and it prevents consumption from rising. Though there is a conflict between 'the elite' (and 'their allies in the intelligentsia') and the working class, 'the elite' lacks any legitimacy as a ruling class and its powers over the redistribution of surplus are severely restricted by the producers (i.e. the workers).

Ticktin's analysis is quite baffling as a 'Marxist' interpretation. Nowhere do we have any discussion of the class structure of the society: we are unable to link 'the elite' to any class formation. While one may concede that a 'classless' formation may prevail for a short period of time in the transition between modes of production, in a Marxian analysis there is no reason to suppose that such a formation may have any permanence. Yet the Soviet Union has been in existence for more than sixty years and appears to be going strong. While such formations as barbarism which followed Roman civilization may have been moribund, it is quite another thing to assert that Soviet-type societies are so. The Soviet model is dynamic in the sense that it provides a challenge to capitalism on a world scale, as the revolutions in China, Cuba and other parts of Asia and Africa bear out. To characterize 'waste' as the central economic feature of Soviet-type societies is overstated: the Soviet Union has risen from an underdeveloped country to the world's second largest economy. The concept of 'waste' is also ambiguous; it is sometimes used to describe deficient products (*brak*) and at other times refers to the tendency of the system to over-accumulate, to devote resources to wasteful activities.[35]

Depending on how one defines it, 'waste' has been generated by feudal and capitalist societies (see above p. 76) – it is an effect of a class structure, not a cause of it. The instability which Ticktin asserts exists is more latent than apparent and there is no discussion of class consciousness, or any explanation of its absence.

The attempt to distance Soviet-type societies from the modes of production of capitalism and socialism, and from the social formation of the transitional society, finds more coherent expression in the fourth model – that of a novel mode of production.

Bureaucratic Collectivism as a Mode of Production

The permanence of Soviet-type societies, their ability to reproduce themselves and to spread to other countries, in addition to some of the criticisms made above of the traditional critical Marxist positions, has led to the rise of the concept of bureaucratic collectivism, not just as a social formation transitional between capitalism and socialism, but as an alternative mode of production to capitalism. 'Bureaucratic collectivism' is held by Carlo[36] to apply to European Soviet-type states and China is excluded, whereas Melotti[37] restricts the term to those societies which he claims have arisen out of the Asiatic mode of production – Russia and China in particular.

Carlo argues that Soviet-type societies cannot be capitalist because there is no exchange of commodities, no competition of capitals and no category of surplus value. Like Mandel and Ticktin, he argues that the economy is dominated by the production of use values.[38] But like the state capitalist and 'transitional' theorists, Carlo denies that socialism has been achieved, for exploitation of the 'surplus labour of subordinate classes' by a dominant class occurs and the working class is 'alienated' from the 'productive apparatus'. While the 'Soviet system exhibits certain features similar to feudalism (the fusion of public power and control)',[39] it is not feudal. Feudalism is based on an agrarian society and production is for immediate consumption. Furthermore, Soviet-type societies are not segmented but centralized, expanded production and planned mass production being dominant.

For Carlo the Soviet system is one of 'bureaucratic collectivism'; it is a system 'dominated by the collective property of a central political class bureaucracy'.[40] The principal features of this system are:

1 Property is owned by a class as a whole, and not by its individual members.
2 The economy is run to a plan and is insulated from the market and the free-for-all of competing funds.

3 The commanding position of the state is utilized for the extended reproduction of use-values (and not exchange-values, as in capitalism).

4 The exploitation of man by man is a direct process, operating by the appropriation and distribution of part of the total surplus product through the plan (and not through individual producers and the market, as happens with the profits of capitalism).

5 Political and organic power is completely centralized.[41]

Melotti takes up the point of the origins of bureaucratic collectivism and traces it to countries 'based on the Asiatic mode of production'. 'Bureaucratic collectivism is the typical form of development of countries based on the Asiatic or semi-Asiatic mode of production that have not been subject to the capitalistic mode of production as a prolonged and penetrating external influence ... For those countries the impact of capitalism was enough to upset their centuries-old stagnation, but not enough to draw them into the Western stream of development.' The forces which hinder the development of capitalism encourage the formation of bureaucratic collectivism. Countries such as Russia, China, Vietnam, Egypt and Iran move from the Asiatic mode to bureaucratic collectivism. This novel mode of production is an alternative mode which ensures 'an expanded form of reproduction and updating the relevant social structures and superstructures accordingly'.[42] Rather than the progression from slave-based society to feudal society to developed capitalist society which characterizes European development, Melotti postulates a progression from semi-Asiatic society (Russia) or Asiatic society (China, Egypt) to bureaucratic collectivism.[43]

Bureaucratic collectivism then is an alternative mode of industrialization to capitalism. It is not 'retrograde' for it ensures the 'maximum development of the social forces of production'; like capitalism, it does 'a good job, as is shown by ... its stream of successes in science, technology, education and culture'.[44] In turn, Melotti believes that capitalism and bureaucratic collectivism will be superseded by socialism.

Whilst one might concede that Soviet-type societies have not 'transcended' capitalism to become a full communist mode of production, one cannot be convinced by Melotti's argument that such states are merely 'parallel socio-economic formations which in different circumstances perform much the same function' as capitalism'.[45] The Soviet Union does not extract surplus value from the working class, the law of value does not operate, a *capitalist* class living on surplus does not exist, and a form of state planning supersedes the capitalist market and its attendant evils of underemployment of labour and capital. The working class is the only legitimate source of state power. None of these things may be said of the capitalist mode of production. Hence in terms of fundamental criteria used by Marxists, such societies are not 'parallels' or alternatives to capitalism as a means of industrial development.

State Socialist Society as a Social Formation

The attempts we have discussed above to locate the Soviet Union in a Marxist paradigm of society have led to contradictory and bewildering accounts. The evolution of the Soviet Union and the other socialist countries cannot be fitted into the concept of the mode of production devised by Marx and Engels. The Soviet Union is of neither the capitalist nor the communist mode of production. It is also not 'transitional' between modes of production: transitional societies are *temporary* and the dynamics of such societies lead to the dominance of one mode over the remnants of another. Transitional societies do not reproduce themselves as such. In this book it is shown that the social and economic institutions of the USSR *reproduce* themselves and are likely to continue to do so.

The Soviet Union may be defined as a state socialist social formation. By a 'social formation', I refer to *an ensemble of forces of production relations, and a superstructure not being in correspondence with the basis but being capable of reproduction*. It is a mixture of pre-capitalist, capitalist and communist components. The label of 'state socialist' brings out the role of the state (government and party) in defining the course of development, in directing the society towards the goal of communism.

None of the theorists discussed above, including Ernest Mandel, is able to point to unambiguous *socialist* elements in the Soviet Union. The points made above concerning ownership relations, the absence of a process of exchange and extraction of surplus value lead one to identify the socialist component in the ownership relations to the means of production. This does not mean that all relationships are socialist, but it does mean that a form of planning, however inadequate, differentiates Soviet-type society from capitalist. It also provides a dynamic: the dominant institutions support these relationships and, more or less, actively attempt to steer the society to socialism. It is the absence of this recognition that creates ambiguity in Mandel's conception. A transitional society must be in transit to something, and it cannot be in the direction of socialism unless a socialist dynamic may be located. The absence of structural unemployment, the guarantee of job security together with the elimination of economic rent and relatively narrower income differentials than under capitalism are major effects of the socialist component which have to be given prominence in any account of these societies. Hitherto, the maintenance of sustained economic growth, coupled with a fully employed though low –

pay economy, is a major distinction between the Soviet economic system and that of the West.

The critical theorists we have discussed are correct to point out the immature level of productive forces. The considerable reliance on the importation of Western technology in recent years, the utilization of techniques developed under capitalism as well as the slow-down in the rate of growth of the economy is evidence of this immaturity. This backwardness creates contradictions in the society. These contradictions are reflected in the character of the superstructure. The state is a crucial element here. Soviet writers on 'developed socialism' do not view the state apparatus critically. They assume that there is a necessary correspondence between state, economy and civil society. There is an absence in their work of a political sociology of existing socialism. 'Critical' Western Marxists, on the other hand, conflate state and economy and posit an antagonistic contradiction between state and civil society. But the existence of nationalized property does not eliminate the distinction between the political and the economic.

State and Economy

Analytically, 'the state' either under capitalism or in a transitional society, is not concerned with the material production of commodities; accumulation does not accrue to the state. Production and accumulation are the functions of the economy. A government institution may organize an industrial undertaking, but this does not make it part of the state. Nationalized British Leyland or British Rail are not analytically part of the state: they are government-run parts of the economy. The *state* under capitalism is distinguished by its role of safeguarding the reproduction of relations to the (capitalist) means of production. It ensures consensus through laws and socialization. The state in Soviet society has the task of maintaining and creating socialist relations to the means of production. The economy is composed of those ministries concerned with production and distribution of goods and services. The fact that the institutions are publicly owned does not change their functioning in the economy. The state in Soviet-type societies is composed of the ideological apparatuses, the institutions of enforcement and socialization (education and the media).

This approach not only classifies conceptually the nature of the transitional society, but also points to areas of contradiction, not just in the abstract but in terms of the institutional arrangements. Rather than there being a unitary 'bureaucracy' having, in the words of Binns and Hallas, 'a monopoly of decision-making, of power',[46] the 'bureaucracy' may be seen to be composed of two major institutional clusters, the state and the economy. The politics of Soviet-type societies may be usefully thought of in these terms. The necessity of the economy to accumulate and to achieve the levels of advanced capitalism build in tendencies to operate like capitalist societies in terms of wage differentials, discipline of labour, and work processes (e.g. Taylorism). The contradiction between plan and market, in terms of practical politics, may be seen to operate between state and economy. The state, in a transitional society, ensures the continuation of the structure of socialist relations to the means of production, but the economy produces and distributes according to bourgeois principles. Accusations by such writers as Bettelheim that Soviet-type societies 'slip back' into capitalism involve no more than recognition that the economy operates more like capitalist processes – and ignore the defence of the framework of the economy by the state.

The apparatus of government under state socialism cannot merely be characterized as 'bureaucratic', 'a bureaucratic deformation' or 'dictatorial'. The lack of popular control of the state, or absence of organs of people's power which replace the state, must be attributed to two features in the evolution of these societies. First, in the international context, emerging socialist societies have been confronted with militarily powerful capitalist states; Soviet military expenditure is a response to the threat to the USSR's political integrity. Second, a popular participant culture may arise only on the basis of a high level of political competence on the part of the masses. Writers such as Melotti bring out the 'subject' nature of the political culture inherited from the previous social formation or mode of production. What ought also to be emphasized is the way that citizen participation has been encouraged in Soviet-type states. Soviet writers believe that under developed socialism the working class will have a higher political consciousness. But participation is to flourish in a context of 'the centralization of administration'[47] and under the direction of society by the party and government apparatuses. Such forms of mobilization may have outlived their purpose, and current developments may require a greater call on popular 'inputs' to the political system. This is the gist of criticisms of the inadequacies of the planning system by 'critical' Soviet writers, such as Zaslavskaya, when they complain that the 'system of production relations is outdated' and that economic management is unable 'to ensure the complete and efficient utilization of the working and intellectual potential of society'.[48]

The 'inherited culture' of the Soviet Union must also be taken into account.[49] The pre-revolutionary culture becomes absorbed by the state, which is the embodiment not only of Marxist–Leninist beliefs but also of traditional ones. Also, and this is where traditional bureaucratic structures are important, the procedures of the pre-revolutionary social formation are adopted by the incumbents of power after the revolution. While Lenin is acknowledged as having recognized the dangers of 'bureaucratic socialism', many contemporary Soviet writers (unlike Zaslavskaya) are perhaps too complacent that bureaucratic control by elites cannot occur under socialism.[50] The low level of the political and social consciousness of the masses, the lack of a deep socialist ethos, therefore, become a barrier to the development of a socialist consciousness. Contradictions then may be located, not only between state and economy, but also between social institutions of the superstructure. The political and ideological apparatuses of the state may not be hegemonic in their role of creating socialist relationships, but may have to compromise with the forces of coercion, and with inbuilt traditionalism in institutions such as the family, and with the interests of professional groups.

Conclusions

We may summarize our discussion of the transitional society as follows. First, Soviet society is not characterized by class conflict relations, as understood in traditional Marxist analysis. The relations to the means of production are socialist in the sense of there being collective ownership of the means of production. Second, the productive forces, due to the historical trajectory of the USSR, are at a level lower than those of the advanced capitalist states. Third, Soviet society is not a class*less* society. It is a unitary class society involving the domination of the state acting on behalf of the working class. Fourth, planning has replaced the market: there is no production for profit or exchange; full employment has eliminated the 'reserve army' of labourers and ensures a different kind of labour process than under capitalism. Fifth, in a classless society there are fully congruent relationships between the basis and the superstructure; this is not the case in the USSR at present. Sixth, the pattern of distribution of various types of commodities (goods and education) is unequal and entails status differentiation and inequality of opportunity. This gives rise to various forms of hierarchy: to the rankings of occupations in terms of attractiveness and to consumption difference between various social strata. Seventh, the other forms of incongruity are of a cultural kind and represent forms of activity developed in pre-revolutionary Russia. Finally, these kinds of inequalities and incompatibilities, it should be emphasized, are of a qualitatively different kind from notions of class conflict developed by traditional Marxists. In the next chapters we shall discuss further the cultural conditioning and various forms of differentiation and inequality.

NOTES

1 V.S. Semenov, *Dialektika razvitiya sotsial'noy struktury sovetskogo obshchchestva,* 1977, p. 103.
2 A. Zdravomyslov, 'Metodologicheskie problemy izucheniya sovetskogo rabochego Klassa'. *Kommunist,* no. 9, 1978, pp. 127–8.
3 Semenov, *Dialektika...*p. 143. For a more developed treatment of 'developed socialism' see D. Lane, *State and Politics in the USSR,* chapter 5. Much of the following is based on my article 'Western "Critical Marxist" Interpretations of Socialist Societies,' *The Insurgent Sociologist,* vol. 12, no. 1–2 (1984), pp. 101–112.
4 For more detailed and extended accounts, see Paul Bellis, *Marxism and the USSR: the theory of proletarian dictatorship and the Marxist analysis of Soviet society* (1979).
5 T. Cliff, *Russia: a Marxist Analysis* (1963), p. 101.
6 Ibid., pp. 105–7. Italics in original.
7 Ibid., p. 122.
8 Ibid., p. 155.
9 Ibid., pp. 160–61.
10 P. Binns and D. Hallas, 'The Soviet Union: State Capitalist or Socialist', *International Socialism,* no. 91 (1976), p. 25.
11 Ibid., p. 21.
12 P. Binns and M. Haynes. 'New theories of Eastern European class societies', *International Socialism,* Series 2, no. 7 (1980), p. 19.
13 Ibid., pp. 33–5.
14 See D. Lane, 'Marxist Class Conflict Analysis of State Socialist Society', in R. Scase, *Industrial Society: Class, Cleavage and Control* (1977), pp. 175–6.
15 K. Marx, *Capital* (1962), vol. 13, chapter XLIX.
16 Ibid., p. 799.
17 P. Sweezy and C. Bettelheim, *On the Transition to Socialism* (1971), p. 4.
18 L. Trotsky, *The Revolution Betrayed: The Soviet Union, what it is and where it is going* (1945), pp. 248–9.
19 E. Mandel, 'Ten theses on the social and economic laws governing the society transitional between capitalism and socialism', *Critique,* no. 3 (1974). E. Mandel, 'Once again on the Trotskyist definition of the social nature of the Soviet Union', *Critique,* no. 12 (1980).
20 E. Mandel, 'Ten theses on the social and economic laws ...', p. 6.
21 Ibid., p. 8.

22 Ibid., p. 3.

23 Ibid., pp. 10, 15, 16.

24 E. Mandel, 'Once again on the Trotskyist definition of the social nature of the Soviet Union', *Critique*, no. 12, (1980), p. 20.

25 For an interesting discussion of Trotsky in this connection, see B. Knei-Paz, *The Social and Political Thought of Leon Trotsky* (1978), pp. 390–91.

26 H. Ticktin, 'Socialism, the market and the state', *Critique*, no. 3 (1974), p. 66.

27 S. Meikle, 'Has Marxism a future?', *Critique*, no. 13 (1981), p. 107.

28 H. Ticktin, 'Socialism, the market ...', p. 46.

29 H. Ticktin, 'The class structure of the USSR and the elite', *Critique*, no. 9 (1978), p. 48.

30 Ibid., p. 43.

31 H. Ticktin, 'Towards a political economy of the USSR', *Critique*, no. 1 (1973), p. 34.

32 Ticktin, 'The class structure of the USSR ...', pp. 44, 46.

33 Ticktin, 'Towards a political economy ...', p. 22.

34 Ticktin, 'The class structure of the USSR ...', p. 51.

35 See, for example, D.A. Filtzer, 'The concept of waste as a category of the political economy of the Soviet Union: the example of the 1930's', duplicated paper, Centre for Russian and East European Studies, University of Birmingham (1982).

36 A. Carlo, 'The Socio-economic Nature of the USSR', *Telos*, no. 21 (1974).

37 U. Melotti, *Marx and the Third World* (1977); U. Melotti, 'Socialism and Bureaucratic Collectivism in the Third World', *Telos*, no. 43 (1980).

38 A. Carlo, 'The Socio-economic Nature of the USSR', p. 21, 22.

39 Ibid., p. 44.

40 Ibid., p. 45.

41 Cited by U. Melotti, *Marx and the Third World* (1977), pp. 147–8.

42 Ibid., pp. 149, 150–51.

43 See ibid., pp. 25–7.

44 Ibid., pp. 154–5.

45 Ibid., p. 154

46 P. Binns and D. Hallas, 'The Soviet Union: State Capitalist or Socialist', *International Socialism*, no. 91 (1976), p. 22.

47 P. N. Fedoseev, 'Aktual'nye problemy obshchestvennykh nauk', *Kommunist* no. 5 (1975), p. 33.

48 T. Zaslavskaya, 'The Novosibirsk Paper', p. 1. Reprinted in *Survey* vol. 28 no. 1 (1984) pp. 88–108. See also above chapter 2.

49 See D. Lane, *State and Politics in the USSR*, Part I.

50 G. Shakhnazarov, 'O demokraticheskom tsentralizme i politicheskom plyuralizme', *Kommunist*, no. 10 (1979), p. 104.

BIBLIOGRAPHY TO
PART I:

This bibliography does not include all references cited in the text. It is intended to assist the reader who wishes to pursue further study. Under 'Introductory' are listed works dealing with general themes; under 'Basic' are articles and books that are reliable guides to particular topics. 'Specialized' includes literature involving a more detailed treatment and which might be consulted by the specialist.

Introductory

Berliner, Joseph S. 'Managing the USSR Economy: Alternative Models', *Problems of Communism*, vol. 32, no. 1, Jan.–Feb. 1983.

Brown, E.C. *Soviet Trade Unions and Labor Relations*. Cambridge, Mass.: Harvard University Press, 1966.

Ellman, Michael. *Economic Reform in the Soviet Union*. London: Political and Economic Planning Broadsheet 509, 1969.

Granick, D. *Management of the Industrial Firm in the USSR*. New York: Columbia University Press, 1954.

Granick, D. *The Red Executive*. London: Macmillan, 1960.

Kaser, Michael. 'Economic Policy', in A. Brown and M. Kaser, *Soviet Policy for the 1980's*. London: Macmillan, 1982.

Kaser, Michael. 'The Economy: A General Assessment', in A. Brown and M. Kaser, *The Soviet Union Since the Fall of Khrushchev*. London: Macmillan, 1982, 2nd edn.

Lane, David. 'Marxist Class Conflict Analysis of State Socialist Society', in R. Scase, *Industrial Society: Class, Cleavage and Control*. London: Allen and Unwin, 1977.

Lane, David and O'Dell, Felicity. *The Soviet Industrial Worker*. Oxford: Martin Robertson, 1978.

Lavigne, M. *The Socialist Economies of the Soviet Union and Europe*. Oxford: Martin Robertson, 1974.

McAuley, A. 'Social Policy', in A. Brown and M. Kaser, *Soviet Policy for the 1980's*. London: Macmillan, 1982

Nove, Alec. *The Soviet Economic System*. London: Allen and Unwin, 1977.

Ruble, B.A. *Soviet Trade Unions*. Cambridge: Cambridge University Press, 1981.

Smith, Hendrick. *The Russians*. London: Sphere Books, 1976.

Spulber, Nicholas. *Socialist Management and Planning*. Bloomington: Indiana University Press, 1971.

Steele, Jonathan and Abraham, Eric. *Andropov in Power*. Oxford: Martin Robertson, 1983.

Basic

Azrael, J.R. *Managerial Power and Soviet Politics*. Cambridge, Mass.: Harvard University Press, 1966.

Bellis, Paul. *Marxism and the USSR: the Theory of Proletarian Dictatorship and the Marxist Analysis of Soviet Society*. London: Macmillan, 1979.

Bergson, Abram, and Levine, Herbert S. (eds). *The Soviet Economy: Towards the Year 2000*. London: Allen and Unwin, 1983.

Berliner, J.S. *Factory and Manager in the USSR*. Cambridge, Mass.: Harvard University Press, 1957.

Block, Herbert. 'Soviet Economic Growth – Achievements under Handicaps', in Joint Economic Committee US Congress, *Soviet Economy in a New Perspective*. Washington DC: US Congress, 1976.

Brus, W. *The Economics and Politics of Socialism*. London: Routledge, 1973.

Brus, W. *Socialist Ownership and Political Systems under Socialism*. London: Routledge, 1975.

Burnham, James. *The Managerial Revolution*. Harmondsworth: Penguin, 1945.

Cliff, T. *Russia: a Marxist Analysis*. London: Socialist Review Publishing Co., 1963.

Edwards, Imogene et al. 'US and USSR: Comparisons of GNP', in Joint Economic Committee US Congress, *Soviet Economy in a Time of Change*, vol. 1. Washington DC: US Congress, 1979.

Ellman, Michael. *Planning Problems in the USSR*. Cambridge: Cambridge University Press, 1973.

Ellman, Michael. *Socialist Planning*. Cambridge: Cambridge University Press, 1979.

Grossman, G. 'The "Second Economy" of the USSR', in *Problems of Communism*, no. 5, 1977.

Hough, Jerry F. *The Soviet Prefects: The Local Party Organs in Industrial Decision-Making*. Cambridge, Mass.: Harvard University Press, 1969.

Joint Economic Committee US Congress. *Soviet Economy in the 1980s: Problems and Prospects*. Washington: US Government Printing Office, 1982.

Joint Economic Committee US Congress, *USSR: Measures of Economic Growth and Development*. Washington: Government Printing Office, 1982.

Joint Economic Committee US Congress, *Soviet Economy in a Time of Change* Washington: US Government Printing Office, 1979.

Kahan, A. and Ruble, B.A. (eds.). *Industrial Labor in the USSR:* New York: Pergamon Press, 1979.

Knei-Paz, B. *The Social and Political Thought of Leon Trotsky*. London: Oxford University Press, 1978.

Kogan L.N. and Merenkov, A.V. 'Kompleksnye brigady: mneniya, otsenki, opyt vnedreniya', *Sotsiologicheskie issledovaniya*, no. 1, 1983.

McAuley, Mary. *Labour Disputes in Soviet Russia, 1957–1965*. Oxford: Clarendon Press, 1969.

Mandel, E. 'Ten theses on the social and economic laws governing the society transitional between capitalism and socialism', *Critique*, no. 3, 1974.

Nove, Alec. *The Economics of Feasible Socialism*. London: Allen and Unwin, 1983.

Pitzer, John. 'Gross National Product of the USSR, 1950–80', in Joint Economic Committee US Congress, *USSR: Measures of Economic Growth and Development, 1950–80*. Washington DC: US Congress, 1982.

Richman, B.M. *Soviet Management*. Englewood Cliffs, N.J.: Prentice-Hall, 1965.

Schroeder, Gertrude E. 'Soviet Living Standards: Achievements and Prospects', in Joint Economic Committee US Congress, *Soviet Economy in the 1980's: Problems and Prospects* Part 2. Washington DC: US Congress, 1982.

Schroeder, Gertrude E. 'Soviet Economic "Reform" Decrees: More Steps on the Treadmill', in Joint Economic Committee US Congress, *Soviet Economy in the 1980's: Problems and Prospects*, Part 1. Washington DC: US Congress, 1982.

Schroeder, Gertrude and Severin, Barbara S. 'Soviet Consumption and Income Policies in Perspective', in Joint Economic Committee US Congress, *Soviet Economy in a New Perspective*. Washington DC: US Congress, 1976.

Semenov, V.S. *Dialektika razvitiya sotsial'noy struktury sovetskogo obshchestva*. Moscow, 1977.

Shakhnazarov, G. 'O demokraticheskom tsentralizme i politicheskom plyuralizme', *Kommunist*, no. 10, 1979

Sweezy, P. and Bettelheim, C. *On the Transition to Socialism*. New York: Monthly Review, 1971.

Ticktin, H. 'The class structure of the USSR and the elite', *Critique*, no. 9, 1978.

White, Stephen, 'The USSR. Patterns of Autocracy and Industrialism', in A. Brown and J. Gray, *Political Culture and Change in Communist States*. London: Macmillan, 1977, pp. 25–65.

Specialized

Andrle, V. *Managerial Power in the Soviet Union*. Farnborough: Lexington Books, 1976.

Batkaev, R. and Semin, S. 'Shchekinski metod v usloviyakh sovershenstvovaniya khozyaystvennogo mekhanizma', *Sotsialisticheski trud*, no. 1, 1983.

Becker, Abraham, S. 'Military Allocations and Burden', in Joint Economic Committee US Congress, *Soviet Economy in the 1980's: Problems and Prospects*, Part 1. Washington DC: US Congress, 1982.

Binns, P. and Hallas, D. 'The Soviet Union: State Capitalist or Socialist', *International Socialism*, no. 91, 1976.

Binns, P. and Haynes, M. 'New theories of Eastern European class societies', *International Socialism*, Series 2, no. 7, 1980.

D.F. Burton, 'Estimating Soviet Defense Spending: *Problems of Communism*, vol. 32, no. 2, 1983. pp. 85–93.

Bush, Keith. 'Retail Prices in Moscow and Four Western Cities in May 1976', *Osteuropa: Wirtschaft*, no. 2, 1977, pp. 122–41.
Bush, Keith. 'Rents and the Social Contract in the USSR', Munich RFE-RL 410/82, 1982.
Bush, Keith. 'Retail Prices in Moscow and Four Western Cities in March, 1982', Munich: RFE-RL, June 1982.
Bush, Keith and Tenson, A. 'Indicators of Living Standards in the USSR and Eastern Europe', *Radio Liberty Research*, Munich, RL 101/77, May 1977.
Carlo, A. 'The Socio-economic Nature of the USSR', *Telos*, no. 21, 1974.
Ellman, Michael. 'Seven Theses on Kosyginism', *De Ekonomist* (Leiden) vol. 125, no. 1, 1977.
Ellman, Michael. *Full Employment: Lessons from State Socialism.* Leiden/ Antwerp, 1979.
Fedoseev, P.N. 'Aktual'nye problemy obshchestvennykh nauk', *Kommunist*, no. 5, 1975.
Gorlin, Alice C. 'Industrial Reorganisation: The Associations', in Joint Economic Committee US Congress, *Soviet Economy in a New Perspective.* Washington DC: US Congress, 1976.
Gosudarstvenny byudzhet SSSR i byudzhety soyuznykh respublik 1976–1980g. Moscow, 1982.
Grossman, G. 'A Note on Soviet Inflation', in Joint Economic Committee US Congress, *Soviet Economy in the 1980's: Problems and Prospects*, Part 1. Washington DC: US Congress, 1982.
Hanson, P. *The Consumer in the Soviet Economy.* London: Macmillan, 1968.
Hanson, P. 'Success Indicators Revisited: The July 1979 Soviet Decree on Planning and Management', *Soviet Studies*, vol. 35, no. 1, Jan. 1983.
Hill, S. *Competition and Control at Work.* London: Heinemann, 1981.
Hindebrandt, Gregory G. 'The Dynamic Burden of Soviet Defense Spending', in Joint Economic Committee US Congress, *Soviet Economy in the 1980s: Problems and Prospects.* Part 1. Washington DC: US Congress, 1982.
Howard, David H. 'A Note on Hidden Inflation in the Soviet Union', *Soviet Studies*, vol. 28, no. 4, 1976, pp. 509–608.
Katsenelinboigen, A. 'Coloured Markets in the Soviet Union', *Soviet Studies*, vol. 29, no.1, 1977, pp. 62–85.
Mandel, E. 'Once again on the Trotskyist definition of the social nature of the Soviet Union', *Critique*, no. 12, 1980.
Melotti, U. *Marx and the Third World.* London: Macmillan, 1977.
Narodnoe khozyaystvo SSSR 1922–1982. Moscow, 1982.
O'Hearn, D. 'The Consumer Second Economy', *Soviet Studies*', vol. 32, no. 2, 1980.
Pravda, A. 'Spontaneous Workers' Activities in the Soviet Union', in A. Kahan and B.A. Ruble, *Industrial Labor in the USSR.* New York: Pergamon Press, 1979.
Ruble, B.A. 'Soviet Trade Unions and Labor Relations after "Solidarity"', in Joint Economic Committee US Congress, *Soviet Economy in the 1980's: Problems and Prospects*, Part 2. Washington DC: US Congress, 1982.

Schachtman, Max. *The Bureaucratic Revolution*. New York: Donald Press, 1962.
Shaffer, H.G. (ed.). *Soviet Agriculture: An Assessment of its Contributions to Economic Development*. New York: Praeger and Oxford: Martin Robertson, 1977.
Shalaev, S. 'Sovetskie profsoyuzy v obshchestve razvitogo sotsializma', *Pravda*, 12 October 1983.
Shapiro, L. 'Razvitie brigadnoy formy organizatsii i stimulirovaniya truda', *Planovoe khozyaystvo*, no. 7, July 1983.
'Shchekino Experiment is Ten Years Old'. *Pravda*, 28 March 1977. Summarized in *Current Digest of the Soviet Press*, vol. 29, no. 13, 1977.
'Text of the Model Collective Farm Charter', *Current Digest of the Soviet Press*, vol. 21, no. 50, 1969.
Ticktin, H. 'Towards a Political Economy of the USSR', *Critique*, vol. 1, no. 1, 1973, pp. 20–41.
Ticktin, H. 'Socialism, the market and the state', *Critique*, no. 3, 1974.
Trotsky, L. *The Revolution Betrayed: The Soviet Union, what it is and where it is going*. London: Pioneer Press, 1945.
United States Congress, Joint Economic Committee. *Soviet Economy in a Time of Change*. Washington DC: US Congress, 1979.
'Ustav professional'nykh soyuzov SSSR', in *Spravochnik profsoyuznogo rabotnika*. Moscow, 1962.
'Ustav professional'nykh soyuzov SSSR', Printed in *Materialy XVI s''ezda professional'nykh soyuzov SSSR*, Moscow, 1977.
Wädekin, K.E. 'Income Distribution in Soviet Agriculture', *Soviet Studies*, vol. 27, no. 1, 1975.
Yanowitch, M. (ed.). *Soviet Work Attitudes – The Issue of Participation in Management*. Oxford: Martin Robertson, 1979.
Zdravomyslov, A. 'Metodologicheskie problemy izucheniya sovetskogo rabochego klassa', *Kommunist*, no. 9, 1978.
Zdravomyslov, A.G., Rozhin, V.P., and Yadov, V.A. (eds). *Man and His Work*. New York: International Arts and Sciences Press, 1972.

Part II
SOCIAL RELATIONS

4

POPULATION AND THE FAMILY

The family is a universal social phenomenon, and may be defined as a more or less permanent bio-social group composed of at least two cohabiting adults of the opposite sex together with children, towards whom they act as parents. The family has four major functions: the physical reproduction of individuals, the nourishment and maintenance of children, the socialization of children (that is, the teaching of social behaviour and mores), their placement in the occupational system or status hierarchy.[1] In modern times the family also serves to provide companionship for its members: it is, as Parsons has put it, 'a haven of emotionality', helping its individual members to face an impersonal external world. None of these functions, of course, is exclusive to the family. Reproduction may be secured by a single mother with no permanent attachments; the maintenance of children may be the responsibility of children's homes or orphanages; socialization may be performed by the church and/or mass media; and occupational placement is often done via the educational system. Nevertheless, in all societies, including the USSR, the family fulfils, to a greater or lesser extent, all these functions.

To avoid confusion, we must distinguish between two kinds of family structure: the nuclear or conjugal, consisting of husband, wife and the children to whom they act as parents; and the consanguine, consisting of a group of blood relatives, forming several conjugal units. Hence, though every adult is a member of one consanguine family, he or she is a member of two conjugal families: a family of orientation, in which he or she is born and reared, and a family of procreation established by marriage and the birth of offspring (or adoption). Though there are many types of family in the USSR, over the last one hundred years the typical family structure has changed from that of the larger family grouping of several conjugal families (the consanguine unit) to the more independent or 'nuclear' family. This shift parallels the movement from a predominantly peasant agrarian society to an urban-industrial one.

The Traditional Russian Family

During the nineteenth century, the Russian Empire was predominantly rural. The peasant family was monogamous – at least in the European areas of the country – and based on the larger consanguine unit, which was both patriarchal and authoritarian: the head of the family was the grandfather, his eldest brother or son. Relations between spouses followed the same pattern: 'The wife is obliged to love, respect and obey her husband implicitly and must please and follow him in every way.'[2] The family also served to transmit property, which was legally vested in the family head, and as the basic work unit: usually, the fields were tended collectively. The peasant remained largely untouched by educational and government institutions, and the chief, non-familial influences on peasant life were the church and, perhaps, army service. The role of property for the peasant was less important than in Western Europe: until the Emancipation of the Serfs in 1862, the peasant was 'bound to the land', and even after that date most land was owned by the commune and was not transferred through families. For the townsmen and other permanent urban dwellers, family life approximated to that of Western Europe; and for the bourgeoisie it remained important in the transfer of property.

During the nineteenth century, the population grew rapidly following the pattern of other developing industrial nations, with a high infant mortality rate and a higher birth rate: in 1913 the birth rate was 47 per thousand of the population and the death rate 30.2.[3] Consequently, the population grew, mainly due to an increase in the number of live births, and large families predominated, especially in the countryside.

With the development of industry and commerce, the *Gemeinschaft* (or communal) relations of the peasant family broke down. Men moved to the town for work, thus breaking the geographical unity of the family, and though wife and children remained in the village, where the new town worker may have been legally domiciled, urban life began to assert its values within the village community. The traditional male head lost much of his power because of the comparative wealth of his sons who now worked in the town and sent money to the country.[4] The growth of towns encouraged a larger market for agricultural produce which tended to undermine the peasant subsistence economy.

In the non-European areas of Russia, many different forms of family life existed. Polygamy was general, and many brides married under sixteen years of age. Marriage contracts were arranged through parents, and patriarchal authority predominated. In Central Asia, family structure was usually organized on a consanguine basis. Kislyakov has shown that among the Tadzhiks, even in the early 1930s, family units could number up to 50 strong, and in Turkestan, in the early 1940s, similar large family units were found.[5] But there were exceptions: already in the nineteenth century the Kirghiz had developed a more nuclear family structure.[6]

Soviet Marxist Ideology of the Family

After the October Revolution, the attitude of the Soviet government to the family was determined, like all policy matters, partly by Marxist theory and partly by expediency. Marx and particularly Engels had attempted to explain the various forms of family life in terms of the requirements of the economic structure of society.[7] Under capitalism, Engels maintained, monogamy allows the regular transfer of property from father to son, thereby strengthening the motive for capitalist accumulation. Spouse relationships are not based on equality but on the subjugation of the female by the male. Love, at least for the property-owning or bourgeois family, rarely exists: the sexual relationship between husband and wife is a form of legalized prostitution which takes place alongside frequent sexual liaisons outside marriage.[8] As Engels put it in his description of the bourgeoisie: 'the wife differs from the ordinary courtesan only in that she does not hire out her body like a wage worker, but sells it into slavery once for all',[9] and, in *The Communist Manifesto* Marx stated, 'bourgeois marriage is in reality a system of wives in common . . . .'[10] They both believed that for the subject class – the proletariat under capitalism – family relationships were sustained more by love and less by property relations, because the workers were propertyless. The wife is less subjugated by the husband, since industrial conditions enable her to take up paid employment. To this extent, therefore, no economic basis exists for the exploitation of one sex by the other,[11] and mutual love is more common. On the other hand, the brutalizing effects of industrial capitalism, the ruthless and merciless employment of women and children degrade family relationships. Nevertheless, under capitalism, the growth of wage labour and the industrial employment of both men and women create a basis for equality between spouses.

Engels also applied his analysis to the exploration of family life under socialism. Given the abolition of private wealth – which lay at the root of the prostitution (i.e. sexual relations without love) of monogamous marriage – prostitution itself, he argued, would disappear. But monogamy, as a form of social relationship, would prevail: in fact, only under socialism would monogamy 'finally become a reality'.[12] Women would have equality with men: the care of children and housekeeping would be the concern of society. Contracting out of marriage, which was extremely difficult in Engels's day, would be easy and available to either spouse.

Marriage would be a union reflecting free choice between partners and based on individual sexual love.[13] 'The monogamous family has improved greatly since the commencement of civilisation, and very sensibly in modern times, it is at least supposable that it is capable of still further improvement until the equality of the sexes is attained.'[14] Such unions would lose the element of patriarchal dominance. Women would enjoy economic independence and the burdens of child care would become the prerogative of the state. Engels, in Besemeres's words, at times 'betrays a romantic, not to say ingenuous, enthusiasm for the joyous potentialities of marriage if and when it were to be stripped of economic calculation and based on what he called individual sexual love'.[15]

The chief points embodied in Engels's works may be summarized as follows. Under capitalism, monogamy has an economic foundation necessary for the transmission of property and is corrupted by private wealth. It also provides for the fulfilment of human love, which exists more in working class families than among the capitalists themselves. Under socialism, the monogamous family would continue, but entry into and release from marriage would be based on individual free choice unrestricted by legal barriers and property considerations. The burden of child care would be shouldered by the government.

Soviet Family Policy Since 1917

Soviets communists in the days after the Revolution interpreted Marxist theory in different ways. Alexandra Kollontay argued for a looser family union based more on sexual desires.

The old type of family has seen its day ... [it] needlessly holds back the female workers from the more productive and far more serious work. Nor is the family any more necessary to the members themselves, since the task of bringing up children ... is passing more and more into the hands of the collectivity.[16]

The status of sexual love for 'left-feminists' like Kollontay was symbolized by the saying that having sexual intercourse should be like drinking a glass of water. In the days of the Civil War such views were cited to justify promiscuity, 'free love' and the 'nationalization of women': for example, in Vladimir, a decree was passed making every virgin over eighteen years state property. This, of course, was not official Leninist policy, but a popular vulgarization of Marxism.

Lenin's views on marriage and the family were conservative. He opposed Kollontay's ideas of radicalizing sexual relations and instead favoured the pedestrian notion of 'a proletarian civilian marriage with love'.[17] He also believed that the source of liberation was paid employment and supported women's rights to divorce.

The period following the October Revolution was one of relatively unrestricted sexual activity: many families broke up and children were often conceived outside marriage.[18] The breakdown of traditional morals was not due soley to the actions of the communist government; it was as much the result of the breakdown of the old society, and the impact of war and revolution. One should not, however, exaggerate the extent of this dislocation. It was greatest in the towns. In the countryside, and the non-European areas, family life was less affected. Nevertheless, where it became common, uninhibited sexual activity caused concern and some communists called for the sublimation of the sexual drive. Opposing the 'old wives tale' that sexual indulgence was necessary to health, Semashko wrote in *Izvestiya*: 'Drown your sexual energy in public work .... If you want to solve the sexual problem, be a public worker, a comrade, not a stallion or a brood-mare.'[19]

In addition to the changes that took place in ownership and the control of the economy, legislation was enacted specifically concerning the civil status of husband, wife and children. This reflected thinking more conservative than the views held by Kollontay. The legislation of 1917 and 1918,[20] by abolishing inheritance of property, the legal differences between husband and wife and the distinction between legitimate and illegitimate children, set out to weaken family bonds (to 'obliterate' the capitalist family); but it by no means abolished the family as a social institution. Instead, it reflected Lenin's view of a 'proletarian civilian marriage with love'. While inheritance was abolished in 1918 and property was transferred to the state, by 1922 one could inherit personal possessions of up to 10,000 rubles, and after 1926 the upper limit was abolished. (Private ownership of the means of production remained, of course, illegal.)

The principal aspects of Soviet family legislation (the foundation of a 'socialist' family) were designed to sustain the principle of monogamy; to recognize *de facto* or common-law marriage – if registered at the registrar's office or if proven in court of law; to abolish all class, national or religious restraints on marriage; to allow easy divorce – through the court if one spouse desired it, through the registry office if both agreed; to equalize the legal status of husband and wife (especially with respect to property and children); and to recognize birth as the basis of the family (whether the parents were legally married or not). In 1920, abortion was legalized.

In the Asiatic parts of the country, the Bolsheviks were confronted with extended family structures based on tribal and feudal forms of social organization. Women were a subject class. Here, as in the European western areas of the country, laws were passed outlawing traditional forms of female bondage: the 'bride price' was abolished and the minimum age of marriage was raised. The communists organized mass political activity, called the *khudzhum*, which set out to mobilize native women to oppose traditional practices by, for example, organizing the ceremonial burning of veils. The laws doubtless reduced the incidence of certain practices, but customs are not changed at a stroke and patriarchal attitudes remained dominant.

The Code of 1926[21] contained provisions similar to the above and gave legal status both to registered marriage and marriage in 'common law', the latter being a union where 'the fact of cohabitation, combined with a common household ... the manifestation of marital relations ... could be shown' (Article 11). Soviet legislation differed from that of Western states at that time in that children of 'common law' marriage were given the same rights before the law as those of 'civil law' marriage. In this way the Soviet state sanctioned many unions which had occurred outside the framework of state legality. The decree of 1917 had made marriage a civil and not a religious procedure. Yet in 1925 about a third of urban marriages were still performed in church[22] (and the comparable figure in the countryside must have been about three-quarters). The effects of the 1926 Code were to allow marriages to be both easily formed and ended.

If by marriage we mean the regular cohabiting of a man and woman with the intention of founding a family, then the Soviet practice during these times would properly be defined as 'marriage'. If, however, we wish to restrict the usage to unions given public recognition and conferring a special legal status on children of marriage, then Soviet 'marriage' between 1926 and 1944 might be excluded. Kingsley Davis, for example, has argued that control by society over parenthood (as distinguished from control over sexual relations) and the legal obligations and rights associated with it are the most important attributes of the family.[23] It could be argued that Soviet family law did not distinguish closely between such unions and other less permanent liaisons, for both parents and offspring could claim that a 'common law' marriage had taken place. Therefore, it might be said, 'marriage' as an institution did not exist. It is perhaps best, however, to adopt a wider definition of the family. It seems arbitrary to define marriage as a sociological phenomenon in terms of Western (and particularly Catholic) conventions. The Soviet family, during this period (1926–1944), was certainly of a looser, more informal 'common law' type than in Western states.

Up to 1944, when the laws were changed again, Soviet law was permissive and tended to encourage family disintegration. A weakened family unit was in the interests of the new regime in that it made easier the accomplishment of social change. By weakening the family, with its relationships over which the state could have no direct control, the socializing influence of the parents and many of their traditional (or anti-socialist) values were minimized. As a result, the individual became more open to pressure from other social institutions. And the 1930s were indeed a period of tension between parents and children.

Inkeles and Bauer give examples of the intergenerational conflicts reported by post-1945 Russian émigrés.

. . . We can understand why conflicts over religion and political belief permeated the reports on family life given by those from peasant and worker backgrounds. From the parents' point of view, it seemed that their children were being torn away from them and won over to or at least significantly influenced to be irreligious and to support the Communist regime. The children, in turn, often felt their parents to be backward or ignorant, and thus were alienated from them. This was especially evident when the children were advancing themselves and thus coming ever more under the influence of values which ran counter to those of the parents. A Komsomol [Young Communist League] member, who was a student at the time the war began, reported that when he came home from school he demanded that the ikon which his peasant mother kept in plain sight be removed from the home. 'When younger', he said, 'I had been afraid to discuss the matter with them, but growing older and being away from home I found the courage to do this.' He hid the ikon, but his mother found it, and after a scene he agreed not to remove it again. Thus a resolution was achieved, but it is clear that the residue must have been a sense of alienation between parent and child.[24]

The economic and legal position of women was transformed: industrial employment was thrown open to them and they had the same rights as men before the law.[25] In spite of this, during the inter-war period, the tasks of child minding and upbringing were still the main responsibility of the wife: in 1927, there were only 2,100 kindergartens.[26] The wife, sometimes helped by her mother or mother-in-law, looked after the children and was responsible for the household: and her duties included the latter whether she worked or not.

From 1935 onwards, a different policy emerged, although the chief provisions of the 1926 Code were kept intact until 1944. A number of decrees were introduced designed to strengthen the family: in that year, parents were made responsible for the disorderly conduct of their children; divorce was made more difficult and expensive in order to discourage marital instability and, in 1936, abortion became a criminal offence. In 1942, single persons and married couples without children were additionally taxed. In 1944 a wholesale restructure of state policy on the family took place. The deprivation and chaos of the war had led to many pre- and extra-marital sexual relations: some four million Soviet women had children with no legal father.[27] The main provisions of the 1944 decree were four-fold: only registered marriages were recognized; divorce was made much more expensive[28] and obtainable only through court action; the family was strengthened – children born outside wedlock had no right to the father's name, or his possessions, and the father had no legal obligations to maintain them. (On the other hand, the mothers of such children received a state grant.)

Official attitudes to sex and marriage had also changed. The radicalism advocated by some Bolsheviks in the early revolutionary years was replaced by taboos on sexual libertarianism. An almost Victorian attitude to monogamy and child rearing became the norm. 'The purpose of marriage was declared to be the creation of a "strong, many-childrened family", unmarred by the "obscenity" of bourgeois divorce, a family which was at once loyal to itself and loyal to the state.'[29] In 1949, rights and duties arising from 'de facto' marriages were annulled. In addition, divorce was made even harder to obtain.

After Stalin's death a liberalization in family matters gradually set in once more. In 1954, women were exonerated from criminal responsibility for abortions performed on them and, in 1955, abortion was legalized. On 10 December 1965, a decree eliminated the need to publish a notice of divorce in the local press, and the second (or final) hearing is now conducted in the people's court. The cost of divorce was reduced marginally: the 40 ruble publication fee was abolished, but other costs remained.[30] New restrictions on divorce were, however, introduced in 1968, when a new family law was introduced. The law on marriage and the family[31] decreed that children born outside marriage have the right to the father's name if paternity can be established – either by a joint statement or through the court. This measure was designed to strengthen an unmarried mother's rights for her children. Now, a husband cannot start divorce proceedings without his wife's consent if she is pregnant or during the year following the birth of a child.

The legal position of the Soviet family between 1917 and that of the Constitution (or Fundamental Law) of 1977 has thus turned full circle: from being weakened to being strengthened by state laws. Article 53 of the Constitution of 1977 says that:

The family is under the protection of the state. Marriage is entered into with free consent of the woman and the man; spouses are completely equal in their matrimonial relations.

The state aids the family by providing and developing an extensive network of child-care institutions, organising and improving the community services and public catering, and by providing allowances and benefits for families with many children, and by paying benefits on the birth of a child.

The history of the Soviet family since the revolution helps to illustrate that the character of the family is determined by other institutions, particularly the political and economic. The measures passed since 1944 to strengthen the Soviet family are an indication of the Soviet belief that new families are no longer likely to inculcate values at variance with the dominant ideology; rather than being a potential opposition to the regime, their conservatism helps to sustain it. Though Kollontay's proposals are still occasionally voiced in the USSR, they are regarded as eccentric.[32] In the USSR the driving agents of social change were located in the political system: the character of the family changed in response to it. But it has not changed completely and it plays as we shall see later an important role in socializing children with pre-revolutionary traditional mores.

Population Structure and Change

Family policy is shaped not only by ideal considerations, but also by the government's need to ensure a certain level of population in order to facilitate the replenishment of this crucial national resource. There can be no doubt that demographic considerations have played an important role in shaping social policy on the family. An American authority on the Soviet family has interpreted the 1936 and 1944 legislation as 'marked extension(s) of Stalin's social engineering for a strong family, and, especially, for a higher birth rate'.[33] It is pertinent, then, to consider the first function of the family mentioned above – the physical reproduction of the population. Here we shall consider its size, age and gender division and in chapter 6 we shall examine in more detail its national and ethnic divisions.

Basic data on the population since 1897 are summarized in table 4.1. Study of the table shows that population has doubled by 1979. The Second World War exacted a toll of some 20 million citizens, illustrated by the net

TABLE 4.1: POPULATION GROWTH OF RUSSIA AND USSR (CURRENT BOUND-ARIES)

Year	Total Population (millions)	Periods	(Years)	Annual Average Growth (millions)
1897	125.0	1897–1913	(16)	2.3
1913	159.2	1913–1926	(13)	0.64
1926	167.6	1926–1939	(13)	1.95
1939	193.0	1939–1950	(11)	−1.02
1950	181.7	1950–1959	(9)	3.0
1959	208.8	1959–1970	(11)	2.9
1970	241.7	1970–1979	(9)	2.3
1979	262.4	1979–1983	(4)	2.2
1983	271.2			

Sources: Naselenie SSSR (Moscow, 1980), p. 3. SSSR v tsifrakh (1983). Calculations added.

TABLE 4.2: CRUDE BIRTH RATE* IN USSR, USA AND ENGLAND AND WALES

	1913	1940	1958	1964	1978	1981
USSR	45.5	31.3	25.3	19.7	18.2	18.5
USA	35.0	17.9	24.3	21.7	15.3	15.9
England and Wales	24.3	14.6	16.8	18.4	12.3	13.1

*per thousand of total population

population loss between 1939 and 1950. Territorial changes[34] following the Second World War made good some of these losses. The years of peace have witnessed the replenishment of the population stock – but not at an even rate and not without regional disproportions.

The underlying dynamics of population growth may be considered by studying birth and death rates. Countries undergoing modernization normally experience population growth through a rising birth rate and declining death rate; after an initial rapid rise in population (due to the rise in births), and following an ageing of the population, the *rate* of growth tends to fall. Table 4.2 illustrates these tendencies for the Soviet Union, the USA and England and Wales for selected years between 1913 and 1981.

The fall in birth rate follows a pattern similar to that of Western societies, as can be seen from table 4.2. The Soviet birth rate fell from 45.5 in 1913 to 19.7 in 1964, a figure below the American equivalent for the latter year. By 1982, the Soviet birth rate had fallen slightly to 19.0.[35] These figures, it should be remembered, are insufficient for a detailed analysis of fertility, which is affected by changes in the proportion of sexes of different ages and the age of marriage. The large number of men killed in the war not only reduced the birth rate during the period 1941–45, but also had effects for twenty years afterwards. It has meant that the male death rate was 'artificially' reduced from about 1960 to the early 1980s as fewer men than usual were between the age of 60 and 80 years (see table 4.3). The trend towards declining fertility was reversed in the late 1970s, and stable fertility rates are now forecast. The effects of the decline in the

TABLE 4.3: CRUDE DEATH RATE* IN USSR, USA AND ENGLAND AND WALES

	1913	1940	1958	1964	1978	1981
USSR	29.1	18.1	7.2	7.0	9.7	10.2
USA	13.2	10.8	9.5	9.6	8.8	8.6
England and Wales	14.2	14.4	11.7	12.2	11.7	11.8

*per thousand of total population

birth rate will mean that between 1986 and 1990 there will be a decrease in the Soviet Union's working population of some one million.[36]

Infant mortality has also followed the long-term downward trends of other Western countries. In the late 1950s, there were 40.6 deaths per thousand births of children aged under one year in the USSR, compared to 29.5 in the USA: by 1970, the Soviet infant mortality rate had fallen to 25. In the 1970s, however, concern was expressed in the West that the Soviet infant mortality rate had risen again. In 1974, the overall figure was 27.9;[37] and since this date, no further figures have been published, though Davis and Feshback have estimated that it rose again to 29.4 in 1975 and to 31.1 in 1976.[38] These writers attribute this not only to the deterioration in health care, the prevalence of continual abortions, the break-up of the extended family and the high female labour force participation rates, but also to bad diet, poor public sanitation in most areas, inadequate medical supplies and epidemics of powerful strains of influenza leading to pneumonia.

In the absence of detailed statistics for the late 1970s and early 1980s, one cannot be sure of identifying a long-term trend. The cited causes for the increase in deaths are also open to question. Jones and Grupp, however, in a detailed analysis of statistical reporting, argue most convincingly that much of the increase in the reported infant mortality rate is due to better statistics in the Central Asian parts of the country. A higher rate of hospitalization has led to fuller recording of infant deaths. Also, techniques for keeping babies alive at birth lead to the registration of their subsequent deaths as infant mortality rather than still birth. Jones and Grupp conclude that in the European areas infant mortality stagnated or declined in the late 1970s; the real infant mortality rate in the 'southern tier' also declined – though recorded rates increased.[39]

Accompanying the fall in the birth rate has been a shift in the share of the population from rural to urban. In 1913, 82 per cent of the population was rural, falling to 67 per cent in 1940, 60 per cent in 1951, 50 per cent in 1961, 43 per cent in 1971 and 35.6 per cent in 1983.[40] With urbanization, the size of the family in the USSR has fallen. In 1939, its average size was 4.1 with 3.6 in urban and 4.3 in rural areas. In 1970, the census showed that the average size had declined to 3.7 with 3.5 in the town and 4.0 in the countryside. There were still important differences between the Republics. By 1979, average family size in the USSR had fallen to 3.5. In Tadzhikistan it was 5.7; in Uzbekistan 5.5; in the Russian Republic 3.3; in Latvia 3.1; and in Estonia 3.1. Table 4.4 shows the average family size in the last three censuses and the distribution of large and small families in 1979.[41] The table shows the very large families in the Central Asian parts of the country, a point we shall consider in more detail below (see p. 218).

TABLE 4.4: SIZE OF FAMILY IN UNION REPUBLICS OF USSR, 1959, 1970, 1979

				Percentage of Families		
		Average		*in 1979 consisting of*		
Republic		*Family Size*		*2 or 3*	*4 or 5*	*6 or more*
	1959	*1970*	*1979*	*Members*	*Members*	*Members*
Armenia	4.8	5.0	4.7	26	44	30
Tadzhikistan	4.7	5.4	5.7	27	27	46
Uzbekistan	4.6	5.3	5.5	28	29	43
Turkmenia	4.5	5.2	5.5	29	28	43
Azerbaidzhan	4.5	5.1	5.1	30	32	38
Kirgizia	4.2	4.6	4.6	39	32	29
Kazakhstan	4.1	4.3	4.1	46	36	18
Georgia	4.0	4.1	4.0	41	42	17
Moldavia	3.8	3.8	3.4	59	33	8
Belorussia	3.7	3.6	3.3	61	34	5
Russia	3.6	3.5	3.3	63	32	5
Lithuania	3.6	3.4	3.3	61	34	5
Ukraine	3.5	3.4	3.3	62	33	5
Latvia	3.2	3.2	3.1	68	29	3
Estonia	3.1	3.1	3.1	67	30	3
USSR average	3.7	3.7	3.5	59	32	9

Source: A. Volkov, 'Sem'ya kak faktor izmeneniya demograficheskoy situatsii', *Sotsiologicheskie issledovaniya*, no. 1 (1981), p. 35.

Of the 66 million family units in 1979, 29.6 per cent were composed of two persons, 28.8 of three persons and 22.9 of four individuals.[42] As in Western societies, a trend towards small nuclear family units has occurred. By 1962, the single child family was most typical as shown by table 4.5. This table may underestimate family size, as it includes only children under 16 years of age. The figures confirm that the family is still relatively large in

TABLE 4.5: NUMBER OF CHILDREN UNDER SIXTEEN IN FAMILIES OF DIFFE-RENT SOCIAL GROUPS

	*1962 study**			*1978 study*[+]	
	Manual Workers	*Collective Farmers*	*Non-Manual Workers*	*Manual and Non-Manuals*	*Collective Farmers*
	%	*%*	*%*	*%*	*%*
All families having children	100	100	100	100	100
With one child	46	40	50	57.4	39.9
With two children	39	32	41	31.8	30.2
With three children	12	19	8	6.4	14.6
With four or more	3	9	1	4.4	17.3

Sources: * *Zhenshchiny i deti v SSSR*, Statisticheski sbornik (1963), p. 68.
          † *Deti v SSSR*, Statisticheski sbornik (1979), p. 9.

the countryside, where in 1978, 31.9 per cent of all families had three or more children. Non-manual workers have the smallest families – half having only one child. This tendency towards smaller families has established itself despite substantial financial aid given to, and orders[43] bestowed on, mothers who beget large families. By 1978, 57.4 per cent of families of manual and non-manual workers having children had only one child; for collective farmers, the figure was 39.9 per cent.

Birth Control

Several factors play a part in determining family size. The lowered birth rate has not simply been due to publicity about, and the availability of, contraceptives. Birth control is widespread in the USSR. Condoms and the IUD are universally available, although birth control pills are not widely used. However, knowledge about contraception is at a low level, leading to the creation of a large number of unwanted pregnancies.[44] One survey showed that only half of the couples wishing not to conceive used contraceptives.[45] Abortion, which was legalized between 1920 and 1936 and again after 1955,[46] is the chief method of birth control. Abortions are carried out for pregnancies not exceeding twelve weeks (save for overriding medical reasons). Women remain in hospital for observation for three days. For women in employment the operation costs 5 rubles; for those with low income it is free.[47] It has been estimated that the ratio of abortions to live births is between 2.5 and 3.0 to 1.[48] Kharchev and Matskovski[49] cite data to the effect that, of a group of women surveyed in Moscow, 10 per cent had had five or more abortions. But Soviet women are discouraged from having abortions, particularly on health grounds. The lack of privacy concerning hospitalization also leads to illegal abortions – one Soviet estimate puts the figure at 15 per cent of all abortions.[50] The service is considered by some Western writers to be inefficient and involving pain and distress to the woman. Reliance on abortion may be considered to be partly due to the preference in a peasant society for a trusted method rather than a new and unknown possibility. Perhaps more important is the government's pro-natal policy and the lack of oral contraceptives. It has also been suggested that the government is reluctant to promote the separation of sex from reproduction[51] and that this fear is conditioned by a concern for the stability of the family.

The widespread employment of women also works against the large family. Studies show an inverse relationship between the female employment rate and the birth rate: the higher the former, the lower the latter. It is clear, too, that couples now want to rear a small family as a way of life. In one large-scale study of women's preferences for size of family, 43.5 per cent surveyed wanted one or two children, 39.4 per cent sought three and 6 per cent wanted five or more. However, in another survey of women working at eleven Moscow factories, it was found that 60 per cent thought that two children 'made the best family', 36 per cent were for three and only 3 per cent favoured a one child family. The authors of the study point out, though, that in fact 17 per cent of the women surveyed had no children, 64 per cent had one child and 18 per cent had two. A sample survey of Moscow families with an average married life of 11.2 years, found that 61 per cent had one child, 30 per cent, two, 8.5 per cent, three and 0.5 per cent, four children. The average number of children was 1.4 per family.[52]

Family size is one area of policy in which a government finds it extremely difficult to exercise control. Although having children has been regarded since the revolution as a right of the citizen, the falling birth rate induced the government to prohibit abortion (in the 1930s and 1940s) and to give family allowances. Nevertheless, the size of the Soviet family seems to have followed the pattern of other industrialized countries, and there is an inverse relation between income and fertility and between income and infant mortality.[53] As in the West, too, the role of the family in the provision of maintenance during sickness, incapacity and old age has declined. Social security covering illness, maternity, industrial injury, family allowances, old-age, self and dependants' disability is provided by the government through the trade union organization.[54] The decline in the birth rate, particularly in the European areas of the USSR, and (as we shall discover below) the increased divorce rate have led to developments in Soviet demographic policy in the 1980s designed to 'strengthen the family as a most important kernel of socialist society'.[55]

Entry to Marriage

Until 1968, the legal minimum age of marriage varied from one republic to another: in some, girls under 16 could legally marry. The All-Union law[56] on marriage and the family (1968) made the minimum age 18 for men and women, but republics were given the right to lower the minimum by two years.

The age of marriage in the USSR as a whole has fallen and approximates that of advanced capitalist countries. The ages of those marrying in 1980 are shown in table 4.6; 72.7 per cent of the brides and 62.1 per cent of the grooms married under the age of 25. There is a tendency at all ages for the grooms to marry younger brides and for the age of marriage for women to be getting younger. Table 4.7 illustrates the increase in the proportion of early marriages. In 1980, 65 per cent of men marrying in the 30–34 age group married women under 30 years of age.[57] This is due to the imbalance

TABLE 4.6: AGE OF MARRIAGE OF BRIDES AND GROOMS IN THE USSR, 1980 (000's)

Age of Grooms	Total Marriages	Age of Brides										
		Under 20	20–24	25–29	30–34	35–39	40–44	45–49	50–54	55–59	60 and older	Age not known
	2724·6	756·1	1226·2	328·4	135·1	53·6	65·9	40·1	44·9	30·0	44·0	0·3
Under 20	147·5	105·5	39·3	2·4	0·3	0·0	0·0	0·0	—	—	—	0·0
20–24	1546·0	568·2	877·5	89·6	9·5	0·8	0·2	0·1	0·0	0·0	—	0·1
25–29	516·5	75·1	256·6	143·7	35·0	4·4	1·4	0·2	0·0	0·0	0·0	0·1
30–34	176·7	6·3	42·8	65·7	46·0	10·1	4·8	0·8	0·1	0·1	0·0	0·0
35–39	71·0	0·7	6·3	15·9	21·8	13·0	10·1	2·4	0·7	0·1	0·0	0·0
40–44	81·7	0·2	2·8	8·4	16·8	15·8	24·4	8·9	3·7	0·6	0·1	0·0
45–49	44·7	0·1	0·5	1·8	3·8	5·8	13·2	10·7	6·9	1·6	0·3	0·0
50–54	46·2	0·0	0·3	0·6	1·4	2·7	8·5	10·7	15·1	5·6	1·3	0·0
55–59	27·3	0·0	0·1	0·2	0·3	0·7	2·1	3·8	9·7	7·6	2·8	0·0
60 and older	66·8	0·0	0·0	0·1	0·2	0·3	1·2	2·5	8·7	14·4	39·4	0·0
Age not known	0·2	0·0	0·0	0·0	0·0	0·0	0·0	—	0·0	0·0	0·0	0·1

Source: Vestnik statistiki, no. 11 (1981), p. 73

TABLE 4.7: AGE OF MARRIAGE IN THE USSR, BY COHORT OF WOMEN

Date of Birth	Proportion (%) Married by the Age of:	
	22 years	24 years
1931–35	40.1	62.5
1936–40	50.2	71.2
1941–45	55.2	74.2
1946–48	54.4	74.9
1949–51	57.7	76.1
1952–54	58.1	76.0

Source: Volkov, 'Sem'ya kak faktor izmeneniya...', p. 36. Based on data collected in 1978.

in numbers between the sexes resulting from population loss during the war: in 1959 there were 20.7 million more women than men; by 1983, this excess had fallen to 17.4 million. It has the unfortunate demographic and social effect of leaving a high proportion of older women with no husband.

Divorce

Earlier we noted the changes in the regulations for divorce: we saw that the 1944 decree made divorce more difficult and that the 1968 law gave certain safeguards to pregnant wives. In addition, the 1968 law gave a divorced partner, of either sex, the right to maintenance by the other if he (or she) becomes incapacitated within a year of divorce. The divorce rate fell in 1944, but then began to rise again, until in 1958 it reached, and in 1960 it surpassed, the 1940 figure (see table 4.8).

In the 1960s Soviet writers claimed that the divorce rate in the USA was twice as high as that of the USSR: one quarter of marriages ended in the divorce court in America, compared with only one in nine in Soviet Russia.[58] Expressed as a proportion (per 1,000) of the population, the comparative figures cited in 1965 were: England and Wales 0.6; USSR 1.6; USA 2.2; France 0.6; West Germany 0.8.[59] Since then the Soviet divorce

TABLE 4.8: DIVORCE RATE IN THE USSR

		(per 1000 of population)		
1940	1.1	1970	2.6
1950	0.4	1975	3.1
1960	1.3	1979	3.6
1965	1.6	1982	3.3

Sources: Narkhoz 1979g (1980), p. 35. Narkhoz 1982g. (1983), p. 30.

rates have shot up to 3.3 in 1982 (in 1980 the comparable figures were 3.01 for England and Wales and in 1981 5.30 for the USA). Such broad comparisons, however, can only be superficial and may be misleading – measuring the ease of divorce, rather than the real level of family disintegration – and are partly determined by the population's age and sex structure. For example, in a very young population there is a lower proportion of marriageable age and therefore, other things being equal, there is a lower divorce rate. The expense involved in getting divorce may encourage separations, and new families may be formed outside formal marriage. Of a survey on divorce carried out in Leningrad, it was reported that 'already one or both of the divorcees have, in one fifth of the cases formed another marriage (in practice) from which they have children.'[60] This poses a problem for measuring family break-up, not only in the USSR, but in all countries where there are impediments to divorce. The amount of 'real' family disintegration in Russia is comparable to that in the USA. In 1978, the official divorce rate showed that, for ever three marriages, there was one divorce[61] and it has been estimated that in Moscow ten per cent of marriages last for less than a year.[62] Again, such data may be misleading: if one considers the number of divorces per year to the number of married couples one has a better measure of family break-up. In 1938–39, the figure for the USSR was 4.8 per 1000; in 1958–59, 5.3; in 1969–70, 11.5; and in 1978–79, 15.2.[63] One major effect of the relatively high divorce rate is a large number of single-parent families: yearly about 350,000 children are separated from one of their parents, usually the father.[64] In Central Asia, the divorce rate is two to three times lower than in the European areas.

Soviet researchers have attempted to determine the causes of divorce. Determining the 'real' factors is a difficult task; expressed opinions by divorcees tend to exculpate their own faults, and respondents may point to the immediate causes of marital breakdown rather than long-term underlying changes in relationships. In table 4.9 are assembled the results of three major Soviet surveys. Despite the fact that they are empiricist, some interesting points emerge. Personal incompatibility was cited overall as the major cause of break-up, though in research study 'C', drunkenness was considered the major cause by wives and the courts. A survey of 168 couples of manual class background and 183 of non-manual couples seeking divorce found that in the former drunkenness and alcoholism was the main reason cited for divorce (59.5 per cent of cases), while among the non-manuals reasons of a psychological character took first place (i.e. incompatibility, conjugal infidelity).[65] For a fuller understanding of the reasons given for divorce it is necessary to consider the nature of the relationships in, and strains put upon, the family unit.

TABLE 4.9: MOTIVES FOR DIVORCE

Motives	A	B		C		
		Husband	Wife	Husband	Wife	Court
Absence of compatible views and interests (including religious differences)	33.9	—	—	—	—	—
Incompatible characters	28.2	63	27	22.2	6.7	15.1
Infidelity	24.4	51	28	15.3	12.6	9.4
Absence or loss of feelings of love	23.5	—	—	12.3	8.6	5.3
Flippant attitude to material responsibilities	23.5	—	—	—	—	—
Bad relationships with parents (interference by parents or other kin)	22.0	—	—	11.3	4.4	5.3
Drunkenness	21.5	11	111(sic)	10.6	44.3	38.7
Assault, cuelty, fighting	16.6	—	—	0.6	5.6	3.6
Absence of normal living conditions	14.4	—	—	0.5	0.3	0.3
Sexual or physiological inadequacies	6.0	—	—	—	—	—
Impossibility of having children (infertile)	5.4	—	—	1.0	1.7	0.8
Lack of desire to have children	5.0	—	—	—	—	—
Illness of spouse	3.7	6	3	2.6	1.7	2.1
Entry to marriage without love or a thoughtless marriage	—	—	—	4.5	2.0	8.5
Sentence of spouse to three years' imprisonment (loss of freedom) or more	—	—	—	2.1	2.6	3.3
Long separation for objective reasons				3.1	3.8	5.4

Source: A 168 respondents; B 170 respondents: C 83 respondents. Data cited in A.G. Kharchev and M.S. Matskovski. *Sovremennaya sem'ya* (1978), pp. 141–2.
Notes: Figures are percentages of responses. They do not sum to 100 due to multiple answers.

Family Relations

What does marriage mean in terms of interpersonal relations? Soviet historical materialism defines relations generally under socialism as 'based on principles of comradely co-operation and mutual assistance'.[66] Sverdlov applies this view to the Soviet family:

The Soviet family, the latest type of family in the history of humanity, is based on entirely new principles compared with other types ... In a society based on exploitation, all the natural and necessary human relationships, including family relationships are wholly subordinated to the laws of private ownership. In a society with antagonistic classes, love and the interests of preserving private property contradict each other to a large extent. The family in socialist society is of an entirely different nature.

Socialist society has brought about conditions for a really free marriage. Consolidation of the socialist system, the growing well-being of the people and the emancipation of women mean that the overwhelming majority of marriages in the USSR have nothing to do with considerations of gain. Mutual love of men and women and the affection for children is the guiding force of marriage in the Soviet Union. Here, as Marx put it, family life for the first time becomes the life of the family, the *living love*.[67]

Unfortunately, Sverdlov provides no empirical data to substantiate his *a priori* generalization. In fact, Soviet families differ in character, both between ethnic areas and between social strata, though there is a general tendency in the USSR to a movement from a 'traditional' to a 'democratic' family structure. Kharchev and Matskovski note, however, that there are many insufficiencies among families in support of democratic relationships[68] (meaning that authoritarian and male chauvinist views persist).

In the countryside, some traditional practices have continued into the Soviet period. The traditional marriage ceremony and ritual is still performed and the agreement of parents for marriage is still sometimes formally required.[69] Even in 1983, the traditional practice of abduction of a girl was reported in Kirgiziya. A respondent wrote to *Komsomol'skaya Pravda*: '[Abduction] is what happened to me a year ago. But I said that I could never be the wife of someone I didn't love. The man who abducted me begged me to stay with him. Nevertheless, the next day I left. The old women cursed me and gloated over my misfortune: "Who will have you now?" they said.'[70] But important changes have taken place in the countryside. Patriarchal authority has crumbled: in the collective farm the individual rather than the head of household is the unit of payment for work. Choice of occupation, spouse and leisure pursuits are now generally regarded as the right of individual members – and not of the family as a whole.

Romantic love is often the basis for marriage. Soviet sociologists have studied people's expressed motives for getting married. A number of researches are summarized in table 4.10. Examination of the responses noted in that table shows the great weight put on 'love', a community of interests and mutual understanding. Study of Leningrad inhabitants (A) and collective farmers in Orenburg province (B) indicate greater similarities than differences; 'on the advice of, or at the request of, parents' as a motive for the collective farmers (5.2 per cent men, 7.6 per cent

TABLE 4.10: MOTIVES FOR GETTING MARRIED

Motives for getting married	Research Studies 'A'		'B'	
	Men %	Women %	Men %	Women %
Love	39.1	49.6	55	46.6
Community of interest and views	26.1	28.5	—	—
Feeling of loneliness (i.e. a fear of being lonely)	14.1	4.7	—	—
Feeling of compassion	7.4	3.1	—	—
Probability of imminent birth of a child	6.7	4.3	—	—
Accident (sluchaynost')	4.0	2.4	—	—
Material security of future husband (or wife)	—	3.1	—	—
Mutual attraction and sympathy	—	—	25.5	30.8
Outward attractiveness	—	—	9.0	8.4
At the request (or on advice) of parents	—	—	5.2	7.6
Moral considerations (kindness)	—	—	5.2	6.6
Other considerations	0.6	3.1	—	—

Source: 'A' Study of 350 respondents in Leningrad.
'B' Study of collective farmers in Orenburg.
Data cited in A.G. Kharchev and M.S. Matskovski, Sovremennaya sem'ya i ee problemy (1978),
p. 87.

women) reflects the hangover of patriarchal authority. A study of 15,000 persons in Perm conducted in the 1970s found that 70 to 80 per cent of the respondents married for 'love or infatuation', 15 to 20 per cent out of custom ('everyone does') and from 3 to 10 per cent for economic reasons or convenience. Another study completed in Minsk found that initial feelings of infatuation lasted only for the first few years of marriage and were then replaced by other feelings: 'habit, sense of family responsibility, resignation, or combinations of these elements'. Mutual love and a community of interest is paramount in mate selection. In another Leningrad study, 'Equality' is only stated by 13.2 per cent of the couples to be a prime condition for a happy marriage.[71]

Such popular Soviet films as Ballad of a Soldier and plays such as Warsaw Melody emphasize the romantic and emotional ties between the sexes which are probably still more typical in the town. In Ryazanov's film, Station for Two (1983), the principal characters are two middle aged people (waitress and musician) whose marriages had broken down. The film portrays a Soviet world of impersonality, of human relations that lack spontaneity and love; it shows the absurdity of mercenary and bureaucratic transactions. This is only transcended by the emotional interaction of the two characters. The romanticism of the film had great appeal in Moscow – it played concurrently to full houses in over twenty cinemas – but at the Cannes film festival it was dismissed as simplistic.

The urban family as a unit provides love (or emotional satisfaction) and companionship for its members. It is not as 'isolated' from other social organizations as in the West. The mass-produced private car which binds the nuclear family in the West has yet to appear in large numbers in the USSR. The 'companionship' role between spouses and children in the Soviet Union is less important than in the Western nuclear family. Collective activity (for example, leisure pursuits and holidays) is often organized by social clubs, trade unions and schools. The members of families often take their holidays separately: husband and wife may attend a union rest home, and the children a Pioneer or *Komsomol* camp. Soviet commentators have pointed to the lack of contact between children and adults. Children, it is said, often grow up to be 'selfish and egocentric'.[72] With the greater development of an adequate housing stock, the family is becoming more nucleated. This in turn has had a harmful effect on child rearing. As Yuri Ryurikov has expressed it: 'One of the most serious changes wrought by urbanization is the weakening of social ties in everyday life. With the breakup of extended families and the disappearance of communal apartments, mutual assistance among relatives and neighbours is disappearing. Our daily life is broken down into tens of millions of tiny and virtually unconnected facets. The isolated life of today's family does little to instil a spirit of collectivism and comradely mutual assistance.'[73]

Domestic Work

Urban spouses often specialize in their marital roles, cooking and cleaning being the wife's tasks and decorating that of the husband. Equality and consideration often characterize marriage. A marriage between a university professor's daughter and an army officer has been described as follows: 'Relations between them were very affectionate and they did a lot of things together, though she did not share his occupational life. Surprisingly, he was more for equal rights in the marriage than she, who preferred to be somewhat subordinate and made no use of the liberties he was ready to extend to her.'[74] This is a somewhat idealized position. Research has shown that there are often role conflicts between husband and wife. The traditional role of the husband is that of breadwinner; and as a high proportion of women are in employment, they have to fulfil this role together with those of wife and mother.

An area of role strain between husband and wife takes place over the division of housework. Studies show that wives bear the burden of housework and that this is resented. Lapidus has constructed a most useful table based on seven studies of the use of time by men and women (see table 4.11). The ratios show a slightly lower figure for women for 'working time' and 'physiological needs', and a much lower frequency for the use of

TABLE 4.11: TIME BUDGETS OF MALE AND FEMALE WORKERS

Category	Per cent of week directed to given activity (average)		Ratio of time spent by females in given categories to that of males
	Males	Females	
Working time	30	29	0.96
Physiological needs	41	39	0.95
Housework	8	19	2.37
Free time	21	13	0.62

Notes: Working time includes time at work and travel to work. Physiological needs include eating, sleeping, washing, etc. Housework includes shopping, food preparation, housework, care of children. Free time includes hobbies, public activities, study, amusement, activities with children, rest.
Source: G.W. Lapidus, *Women in Soviet Society* (1978), p. 271.

leisure; on housework, however, women spend more than twice the amount of time than men. On average, studies show that women spend 28 hours a week on such activity, compared to only 12 hours by men.[75] Housework is still considered to be 'women's work' by men. Inequalities in the distribution of housework between spouses are shown in table 4.12. Considering the figures on 'domestic work as a whole', we see the very great disparity between men and women – 0.55: 3.15 and 1.25: 5.30 hours. Women are particularly adamant that men should share in household tasks. Only 15 per cent of women surveyed felt that housework was women's work, and these were mainly older women with low educational standards.[76]
Research has also shown that, where housework is done mainly by the

TABLE 4.12: TIME SPENT ON DOMESTIC DUTIES IN THE USSR (IN HOURS AND MINUTES)

Kind of Work	Married Women		Married Men	
	Work Days	Days off Work	Work Days	Days off Work
Preparing food, Washing dishes, etc.	1.15	2.10	0.14	0.18
House cleaning	0.40	1.00	0.11	0.24
Shopping	0.55	1.30	0.21	0.29
Looking after children	0.25	0.50	0.09	0.14
Domestic work as a whole	3.15	5.30	0.55	1.25

Source: B.M. Levin, *Motivatsiya zhenskogo truda i semeyno-bytovye otnosheniya* (1970), p. 7. Cited in E. Novikova, V.S. Iazykova and Z.A. Iankova, 'Women's Work and the Family', printed in *Problems of Economics*, vol. 24, Nov. 1981), p. 171.

wife, only 58.9 per cent of marriages are 'happy or satisfactory'. In those cases where the husband helps the wife, the figure rises to 88.1 per cent and where they undertake the work equally it rises to 94.4 per cent.[77]

Policy is to try to transform 'domestic labour' by extending the service sector and reducing time spent on it by the provision of mechanical household appliances. The problem here is that mechanization of housework has not compensated for other changes in the nature of domestic labour and has in effect only marginally reduced the amount of time spent on it. One contemporary Soviet survey claims that women spend as much time on domestic chores as in the 1920s. The work is lighter, but time spent on shopping has increased.[78] Also there is consumer resistance to public service provision: of people polled in the USSR a majority found that eating out was expensive, it did not save time and the meals were of low quality.[79] Cafeterias lacked children's menus and the premises were unsuitable for family meals.

More traditional views in the Soviet Union, rather than stressing the greater equality of women entailing a change in the roles of men, support role differentiation. In his discussion of American society, Talcott Parsons has argued that the division of sex roles in the occupational sphere is a mechanism which minimizes rivalry and promotes family stability. Women are more often occupied in menial jobs and therefore do not rival husbands.[80] A useful test of this proposition is the case of the USSR, where women enjoy a greater parity with men in the professional occupational sphere. They account for 59 per cent of the 'specialists' (i.e. professional employees with higher education): 68 per cent of doctors,[81] 71 per cent of teachers, 65 per cent of economists and 33 per cent of engineers.[82]

The major burden of women lies with the combination of roles of housekeeper, wife, mother and worker. Most women still perform their traditional roles in addition to full-time employment: 82 per cent of all Soviet women under 55 are in paid employment,[83] twice the proportion in Western societies. Not only does this create stress and tension in marriage, but it reduces the advancement of women in careers: only 9 per cent of directors of enterprises are female, 12 per cent of foremen (*mastery*) in the building industry, and 28 per cent of heads of secondary schools.[84] In 1980, only 1.9 per cent of collective farm chairpersons were women, and 7.3 per cent were deputy chairpersons.[85]

Present policy is moving in the direction of enhancing the status of a wife and her role as mother. Parsons' observations are echoed in some Soviet discussions of the instability of family life. A writer to the paper *Literaturnaya Gazeta* (7 Sept 1977, p. 12) complained that his wife refused to do housework and to look after children. In the reply, it was pointed out that it was a general problem of upbringing which did not prepare girls for the role of wife and mother. An article in the press points out that lack of understanding often results from spouses who feel socially and economically equal; a woman's desire for independence and a career is not appreciated by many husbands. Another author in the same journal argues that married women with children should stay at home until their offspring are seven years old. In such articles a greater emphasis is now put on women being feminine as well as being workers. Such 'femininity' involves women having specific roles – child care, housework. In the letter columns to the newspaper, *Literaturnaya Gazeta*, the male correspondents advocated bringing up girls with the feminine attributes of 'modesty, timidity and homeliness', boys should be 'courageous, hard, principled and responsible.'[86] This policy is also supported by demographers, who advocate a 'pronatalist' policy. It is especially directed towards the raising of the birth rate – 'regardless of any considerations that may be advanced from an economic, ecological, sociological or any other point of view'.[87] Such considerations, of course, involve women becoming more dependent on men – even if substantial financial rewards are given for child bearing. Support for the more traditional position of women in society comes from a group of anti-Marxist Christian feminists in the Soviet Union. The social ethic of this group may be gleaned from the following: 'I consider that a woman is first and foremost a mother and therefore her role is a protective one: to protect the home from harm. But these days women find themselves mothering their husbands as well as their children. I believe that our movement must fight for the rebirth of men, for we women have got tired of carrying the *whole* burden on our own shoulders. We want to be wives as well as mothers.'[88]

Sexual Relations

Sexuality and sexual relations now figure more prominently in Soviet research into family life. Kon, in generalizing about sexual behaviour in the Soviet Union, has pointed to trends which are universal to industrial society: the acceleration of adolescents' sexual maturation, the lowering of the age of initial sexual experience, the lessening of differences in sexual behaviour of men and women, the liberalization of sexual morality, 'an increase in the significance of sexual factors in marriage', 'the separation of motives for sexual behaviour from child bearing; the individualization and growing variety of erotic techniques, the increasing sexual activeness of women ... ' Kon refers to the greater experience of orgasm by women, and to expectations of sexual fulfilment in marriage. There is a greater role played by choice of partner, a recognition of the 'potentially temporary nature of the marital union'.[89]

The extent of pre-marital sexual relations is indicated by a study which showed that 29 per cent of first births took place within eight months of marriage; of married mothers under 19 years of age the proportion rose to 53 per cent. One study showed that 12.5 per cent of births were outside of marriage, 15.2 per cent of babies were born in the first few months and in 4.4 per cent of cases marriage occurred after birth.[90] A longitudinal study conducted in Leningrad showed that, of first-born babies registered in the month of December, in 1963, 24 per cent were conceived before marriage, in 1968 the figure was 23 per cent, in 1973, 28 per cent, and in 1978 it rose to 38 per cent.[91] Nationally, the 1979 census found that, of a total of 23.8 million family units, 2.5 million (or 14%) were composed of a child (or children) and one parent.[92] Between 1970 and 1978 it has been estimated that the number of children born out of wedlock doubled.[93]

In decrying marital infidelity, Sergei Chuprinin in *Literaturnaya Gazeta* complains about the number of erotic scenes in Soviet novels. The following is an example of his concern from the magazine *Ural* (no. 5, 1981):

Chuvilin's heart was pounding. At the far end of the room, in a crimson haze, his Vera was undressing ... Vera crossed her arms and took off her dress. Then she unfastened her brassiere and took it off. Her ample breasts, filled with the juice of life, revealed themselves to Chuvilin's clouded gaze. Vera stood there in nothing but her slippers. Chuvilin reached out towards her ...[94]

The emphasis we saw above on romantic love (which is expressed in sexual intimacy) is a weak one to sustain a lasting union. The economic, domestic and child rearing functions of the family create tensions which 'romantic love' are unable to contain. Marriages collapse. Kon argues that in the Soviet Union there has been a tendency for younger people not to become involved in a legally sanctioned marriage. Men, he points out, do not want the responsibility of marriage and are able to fulfil their sexual needs by having sex 'on the side'. Also, many people now cohabit rather than make legal marriages.[95]

As may be inferred from the above, expectations for sexual relations vary between the sexes. One Soviet study of manual and non-manual workers in Leningrad found that 91 per cent of the males thought sexual intercourse to be all right if based on love and 60 per cent thought it all right if it took place with a friend: of the women interviewed, 81 per cent thought it was possible for them to have intercourse if based on love and only 14 per cent thought it desirable with an acquaintance.[96] Here one sees a different attitude to sex by men and women, with greater expression of the need for sexual relations as self-gratification by men. The differences are also brought out in table 4.13. Women are restrained more by moral

TABLE 4.13: FACTORS RESTRAINING MEN AND WOMEN FROM PRE-MARITAL RELATIONS

	Men (%)	Women (%)
Moral considerations	24.4	34.5
Lack of sexual need	3.5	34.1
Fear of consequences	6.7	11.6
Fear of disclosure of relations	3.7	4.4
Absence of opportunity	48.5	4.8
Other reasons	5.1	8.4

Source: A.G. Kharchev, Brak i sem'ya v SSSR (M. 1979), p. 195.

considerations and lack of need, whereas for men the main factor was 'lack of opportunity'. This shows not only a dual standard, but also unequal sexual satisfaction by women.

Socialization of Children

One of the major activities of the family is the socialization of children. Compared to the USA and Great Britain, the family, at least on the surface, has less power in the USSR to influence the informal ways children learn to deal with problems and adopt attitudes. This is because to a much greater extent than in Western societies, the government is responsible for comprehensive services of child welfare and for the provision of social and cultural amenities for young people.

As a larger proportion of married women work in the USSR than in Great Britain or the USA, the government provides collective child care. More than 82 per cent of all women in the 15 to 55 years age group are at

TABLE 4.14: PROPORTION OF CHILDREN UNDER SEVEN IN REGULAR PRESCHOOL INSTITUTIONS: URBAN AND RURAL.

	1940	1960	1970	1977
In urban areas, 000's	1,422	3,565	7,380	9,800
% of total	73	82	80	77
In rural areas, 000's	531	863	1,901	2,872
% of total	27	18	20	23
Rural population as a proportion of the total population (%)	67	50	44	38

Note: By 1981, a total of 14.8 million children attended preschool institutions compared to 11.5 million in 1975.
Source: Narkhoz 1922–82 (1982), p. 451.

work; about 70 per cent of children under 16 have mothers who work. Though the Soviet authorities have made great efforts to provide collective care for young children, the burden of their upbringing often falls on the family (usually the grandmother) or neighbours. Table 4.14 shows the number and proportion of children in full-time preschool institutions in urban and rural areas. Examination of the table shows that the proportion of children at preschool institutions has remained fairly constant from 1940 to 1977–a rise from 73 per cent in urban areas in 1940 to 77 per cent, compensated by a fall from 27 per cent to 23 per cent in rural areas. Hence quite large numbers of children are not socialized in the preschool institutions. These are largely drawn from the families of the lower educated and rural and manual occupations. In 1974–75, it was found that although 50 per cent of children with fathers having only primary education went to preschool groups the number rose to 88 per cent for children with fathers in the higher educational category.[97] After reaching school age, provision for the children takes the form of a developed network of nearly 5,000 'palaces of culture'. In 1981, over 12 million attended pioneer camps[98] and over 11.3 million children were in 'extended-day schools' (from 9 a.m. to 6 p.m.).[99]

Since 1944, children may be adopted 100 or reared in a children's home. The local authority also has the right to deprive a family of its children if it considers them to be in need of care and protection. Many of them go to boarding schools although they may go home at weekends. Few staff live on the premises and the staff–pupil ratio appears to be less favourable than in good English private boarding schools. In 1975, there were 750,000 children in Soviet boarding schools,[101] about 1.8 per cent of the school population. Most of these had only one parent: of 422 children in one Leningrad boarding school, 325 had only a mother, 15 only a father and 16 were orphans.[102] Since the 1960s, policy has turned to providing 'extended-day' facilities. These provide supervision in school for most of the day and outside formal school hours. In 1975, places were available for about 19 per cent of the pupils.[103] The family, however, has an important part to play in the process of socialization. As some Soviet writers put it: 'Among the freedom, rights and duties of Soviet citizens listed in the new Constitution of the USSR there is, for the first time in history, the obligation "to be concerned with bringing up children, preparing them for socially useful labour, and rearing them to be worthy members of socialist society" ... Upbringing has become a prime function of the Soviet family, and the harmonious blending of public and family forms of upbringing has become a characteristic trait of the Soviet way of life.'[104] In practice, the kind of upbringing a child has will depend on the kind of parents he or she has.

In generalizing about 'the family' one might bear in mind that there are different social milieux in which families are located and that the form of socialization of children varies in different types of families. Among urban families, and perhaps particularly among the middle class, children become the centre of attention, and the family is often 'child-centred'. Children in such homes are planned and very much loved. A nurse married to a university lecturer recalls: 'Because we had a dearly loved only child, we lived and worked for him. He was the main aim of our life. My husband and I wanted to make him a decent, honest and diligent man.'[105] Hendrick Smith has observed that urban children are spoiled and that parents are permissive. 'Several times I saw children act fresh, come and go haphazardly from the table, ignore repeated parental requests to eat, to be quiet, to sit still and the parents let it go . . . Nor is this just laxity in a few random families. A Moscow kindergarten director asserted to me that one major justification for Soviet kindergartens was to socialize "only" children spoiled at home.'[106] Concern about education and an intense desire for upward mobility are characteristics of such families.

Here again, the small child-centred family like that in the West supplies an aim in life for the parents and provides them with emotional satisfaction. It is difficult to know whether values stemming from the family influence the child more than those of the environment outside. The incidence of religious views is probably an indication of still strong family influence (see chapter 7 on religion). Other conflicts, perhaps of a more political nature, may take place: for example, the condemnation by the young of a parent's involvement in affairs during Stalin's time; or criticisms by parents of the more permissive youth culture. The Soviet film *Private Lives,* for instance, shows the complete lack of understanding shown by a redundant ex-Stalinist factory manager for his unemployed, idle, ambitionless, pop-loving, pleasure-seeking son and his friends.

In the professional career-centred family both parents work and are to varying degrees engrossed in their profession. The mother suckles the child for six months or so, and may even take a year off work. The child is well cared for and loved. But a surrogate quickly enters his/her life. This is either the staff at the local *yasli* (or nursery) or, perhaps more frequently, a grandmother. Sometimes a private children's nurse is employed. The surrogates have an important influence in the formative years and the role of factors outside the home is extremely strong. The following extract, cited disapprovingly from *Izvestiya,* is indicative of this type of family (conversation overheard in subway):

'Your little Andrei will be starting school already, no doubt.'
'Yes, he will. Only I won't see him. I'll be away on business then.'
'Oh, but who will take care of him?'

'Who else? His grandma – my mother-in-law, who's one of the great martyrs of all times. But anyway, he's better off with her. He hardly even knows me . . .'[107]

In spite of this, throughout a child's life the mother plays a greater role than the father. Studies in the Soviet Union have shown that in discussions with children about family affairs mothers participated more than fathers (75.4 against 67.2 per cent); read books or saw plays (56.7 and 25 per cent); as the Soviet authors point out, 'All this is indicative not only of the mother's authority in the eyes of her children but also of her great educational potential.'[108]

A study by Urie Bronfenbrenner brings out a greater congruence of influences on the child in the USSR than in the USA: ' . . . from a cross-cultural perspective, Soviet children, in the process of growing up, are confronted with fewer divergent views both within and outside the family, and in consequence, conform more completely to a more homogeneous set of standards.'[109] Since 1968, however, Bronfenbrenner goes on to suggest that Soviet official attitudes are moving to develop 'individual personality', and that there is a shift towards greater individuality and independence, rather than dependence and conformity. However, he concludes that 'Soviet children of the future will continue to be more conforming than our own . . . This means also that they will be less anti-adult, rebellious, aggressive and delinquent.'[110] The kinds of values espoused by the authorities in child socialization have been analysed by O'Dell in her study of children's literature. Soviet patriotism is a 'prime virtue' and is the embodiment of collectivism. 'Love of work' and discipline (submission to leadership) are also important, 'equality' and non-acquisitiveness are not emphasized, whereas politeness and the 'presentation of attitudes to women and to home life differ only in certain points of emphasis from Western bourgeois norms.'[111]

Not all families, of course, are oriented to the desired 'lofty socially meaningful goals and ethical ideals': some place 'consumer interests to the forefront' and other families ('problem families') are completely inadequate with 'low levels of social and emotional activity . . . [where] there are more chances for the development of a mostly deficient personality'.[112] We know very little about the number of families of different types.

The family shares in the socialization of the child with other social institutions which engender attitudes of greater conformity than in the West. Perhaps the most important difference with the West is the career interests of both parents. Talcott Parsons has argued that only *one* of the members of a family has an occupational role which is of determinate significance for the status of the family as a whole. 'The wife and mother is either exclusively a "housewife" or at most has a "job" rather than a "career".'[113] This view must be modified in the light of Soviet experience.

The larger number of married women in paid employment and in professional and higher 'specialist' jobs, reflecting more equal educational opportunities, distinguishes the Soviet family from its Western counterpart. Many middle class Soviet women are 'career' women, though they do not achieve the high authority positions which are largely still the prerogative of men (see also chapter 5 below).

Conclusions

Let me now sum up the principal characteristics of the family in the USSR. Over the past fifty years or so, the main change has been away from the consanguine family structure to a smaller and more homogeneous nuclear unit. Important differences in family size remain on an ethnic basis which are discussed below (chapter 6). Spouse relations have changed. Woman is now equal in rights – before the law – with man: she is usually a breadwinner, like her husband, but she is still mainly responsible for household chores. Family relationships are more 'democratic': children are more independent, more performance-oriented. The functions of the Soviet family have followed the trend of its counterpart in the West although the family has lost its control over 'placement' in the important sense that property is owned not by the family but by the government; and socialization is more the prerogative of the state. Its main function is the provision of regular sexual gratification between the spouses, procreation and maintenance of children between its members. The state assists rather than replaces the family. This 'assistance' is of a similar kind to that provided in advanced Western European states. While the monogamous family exists under Soviet Communism, we cannot conclude that society must necessarily be dependent on it. The USSR has never seriously attempted to experiment with different forms of group living. Housing is still designed with the monogamous family unit in mind, and the growth of the housing stock will enhance the nucleation of the Soviet family.

How have the polity and family interacted over the years since 1917? In the days after the October Revolution, the communist powers took measures to weaken the solidarity of the family. Its economic power vested in the control of property was irrevocably broken. The law gave it no support; divorce was easily available; children born in wedlock had no greater status than children born out of it. Probably more important, however, has been the influence of industrialization and urbanization, which has resulted in the smaller family, the working wife and 'achievement-oriented' children. From 1936, and even more so from 1944, the Soviet political system attempted to strengthen the family. Marriage has been given civic recognition, divorce made more difficult to achieve, and stable parenthood encouraged. As a socializing agency, the family in the decades immediately after the revolution was potentially more hostile to the Soviet state: in it were embodied the values of the 'ancien régime'. Today, shorn of its wider functions, indoctrinated with Soviet norms, the family can be relied upon by the regime for support. It is not, however, completely adequate to fulfil the various demands of Soviet society:[114] there remain incongruent traditional attitudes, and the demographic needs of the country for a higher birth rate have not been met. Rather paradoxically, the greater independence achieved by women has not been fully accepted by men, whose expectations of a woman's role are still traditional in many ways. Married women then find that they have four roles: paid worker, spouse, mother and housewife. These demands and the incompatibility of expectations of husbands often give rise to strain and family break-up. In the 1980s, many articles in the Soviet press concentrate on the role of women as mother and wife and there is a growing tendency to emphasize women's expressive roles.

NOTES

1 Kingsley Davis, *Human Society* (1959), pp. 394–5.
2 *Svod zakonov Rossiyskoy imperii*, (1857), vol. 10, part I, p. 18. Cited by A.G. Kharchev, *Brak i sem'ya v SSR* (1964).
3 In 1913, it was estimated that the infant mortality rate was 273 per thousand. *Narkhoz v 1968g* (1969), p. 36.
4 For an example of this, see E.W. Burgess and H.J. Locke, *The Family* (1945) pp. 180–2, and D. Lane, *The Roots of Russian Communism* (1975), pp. 145–6.
5 N.A. Kislyakov, 'Sem'ya i brak u Tadzhikov', *Trudy instituta etnografii*, vol. 44 (1959) p. 31.
6 Kharchev, *Brak i Sem'ya v SSSR*, p. 131. See also O.A. Sukhareva, M.A. Bukzhanova, *Proshloe i nastoyashchee seleniya Aykyran* (1955), S. Lyubimova, *V pervye gody* (1958).
7 I cannot consider here how this theory is related to the various stages of society. Suffice it to say that in the first form of primitive communism there was complete sexual licence with no marriage and family bonds. This developed into group marriage distinguished by the absence of incest. A third type was that of monogamy, which was the dominant family form under capitalism.
8 F. Engels, 'The Origin of the Family, Private Property and the State', Marx and Engels, *Selected Works* (1951), vol. 2, pp. 208–9.
9 'The Origin of the Family', Marx-Engels, *Selected Works* (1951), vol. 2, p. 209.
10 'The Communist Manifesto', Marx-Engels, *Selected Works,* (1951) vol. 1, p. 224.
11 Engels, 'The Origin of the Family', p. 210.
12 Ibid., p. 213.
13 Ibid., p. 218.
14 Ibid., p. 219.
15 J.F. Besemeres, *Socialist Population Politics* (1980), p. 15.
16 A. Kollontay, *The New Morality and the Working Classes* (1918).
17 Besemeres, *Socialist Population Politics*, p. 17.
18 The Petrograd Commission for Juvenile Affairs from 1918 to 1924 handled some 35,000 cases, most of which concerned homeless children; Kharchev, *Brak i Sem'ya v SSSR*, p. 138.
19 *Izvestiya*, 15 May 1925, cited in E.H. Carr, *Socialism in One Country*, part I, (1958), pp. 33–4.
20 See G. Sverdlov, *Marriage and the Family in the USSR* (1956).
21 Code on Marriage, The Family and Guardianship of RSFSR. On Soviet family law see E.L. Johnson, *An Introduction to the Soviet Legal System* (1969).

22 Speech delivered to the Second Session of the Central Executive Committee of the RSFSR. Reprinted in R. Schlesinger, *The Family in the USSR* (1949), p. 84.

23 Kingsley Davis, *Human Society* (1959), pp. 400–1.

24 *The Soviet Citizen* (1959), p. 216.

25 In 1928 women constituted 24 per cent of the employed population, 39 per cent in 1940.

26 28,400 in 1945, 43,600 in 1960, *Narkhoz v 1968g* (1969), p. 676.

27 Gerhard Neubeck, 'Notes on Russian Family Life Today', *Acta Sociologica*, vol. 8 (1965), p. 324.

28 From 1936 to 1944, the cost of a divorce was 50 rubles on the first occasion; 150 rubles on the second and 300 rubles on the third; there was no formality – divorce was registered, expressing the wish of the couple concerned. After the 1944 decree, marriage breakdown had to be shown before the People's Court and (if accepted) before a Higher Court. A fee of 100 rubles was payable, plus the cost of publicity (i.e. newspaper notices, etc.) of the case. In the event of a divorce being given, either or both parties were to pay a sum ranging from 500 to 2,000 rubles decided by the court. The payments are here shown in old rubles (10 old rubles equals 1 new ruble). In 1940 the estimated average weekly wage was 8.2 new rubles, in 1946, it was 12 rubles.

29 Besemeres, *Socialist Population Politics*, p. 23.

30 *Vedomosti verkhovnogo soveta SSSR*, no. 49 (1965), point 275.

31 Articles 16 and 17.

32 See S. Strumilin, 'Rabochi byt i kommunizm', *Novy mir*, no. 7 (1960).

33 P. Juviler, 'Family Reforms on the Road to Communism', in P. Juviler and H. Morton, *Soviet Policy-Making: Studies of Communism in Transition* (1967), p. 33.

34 To the territory of the USSR were added the Baltic States, Bessarabia, Karelia, Bakovina and some parts of the east of Poland.

35 *Narkhoz SSSR v 1978g* (1979), p. 83, *SSSR v tsifrakh v 1982g* (1983), p. 18.

36 Further data see V.I. Perevedentsev, 'Population Reproduction and the Family'. Abstract in *CDSP*, vol. 34, no. 19. p. 5.

37 Figures for USA in 1959 and USSR 1958–9. Cited by J.W. Brackett, 'Demographic Trends and Population Policy in the Soviet Union', in Joint Economic Committee US Congress, *Dimensions of Soviet Economic Power* (1962), p. 499. For 1974, *Narkhoz SSSR v 1975g* (1976), p. 40.

38 C. Davis and M. Feshback, *Rising Mortality in the USSR in the 1970s* (1980), p. 2.

39 Ellen Jones and Fred W. Grupp, 'Infant Mortality Trends in the Soviet Union', *Population and Development Review*, vol. 9, no. 2 (1983), pp. 213–46.

40 Narkhoz v 1979g (1980), p. 7. *SSSR v tsifrakh v 1982g* (1983), p. 7.

41 A. Volkov, 'Sem'ya kak faktor izmeneniya demograficheskoy situatsii', *Sotsiologicheskie issledovaniya*, no. 1 (1981), p. 35. See abstract in *Current Digest of the Soviet Press*, Vol. 33, no. 9 (April 1981).

42 *Vestnik statistiki*, no. 11 (1981), p. 60.

43 Mothers who give birth to and rear ten children have the title 'Heroine Mother'.

44 See A.G. Kharchev, *Brak i sem'ya v SSSR* (1979), pp. 207–8.
45 B. Holland, '"A Woman's Right to Choose" in the Soviet Union', in J. Brine et al., *Home, School and Leisure in the Soviet Union* (1980), p. 62.
46 Abortion was made legal in 1955 due mainly to the prevalence of criminal abortion taking place outside hospital. It was considered a temporary measure until contraception, which is now encouraged, could be effective.
47 Barbara Holland, '"A Woman's Right ...",' p. 63.
48 Data cited in Richard Johnson, 'Abortion in the USSR', RL 243/82 (1982), pp. 4–7.
49 A.G. Kharchev and M.S. Matskovski, *Sovremennaya sem'ya* (1978), p. 154.
50 Cited by Holland, '"A Woman's Right to Choose" in the Soviet Union', p. 63.
51 Holland, ibid. M. Sonin, 'Demographers' New Findings Leave Policy Needs Unanswered', *CDSP*, vol. 33, no. 44 (2 Dec. 1981), p. 11.
52 Surveys reported in E.E. Novikova, U.S. Iazykova and Z.A. Iankova, 'Women's Work and the Family', *Problems of Economics*, vol. 24 (Nov. 1981), pp. 180–1.
53 James W. Brackett, 'Demographic Trends and Population Policy in the Soviet Union', in Joint Economic Committee US Congress, *Dimensions of Soviet Economic Power* (1962), p. 544.
54 For details of amounts paid see *Gosudarstvennoe sotsial'noe strakhovanie* (1965).
55 Cited by Volkov, 'Sem'ya kak faktor izmeneniya...', p. 34.
56 *Basic Principles of Legislation on Marriage and the Family*. Reprinted in W.E. Butler, *Studies on the Socialist Legal System*, (1981), Legislation on Social Development and Culture. vol. 2.
57 Based on data in *Vestnik statistiki*, no. 11 (1981), p. 73. See table 4.6.
58 G.M. Sverdlov, 'Zakon o razvode ...', *Sovetskoe gosudarstvo i pravo*, no. 10 (1964), p. 33.
59 Figures for 1965, *Narodnoe khozyaystvo SSSR v 1965g* (1966), p. 117.
60 A.C. Kharchev, *Brak i sem'ya v SSSR* (1964), p. 212.
61 Cited by Volkov, 'Sem'ya kak faktor izmeneniya...', p. 38.
62 *Literaturnaya Gazeta*, 3 September 1969.
63 Volkov, 'Sem'ya kak faktor izmeneniya...', p. 38.
64 V.A. Sysenko, 'Razvody: dinamika, motivy, posledstviya', *Sotsiologicheskie issledovaniya*, no. 2 (1982), p. 99.
65 Ibid., pp. 101–2.
66 *Fundamentals of Marxism–Leninism* (1961), p. 695.
67 G. Sverdlov, *Marriage and the Family in the USSR* (1956), pp. 5–6.
68 Kharchev and Matskovski, *Sovremennaya sem'ya* (1978), p. 40.
69 P.I. Kushner, *Selo Viryatino v proshlom i nastoyaschem* (1958), p. 226.
70 Summary in *CDSP*, vol. 35, no. 20 (15 June 1983), p. 5.
71 A.G. Kharchev, *Brak i sem'ya v SSSR* (1964), p. 179.
72 Yu. Ryurikov, 'Family Matters? No, Matters of State'. Extract in *CDSP*, vol. 34, no. 48 (29 Dec. 1982), p. 1.
73 Ibid, p. 2.

74 Report by returned German POW, cited in Geiger, *The Family in Soviet Russia* (1968), p. 222.

75 G. Lapidus, *Women in Soviet Society* (1978), p. 270.

76 E. Novikova, V.A. Iasykova, A.A. Iankova, 'Women's Work and the Family', *Problems of Economics*, vol. 24 (Nov. 1981), p. 172.

77 Data cited by Kharchev and Matskovski, *Sovremennaya sem'ya*, pp. 92–3.

78 *Gudok*, 8 March 1979. Cited by A Tenson, 'A Soviet Woman's Work is Never Done', FRE/RL Research, RL 180/79 (12 June 1979).

79 Novikova et al., 'Women's Work and the Family', p. 169.

80 T. Parsons, 'The Kinship System of the Contemporary United States', *Essays in Sociological Theory* (1964), pp. 192–3.

81 *Zhenshchiny v SSSR* (1983), pp. 12, 13. Data for 1981.

82 *Zhenshchiny SSSR* (1975), pp. 78, 86. Data for 1974.

83 Ryurikov, 'Family Matters?...', p. 1.

84 *Zhenshchiny* (1975), pp. 80, 86.

85 *Narkhoz v 1979g* (1980), p. 313.

86 *Smena* (Dec. 1970 and May 1970) *Literaturnaya Gazeta*, no. 47. November 1976, p. 11.

87 B. Urlanis, *Problemy dinamiki naseleniya SSSR* (1974), p. 283. Cited by G.W. Lapidus, 'Introduction', *Problems of Economics*, vol. 24 (1981), p. xxxvi.

88 'Soviet Feminism – What Future for Marxism?' *Women in Eastern Europe*, no. 4 (March 1981), p. 11.

89 I. Kon, 'Studying Sexual Behaviour in the USSR', *Voprosy filosofii*, no. 10 (1981). Summary in *CDSP*, vol. 33, no. 50, 1981, pp. 9–10.

90 Data cited by A.G. Kharchev, *Brak i sem'ya v SSSR* (1979), p. 206.

91 I. Kon, 'O sotsiologicheskoy interpretatsii seksual'nogó povedeniya', *Sotsiologicheskie issledovaniya*, no. 2 (1982), p. 115.

92 *Vestnik Statistiki*, no. 4 (1983), p. 71.

93 M. Bedny, *Meditsinskaya gazeta*, 9 Sept. 1983. Abstracted in *CDSP*, vol. 35, no. 37, 1983, p. 11.

94 'Spicing it UP', *Literaturnaya Gazeta*. Abstract in *CDSP*, vol. 34, no. 13 (28 April 1982), p. 7.

95 I. Kon, 'O sotsiologicheskoy interpretatsii seksual'nogo povedeniya', *Sotsiologicheskie issledovaniya*, no. 2 (1982), p. 115.

96 Data cited by A.G. Kharchev, *Brak i sem'ya v SSSR* (1979), p. 195.

97 F.R. Filippov, 'Deti v strane razvitogo sotsializma', *Sotsiologicheskie issledovaniya* no. 4 (1979), p. 56.

98 *Narkhoz 1922–1982* (1982) p. 505.

99 Report on fulfilment of State Plan 1981, *Soviet News* (13 April 1982) p. 118.

100. See Article 24 of *Basic Principles of Legislation on Marriage and the Family*. Reprinted in W.E. Butler, *Studies on the Socialist Legal System* (1981) vol. 2: *Legislation on Social Development and Culture*.

101 J. Dustan, 'Soviet Boarding Education', in J. Brine, et al., *Home, School and Leisure in the Soviet Union* (1980), p. 133.

102 A. Kharchev, *Brak i sem'ya v SSSR* (1964), p. 273.

103 Dunstan, 'Soviet Boarding Education'.
104 Novikova, Iazykova and Iankova, 'Women's Work and the Family', p. 173.
105 Cited by K. Geiger, *The Soviet Family* (1968).
106 Hendrick Smith, *The Russians* (1976), pp. 194–5.
107 'A Child is not a thing, and Grandma is not a storage locker', Excerpt in *CDSP*, vol. 34, no. 38 (20 Oct. 1982), p. 20. See also details given of child socialization in U. Bronfenbrenner, *Two Worlds of Childhood: USA and USSR* (1971), chapters 1–3.
108 Novikova et al., 'Women's Work and the Family', p. 176.
109 U. Bronfenbrenner, *Two Worlds of Childhood*, p. 81.
110 Ibid., p. 90.
111 F. O'Dell, *Socialization through Children's Literature* (1978), pp. 185–9.
112 Novikova et al., 'Women's Work and the Family', p. 182.
113 'The Kinship System of the Contemporary United States', *Essays in Sociological Theory* (1964), p. 192.
114 See A.G. Kharchev, *Brak i sem'ya v SSSR* (1979), p. 363.

5

SOCIAL STRATIFICATION AND CLASS

Many radicals seek, in one way or another, to make society more equal, to reduce the distance between social strata: to give the powerless more power, the poor more riches, the social outcasts more status. More traditional and conservative people regard these objectives as Utopian: inequality is a 'natural' state of the human race, they say, and attempts to create conditions of equality are doomed to failure. Also, the liberal will point to the fact that equality can only be achieved at the expense of other cherished values: freedom for the individual – to excel, to own property, to exercise the right to private education and personal medical care – is severely constrained by egalitarians seeking the imposition of their own collectivist values. Yet another position is that of the contemporary social democrat who vehemently denounces inherited or ascribed inequality (of wealth, of privileged education, of ancient title) and contrasts this with inequality of achievement or of merit based on individual performance.

The sociologist may also have his own values about the normative distribution of resources and the class structure, but he is concerned to make a detached description of the sources and extent of social inequality as well as to explain why social stratification comes about. Is it a necessary condition to maintain the equilibrium of a social order? Is it a functional requirement necessary 'to ensure that the most important positions are conscientiously filled by the most qualified persons'?[1] Or is it a process by which the privileged have seized an unfair share of the desirable things in life and, thereafter, by force and fraud (of which the ideology of inequality is a part), maintain a *status quo* which is mainly in their own interests?

Two distinctive approaches to social inequality may be delineated. The first is a Marxist one which emphasizes class relationships and the second is adopted by 'bourgeois' sociologists who see stratification as a manifold pattern of hierarchy and social division including status, power, wealth and income. In developing a social and political policy, Soviet Marxists have emphasized class position in terms of ownership relations: their major objective was to destroy private ownership and to replace it with collective ownership. Other types of inequality (distributive, power and status) are seen as largely dependent on such class relations.

Non-Marxist sociologists see inequality much more widely in terms of social stratification. This has as its focus the division of society into a hierarchy of strata, each having an unequal share of society's power, wealth, property or income and each enjoying an unequal evaluation in terms of prestige, honour, or social esteem. Studies of stratification attempt to delineate the 'socially important' groups, to determine the relations between political privilege, economic inequality and social rank. In this chapter we shall consider first Marx's attitudes to class, second, the policies adopted by the communists after the revolution, third, the profile of the main social groups today (intelligentsia, workers and peasants) and finally, the implications of Soviet experience for the process of social change.

Bolshevik Policy 1917 to 1936

Marx and Engels made ownership the fundamental determinant of class position. The version of Marxism adopted by the Soviet leadership is briefly as follows (see also above chapter 3). The owners of the means of production constitute the ruling class over the non-owners. Originally, the division of labour in society gave rise to economic classes. Associated with class position and dependent on it are social status and political power. In capitalist society, the industrial *bourgeoisie* owns the means of production and employs labour; the state functions to reproduce the bourgeoisie's domination; its wealth gives access to culture and education and gives rise to a style of life. The *proletariat* is distinguished by the fact that it sells its labour power on the market (where it has a bargaining disadvantage); it has little participation (power) in the affairs of the state; it is deprived educationally and culturally. For Marx, class, power and status in capitalist society are inextricably related and are highly correlated.

Under capitalism, the domination of the bourgeoisie and the capitalist state ensures systematic inequality between classes: libertarian and social-democratic attempts to 'introduce equality' therefore are sure to fail within the context of the capitalist system. Unlike traditionalists, however, Marxists have a vision of the egalitarian society under socialism. In the *Communist Manifesto* Marx wrote: 'When in the course of development class distinctions have disappeared and all production has been concentrated in the hands of a vast association of the whole nation, then public power will have lost its political character.' Hence the assumption made by the early Soviet Marxists was that the abolition of private property and of the capitalist class based on it would entail the elimination of political and social inequality. Only in communist society would '...all the springs of co-operative wealth flow more abundantly – only then can ... society inscribe on its banners: From each according to his ability, to each according to his needs!' Under communism, there would be no division of labour and therefore no antithesis between mental and manual labour.[2] From the point of view of social stratification, the October Revolution was to create conditions for a truly equal and classless society. In place of a system of stratification determined by class relations and by the forces of the market, it was thought that social relations would be determined by the ideology and goals of the Communist Party.

After the revolution, the Bolsheviks' main concern was to abolish the ownership relations on which capitalism rested. Nationalization of property, the seizure of land and factories, helped destroy the old possessing classes and the middle strata associated with them. But before and during the New Economic Policy private ownership and private trade continued. In market terms, separate classes still existed: the proletariat and a property-owning class (particularly among the peasantry).

The proletariat was, in theory, the political base of the new order. To safeguard the revolution the Bolsheviks thought it necessary that the proletariat act initially as the *ruling class*. During the period up to 1936, the official definition of Soviet society was that of 'the dictatorship of the proletariat'. From the communist viewpoint the proletariat consisted of three strata – workers, landless peasants and employees. The strata hostile to the proletariat were made up (during the New Economic Policy, 1921–28) of private traders (*nepmen*), rich peasants (*kulaks*) and the technical intelligentsia having sympathy for a bourgeois order. These 'hostile' groups had restricted political rights: they were barred from official positions, some had no vote and could not join the Communist Party.[3]

In terms of social esteem a most complex situation existed: the values of the old regime still lingered on in people's consciousness, while the communists attempted to assert the mores of a new order. Official policy was egalitarian, an attempt was made to give higher status to skilled and unskilled factory workers. In April 1917, Lenin had said that the pay of officials must not exceed that of 'competent workmen'. The status of the old managerial and executive groups was undermined: for example, in 1917, the Council of People's Commissars fixed salaries at 500 rubles basic for Commissars. Soviet policy was to reduce high salaries to the earnings of the average worker.[4] Wage differentials were reduced, giving government employees the salary of the lowest category of office worker, 350 rubles a month.[5] This, however, should not be taken as the 'introduction of communism'; wage equalization and the rationing that went with it were temporary measures intended to distribute the scarce resources available under 'War Communism'.

In January 1919, a wage scale approved by the Second Trade Union Congress laid down wages of the highest grades of workers and employees at only 1.75 times those of the lowest paid grade in each category – a drastic reduction in the differentials pertaining before the revolution.[6] In practice, however, it was difficult to enforce these trade union statutes and the wages of 'scarce' workers went above the ceiling. In 1921, when Lenin introduced the New Economic Policy, a wage structure with 17 divisions covered all grades of workers and employees. The differentials were widened; highly skilled workers received 3.5 times the wage of the lowest category and the ratio of the highest salary to the lowest was eight to one.[7] It is interesting to note that in the 1920s the differentials between workers followed a ranking similar to the pre-revolutionary pattern: printers, tanners and workers in the food industry receiving more than miners, metallurgists and engineers.[8] Here is an example of the way the forces of tradition were stronger than Bolshevik policy at this time. In 1926 the law was again changed and differentials were reduced to much below the pre-war levels. This was part of a policy by the communists to ameliorate the position of the poorest people. Even so, as Bergson has pointed out, income inequality among Soviet industrial workers in 1928 'was closely proximate to that among American industrial workers in 1904'.[9]

Until the time of Stalin's leadership, the Soviet Bolsheviks gave priority to the political tasks of maintaining their hegemony, which they thought would ensure the dissolution of the capitalist class. Within this context, they tried to minimize other social differences: they opened up higher education to the children of previously deprived strata, they improved the position of women, they tried to reduce wage differentials. They conceded that the traditional attitudes of the population would mean that various kinds of equality would take a considerable time to be achieved. Under Stalin, however, the subscription to egalitarian goals was replaced by a legitimation of social, political and economic inequalities under socialism. Only under full communism, Stalin argued, would individuals receive according to need, under socialism wages must be paid according to work performed. The 'Marxist formula of socialism' stated: 'From each according to his ability, to each according to his work.'[10]

In 1932, in an interview with Emil Ludwig, Stalin made clear his views on egalitarianism.

The kind of socialism under which everybody would get the same pay, an equal quantity of meat and an equal quantity of bread, would wear the same clothes and receive the same goods in the same quantities – such a socialism is unknown to Marxism.... Egalitarianism owes its origin to the individual peasant type of mentality, the psychology of share and share alike, the psychology of primitive 'communism'. Egalitarianism has nothing in common with Marxist socialism. Only people who are unacquainted with Marxism can have the primitive notion that the Russian Bolsheviks want to pool all wealth and then share it out equally. That is the notion of people who have nothing in common with Marxism.[11]

Accordingly, a steeper gradation between skills and occupations was introduced and wage ratios increased between the lowest and highest paid.[12] Stalin's immediate justification for the change was the need to reduce labour mobility and to introduce incentives for the unskilled to become skilled – a policy vindicated, at least in part, by the most authoritative Western writer on this subject.[13]

In other ways, too, Soviet policy changed. Formal ranks were reintroduced into the army; the 'proletarianization' of higher education was relaxed; charges were later introduced for higher education; and a status differentiation in the form of awards and medals was introduced. In 1927, for instance, the award of Hero of Labour was introduced, the Order of Lenin in 1930, the title of Honoured Artist of the RSFSR in 1931; by 1944 medals were also awarded to mothers who had raised five or six children. Some of these 'Orders' also entailed financial rewards: for instance, time necessary for full pension was reduced by one-third, some gave rights to free travel. But the number of awards given was relatively modest in the pre-war period: in all there were 1,900 between 1918 and June 1941, a total which rose to 50,700 between 1941 and 1945 and 196,600 between 1946 and 1957.[14] Hereafter the number of decorations decreased (and under Khrushchev not one new Order was introduced).

Post-revolutionary experience, therefore, saw, after an initial egalitarian phase, the assertion of wage inequality. The Russian communists, in this sphere of social life as in others, found themselves faced with introducing socialism in a backward underdeveloped country. Without the economic basis provided by an advanced industrial economy, a system of differentiation based on egalitarianism could not come to fruition, especially when introduced after a revolution, a civil war, a general famine and economic collapse. In practice, the inequality between occupational strata of other industrial societies became also a characteristic of Soviet Russia. As Robert Hodge and others have suggested, economic development depends upon the recruitment and training of men in skilled, clerical and administrative positions, and a system of differential social evaluation is therefore a necessary condition of rapid industrialization.[15]

To attract workers to the industries essential for the industrialization effort, wages in them were increased. In 1934, the highest wages were paid in engineering, followed by the power industry, ferrous metallurgy, oil, coking, iron ore and coal industries.[16] While it is sometimes thought that Stalin personally created a system of severe social inequality, it is more accurate to view the changes in social stratification of the early 1930s as determined by the demands of industrialization and the forces to which they gave rise. The centrally *administered* economy recognized these demands. In doing so a system of wage payment was introduced in which 'the principles of relative wages in the Soviet Union are also capitalist principles.'[17] The Soviet labour system under Stalin was not, however, solely based on financial incentives to stimulate supply. Coercion was also used. Labour camps were organized in the east and north and approximately five million people laboured on construction projects.[18] This is quite exceptional in a modernizing society and is a throw-back to similar, though smaller, developments which had occurred under the Tsars.

The USSR as a Socialist State

In 1936 the USSR was proclaimed a 'socialist society'. In Soviet Marxist terms this implied that no antagonistic class relationships existed. In nationalizing the land and large factories the owners of the means of production had been expropriated and Stalin believed that the crash industrialization programme had created the material basis of a Socialist system (see above, chapter 3). But inequality persisted. Under socialism men were paid according to their work. The 1936 USSR Constitution defined three friendly co-operative groups each with full civil rights: the workers, the intelligentsia (sometimes called employees or non-manual workers) and the collective farm peasantry. The first two groups are the main subdivisions of the working class which is seen in a firm friendly union with the collective farm peasantry. Two social (but not antagonistic) 'classes' therefore exist, differentiated by their relationship to the means of production. Though the means of production (the land) on collective farms is owned by the government, the products of collective farms belong to collective farmers: they are sold to the government and the proceeds of sales are distributed by the collective farm.

The social structure of Soviet *socialism* (not communism) involving social inequality is not as contradictory as is sometimes supposed. In Soviet terms, property relations have been changed: private ownership has been abolished. But this does not imply that inequality has been eliminated. Unequal incomes giving rise to privileges in consumption and status differences have been officially admitted, with differential access to power position, or political stratification. Wesolowski[19] claims the authority of Engels to assert that a hierarchy of command positions is necessary for the organization of a modern economy. To understand adequately the process of social stratification, much more than a crude mechanical relationship between ownership relations, on the one hand, and honour and political power, on the other, is required. We must bear in mind that in the USSR 'socialism' is defined in terms of Marxist categories of modes of production, derived from the character of ownership relations to the means of production. In Western social-democratic theory, socialism is *defined* in terms of equality.[20] In practice, however, Western social-democratice parties are more democratice in ideals than they are socialist, and policy is geared to the reduction of distributive differentials and the promotion of equality of opportunity. Class conflict is regarded as something which was part of early industrialization and has been superseded by a partnership between management and employees in a 'mixed' economy of government and private enterprise.

Social Stratification in Modern Russia

In the sense that Soviet sociologists use the term, there can be no class conflict in a state socialist society. This does not mean, even in theory, that there is complete harmony, or that no system of social stratification prevails. An authoritative article in the Soviet journal *Kommunist* alludes to differences of interest inherent in present Soviet society. Glezerman quotes Lenin's description of social classes as 'large groups of people differing from each other by the place they occupy in the historically determined system of social production, by their relation (in some cases fixed and formulated in law) to the means of production, by their role in the social organisation of labour, and, consequently, by the dimensions and mode of acquiring the share of social wealth of which they dispose.'[21] This definition of class is much wider than Stalin's interpretation of Marx defined above in strict terms of ownership. The place one occupies in 'the social organization of labour' and 'the dimensions and mode of acquiring the share of social wealth' of which one disposes may be independent of one's ownership relations. Here the division of labour is a basis for differentiation.

Glezerman continued by defining four main kinds of social distinction under socialism: first, a class division proper between workers and peasants; second, differences between rural and urban populations; third, those between manual and mental labour; fourth, those between 'people of different trades, skills and incomes within the working class, peasantry, intelligentsia and office workers'. These distinctions are quite useful and they also alert us to the bases on which Soviet data are collected. Manual and non-manual *workers* include all engaged in state and co-operative institutions, and members of collective farms regularly employed in industry, building, transport (etc.) and only partly or not at all employed on the collective farm. Collective farmers include members of the *kolkhoz* and their families engaged in agricultural production.[22] A collective farmer is in a different *class* because he is not employed by an enterprise for a wage; he is a member of the collective which owns the seeds and their produce and the agricultural machinery. In 1983 manual workers totalled 61.2 per cent, non-manuals 25.9 per cent and collective farmers 12.9 per cent of the population. (These figures include non-working members of families.)[23]

In Soviet society, status or power ranking is not part of the official ideology. The classes of peasantry and workers live in 'friendly collaboration', only distinguished by the leading role of the working class in building communism. As Ossowski has pointed out, the Soviet image of contemporary Russia 'is of a society without class stratification ... nor are there upper classes and lower classes in the sense in which we encounter them in the American scheme of gradation ... In the Soviet Union economic privileges and discriminations have, in accordance with Soviet doctrine, nothing in common with class divisions.'[24] The grading or ranking of individuals into groups of superior or inferior status is alien to the Soviet concept of socialism. Sociological work investigating such grading therefore is not carried out – or is done only indirectly, unlike in the United States, where a plethora of empirical work has been carried out into status differences. It is not quite true, however, to assert, as does Ossowski, that Soviet writers are blind to social stratification. The division of labour, type of employment, level of training and education are widely recognized by Soviet sociologists and philosophers as underpinning social differentiation. Under developed socialism cognizance is taken of differences *within* (rather than between) the classes of workers, collective farmers and the social stratum of the intelligentsia.[25]

The Soviet 'Intelligentsia', Non-manual Workers

The social category of 'intelligentsia' is one which does not fit neatly into a Marxist classification. Historically, the term was applied to a social group which arose in Russia and Poland in the late nineteenth century. It was differentiated by its function of creating and consuming cultural goods and services; the intelligentsia also had an important role as political critic and defender of the cultural heritage (in Poland the intelligentsia has shown a close affinity with Polish national aspirations).[26] Historically, the intelligentsia was recruited from the sons of the gentry; they adopted a particular urban life style and typically entered the professions of creative writer, poet and social critic. They were therefore outside the major Marxist categories of worker and capitalist, though they possessed some cultural capital, which they embodied in products such as books which they sold. However, they were not members of the proletariat for they were not employed and did not create surplus value.

A Soviet theorist notes that under socialism the division of labour gives rise to a 'qualitative difference' between non-manual and manual labour[27] which is abolished only under communism. Such a definition of 'mental labour' includes a very wide range of employees – from storemen to government ministers. Sometimes, the term *intelligentsia* is restricted to an exclusive group of specialists possessing higher educational qualifications, and the word *sluzhashchie* is used to describe unqualified or junior white collar workers. The 'qualitative difference' referred to above has to do with the fact that some strata of non-manual workers are in positions of authority. Their activity gives them certain prerogatives in defining policy and they also have the responsibility of executing the decisions of the higher administration which again involves command over other people. In addition to this, I would add that the more pleasant work environment, the higher educational qualifications required and the daily use of words rather than products give rise to a peculiar way of life, distinct from that of the manual workers.

The literature on the subject of the intelligentsia is highly ambiguous. In the widest sense the *intelligentsia* and *sluzhashchie* are synonymous – 'non-manual workers'. But the more proper use of the term 'intelligentsia' refers to a highly qualified creative executive and technical stratum. Llyod Churchward has provided a useful classification of the 'main social functions of the Soviet intelligentsia'. These are:

(1) organization and development of the productive process (production and preservation of human resources, research and development, scientific organization of labour),
(2) organization of culture (management of communications, propaganda and enlightenment, promotion of art and literature),
(3) theorizing and generalizing social experience (criticism and policy review),
(4) system maintenance and system adaptation (political socialization, political recruitment, political legitimation).[28]

Churchward here is accepting the narrow definition of intelligentsia which sees this group as occupying the leading administrative, scientific, executive and cultural roles in society. He, like Soviet writers, does not regard a defining characteristic to be that of a 'radical critic'.

TABLE 5.1: GROUPINGS OF PERSONS HAVING POSITIONS OF RESPONSIBILITY
AND LEADERSHIP IN THE USSR

	000s
Chiefs of organs of government administration and their structural sub-divisions	210.8
Chiefs of Party, Komsomol, trade unions, other social organizations and their structural sub-divisions	194.9
Chiefs of enterprises, collective farms and their structural sub-divisions	1,570.1
Chiefs in research and teaching institutions (excluding primary schools)	633.2
Chiefs and their assistants in publishing	39.2
Directors in culture and art	20.7
Directors and chiefs in trade and catering	463.3
Heads of planning, finance and economic institutions	85.8
Chief doctors and other leaders in medicine	57.7
Leading specialists among engineering-technical employees	282.2
	3,547.9

Source: *Itogi vsesoyuznoy perepisi naseleniya* (1970), vol. 6, Table 2.

The size of the intelligentsia depends on how one defines it. In table 5.1 are shown those groups of men and women who occupy a position of authority – as defined by the 1970 census (comparable data for 1979 have not been published). They total 3.5 million. Mervyn Matthews has narrowed down these groups to an occupational elite of about a quarter of a million. These are men and women who have responsible posts and earn at least an estimated 450 rubles per month – at the time of his study (early 1970s) about four times the average wage. These include party officials (95,000), government, trade union and Komsomol officials (60,000), intellectuals (43,000), factory managers (22,000), military, police and diplomatic service (30,000).[29]

If we consider the population stock of professionals with higher and specialist secondary education, the total size of the intelligentsia was 46.2 million in 1982: 20.4 million with higher and 25.8 million with secondary specialist education. As for non-manual workers in general, that is, those occupied in mental as opposed to manual work, this group as a statistical category numbered 34.7 million in 1982 (25.3 million in 1970); that is, 30.1 per cent of the employed population (28 per cent in 1970).[30] These data illustrate the important changes which have taken place in the Soviet social structure in the last half century. (In 1959, only 1.2 million people had higher education.)

The differences (social, political and economic) between the lower non-manuals and the upper cadres are so great that I would suggest that the latter ought to be defined as 'the intelligentsia'. Another distinction may be made between lower non-manual employees in culture, administration and politics (e.g. librarians, trumpet players, local government clerical assistants, trade union functionaries) and those in industrial production. The latter include an important group of 'engineering-technical workers' (ITR's) – men and women with specialist qualifications – working in production (e.g. mechanical, electrical and petroleum engineers). Such employees should, in my view, be regarded as non-manual members of the working class, employed in production.

As to the political role of the intelligentsia, Marxist champions of Soviet-type societies would argue that only under socialism does the intelligentsia become an integral part of society. It serves the nation. This is possible because there is no ruling class exploiting the masses. The 'intelligentsia' then is distinguished by virtue of its role in the division of labour. Differences in income and consumption correspond to differential contribution to the national product; the argument is similar to that which we encountered at the beginning of the chapter: social differentiation is necessary for the effective and efficient operation of the economy.

The Intelligentsia as a 'Cultural Bourgeoisie'

This line of approach has been strongly criticized by some dissident critics and by Western sociologists such as Alvin Gouldner.[31] They suggest that the functional roles described by writers such as Churchward point not only to the crucial activities of this group, but also put it in a position of potential if not actual domination. Daniel Bell[32] and Alvin Gouldner consider as a defining characteristic of the intelligentsia the possession of knowledge or 'cultural capital'. For Bell, the possession of scientific knowledge and particularly that which assists planning the economy is crucial in defining its potential political role – computer scientists, those who understand cybernetics and econometrics. Such knowledge gives control. For Gouldner, cultural knowledge is of much wider significance. It includes all who have higher educational qualifications in arts, social sciences and the natural sciences.

These writers see the intelligentsia as playing an increasingly dominant role in modern society. As far as Bell is concerned, these new middle strata do not become a ruling class: in the West, they join the traditional holders of property and those with political office. They become an important constituency of the ruling elites. By virtue of their knowledge they are able to influence and veto the other groups. Alvin Gouldner takes a more radical view of the 'New Class' which he sees as a contender for power in its own right. Referring to both Soviet and Western society, he emphasizes the fact that the possession of cultural capital turns the intelligentsia into a cultural bourgeoisie – its power is derived from its control of 'special cultures, languages and techniques' that generate a stream of income which it appropriates. Its income is legitimated by credentials gained in the educational system. It has a monopoly of skills and professionalism: these are the key to productivity and economic growth. This group develops a consciousness through the 'culture of critical discourse': a kind of ethos surrounding the use of knowledge, it gives rise to a class ideology. This new class of intellectuals has power through (1) its management of the means of production and administration, and (2) its acquisition of control over the means of communication and violence. It despises formal bureaucrats and political chiefs who are intellectually incompetent.

These arguments appear particularly persuasive in relation to state socialist societies. The crucial difference compared to capitalism is that the property-owning or 'moneyed bourgeoisie' has been destroyed. This approach has been developed with respect to socialist societies by two Hungarian dissidents, Konrad and Szelenyi. They reason that the intelligentsia is forming an exploiting dominant class. They argue that, with the abolition of capitalism (and capitalists), the intelligentsia is in a position to direct society, as social planning is guided by technical experts. It is this group which has the legitimized right to dispose of surplus product.[33] Their argument is not a Marxist one, for, rather than conceiving of the ruling class in terms of ownership, they see it in terms of authority and in the control of distribution of the social product. In the vein of radical American sociologists, such as Wright Mills, they conceive of a ruling class made up of three distinct but united groups of intellectuals: economists and technocrats, the administrative and political bureaucracy (including police and military) and the ideological, scientific and artistic orders. As they put it: 'The ideologue, the policeman and the technocrat are mutually dependent on one another and are impregnated with one another's logic.'[34]

There can be no doubt that the intelligentsia – in the sense of a group having academic credentials – does provide the basis of political leadership and in many respects is a social and political elite. The party leadership is staffed by 'intellectuals': in 1981, 90 per cent of the members of the Central Committee of the party had higher education. The Academy of Sciences is closely linked to the party and government apparatus. Members of the intelligentsia play an important role on advisory committees. They are also able to formulate ideas about the political system.[35] It is an overstatement, however, to suggest that the 'intelligentsia' can be considered to be a political ruling class. The intelligentsia, as defined by Konrad and Szelenyi, includes people from the arts, science, administration, economy, police and party. Each of these groupings has a different view of the world, which precludes the formation of a common class identity. The cultural and scientific intelligentsia are restricted by the political authorities (particularly the political police) over their work: censorship and restriction of foreign travel curb their activity. Knowledge and indispensability cannot be equated with political power. The ideological, scientific and artistic intelligentsia is very much under the direction of the political apparatus. The outlook of intellectuals in the sciences and humanities tends to conflict with the military and police. It is doubtful whether the three sections of 'the intelligentsia' concurred over the Soviet invasion of Afghanistan and Czechoslovakia. There are important distinctions to be made between the ruling bureaucracy and the creative intelligentsia: these have to do with ways of thinking and acting, as well as life styles. A criticism I would make of the 'intelligentsia as a ruling class' theory is that it conflates into one political and social group a category of persons who share in common only a higher education, a white collar occupation and some authority position. Whilst these attributes give them privileges, they do not provide sufficient conditions for the formation of a ruling class. They lack a homogeneous political consciousness, unity of action and a common ideology in opposition to the masses. 'The masses' may be divided into two major social groups and it is to a consideration of these that we now turn.

The Working Class in Production

The 'working class' cannot simply be identified with manual workers.[36] It is true that in the early days of the industrial revolution, production was characterized by relatively large labour armies performing manual work with low levels of capital. Such workers sold their physical labour for wages. The development of the productive forces, however, leads to a decline in the proportion of workers in production who utilize manual skills and to a rise in the number of employees who perform 'mental labour'; that is, they bring knowledge to oversee machines and processes of production. In this way non-manual labour replaces manual. The activity of 'manual workers' also changes: the proportion of those performing physical work (dockers, draymen, labourers) declines, while those with manual skills and knowledge (turners, lathe operators, milling-machine operators) increases, as does the proportion of those whose work requires mainly knowledge (electricians, furnace-men, laboratory assistants). With the development of the means of production, the boundaries then between 'manual' and 'non-manual' workers become more blurred.

It may, therefore, be misleading to define the social structure as being divided into two distinct groups of 'manual' and 'non-manual' workers. It may be more appropriate to distinguish between those groups of non-manuals whose role it is to reproduce relationships to the means of production (i.e. in politics, education, administration and culture) and workers who are in production and whose labour is embodied directly or indirectly in products (goods and services) which are exchanged. The former group includes not only the 'cultural' intelligentsia, but also those engaged in the apparatuses of coercion (police, law) and socialization (education, media). The second category includes those strictly non-manual workers who oversee, check and supervise machinery as well as specialized skilled workers who combine manual and non-manual roles such as installers, setters and repairers of high technology. All workers in production enterprises may be considered as part of the working class in the sense that they share the same relationship to the means of production, they are all wage-labourers, and they all contribute to production. This definition would include technical and managerial staff – for they too contribute to output.

Soviet statistics, however, differentiate between *rabotniki* (employees) and *rabochie* (workers), the former being non-manual and the latter manual. Soviet statistics also include, in the working class, manual workers employed in *state* farms: i.e. industrial type production on the land. In 1981 the employed manual working class totalled 79.6 million: 30.6 million in industry, 10.8 in agriculture (i.e. on state farms), 9.6 million in transport and communications, 8.5 million in building, 7.7 million in trade, catering and supply, 3.7 million in housing and utility services and 8.4 million in health, education, culture and administration.[37] In the different sectors of the economy manual and non-manual workers in 1982 had the following distribution: industry and building 39 per cent, transport and communication 9 per cent (a total of 28 per cent in 1940), agriculture 20 per cent (54 per cent), and services 32 per cent (18 per cent).[38] The relative decline of employment in agriculture and its rise in manufacture and services are apparent. But the Soviet Union still has a larger agricultural sector and a smaller services one compared to advanced Western industrial states.[39]

A corollary to the rapid industrialization of the USSR has been the swift growth of the working class. This has resulted in a tremendous inflow of peasants into urban industrial work. In 1928 manual workers (including members of families) came to 12.4 per cent of the population. By 1939 this figure had risen to 33.7 per cent and by 1982 to 60.9 per cent.[40]

The Soviet working class has a heritage of peasant background and a comparatively low level of education. A survey of Leningrad workers in 1963 showed that, of those in the 26–30 age bracket, 77.7 per cent had under ten years of education; of those aged 41 to 50, 50.0 per cent had less than seven years' education.[41] (In Britain a full nine-year education was introduced in 1918 and ten-year in 1945.) Even in 1976–77, skilled manual workers had only 8.9 years of education, and the most highly skilled workers (such as toolmakers) had only 9.1 years. In the Soviet Union as a whole, in 1979, 80 per cent of Soviet manual workers had seven or more years of education, but of these, 45 per cent had only 'incomplete secondary'.[42]

Such a large number of raw peasant recruits forming a relatively large proportion of the urban manual working class led not just to 'islands' of peasant culture within the working class, but played a major part in its creation. Such immigrants were less adaptable to urban and factory culture. Their rudimentary educational levels gave rise to work skills based on rote learning and they had difficulty in accommodating to the rhythm of production. Their work discipline was bad – they were subject to poor time-keeping and drunkenness. Their productive potential was lower than that of a more settled urban working class, and one which had been recruited from craft artisans. The rural background of the working class has had effects which continue into the 1980s – in the form of low skill levels and poor labour discipline.[43]

The Soviet working class is stratified in many ways. First, conditions and wages vary by industry. At the top is the coal-mining industry: in 1980, when the average national wage was 168.9 rubles per month, in the mining industry it was 298.9 rubles, while workers in cultural institutions (i.e. librarians, museum and art gallery employees) averaged only 111.3 rubles.[44] Underground miners also have longer holidays, better access to health resorts, and the right to retire five years earlier than other workers.

Second, workers are classified by level of skill. Jobs are defined as requiring a worker of a particular grade of skill. Payment for work is linked

TABLE 5.2: EDUCATION OF WORKERS IN LENINGRAD MACHINE-TOOL INDUSTRY

Socio-occupational group	Education (years of school)		
	1965	1970	1976–77
Unskilled workers	6.5	5.6	7.7
Skilled machine operatives	8.2	8.4	8.7
Skilled manuals	8.3	8.7	8.9
Highly-skilled workers (mental and physical labour)	8.7	9.8	9.1

Source: Adapted from N.P. Konstantinova, O.V. Stakanova and O.I. Shkaratan, 'Changes in the Social Characteristics of Workers under Developed Socialism', in Soviet Sociology, vol. 17, no. 4 (1979), p. 15.

to the complexity and arduousness of labour performed. Piece-work is widespread and rewards workers for the quantity of output. Typically, in a given industry there are six grades of skill; a worker will be paid according to the skill rating of his job. For instance, a time-worker in the chemical industry in 1975 on grade 1 would receive 41.8 kopecks per hour; on grade 6 he would earn 71.7 kopecks. If the work was of a 'heavy and harmful' nature the tariff would rise to 47.1 and 80.7 kopecks respectively, and if it were 'especially heavy and harmful' it would warrant a tariff range from 52.1 to 89.3 kopecks.[45]

The level of skill of manual workers is increasing and the numbers of unskilled workers are on the decline. In 1979, for instance, 26 per cent of industrial manual workers were 'low and unskilled', 51 per cent were semi-skilled and skilled and 23 were highly skilled; comparative figures for 1962 were 38 per cent, 49 per cent and 13 per cent.[46] In 1982, the distribution of manual workers in industry by skill tariffs was as follows: grade 1 (lowest): 4.9 per cent; 2: 18.3 per cent; 3: 28 per cent; 4: 23.4 per cent; 5: 18.1 per cent; 6: 7.3 per cent.[47]

Third, the manual working class is also differentiated by level of culture defined in the most general way. There seems to be a correlation between level of skill (and education) and consumption of cultural goods. For instance, a study of Leningrad workers in 1976–77 showed that 45.6 per cent of unskilled workers go to the theatre several times a year; the proportion rose to 62.1–66.8 per cent for skilled, and 73.2 per cent of the highly skilled. Similarly, 18.2 per cent of unskilled workers do not read books, compared to only 4–5 per cent of the skilled.[48] There is also an important difference between the political identity of different groups of workers: Shkaratan, in an empirical study of Leningrad engineering workers, found that in 1967, 13.8 per cent of unskilled manual workers were party or Komsomol members, but this figure rose to 37.4 per cent for skilled manuals and 39.5 per cent for semi-skilled operatives.[49]

The Political Significance of the Working Class*

The preamble to the Soviet Constitution defines the working class as the 'leading force' in Soviet society. In the quest for the building of communism, the interests of the party, the government and the working class are considered to be one. In what ways then may we consider the Soviet working class to be different from that under capitalism? At the outset, and in partial agreement with Shkaratan, we may identify four major features.

*The following section draws from D. Lane and F.O'Dell, *The Soviet Industrial Worker: Social Class, Education and Control* (1978).

First, for more than 50 years, the Soviet worker has been employed in state-owned industry: he has not been subject to the process of the market as understood in Western states. While the *process* of production has been very much on Western lines, the *class ownership* relationships to the means of production are quite different. In discussing the class structure of a society one should not conflate these two separate phenomena.

Second, the political conjunction of the industrial worker is also at variance with that of the Western worker. The class values of the rulers are legitimated by reference to the working class as a whole. There is a socially structured political monopoly of organization by the party which limits the independence of industry-based unions. Trade unions in Russia have never had the political saliency that they have had in the West, and the Communist Party (then RSDLP) preceded the growth of unions. In Britain the Labour Party developed out of the unions. The industrial working class provided the political class support for the October Revolution and the single ruling party has recruited large numbers of workers (or ex-industrial workers) to its ranks. In recent years policy has been to increase the number of manual workers in the party. By 1983, they totalled 44.1 per cent of all members. Between 1976 and 1980, 59 per cent of new admissions to the party were manual workers, 10.3 per cent were collective farmers, 25.4 per cent were engineers (ITR's) and other professionals (doctors, teachers).[50] At least 10 per cent of all manual workers and a third of all engineers are party members.[51]

Third, the Soviet Union has maintained itself against foreign invasion and, unlike other socialist countries of Eastern Europe, has repelled a premeditated attack and defeated a leading capitalist power. This has led to a closer identification in the USSR of the working glass and peasantry with the nation. As in other states where the party is identified with national liberation (China, Vietnam), the party acts as a symbol of national identity.

Fourth, the Russian worker both before and after 1917 has had no experience of a bourgeois system of industrial relations. As a consequence of the absence of unions based on trades, there is less competitiveness between strata of the working class. Work discipline is more lax than under capitalism. This has been conditioned by rapid extensive economic growth leading to the recruitment of the working class from the peasantry; by the absence of structural unemployment and inflation; and by generally rising standards of living. It must be emphasized that the present industrial working class has been recruited from one of the most culturally backward peasantries in Europe.

All this does *not* mean, however, that the Soviet working class is homogeneous; that strata are undifferentially identified with the party and the state; that work is universally regarded as community service; or that there are no conflicts between various groups within the working class. But I would argue that the class structure and political culture preclude a major collision between the working class and the state comparable to that predicted by Marxists between bourgeoisie and proletariat under conditions of modern capitalism.

Soviet organizational structures demand a greater level of formal commitment or participation by the worker (manual and non-manual) than in the West. General levels of participation and involvement in the USSR are higher than here. While calling for caution in interpreting the data collected by Soviet sociologists about the quality of commitment and the extent of participation, the *trend* is clear. White, in reviewing numerous Soviet empirical studies, concludes: 'The average amount of time devoted to socio-political activity is estimated to have increased almost seven times over the period of Soviet rule, while the proportion of working people involved is estimated to have increased eighteen times over the same period.'[52] These forms of participation, it must be emphasized, are subject to important variations between groups of workers. Of the participant respondents in Mukhachev and Borovik's survey, 38 per cent were party members, and 58 per cent were manual workers.[53] This shows important stratification of activity within the enterprise where, of the work force as a whole, 14.6 per cent were party members and 75 per cent were manual workers. By averaging the results of ten different Soviet studies of socio-political activism, we see that the average level of participation for technical staff was 68 per cent and for manual workers 35 per cent.

It must be borne in mind that these data all show that many employees, especially among the manual workers, do not participate and many do not think that it is necessary to do so. Even so, the point should not be lost sight of that the institutional arrangement and levels of social, political and economic participation in the enterprise are much higher than in industrial enterprises in the West (e.g. four million trade unionists help administer the social security benefits system in their spare time). Empirical data also show that Soviet workers compared to the Polish have a higher assessment of their ability to participate in decision-making in the factory.[54] And one must appreciate the difficulties involved in assuring the active participation of workers with a low cultural level and lack of a tradition of democracy.

Alienation

How these forms of industrial organization and means of participation influence the level and kinds of alienation of the industrial worker is again difficult to ascertain with accuracy. Many contemporary Western studies of alienation analyse components of workers' attitudes independently from ownership relations. Blauner,[55] for instance, identifies four components of alienation: powerlessness, meaninglessness, social isolation and self-estrangement. This is, to be charitable, a re-interpretation of Marx, for Blauner considers the essence of alienation, or rather of attitudes towards and happiness in work, to be derived from technological factors, not social relations derived from forms of property. This is not the same as the essential macro-system conditioning of alienation meant by Marx. It is important not to confuse these two kinds of relationships. 'Alienation', in the sense of dissatisfaction with work, with instrumental attitudes, with forms of 'powerlessness' over the work situation, *is* still a feature of the Soviet worker and in some ways is comparable to workers' attitudes revealed by Western non-Marxist studies.

Data collected by Zdravomyslov and Yadov,[56] for instance, help to show the extent of dissatisfaction by workers with their work, and this may be used as an index of motivational commitment. Again, caution is necessary in interpreting the published results and one should focus on the different responses of various groups and the rankings, rather than on absolute levels. The authors found that satisfaction with occupation varied from a negative attitude among unskilled manual labour to a highly positive one among the highly skilled. The 'social significance of work' is another measure of worker attitude, and here again we find that the more highly qualified workers (especially panel setters) had positive attitudes, while the unskilled manual workers did not, and the machine operators also had a low score.

These results are not dissimilar to those revealed by studies of workers conducted in the West. Greater dissatisfaction exists among unskilled workers doing repetitive jobs than among more skilled workers; political activity is greater among skilled than unskilled, and non-manuals rather than manuals. Such dissatisfaction, in my view, is determined partly by the technology of modern industry which – in both the USSR and the West – requires some workers to be involved in routine production. Many of these workers see factory labour as instrumental. A secondary factor giving rise to job dissatisfaction in the Soviet Union is the incapacity of the system to provide a sufficient number of jobs which require the levels of education and attainment achieved by many youths coming into the labour market. School leavers who want to be engineers do not like the idea of working on a milling machine.

There is then among Soviet industrial workers a certain lack of unity between man and his work, between subject and object. Whether this amounts to the essence of 'alienation' in a *Marxist* sense is debatable; these attitudes are rather evidence of work dissatisfaction. The Soviet worker is still subject to various forms of estrangement from his work, his fellow men and his environment; and some groups of workers may even form an alienative sub-culture. Though the working class has secured the right to employment, it is particularly important to note that the worker does not directly control the means of production. The state rules on behalf of the working class rather than there being direct working class decision-making. To this extent I would disagree with Soviet sociologists such as Shkaratan who say that the Soviet working class is a class 'for itself'. Control of the means of production is essentially centralized and further enhanced by various forms of checking (*kontrol'*) by groups (party and non-party) of workers at the industrial enterprise. Such '*kontrol'* does not articulate the workers' group interest, but seeks to enforce central policy against local deviation (see discussion above, chapter 1).

But workers do have the power to vary levels of work output: any reduction in production is destabilizing for the government and thus indirectly workers have an 'input' role during policy formation: '... workplace behaviour constitutes an ongoing plebiscite, with a permanent place in the formulation phase of public policy.'[57]

What one should perhaps emphasize is the stratification within the work force. This involves forms of 'unequal exchange' between various groups and an imbalance of power and rewards in favour of managerial/executive strata within the enterprise. Though there are exceptions, the more highly skilled and educated workers and employees have greater positive commitment to the work process and participate in 'control' within the framework of Soviet management, and their membership of the dominant party is greater. It is not implied here that there is a complete unity of interest between the various groups working in the Soviet enterprise; there are important distinctions which stem from the social and cultural division of labour, occupation being the most salient and position in the administrative hierarchy being another.

'Ideal Types' of Industrial Worker

Research findings show that the Soviet working class is socially and politically stratified. Lockwood[58] and others have attempted to categorize in British society three main types of working-class milieux: the traditional, the deferential and the privatized. I shall discuss the Soviet working class in terms of these types and then define a fourth ideal type, the incorporated, which I believe is more apposite to the Soviet worker.

The 'traditional' proletarian worker under conditions of modern capitalism is part of a highly homogeneous social group with respect to life styles. Also, he sees society in essentially dichotomous power terms; of 'them' and 'us'.[59] Alec Nove has attempted a similar type of power analysis of Soviet society, in which he makes a 'qualitative distinction between ... "we" and "they", between rulers and ruled ...' Nove asserts that this imagery of society 'impregnates people's consciousness in the Soviet Union'.[60] No evidence is marshalled to support this contention, and I feel that the centre of gravity is misplaced in this model. While it may apply to the attitude of the masses to the political elite – because of its aloofness and distance[61] – this does not operate at the level of the factory, because the managerial and technical staff have roots in and live among the workers. The idea that 'the Russians' are docile and obedient conveyed by Hendrick Smith[62] is no more true than the argument that the British are obedient because they have a habit of forming queues. Soviet factory workers are not particularly docile in their attitude to management, as Soviet studies of 'infractions of discipline' illustrate.[63] Rakovski, a Soviet dissident writer, regards the 'us' and 'them' distinction as being 'primitive' – 'an empty interpretive framework without practical consequences ...'[64] He is correct in this respect.

The Soviet enterprise caters for a wide range of needs of its employees: it has at its disposal housing stock, it may have a Palace of Culture organizing literary, cultural and social events. Soviet sports teams are linked to production enterprises. Leisure activities and holidays are organized by the trade union at the place of work; this organization also sees to sickness and various social security benefits. Voluntary workers from the union administer these activities. Also, party organizations which should unite the workers are located in the enterprise – unlike the dominant parties under capitalism. There is no evidence to suggest that the Soviet working class as such has developed an alternative counter-culture to the dominant one of Marxism–Leninism. There are no groups analogous to unions seeking to bring down the management or government, or even counter-cultures like the 'hooligan' element among British football supporters which epitomize a 'them' and 'us' culture in Britain. Rather, these traditional life styles, which in the traditional proletarian model are thought to support social and political *opposition* to the ruling class in Britain, are in the USSR fostered to provide support by the factory through the *kollektiv*. I would argue that it is not merely 'police coercion' which prevents the rise of a workers' opposition, but positive forms of incorporation which help bind the worker to the system.

One radical critic of Soviet society, Holubenko, sees 'working class opposition [being] expressed principally through so-called "deviance" and "social problems"'. Holubenko points out that drunkenness is the 'most prevalent outlet for frustration'.[65] It is indeed the case that alcoholism is widespread in the USSR. In the early 1970s the USSR ranked fourth for alcohol consumption out of 30 countries (following Portugal, France and Italy); its consumption of strong liquor, however, is the highest in the world.[66] But drunkenness, however important, is not solely an expression of the Soviet working class and is as much a Russian cultural and peasant artefact as a working class one.[67] Some studies suggest that the incidence of drunkenness among the working class is greatest among the least educated and most unskilled strata.[68] In my view the phenomenon is more likely to be explained in terms of traditional Russian culture, the strains of industrialization, and maladjustment of the peasant to urban life rather than as an expression of political discontent. Consumption of alcohol in the USSR varies enormously between different regions. It is highest in the Russian Republic, the Baltic States and Kazakhstan – all areas of rapid urbanization and Russian ethnic presence. In Central Asia and the Caucasus consumption is considerably less than in those areas.[69]

Such 'traditional' attitudes do not appear to be linked to protest in the form of strikes. As noted above (see chapter 1), our knowledge about strikes is extremely fragmentary and unreliable. Alex Pravda[70] estimates that there are about 'a few dozen per year'. Holubenko points out that they take place in 'areas removed from the Moscow-Leningrad region', in the 'periphery' of the country. This again would suggest (as far as our interest here is concerned) that such activity is linked to the newly mobilized working class in these parts, rather than being an expression of traditional forms of solidarity which one might expect in the Moscow-Leningrad areas. Unlike Habermas, who has analysed traditions in terms of supports and buttresses to the dominant culture of capitalism, I see traditionalism at the place of work in the USSR as undermining the system of industrial production. This is because in Russian culture before the revolution there had hardly developed a work ethic comparable to the Western 'Protestant ethic', which underpinned capitalist development.[71]

The 'deferential' worker views his bosses with respect; he perceives himself to be in a legitimately inferior position, and he provides his labour power in return for the traditional expertise and paternalism of the management. I would suggest again that this view of a hierarchical yet complementary relation between management and worker is untrue of the Soviet Union. What does seem to be a feature of the world of Soviet industrial workers is that they are, in Lockwood's terms, brought 'into direct association with (their) employers or other middle class influentials and hinder(ed) from forming strong attachments to workers in a similar market situation to (their) own'.[72] This would suggest that there is an integration of worker and management – but not of the traditionalist deferential type.

The 'privatized' worker is one who is isolated at work and in the community: social divisions are seen in terms of 'differences in income and material possessions'. His work is instrumental, the money nexus predominates: 'the single, overwhelmingly important, and most spontaneously conceived criterion of class division is money, and the possessions, both material and immaterial, that money can buy.' Such workers may be in trade unions but union membership is not the 'symbolic expression of an affective attachment to a working class community but a utilitarian association for achieving the member's private goal of a rising standard of living'.[73] The latter could not be said of trade union membership in the USSR. The privatized worker is apathetic, he does not question the political and social arrangements which confront him: he is 'economistic' in orientation.

Workers who are 'privatized' are apolitical, but it would be incorrect to view such people as being not prone to strike activity. On the contrary, workers' expectations for a higher standard of living may be so strongly internalized that if they are not met – through increases in wages – then intense industrial conflict may occur. Such conflict is essentially economistic and does not entail any criticism of the political order. Much of Holubenko's analysis may be interpreted in this vein. He emphasizes the fact that industrial unrest has occurred 'in response to three basic issues: (a) low wages – in particular a sudden drop in bonuses or in wages due to revised work norms announced by the factory management; (b) food and consumer goods shortages; (c) inadequate housing'.[74] I would emphasize, along with Brown, McAuley, Ruble and Alex Pravda,[75] that strikes in the Soviet Union are exceptional events (see also discussion of disputes, chapter 1, above): not only are they mediated by labour disputes procedures and other methods of control, but the Soviet worker 'lacks any tradition of pressing for improvements'.[76] These positive forms of process have to be considered in addition to coercive threats and draconian penalties for anti-state agitation. Such negative sanctions also lead to compliance on the part of the work force.

The Incorporated Worker

The 'incorporated worker' shares many of the traits we have noted in the above ideal types. The authority structure is accepted. Such workers participate in improving production, and they are closer to the administration both socially and politically than workers in capitalist society. But the 'incorporated worker' does not actively control the administrative system of work which is largely shaped by the political leadership in the context of a legacy of the traditional culture. The trade union developed under the political authorities rather than against them. It is more an aid to management than a defence of strictly workers' interests against management. Its manifold social and welfare activities further the integration of the worker in the factory.[77]

Westergaard has called for attention to be directed to the 'macro-structural' features of societies which promote or hinder class identity and opposition.[78] The structural features of Soviet society undoubtedly inhibit opposition. The threat of sanctions for anti-state activity has been effective in binding the worker to the system. As Hendrick Smith has recalled: 'At factories, farms or power projects . . . workmen or farmers or construction engineers speak proudly of their own chief as "a strong boss" . . . They like the feeling that someone above them is firmly in charge.'[79] What the Soviet political and administrative system has succeeded in doing is to provide mechanisms to integrate a relatively unsophisticated labour force into the industrial system. Its dynamics lead to the incorporation of the natural leaders among the workers: not only by occupational promotion, but also through the party and other organizations, the worker becomes increasingly identified with his society through the factory. As Connor has generalized when discussing the working class in Eastern Europe, 'The most striking fact emerging in a thirty-five year review of workers' political activity . . . even allowing for the massive coercive resources of the regime, is how little organised activity there has been.'[80]

Pravda has put this rather more positively when he concludes that the 'adaptive worker' . . . [is] parochial in outlook, his support for the system is based on national identity and an attachment to a concept of socialism centering on security, stability and relative equality.'[81] The Soviet working class is non-revolutionary for similar reasons, but in a different context, as the British: it is inculcated with pragmatic aspirations, and has a general conception of serving the 'national interest'.[82]

Permanence of employment and a rising living standard are important features of Soviet life which contribute to social stability. In my view inputs of mass loyalty are not absent in the Soviet Union and there is no crisis of legitimacy. Teckenberg has argued that the Soviet working class is 'fragmented and segmented along branch lines' (i.e. according to type of industrial activity), and the 'importance of socially oriented values . . . tends to decrease.'[83] This argument is not convincing. All industrial societies have different labour markets – on a skill, industry or firm basis. The attitudes that workers, as a whole, will adopt cannot be projected from their market position. This is because workers take their attitudes with them to work: they are shaped in the process of socialization. The process of socialization is *relatively* homogeneous in the USSR and is reinforced by the structure of the Soviet enterprise. Variations between industries and between occupational groupings within enterprises do not lead to the perception of a 'common interest' on these bases. Differences in expectations, in patterns of association with friends and in mobility chances do exist, but the evidence does not lead, as Teckenberg suggests, to 'exclude its members from the rest of society'.[84] All societies have forms of 'exclusion' – men and women, old and young, skilled and unskilled, able and handicapped, educated and ignorant – this *per se* does not lead to societal exclusion.

Much more important in the USSR than 'crises of legitimacy' proper, involving political collapse or revolution, are problems of political output. This calls into question the ability of the system to fulfil at various levels the expectations of the population. Consumer demands in the USSR are becoming more sophisticated and the economy needs to adapt to meet them. Aspirational deprivation, where consumer demands rise and supply does not increase to meet it, seems to be a likely development in the USSR. As Connor has aptly put it: 'workers' support for socialism is ... based less on principle than on what it can deliver.'[85] A key problem here is the efficiency of industry. The Soviet state has made its prime objective to secure the loyalty of the working class. In doing so, it has maintained full employment and has tolerated slack labour discipline. A priority has been placed on political security and worker loyalty. Further economic advance may require greater 'flexibility' of labour involving reductions in manning levels and subsequent unemployment. This was a policy advocated in Poland in 1970 but subsequently revoked.[86]

The recent history of the USSR has been characterized by rapid industrialization and the inclusion of rural peasants into the working class and urban society. From the mid-1980s we may expect a greater maturation of the working class. There are likely to be greater demands put on the economic and political system from this quarter. As long as living conditions and consumer standards improve, the working class will be unlikely to manifest any open dissent to the system. Any major upheaval can only come if there is association with other social groupings – say intellectuals or the scientific intelligentsia – and possibly if it is linked to a wider unifying theme like the question of national integrity. There are limits on the extent to which dissatisfaction may lead to systemic confrontation. The values of Soviet society give the working class a leading role in its political organization. The ideology of state socialism gives the working class a legitimacy to press its claims. The authorities are likely to respond to grievances and to compromise with the workers.[87]

The Soviet Collective Farmer (Kolkhoznik)

The rapid industrial growth of the USSR and the emergence of the working class as the largest social group should not detract from the fact that the Soviet Union still has a large rural and agricultural population. In 1983 the rural population comprised 35.6 per cent of the people. In the late 1970s agriculture accounted for some third of the national income; 28.2 per cent in 1981.[88] The 'rural' population is not a homogeneous one: it includes those resident in the village but working in industrial enterprises in local towns and two types of farmers – those employed in 'state' farms (*sovkhozniki*) and collective farmers (*kolkhozniki*).

Soviet classification of social classes is dependent on the individual's relationship to the means of production. To understand the Soviet concept of 'state' and 'collective' farmer one must examine the chief characteristics of the two forms of agricultural production: 'state' and 'collective' farms. On state farms workers are paid a wage, and all proceeds accrue to the state. The farm director is appointed by the state. Such men (*sovkhozniki*) are defined as part of the working class – not the peasantry. On the collective farm, however, the land is collectively tilled. The produce is, in theory, owned by the collective: 'The means of production belong to the state, the produce belongs to the individual collective farms as their own property (as is labour and seeds).'[89] Their class position, therefore, is not that of hired labour; collective farmers (*kolkhozniki*) are in co-operative production and, in Soviet theory, form a separate class. But as ownership of the land is vested in the state, the collective farmers do not form a class with antagonistic interests to the workers; they are a 'non-antagonistic' class forming a 'friendly union' with, although under the leadership of, the working class.

In many pre-industrial societies, the status of 'peasant' is given to those mainly occupied in agricultural work. As a socio-economic group the peasantry has the following characteristics: residence in a rural habitat, labour on the land with the family being the fundamental unit, an ideology of attachment to the soil, to the family and to the local community. The peasantry, as a social group, has a certain self-sufficiency and isolation from the urban social world, but is nevertheless part of a wider society and is to a greater or lesser extent influenced by urban areas. Unlike an agricultural worker, the peasant is largely sustained by the produce from the land he works. Though he may not own it, he determines to a large degree the inputs (both in terms of hours worked and kinds of crops to be produced) and has control over the distribution of products.

In the ways defined above Soviet collective farmers do not constitute a 'proper' peasantry. Basile Kerblay, has pointed out that in the collectivized sector the control over labour input by the peasant has been vitiated: 'his work has become subject to the same direction as in industry, except that its remuneration is still a residual income and not a fixed wage', and a collective farmer, in this respect, 'cannot be considered a peasant'.[90] While it is true that crucial production decisions are taken out of the collective farmers' hands by the Soviet planning agencies, it should not be forgotten that all peasants are subject to urban pressures and especially to market forces and therefore the difference may not be as sharp as Kerblay suggests. But it must be conceded that the Soviet collective farm peasantry, in so far as it works on the collective's land, is not a family work unit, nor has it control over decisions concerning planting. Only in minimal respects has it some of the characteristics of a more traditional 'peasantry'. The collective farmer decides the amount of time he spends and the kinds of crops to be produced on the private plot (about 0.25 hectares in size on average). The farmer is also able to own a limited number of livestock which are pastured on the land of the collective. In 1979, private production came to 26.5 per cent of total agricultural production (in 1960 it had been 35.6 per cent); in 1980 it accounted for 64 per cent of potatoes, 37 per cent of fruit and 31 per cent of meat.[91] The mode of work on plots is manual and much of the farmer's labour is expended in the traditional peasant fashion. The early socialization of children takes place in the family (only a quarter of rural children attend nursery schools) and thus the mores of the traditional peasant are passed on (this is reflected in the higher religiosity of country dwellers; see below chapter 7).

Though the term *krest'yanin* (peasant) is still used to describe the collective farmer,[92] it is inappropriate because so many of the traditional characteristics have been lost. The government has economic control over the collective farmer's work and the contemporary Soviet collective farmer cannot be considered to be part of a qualitatively different social world from the urban workers. The family is no longer the dominant unit of production, and the ideology of 'attachment to the soil' no longer exists; mass education is now widespread, modern communications bring urban culture into the collective farmers' homes and there is constant migration to the town. Popular aspirations are for urban-style consumption goods – televisions, refrigerators and other consumer durables.[93]

To analyse the social strata within the Soviet collective farm, Soviet sociologists use a number of criteria: the character of work, the qualifications and culture and income level of the farmers. Most classifications are based on the nature of work performed. Simush suggests seven groups (see table 5.3). These may be aggregated into three major divisions: the first is agricultural/technical and administrative personnel – the farm chairman and his subordinates, economists, agronomists, vets, mechanics, bookkeepers, teachers and others with middle and higher education. These people make up about 12 per cent of *kolkhozniki*. The second group is constituted of those operating farm machinery (*mekha-nizatory*) – tractor and harvester drivers and machine operators. These total some 20 per cent of the collective farm labour force. The third

TABLE 5.3: SOCIO-ECONOMIC STRUCTURE OF COLLECTIVE FARMERS

	1960 (%)	1974 (%)
Manual unskilled labourers engaged in field work	60.6	48.2
Manual labourers working with animals	18.9	19.9
Manual workers operating machines	7.8	13.6
Manual workers engaged in repair shops, subsidiary works, or buildings	5.2	6.3
Middle level management (foreman)	1.9	2.1
Non-manual personnel (management and collective farm specialists)	2.5	4.4
Non-manual personnel in services	3.1	5.5

Source: P.I. Simush, Sotsial portret sovetskogo krest'yanstva (1976), p. 144.

group are collective farmers being occupied only in physical labour – about two-thirds of the total.

The first two groups by occupation and culture form separate, as it were, non-peasant strata, for they have no particular attachment to traditional forms of land working and have been influenced through training and education by urban values and occupational skills. This has led to the suggestion that such members of the collective farm do not 'belong to the class of kolkhoz peasantry'.[94] Soviet writers particularly (though they are not alone in this respect) argue that the peasantry is 'withering away' and rural life is being 'pulled up' to that of the town. It is argued that this levelling will take place in three principal ways.

First, the 'growing together' of the urban working class and the collective farm peasantry is related to the mechanization of agriculture which will increase the number of machine workers and operators in the countryside (group 2 above). By virtue of their trade such men are 'brought near to the working class'. In other words, a highly mechanized and capital intensive agriculture undermines the traditional and 'peasant' work-ways and the mentality that goes with it, and on this foundation an agricultural working class rather than a peasantry will grow.

On what Soviet writers call the 'development of intra-collective relations' rests the second main way that change in the character of the collective farms is likely to occur. Conditions of production and consumption will approximate the practice in the towns: present policy is to pay wages on guaranteed monthly rates and to provide social services (pensions, allowances and medical care) and membership of the trade union on the same basis as in the town.

Thirdly, the nature of the collective farm is influenced through migration of people from the country to the town. The rural population and that of the collective farms is falling. The level of skill in the countryside rises and labour productivity increases providing a further stimulus to the raising of living standards of the collective farmer into line with workers in the towns.

Differences between Town and Country

Though an equalization is taking place between town and country, in the 1980s there are still significant differences between the social composition of the urban and rural population. This may be illustrated by study of levels of education, sources of income, use of time and party membership for citizens in town and country.

The level of education of collective farmers is considerably lower than that of the working class. As shown in table 5.4, in 1979 one-and-a-half times as many urban workers had a higher and middle education as have collective farmers. Collective farm women were also shown to be underprivileged. While it is true that the age structure of the village influences the figures – the larger number of older, relatively uneducated women to some extent explains the very low number of women with the highest qualifications – it is striking that only 46 collective farm women per thousand of the employed population had higher education compared to 92 per thousand of the same groups of the urban working class.

Table 5.5 illustrates differences in income and expenditure of families of workers in industry and collective farmers. In terms of income the major

TABLE 5.4: EDUCATIONAL LEVEL OF WORKERS AND COLLECTIVE FARMERS IN EMPLOYMENT

| | Per 1,000 persons of a given social group having the following education: | | | |
| | Higher, incomplete higher and middle specialist | | Middle education | |
Social group	1970	1979	1970	1979
Urban Manual Workers				
Both sexes	45	102	191	351
Men	48	109	193	353
Women	41	92	189	350
Rural Collective Farmers				
Both sexes	27	58	74	220
Men	36	70	89	239
Women	19	46	61	201

Sources: Census of 1979. *Vestnik statistiki* (1981), no. 2, p. 63. Census of 1970: *Itogi vsesoyuznoy perepisi naseleniya 1970g*, vol. 5 (1972), p. 46.

TABLE 5.5: INCOME AND EXPENDITURE OF FAMILIES OF INDUSTRIAL
WORKERS AND COLLECTIVE FARMERS

	Workers		Collective Farmers	
	1965	1981	1965	1981
Income				
Wages of family members	73.1	73.8	7.4	9.4
Pensions	22.8	23.5	14.6	19.1
Private farming	1.7	0.7	36.5	26.5
Income from collective farm	—	—	39.6	43.3
Other sources	2.4	2.0	1.9	1.7
	100	100	100	100
Expenditure				
Food	37.9	31.4	45.2	35.0
Purchases of goods	20.8	24.0	22.5	26.2
Social cultural and Services	24.3	23.6	14.0	14.8
(including education and				
other government services)				
Savings	2.8	6.0	8.0	9.1
Taxes	7.2	8.7	1.4	1.5
Other outgoings	7.0	6.3	8.9	13.4
	100	100	100	100

Source: *Narkhoz 1922–1982*, (1982), pp. 422–3.

difference is that about a quarter of the collective farmers' income is derived from personal subsidiary farming. As to outgoings, expenditure on 'social-cultural' and services was lower in collective farmers' families than in the industrial manuals', whereas it was higher for food and other goods. Comparing the data for 1965 and 1981, one sees a narrowing of differentials. Purchase of consumer durables is now similar in town and village. In 1981 per 100 urban families, 95 had television, 93 radios and 572 watches; the corresponding figures for the rural families were: 76, 78 and 420 respectively.[95] In the field of services there is still a great difference between facilities in the town and village. In 1973 in the town, 28 rubles per head were spent on services compared to only 14 rubles in the country.[96] Shops, schools, nurseries, and health service provision is inferior. But one must stress the fact that life in the villages has changed tremendously during the times of Soviet power. Now rural inhabitants regularly read newspapers, listen to radio and watch TV. The cultural impact is particularly important on the young: 'high proportions of young men in particular visit their club cinema two or three times a week and cannot but be influenced by the steady bombardment of urban values and life-styles.'[97]

Studies have also been conducted into the use of time by collective farmers and industrial workers (manual and non-manual). The main differences are in the areas of domestic work where the workers spent 2.31 and 5.22 hours on work days and holidays respectively, compared to 2.08 and 4.13 hours for collective farmers; on private plots workers spent 0.03 and 0.08 compared to 1.17 and 1.51 hours; workers had more 'free time', 3.10 and 7.51 compared to 2.37 and 6.33 hours.[98]

Membership of the Communist Party is an important indicator of the level of political consciousness and social integration of a group in society. In 1982, collective farmers (including non-working members of their families) came to 13.3 per cent of the population and in 1983, they constituted 12.4 per cent of membership of the CPSU.[99] Membership, however, is greater among the personnel with more urban-type occupations. Considering the social background of candidates admitted to the party between 1976 and 1980, 31.5 per cent were farmers who worked on machines, 20.9 per cent were specialists, 19.7 per cent worked with livestock and only 16.3 per cent were engaged on field work.[100]

There have been significant developments in raising the living standard of the villages to that of the towns. Education and income have become more alike. Underprivilege remains which may be particularly located among the manual field workers. They spend more of their time on their private agricultural plots and they have a more traditional type of work. Their educational, cultural and political consciousness is lower than that of the urban worker and of the skilled worker in the collective farm. The collective farm non-manual personnel and the manual *mekhanizatory* are closer to their urban counterparts than they are to the traditional peasant.

Rather than conceiving of the contemporary Soviet social structure as being composed of two friendly classes (workers and peasants) and one stratum (intelligentsia), it is more appropriate to conceptualize a continuum of social groups, ranging from the field workers among the collective and state farmers through the manual trades to the upper professionals and 'top dogs' in authority. It is a system of hierarchy and stratification, rather than one of 'two classes and a social stratum'.

Gender Division

Recurring relationships of domination and subordination between men and women have not played an important part in the analysis by Marxists in contemporary socialist states. Inequality by gender is usually regarded to be a consequence of class relationships. Under capitalism, exploitation takes place only when wage-labourers produce surplus value: i.e. labour is embodied in a good or service which is exchanged on the market and gives rise to profit. In Marx's time the overwhelming majority of women did not produce surplus. They were occupied either in paid domestic labour (as hired servants) or in unpaid domestic work as wives. Engels noted the subordinate position of the wife when in *The Origins of the Family* he said that 'in the family he is the bourgeois; the wife represents the proletariat.'[101] (On women and the family, see above chapter 4.)

The Soviet leaders did not directly confront the problem of patriarchy. Seeing class rather than sex as the crucial division, the Bolsheviks concentrated on abolishing rights over property rather than seeking to alter those structures and roles which gave men superior rights over women. Some of the family's functions were to be taken over by society. Women's equality was to be assured by changes giving equality of rights in family law, citizenship, etc., by the inclusion of women in the work force and in educational institutions. As was noted in chapter 4 on the family, these social changes have had very positive effects on the position of women in the USSR. Nevertheless, much inequality remains and has been generalized into a radical critique by Western feminists. Before considering their views, we may outline some of the forms inequality takes.

Women are clustered in different industries, have lower skill levels and earn less than men. In an authoritative study of the available evidence, McAuley has shown that Soviet women earn between 60 and 70 per cent the salaries of men.[102] This is a similar proportion to women's earnings in Western Europe – in 1975 in Britain they earned 62 per cent of men's. Soviet women are mainly occupied in the sectors of health (84 per cent of the labour force), education (73 per cent), banking and insurance (82 per cent) and trade, catering, procurement and supply (76 per cent). While the average money wage in 1982 was 177.3 rubles, it is important to note that *all* these feminized branches of the economy were below it: the figures are health – 129.5 rubles; education – 137.5 rubles; banking and insurance – 169 rubles; and trade etc. – 142 rubles.[103]

Women are engaged in less skilled work than men. A study by Kotliar and Turchaninova (published in 1975) of female industrial workers pointed out that the educational level of women was higher than that of men: 73.2 per cent of female workers have more than an elementary education compared with 69.8 per cent of males; in machine tools the figures were 77.7 per cent for women and 74.5 per cent for men, while in light industry it was 74.5 per cent and 65.3 per cent.[104] In the 1972–73 academic year, women constituted 50 per cent of students in higher education and 53 per cent in specialized technical schools; in the 1980–81 school year, the figures were: higher education 52 per cent women, middle specialized technical schools 56 per cent,[105] and in trade schools girls made up only 30 per cent of the total.[106] When the authors surveyed the skill levels of men

TABLE 5.6(a): MEAN SKILL RATINGS OF MALE AND FEMALE WORKERS IN INDUSTRY (SURVEYED ENTERPRISES)

Industry	Mean Skill Rating*			Differences in mean skill ratings of men and women workers
	All workers	Men	Women	
Baking	4.0	4.5	3.9	0.6
Meat and dairy	3.5	4.0	3.9	0.9
Textile	3.7	3.8	3.7	0.1
Garment	3.4	—	3.4	—
Machine Building	2.6	3.5	2.1	1.4

TABLE 5.6 (b): MEAN SKILL RATINGS OF MALE AND FEMALE WORKERS IN MACHINE BUILDING FACTORIES (%)

	Total	Skill Ratings*					
		I	II	III	IV	V	VI
Men	100	5.8	17.2	24.6	26.6	21.1	4.7
Women	100	29.1	38.6	26.8	4.4	1.0	0.1
Per cent of women in respective wage grade		89.9	79.9	66.0	22.6	7.8	3.8

Note: * The higher the rating, the greater the skill and consequently the higher the wages.
Source: A.E. Kotliar and S. Ya Turchanina, 'The Educational and Occupational Skill Level of Industrial Workers' in Problems of Economics (1981), vol. 24, pp. 81–2.

and women they found that women were invariably at a lower level than men. Even in the textile industry, which employs a large number of women, the skill level was lower than that of men. The data are shown in table 5.6. The Soviet writer M. Ya. Sonin[107] has generalized the typical skill structure in industrial towns as follows:

	Men (%)	Women (%)
Highly skilled (Grades V–VI)	31	4
Semi-skilled (Grades III–IV)	50	30
Unskilled (Grades I–II)	19	66

The conclusions to be drawn from these data are that men predominate in the high skill and women in the low skill groups, even though the educational level of women is higher than that of men.

In the hierarchy of authority, women also fare badly. In the 1980–81 school year, women constituted 85 per cent of the heads of primary schools, but only 38 per cent and 34 per cent of those of eight-year and ten-year schools respectively. They accounted for 30 per cent of all research students, 28 per cent of all those with lower research degrees (*Kandidaty*), and 14 per cent of those with higher research degrees.[108] On the basis of the 1970 census, McAuley points out that only 13 per cent of factory directors and 27 per cent of the foremen were women, figures falling to 9 per cent and 24 per cent in 1973. In 1982, women made up only 1.64 per cent of state farm directors and 2.15 per cent of chairmen of collective farms.[109] A similar gradation may be discovered in the realm of politics. Women constituted 53.3 per cent of the population in 1980, when they accounted for 50 per cent of local councillors, 36 per cent of deputies to the Supreme Soviets of the Union Republics and, in 1984, 32 per cent of those to the Supreme Soviet of the USSR.[110] In the Council of Ministers in July 1983, there was not one woman. In the Communist Party of the Soviet Union in 1981, 26.5 per cent were women (27.4 per cent in 1983); at the Party Congress in 1981, 28.2 per cent of delegates were women; in the Central Committee only 6 per cent are female; and in the supreme body, the Politbureau, there is not one woman. (In the whole history of the Soviet Union, there has only been one full member of the Politbureau, Furtseva.)

Such data are enough to make the point that in many important fields women do not have equality with men in the USSR. Western feminists therefore come to quite different conclusions about the system of social inequality than do Soviet Marxists. A 'radical feminist' critique of Marxism discounts not only the changes which have taken place in the Soviet Union, but also the class analysis on which they rest. According to Firestone, the 'moving power of historic events [is] the dialectic of sex: the division of society into two distinct biological classes for procreative reproduction, and the struggles of those classes with one another; in the changes in the modes of marriage, reproduction and child care.'[111] This line of approach sees women's subordination to be rooted in 'reproduction, sexuality and the socialization of children'. From this viewpoint, patriarchy is an institutionalized system of domination functioning through sex relationships.

The developments which have taken place in the Soviet Union since the revolution, it is claimed by this school of thought, have not altered the relations between the sexes. The economic and political changes which were associated with socialist development mobilized women that 'sustained and reinforced a pervasive asymmetry of male and female roles. This asymmetry was not merely a consequence of cultural lag but reflected, rather, a coherent, mutually reinforcing and systematic pattern of official perceptions, priorities, and institutional arrangements that impinged on every dimension of social structure.'[112] From this point of view, the place of women in the Soviet Union is subordinate to men. While women have entered the occupational field in great numbers, the traditional definitions of femininity have remained. Women are disadvantaged in that they are expected to maintain their traditional subordinate family roles and are subordinate in power relationships to men: this is particularly the case in positions of authority at work and in politics.

The position of women in the Soviet Union, in my view, is to be understood to lie between these two conceptions of traditional Marxism and radical feminism. It is clear that traditional Marxism does not adequately analyse the basis of women's subordinate position to men. Many feminists, however, in equating the position of women under capitalism to that under socialism, ignore the important and positive changes which have ensued from the abolition of private property. The mobilization of women in the Soviet Union should not be considered merely as a negative form of 'equal liability' with 'an emphasis on the obligation to contribute'.[113] There have been many positive effects of the mobilization process and, as Lapidus concedes, there are positive attributes in the Soviet 'affirmative action' programmes regarding education, child care, conditions of employment and types of employment.[114] They must be seen in the context of a rapidly developing and economically poor society. While the data cited above show inequality, Soviet women fare better in many ways than their counterparts in Western states: many more are in paid employment giving an occupation in the professions, in manual trades, and in politics.

But Soviet women are underprivileged. As we noted in chapter 4 they bear the burden of family chores and greater responsibility for child care. In the economy they are less well paid than men. In the polity they are under-represented. At the root of this is the traditional interpretation of women's biological role. To achieve equality with men, the roles of *men* have to be changed. The traditional Russian culture of male domination cannot be shaken off easily; it seeps from the pores of Soviet society. The lack of political organization of women and the absence of a feminist movement to alert women to the need for further social change is undoubtedly a brake on progress and leads to complacency on the part of the contemporary (male) political leadership.

So far, in our study of the major social strata (intelligentsia, workers, collective farmers, women) we have touched on inequalities in the relationships between groups. Now we turn to consider the distribution of rewards, social hierarchy and social mobility.

Income

Money income is important for two reasons. First, it is instrumental in the provision of a standard of living; it denotes the valuation of a person's labour in terms of the goods and services which may be purchased. Second, the amount of money earned may reflect a society's evaluation of the services performed and thereby it may indirectly be a measure of a person's social standing. High income may distinguish groups of professional and executive workers, but it may not lead to the creation of strata with a definite ranking on a scale of social worth – some being 'superior' to others.[115] One reason for this is that status may be derived from the occupation of a person or from the kinds of goods and services that are consumed. A high status occupation (for instance a physician in the USSR) does not have high financial rewards.

In the USSR 'income' is made up of two components: money earnings and payments in kind. Payments in kind include 'free goods' such as education, subsidized free food, medicine and health care. These non-monetary payments, which figure more prominently in the Soviet Union than in many capitalist countries, come to more than a quarter of the average person's income.[116]

Money earnings have several components. A basic wage linked to a worker's job – the greater the difficulty or arduousness, the higher the pay. In addition there are a number of bonuses – for high quality or the quantity of production, overtime pay and a regional supplement to compensate for inclement conditions. Wages are regarded as an important 'lever' to influence the workers' choice of occupation and place of work. Differential wage rates attempt to attract workers to the more needed occupations and to reward them for improving their skill. The harsher climate and lack of amenities in some parts of the USSR have induced the Soviet authorities to relate pay to various 'zones' of the country. Pay is from 10 to 20 per cent higher in the Urals, Kazakhstan and Central Asia, up to 70 per cent greater in the extreme north, while double pay is earned in the islands of the Arctic Ocean. Extra earnings are also derived from higher qualifications: Doctors of Science receive an extra 100 rubles per month while candidates (a lower post-graduate degree) receive 50 rubles.

Earlier in this chapter we saw that differential rewards, related to skill and output, were sharpened under Stalin. Since the early 1950s, a reversal of this inegalitarian trend has occurred. A measure of this reduction in differentials is the ratio between the top and bottom wage scales. (Manual work is graded for pay purposes into six grades.) Between the 1950s and 1960s the ratio in the ferrous metals fell from 3.6:1 to 2.6:1, in light industry from 2.6:1 to 1.8:1 and in machine tools from 2.5:1 to 2:1.[117] By 1975 differentials had further fallen: in ferrous metals it was 2.1:1, light industry 1.58:1, in machine tools 1.71:1.[118]

The salaries of managerial and technical staffs are also based on skill, responsibility and qualifications. Basic earnings may also be supplemented by payments for inclement working conditions and by bonuses for extra output. The differentials contained in basic wage scales have also shown a decline between the 1960s and 1970s. Directors of the largest enterprises had no increase in basic pay between 1960 and 1975 (i.e. it remained at 300 to 330 rubles per month); at the other end of the scale, however, salaries rose considerably – in grade 7, the lowest, 100–140 rs in 1960 and 150–170 rs in 1975. At the level of shop managers, the top grade rose from 170–210 rs in 1960 to 195–215 in 1975, the bottom grade had an increase from 130–150 rs to 160–170 rs.[119]

The differentials between earnings (in addition to rates) have also narrowed since 1946. The minimum wage has risen from 20 rubles in 1955 to 70 rubles in 1977 (and from 1984, it is to be selectively raised to 80 rubles). The differential between the minimum and the average wage has fallen from 3.6:1 to 2.2:1 between these two dates and rose slightly to 2.5:1 in 1982.[120] The ratios of the lowest earning in the top ten per cent to the highest in the bottom ten per cent (the decile ratio) were as follows: 1946: 7.24:1: 1954: 4.4:1; 1959: 4.2:1; 1964: 3.7:1; 1966: 3.26:1; 1968: 2.7:1; 1975: 2.9:1. By way of comparison, in the United States the decile ratio in 1972 was 4.48:1.[121] These figures, of course, ignore the various non-monetary payments received by managerial staffs (see below). On the other hand, 'transfer payments' (services provided such as pensions and welfare benefits) have also increased from 19 rubles per head in 1950 to 126.5 rubles in 1982 and they bring up the lower incomes.[122] They do show, however, that wage differentials are not great and that they have fallen in recent years. There can be no doubt that in the 1960s and 1970s the narrowing of income differentials was 'enormous'.[123] The differentials between managerial/technical employees, manual workers and office staff are shown on table 5.7. Since the mid-1970s, however, there has been a slight increase in differentials between the lowest and average earnings. This is due to the fact that the minimum wage has remained constant while the general level of wage rates has risen.[124]

As for actual earnings, average monthly money wages for manual and

TABLE 5.7: WAGE RATIOS OF MANAGERIAL/TECHNICAL, MANUAL AND OFFICE WORKERS IN SOVIET INDUSTRY, 1932–1981

	1932	1940	1950	1960	1970	1975	1981
Workers	100	100	100	100	100	100	100
Managerial/Technical	263	210	175	148	136	124	112.7
Office Workers	150	109	93	82	85	82	77.9

Sources: Calculated from *Narkhoz 1922–82* (1982), p. 405 and *Narodnoe Khozyaystvo SSSR* for relevant years.

non-manual workers in 1982 were 177.3 rubles (over double the minimum wage), an estimated real income of 246 rubles including services in kind.[125] (In 1983, 100 rubles exchanged for around 169 dollars or £114.) Figures are also published showing averages for many different sectors of the economy. In 1980, the highest paid workers were in coal-mining (298.9 rubles per month) and the lowest in the sewing industry (136 rubles). (Earnings in different industries have been detailed above in chapter 2.) In 1981, it was decreed that coal miners' wages be raised by up to 27 per cent.

These broad 'industrial' categories obviously mask differences between occupations. Matthews[126] has collected data (mainly from émigrés) on the earnings of party officials: he cites a figure of 600 rubles per month for the secretary of a Union Republic. Of the military elite, a Marshall of the USSR might receive 'up to 2,000 rubles' per month; top academics, such as a director of a research institute, earn a maximum of 700 rubles per month; the editor of a Republican newspaper 500 rubles. The 'basic salary' of a collective farm chairman would be about 180 rubles. No hard data are available for the very top jobs. It is said that a government minister might earn 1,500 rubles and a top party secretary 900 rubles. A composer in a good year might receive 8,000 rubles a month.

In addition to ruble money income, there are other payments for certain elites. These include foreign currency payments available for purchase of superior quality goods in foreign currency shops; other special shops and restaurants are provided for senior officials; special holidays and medical facilities are available to certain managerial and executive groups. Occupational groups have access to housing which favour the academic, political and industrial elites; access to cars is also given to people in high-level posts.[127] These groups undoubtedly have a higher standard of living than the masses. (On income from the black and grey economy, see above chapter 2). At the other end of the scale, a secondary schoolteacher might earn 140 rubles per month, a fork-lift operator 110 rubles, a taxi-driver 140 rubles, a doctor 100–130 rubles (data for mid-1970s).[128]

The perks and privileges of the managerial and political elites are obviously important facts. One must not, however, ignore the equally important point that the general tendency has been towards the reduction of income differentials. We must also bear in mind that among the working class, miners and others in heavy industry receive benefits in terms of better pensions, shorter working hours and superior welfare and holiday facilities. The average working week for adult manual workers in 1981 was 40.6 hours (it was 47.8 in 1955).[129]

The money income of agricultural workers is generally below that of industrial workers. In 1982, the average monthly income of a state farmer was 158 rubles.[130] To this, of course, must be added income from private plots – produce both consumed and sold – which is something of an unknown quantity, but it might increase income by 20 rubles which brings up the wage near to the average (177 rs) of workers and employees. Collective farm incomes have risen rapidly since the 1950s and by 1975 it has been estimated by Western specialists that *kolkhoz* family income was the same as that of a *sovkhoz* family.[131] Since July 1966, collective farmers have been paid at rates similar to those of state farmers. The collective farmer's income is made up of employment outside the farm and of the sale of his own produce, which has been estimated at 27 per cent of his income.[132] By 1981, collective farmers received an income of 122.1 rubles per month from the *kolkhoz,* compared to the average wage of workers in state farms of 152.6 rubles.[133]

Inter-society comparisons are extremely difficult to make. If we take into consideration individual unearned income in capitalist states, the income inequality in Soviet society is certainly less than in most Western states. However great the income of Soviet top dogs, it palls into insignificance compared to the very rich in the West. Paul McCartney, Britain's top earner, receives some £25 million a year – 8,840 times more than the average British wage in 1984. In the USA differentials are similar – Lenski reports that the maximum American income is 11,000 times greater than the minimum and 7,000 times larger than the average. Konstantin Simis has estimated that the top income in the USSR is 60 times the minimum wage. The highest Western calculation based on émigré data is of a comparative Soviet figure of 300 times and 100 times greater than the maximum and average income respectively. (These figures on the USSR include payments in kind.) The late Leonid Brezhnev is reported to have had a fleet of six powerful cars including a Rolls Royce and to have inhabited 'a whole floor' in 'a huge apartment building'. The life style of a Soviet political leader is modest, even frugal, compared to the Duke of Edinburgh or Prince Charles. The British royal family can relax privately in four palaces, four large private homes with 300 staff and can visit their subjects from their own royal yacht, royal train, three aeroplanes, three helicopters, a fleet of private cars and carriages and a choice of horses from several stables.[134]

As in the advanced Western states, the history of Soviet wage and salary rates reflect for the mass of income recipients the forces of demand and supply. With the growing maturity of the Soviet economy, differentials between manual and white-collar workers have shown a similar tendency as in the West – a growing equalization, an improvement in the income of unskilled manual workers at the expense of unskilled and semi-skilled clerical employees. The higher levels of literacy have made less scarce the skills of clerks, and the rise in the numbers of engineers and technicians has also increased their supply in relation to demand. In addition, though, the ideology of 'building communism' together with collective ownership also has an influence on making a lower Soviet income differential. As Wiles and Markowski have concluded, 'capitalism produces extremely rich people with a great deal of capital, and this is the most striking difference between [income distribution under communism and capitalism].'[135]

Social Status

Income is not necessarily correlated with social standing or a person's prestige in a society. Such status may be derived from the evaluation of a person's contribution to society, or to characteristics of a life style, or to types of consumption. As Weber put it: 'status honour is normally expressed by the fact that a specific *style of life* can be expected from all those who wish to belong to the circle ... '[136] Social status is an elusive concept to measure. People do not concur on the criteria of evaluation – occupation, education, external attributes (beauty), income, culture. Also, there is often disagreement on how any given occupation or cultural artefact should be ranked: some rate highly sportsmen and beauty queens, others defer to the scholar or the priest. In Western societies sociologists usually combine a heterogeneous number of measures: people's expressed preferences, years of schooling, an occupational index, and command or authority over other people. In the Soviet Union study of such 'ranking' is not carried out because, as noted above, ideologically the society is considered to be a community (*obshchnost'*) of mutually respected interests. Social 'status' of a hierarchical kind therefore must be inferred from other data. Research conducted in Leningrad illustrates how earnings are related to other factors – education, party membership and voluntary participation in social work. Some of the results of the survey are shown in table 5.8. The striking conclusion to be drawn from the table is the high positive correlation between the four factors: education, wages, party membership and voluntary work. This is shown on the intercorrelation matrix below.

SPEARMAN RANK CORRELATION MATRIX

	Education	Wages	Party Membership	Social work
Education	—	0.52	0.71	0.76
Wages	0.52	—	0.67	0.79
Party Membership	0.71	0.67	—	0.81
Social work	0.76	0.79	0.81	—

TABLE 5.8: SOME ASPECTS OF THE SOCIAL STRUCTURE OF LENINGRAD ENGINEERING WORKERS

Group of workers	Education (Years)	Wages Rubles (monthly)	Party/Komsomol membership (%)	Participation in social work (%)
1. Management (factory directors, shop superintendents)	13.6	172.9	60.8	84.2
2. Workers in highly qualified technical-scientific jobs (designers)	14.0	127.0	40.2	70.4
3. Qualified non-manual workers (technologists, book-keepers)	12.5	109.8	42.8	82.4
4. Highly qualified workers in jobs with mental and manual functions (tool setters)	8.8	129.0	37.6	79.2
5. Qualified workers of superior manual work (fitters, welders)	8.3	120.0	37.4	60.7
6. Qualified manual workers (machine-tool operators, press operators)	8.2	107.5	39.5	54.3
7. Non-manual workers of medium qualifications (inspection and office workers)	9.1	83.6	27.1	54.5
8. Unqualified manual workers	6.5	97.5	13.8	35.1

Source: Adapted from O.I. Shkaratan, 'Sotsial'naya struktura sovetskogo rabochego klassa', Voprosy filosofii, no. 1 (1967), p. 36.

From the data presented in table 5.8 we may make some inference about stratification. At one end of the table (Group 1) we see a group which is highly educated, has high income, very high party/Komsomol membership (60.8 per cent) and good participation in voluntary work. At the other end, the unqualified manual workers seem to constitute a relatively underprivileged group, having low incomes, a very short education (only 6.5 years), a small proportion of party or Komsomol members (only 13.8 per cent), and minimal participation in voluntary work (35.1 per cent). These data, with the positively correlated factors of education, wages, party membership and voluntary work, suggest a 'consistent' system of stratification.

Studies conducted in the West on the prestige given to different occupations show a high correlation between their ranking in the USSR and in other industrial countries. The correlation of matched occupations between the Soviet Union and other countries is highly positive: with Japan it was 0.74, Great Britain 0.83, New Zealand 0.83, United States 0.9 and Germany 0.9.[137] (A perfect match, of course, would be represented by 1.0.) Some notable differences, however, show up in Inkeles's and Rossi's research. The 'worker' was given a relatively higher ranking in the USSR than in USA, Great Britain and New Zealand; and engineers were also given a higher rating in the Soviet Union than in the USA. At the other extreme, farmers were all rated lower in the USSR than in the USA, Great Britain and New Zealand, and surprisingly scientists have less prestige than in the USA. While these findings are of interest, it must be remembered that they relate to the pre-Khrushchev period.

Further data explicitly on the 'prestige' of occupations are available from the study of aspirations of Soviet schoolchildren. Soviet writers insist that their studies do not show a social 'hierarchy' linked to social position, but only the 'preferability' of different occupations.[138] Table 5.9 shows the rankings of jobs on a five-point scale for six surveys. While these surveys, as reported, do not show a very large number of occupations (the unskilled are not represented), a number of general conclusions may safely be made. At the top of children's preferred jobs are those requiring higher educational qualifications – mathematicians, physicists, physicians. At the bottom are unskilled jobs in agriculture and service industries requiring little education.

Distinct 'styles of life' and forms of consumption of commodities are important aspects of status. Soviet studies, while not clearly demonstrating the boundaries between groups, point to some significant differences between them. Table 5.10 shows the different patterns of leisure activity of manual workers, 'specialists' and non-manuals. The cinema was universally the leisure activity put in first place. Study of the index numbers shows

TABLE 5.9: SCALE OF PRESTIGE OF OCCUPATIONS (ON A FIVE-POINT SCALE)

	Middle school leavers 1966	High school leavers (Arbiturienty) 1969	1971	Students 1969	Young workers 1969	Young specialists 1973
Doctor	4.67	4.63	4.58	4.69	4.74	4.53
Scientist	4.16	4.73	4.67	4.65	4.58	4.19
Creative intelligentsia	4.42	4.46	4.55	4.24	4.36	4.42
Lawyer	4.12	4.19	4.37	4.11	4.15	4.27
Engineer	4.52	4.05	4.12	4.30	4.29	3.93
Mathematician	4.24	4.18	4.23	3.90	3.92	—
Economist	3.84	3.83	3.98	3.76	3.82	3.45
Trader	4.15	3.68	3.76	3.79	4.09	3.54
Agricultural specialist	3.69	3.60	3.73	3.58	3.73	3.71
Specialist with animals (*Zootekhnik*)	3.59	3.39	3.51	3.40	3.60	—
Mechanical expert (*Mekhanizator*)	—	3.61	3.75	—	—	3.71
Driver	—	3.35	3.47	3.32	3.49	2.95
Building worker	—	3.31	3.49	3.25	3.95	2.73
Sales person	—	3.12	3.22	—	—	2.82
Fields crops expert (*Polevod*)	—	2.91	3.16	3.47	3.54	3.14

Source: M.Kh. Titma, *Vybor professii kak sotsial'naya problema*(1975), p. 144.

TABLE 5.10: PREFERENCE FOR DIFFERENT KINDS OF CULTURAL ACTIVITY BY SOCIAL GROUPS

	Workers		Specialists (skilled non-manuals)		Unskilled non-manual	
	Index	Rank	Index	Rank	Index	Rank
Cinema	1.00	1	1.00	1	1.00	1
Television	0.61	2	0.51	5	0.68	3
Literature	0.56	3	0.85	2	0.58	5
Popular music/jazz	0.54	4	0.47	6	0.50	7
Music	0.49	5	0.62	4	0.52	6
Circus	0.44	6	0.32	7	0.60	4
Theatre	0.59	7	0.78	3	0.80	2

Note: Based on 981 interviews in the Urals.
Source: Sotsial'naya struktura sotisalisticheskogo obshchestva v SSSR (1976), p. 158.

that the workers were less active in their leisure pursuits than the non-manuals (note the lower scores). In terms of the rankings one notes a distinct preference for theatre by non-manuals; popular music and jazz are ranked more highly by the workers than the other two groups and 'music' was liked more by the specialists. Another study of the audiences at the Chelyabinsk Philharmonic showed that manual workers made up 1.1 per cent of the concert goers, skilled engineering/technical workers 15.3 per cent, skilled non-manuals 31.7 per cent, unskilled non-manuals 2.1 per cent and school pupils 49.2 per cent.[139]

The life styles of the various elite groups (military, political, creative intelligentsia) have not been studied in the Soviet press. Mervyn Matthews[140] has assembled information from émigré reports showing the consumption patterns of the elites. He points out that they have preferential access to transport, housing and medical facilities and enjoy access to better quality consumer goods. They also have access to information not available to the masses, while sessions of Western films are held for specialists in the cultural field. The various elites have summer houses in clusters occupied by other members of their profession. In their life styles the various elites are

able to maintain and enjoy many traditional customs and remnants of pre-revolutionary life-styles which have not survived elsewhere . . . The interiors of their dwellings may be graced with icons, traditional ornaments or embroidery. Their entertaining may be lavish and based on expensive traditional fare – in the case of the Russians, sturgeon, cavier, smoked salmon, vodka, Georgian wines, Armenian cognac, etc. Some holiday patterns, like the use of the *dacha*, also link up with the leisured practices of the last century. The Soviet elite has come to resemble elites in other societies in its protection of cultural heritage.[141]

Social relations between groups involve assumptions about statuses. We have no good studies about the ways that people in different positions treat each other. Literature portrays some relationships but we cannot be sure how typical they are. Solzhenitsyn illustrates a party official discussing his son's marriage:

He was such a naive boy, he might be led up the garden path by some ordinary weaver girl from the textile factory. Well, perhaps not a weaver, there'd be nowhere for them to meet, they wouldn't frequent the same places . . . Look at Shendyapin's daughter, how she'd very nearly married a student in her year at teachers' training college. He was only a boy from the country and his mother was an ordinary collective farmer. Just imagine the Shendyapin's flat, their furniture and the influential people they had as guests and suddenly there's this old woman in a white headscarf sitting at their table, their daughter's mother-in-law, and she didn't even have a passport. Whatever next? Thank goodness they'd managed to discredit the fiancé politically and save their daughter.[142]

While the data available to us do not allow very firm conclusions to be drawn, it does seem likely that, despite the ways in which Soviet society is structurally different from Western industrial systems, 'there is a relatively invariable hierarchy of prestige associated with the industrial system, even when it is placed in the context of larger social systems which are otherwise differentiated in important respects.'[143] Treiman has concluded that prestige hierarchies in traditional, capitalist and socialist societies are similar in ranking of occupations.[144] Our study has indicated that the relatively lower rank given to 'farmers' in the USSR is partly a reflection of the different structure of agriculture and coincides not only with their lower political standing in the USSR, but also with the relatively unskilled work of the collective farmer. The higher status given to 'workers' in the USSR is quite important and shows the influence of political ideology in the social sphere.[145] What is particularly interesting to note in the Soviet case is not only the high status given to the worker, a value engendered by Marxist ideology, but also the high evaluation of professional employees – a factor shared with the West. What is absent in the USSR is a class of persons deriving their income and social position from money capital and ownership and ancient title, and this makes a considerable difference to the structure of the system of social stratification.

On the basis of the data discussed above, Western sociologists have attempted to draw up hierarchies of the major social groups based on a combination of factors – income, life style, patterns of social association and subjective group consciousness. On the basis of a comprehensive study of the available data, Connor defines four general social groups:

1 The *elite* or intelligentsia – encompassing both the political 'rulers' and the specialist creative intelligentsia
2 *Routine non-manuals* – the residual, non-elite white-collar strata
3 *Workers* – manuals outside agriculture, including artisans whether independent or co-operative
4 *Peasants* – manuals in agriculture, whether independent, collective, or wage workers on state agricultural enterprises[146]

This hierarchy seems to me to conflate several important groups into one category. There clearly is a difference between the political elite (particularly those occupying leadership roles in the party) and the creative intelligentsia. There are distinctions to be drawn between engineering/technical/lower managerial workers and manual workers as a whole. The term 'peasant', I have argued, is not appropriate for Soviet agricultural labourers. My own classification is the following:

1 Ruling political leadership
2 Superior creative, technical and academic intelligentsia

3 Engineering/technical/managerial personnel
4 Skilled non-manuals
5 Skilled manual workers
6 Unskilled non-manuals
7 Skilled agricultural workers/collective farmers
8 Unskilled manual workers
9 Unskilled agricultural workers/collective farmers

Social stratification is as much a feature of Soviet society as it is of American. There is an uneven distribution of income, occupations are differentially evaluated, forms of consumption are linked to social position, and various groups – though this has yet to be empirically established – develop a consciousness of their identity *vis-à-vis* other collectivities. There is a scale of evaluation of status linked to education and occupation not unlike that of other industrial societies. There are some differences: these are to do with the traditional sets of values, with the impact of Marxist ideology and with the priorities. determined by the political elites.

Social Mobility

The hierarchical arrangement of Soviet social strata raises the question of social mobility between them. How far are there distinct self-recruiting social layers, and how far are the top positions equally accessible to different social groups lower down the hierarchy?

A major characteristic of Russian and Soviet society since the mid-nineteenth century has been rapid and extensive economic growth. This has brought in its train changes in the occupational and social structure. Social mobility, therefore, is not merely a matter of 'swapping places' between generations, but has to do with structural changes effected by industrialization and the creation of new statuses. Very rapid industrialization, particularly between 1928 and 1939, provided a large number of skilled and executive jobs associated with the factory system. The changes in the broad occupational structure are illustrated by the official figures cited below (table 5.11). Between 1928 and 1939 the proportion of manual and non-manual families rose from 17.6 per cent to 50.2 per cent of the population, though these figures include, of course, workers on state farms.

Between 1928 and 1937 the numbers employed in industrial production increased by 268 per cent and between 1931 and 1961, the number of manual workers increased three-fold, that of engineers five-fold and other non-manual employees by 33 per cent.[147] In addition to the effects of industrialization, the purges depleted the higher ranks of the bureaucracy

TABLE 5.11: COMPOSITION OF SOVIET POPULATION BY BROAD GROUPS
1913 TO 1983

	1913	1928	1939	1959	1979	1983
Manual and non-manual workers	17.0	17.6	50.2	68.3	85.1	87.1
Of whom, manuals	—	12.4	33.7	50.2	60.0	61.2
Collective farmers and co-operative handicrafts persons	—	2.9	47.2	31.4	14.9	12.9
Independent peasants and handicrafts persons	66.7	74.9	2.6	0.3	0.0	0.0
Bourgeoisie	16.3	4.6	—	—	—	—
	100.0	100.0	100.0	100.0	100.0	100.0

Sources: Narkhoz v 1978g (1979), p. 9. *Narkhoz v 1982g* (1983) p. 7.

and provided extra opportunity for upward mobility, and the war, with the huge loss of older experienced manpower, also created greater possibilities for rapid social advance.

The table and figures cited illustrate the changes in the general composition of Soviet society since the revolution. They imply considerable upward social mobility, for the increase in the size of the intelligentsia and working class presumes recruitment from the peasantry, though this does not preclude a high rate of internal recruitment from within the intelligentsia itself. To discover the rates at which different social groups move from one status to another between generations would require a national study of mobility patterns. In the Soviet Union no such study has been attempted and we have to make do with investigations of émigrés which are biased and small-scale research done in the Soviet Union. Such work, though not comprehensive, helps to give a picture of social movement in the USSR. The results of a survey of Russian émigrés show that access to higher education and therefore to high status occupations was differentially related to social background. Inkeles has generalized this tendency by saying that 'as stratification has become institutionalised there has been a noticeable tendency for social mobility to decline and for the system to become less an open class structure.'[148] Those, he argues, who have legitimately acquired privilege in the system will seek to preserve it and pass it on to their children. In 1938, for instance, 47 per cent of the student body was made up of children with intelligentsia background.[149]

We may distinguish two major trends in mobility patterns in the USSR. First, until about the 1950s there was a massive inflow to the towns from the countryside; consequently the working class was formed largely from the peasantry and many of the urban manual workers became non-

TABLE 5.12: SOCIAL COMPOSITION OF YOUNG ENTRANTS OF THE WORKING
CLASS FROM DIFFERENT AREAS OF THE USSR

	Moscow %	Area Chelyabinsk %	Ufa %
From manual worker background	55.8	56.2	58.1
From collective farmer background	15.2	18.7	36.4
From unskilled non-manual background	19.6	16.2	1.8
From professional (*spetsialistov*) background	5.4	8.3	3.3
Others	4.0	0.6	0.4

Source: Sotsial'naya struktura razvitogo sotsialisticheskogo obshchestva v SSSR (1976), p. 183.

manuals. The non-manual strata suffered little downward mobility: sons and daughters largely entered non-manual statuses. There was then both a great deal of upward mobility and inheritance of non-manual positions. Second, since the late 1950s, the rate of economic growth has slowed. This has led to a reduction in the rate of formation of new occupational statuses. There has been a decrease in the rate of inflow from agriculture to industry and there has been a tendency for greater inheritance of their parents' status by both non-manual and manual sons and daughters.

By the mid-1970s, the manual working class was largely self-generating and included even a fair sprinkling of people from a non-manual background. This may be illustrated by those Soviet pieces of research conducted in the 1970s (see table 5.12). Some Soviet research points out that many manual worker fathers are content for their sons to follow in their footsteps. 'Their aspirations for their sons involve higher skill levels, cleaner work, intrastratum mobility rather than exit [from the working class] entirely.'[150] Study of the social background of students in higher educational institutions, however, indicates some upward mobility by the offspring of manual workers. Their share in educational institutions has increased over time. This is illustrated in table 5.13, which also points to the fact that a very high proportion of students hail from non-manual backgrounds. By the mid-1970s, under a quarter of the population was non-manual, but the data show that twice this proportion of students came from non-manual backgrounds. Alex Pravda has calculated the ratios of access of various social groups to full-time higher education (i.e. 'the relative weight of the social group in the student body divided by the group's weight in the population as a whole'). The 'disparity of access' is an index of the difference in opportunity of non-manuals over manuals; it is obtained by dividing the index of access for employee children by that of

TABLE 5.13: SOCIAL BACKGROUND OF STUDENTS IN HIGHER EDUCATIONAL
INSTITUTIONS (VARIOUS YEARS)

	USSR[1] 1965	Sverd-lovsk[2] 1968	Kazak-hstan[2] 1970	USSR[1] 1973	Sverd-lovsk[2] 1974	Kazak-hstan[2] 1974
Children of workers or workers	—	44.6	43.2	—	49.7	48.8
Children of workers	36.5	—	—	43.1	—	—
Children of collective farmers or collective farmers	—	4.9	16.5	—	5.2	9.8
Children of collective farmers	19.7	—	—	18.0	—	—
Children of non-manuals or non-manuals	—	50.5	40.3	—	45.5	41.4
Children of non-manuals	43.8	—	—	38.9	—	—

Sources: [1]Sotsial'noe edinstvo sovetskogo obshchestva (1980), p. 217.
[2]Sotsial'naya struktura razvitogo sotsialisticheskogo obshchestva v SSSR (1974), p. 191.

worker children. Thus an index of 1 gives parity of access for both groups, an index of greater than 1 shows relative advantage to children of non-manual strata. Pravda's calculations give the following statistics: 1960: 3.51 (for USSR, all students in full-time higher education); 1969–70: 3.69 (USSR, first year students); 1975–76: 2.84 (USSR, first year students). The difference is greater in the more prestigious institutions (in Moscow University it was 5.25 in 1973, in medical faculties in the RSFSR in 1978 it was 5.97).[151] There is then both upward mobility on the part of the working class and a positive tendency for the non-manuals' sons and daughters to 'inherit' a non-manual status.

A study by Shubkin in the 1960s showed how the very high aspirations for education (and by extension for a non-manual job) were fulfilled by the children of non-manual employees but not so much by the offspring of the manual workers. In Shubkin's survey, 93 per cent of the school leavers from an urban, skilled, non-manual background sought to continue to study – 82 per cent fulfilled their ambition; the relative figures for the rural, skilled, non-manuals were 76 per cent (aspirations) and 58 per cent (fulfilments), for manual workers in industry and building 83 per cent and 61 per cent, for manual workers in transport and communications 82 per cent and 45 per cent and for agricultural workers 76 per cent and 10 per cent.[152] (See also later studies cited below, chapter 8.)

Advancement to positions of authority in industry would probably be more open to children of manual workers than to those of other strata. In Shkaratan's survey of Leningrad workers, 54.2 per cent of factory chiefs were of manual worker and collective farm family background.[153] Most seem to have worked their way up through the factory. This evidence is corroborated by S.T. Guryanov, who found that, of a thousand workers in a Moscow electrical engineering factory who started work as semi-skilled operators, 14 were promoted after ten years experience to engineer or technical status.[154] E.C. Brown, on a visit to 19 factories, found that at least fourteen of the factory directors had begun as manual workers. 'In their family origin and in part their work experience most of these directors and their chief engineers and other technical and administrative people had a common bond with workers and union officers.'[155]

However, there can be no doubt that in the USSR the social position of parents plays a most important role in determining the education and the subsequent social standing of children. It is not wished to imply that the Soviet regime intentionally restricts mobility. After 1956, tuition fees were abolished in education, though during the Second World War access to higher education (and the top three classes of secondary schools) was made conditional, in most cases, on the payment of fees. In recent years children of lower educational strata (manual workers and collective farm peasantry) have been given special consideration for admission to *vuzy* (higher educational institutions). (See below, chapter 8.)

In the West it is well known that the accessibility of different types of education varies for social groups. Donald Treiman[156] has attempted to generalize the relationship between stratification and industrialization in a number of hypotheses. He has argued the following:

1 that with industrialization, fathers' occupational status becomes less directly influential in determining sons' occupation;
2 that the more industrialized a society, the greater the direct influence of educational attainment on occupational status;
3 that the greater the level of industrialization, the higher the rate of 'exchange' mobility (i.e. 'swopping places' between the children of higher and lower status parents).

As far as our knowledge of the Soviet Union is concerned, little qualification of these hypotheses is necessary. The first hypothesis needs to be rephrased, in order to emphasized that, with industrialization, parental status in the USSR becomes positively more *indirect* in influencing children's occupations. The second hypothesis seems to be valid: as the level of industrialization has increased, educational attainment has been of increasing and direct influence on occupational status. The third hypothesis needs some amendment. It is true that the rate of *internal* stratum recruitment and upward movement increases with industrialization. But there has been little 'exchange' mobility. That is to say: in relation to their parents' social status, children tend to move up the ladder, and very few to the present have moved down. Treiman hypothesizes that there is greater exchange between status positions, with similar movements up and down.

Social stratification based on the division of labour is a common characteristic of all modern urban industrial societies. Exchange mobility is limited because those with scarce skills and specialist training are able, within their family sphere, to perpetuate the advantages which these skills and training give them. The strengthening of the Soviet family has encouraged this tendency, though the family's right to transmit a claim on the appropriation of the social product does not pertain as in the West. The family reproduces human capital. On the other hand, upward social mobility has probably been greater in Soviet Russia than in contemporary Western societies. This upward mobility may only partially be accounted for by 'communist' values. The rapid industrialization process entailed the recruitment, training and upward mobility of lower strata.

Socialism and Inequality

What then are the implications of Soviet experience for the more general questions raised in this book? First, the evidence shows that the USSR is not, and has never been at any time in its history, a society without hierarchically arranged social strata: social inequality is a universal social phenomenon. Second, the forms of social stratification in the USSR differ from those of Western liberal societies. There is no property-owning class; large-scale industrial societies, therefore, can grow and function without the *private* accumulation of property and the inequalities to which it gives rise. This is now an obvious, though most important, conclusion to be drawn from Soviet experience. Third, the functionalists' view that social inequality is necessary – (a) to induce individuals into positions requiring special skills and abilities; (b) to reward them differentially so that their tasks may be efficiently carried out – has been substantiated in Soviet conditions. However, the differentials in terms of economic rewards have been lower in the USSR than under the capitalist form of development. Fourth, political leadership plays an important role in *defining* the inequalities, or the system of positions in which one is rewarded more than in another. In the USSR, engineers, academicians and coal miners get higher pay than physicians. The recruitment of doctors does not depend on a high reward 'commensurate with the sacrifice' necessary to undertake medical studies.[157] This reflects the political priorities of a society, which become embodied in an ideology that justifies a certain income inequality. Fifth, while the political authorities may influence certain kinds of privilege, particularly income and education, they are subject to external social constraints. Some elements of a subjective status hierarchy transcend societies: here control over life itself, exercised by doctors, gives honour; those with technical qualifications in industrial societies and those who transmit knowledge similarly have a high status ranking. Politically too the cultural and technical intelligentsia, while not forming a new 'ruling class', is able to exact material privileges from the political leadership. Sixth, political values may affect the status of occupations: 'the worker' in Soviet society is more highly rated than in liberal-democratic ones. Perhaps more important, public ownership of wealth and the ideology of 'building communism' has had an influence in limiting the range of inequality between the richest and poorest.

To conclude, we may say that state ownership of the means of production and the absence of an antagonistic ascendant class in state socialist society ensures its basic character as a workers' state; as noted in chapter 3 above, its chief forms of *production* are socialist. Western capitalist societies have quite a different basis and dynamic: they are characterized by social classes which have rights over the disposal of property and of income from property; the capital market and the making of profit in the context of a more or less regulated economy are essential dynamics of modern capitalism. Social inequality of one kind or another seems to be inevitable as long as societies are characterized by a division of labour, and as long as the family plays an important role in the maintenance of children. Occupations differentiate the roles of individuals, and, as long as these are specific, intellectual or creative occupations will always be more highly valued by members of society because they are inherently more agreeable; they also promote a way of life culturally distinct from those occupied in routine manual jobs. A necessary condition of a truly classless society is, as Marx has pointed out, the absence of the division of labour. The family, even if its legal rights over property are abolished, differentially socializes children; by doing so, it makes the inculcation of universal social mores difficult. It is a source of cultural capital and makes some children more capable of benefiting from education than others. Thereby inequality is perpetuated. Under the conditions of industrial production known to us, both in state socialist and in capitalist societies, the division of labour is specialized and the family is as persistent as it ever has been.[158]

NOTES

1 Kingsley Davis, *Human Society* (1948), p. 367.
2 'Critique of Gotha Program', in K. Marx and F. Engels, *Selected Works* (1950), vol. 2, p. 23.
3 In addition, the clergy and members of the royal family had restricted political rights.
4 V.I. Lenin, 'The Immediate Tasks of the Soviet Government', *Collected Works* (1965), vol. 27, pp. 249, 581n.
5 See A. Bergson, *The Structure of Soviet Wages* (1954), p. 190.
6 Ibid., p. 182.
7 Ibid., p. 185. See also *Trud i zarabotnaya plata v SSSR* (1968), p. 323.
8 L. Kostin, *Wages in the USSR* (1960), p. 16.
9 *The Structure of Soviet Wages* (1954), p. 92. In the sphere of education, workers and peasants were given preference for admission to higher educational institutions. At the same time laws weakening the family were passed (see above chapter 4).
10 J.V. Stalin, 'Talk with Emil Ludwig', *Collected Works,* (1955) vol. 13, p. 120.
11 Ibid., pp. 120–1.
12 See comparison computed by Bergson, *The Structure of of Soviet Wages*, pp. 101, 118.
13 See ibid., pp. 200–1, 203–4.
14 M. Matthews, *Privilege in the Soviet Union* (1978), p. 122.
15 Robert W. Hodge *et al.,* 'A Comparative Study of Occupational Prestige', in R. Bendix and S.M. Lipset, *Class, Status and Power* (1967), p. 320.
16 L. Kostin, *Wages in the USSR* (1960), p. 16.
17 Bergson, *The Structure of Soviet Wages*, p. 208.
18 S. Wheatcroft, 'On Assessing the Size of Forced Concentration Camp Labour in the Soviet Union, 1929–56', *Soviet Studies*, vol. 33, no. 2 (1981), p. 286.
19 W. Wesolowski, *Classes, Strata and Power* (1979).
20 See Roy Jenkins, 'Equality', in *New Fabian Essays* (1952), p. 69. See also S. Lukes, 'Socialism and Equality', in L. Kolakowski and S. Hampshire (eds), *The Socialist Idea* (1974).
21 G. Glezerman, 'Sotsial'naya struktura sotsialisticheskogo obshchestva', *Kommunist*, no. 13 (1968). V.I. Lenin, *Selected Works*, vol. 3, p. 248. See translation in *Soviet News*, 12 Nov. 1968.
22 P.G. Pod'yachich, *Naselenie SSSR* (1961), p. 154.
23 *Narkhoz v 1982 g.* (1983), p. 7.
24 S. Ossowski, *Class Structure in the Social Consciousness* (1963), pp. 112–3.

25 For a discussion of Soviet views, see M. Yanowitch, *Social and Economic Inequality in the Soviet Union* (1977), ch. 1. Alex Pravda, 'Is There a Soviet Working Class?', *Problems of Communism*, vol. 31, no. 6 (Nov.–Dec. 1982), pp. 1–24. These points are developed further below.

26 On historical evolution of the term, see A. Gella (ed.), *The Intelligentsia and the Intellectuals* (1976), ch. 1.

27 F. Konstantinov, 'Sovetskaya intelligentsiya', *Kommunist*, no. 15 (1959), p. 50.

28 L.G. Churchward, *The Soviet Intelligentsia* (1973), p. 93.

29 M. Matthews, 'Top Incomes in the USSR', *Survey* (Summer 1975) no. 3, p. 13.

30 *SSSR v tsifrakh v 1982 g* (1983), p. 163, *Narkhoz 1922–82* (1982), pp. 42, 399.

31 A. Gouldner, *The Future of Intellectuals and the Rise of the New Class* (1979). G. Konrad and I. Szelenyi, *The Intellectuals on the Road to Class Power* (1979).

32 Daniel Bell, *The Coming of Post-Industrial Society* (1974). Bell's work relates to Western capitalist society, though it is applicable also to socialist states.

33 Konrad and Szelenzyi, *The Intellectuals on the Road to Class Power* (1979), p. 44.

34 Ibid., p. 148.

35 See Churchward, *The Soviet Intelligentsia* (1973), p. 112

36 See discussion in A. Pravda, 'Is There a Soviet Working Class?' (1982), pp. 1–3.

37 *Narkhoz 1922–82* (1982), p. 402.

38 *SSSR v tsifrakh v 1982g* (1983), p. 161.

39 See D.S. Lane and F. O'Dell, *The Soviet Industrial Worker: Social Class, Education and Control* (1978), pp. 10–14.

40 *Vestnik statistiki*, no. 4 (1983), p. 60.

41 L.S. Blyakhman, A.G. Zdravomyslov and O.I. Shkaratan, *Dvizhenie rabochey sily na promyshlennykh predpriyatiyakh* (1965), p. 19.

42 *Vestnik statistiki*, no. 4 (1983), p. 66.

43 L.A. Gordon and A.K. Nazimova 'The Productive Potential of the Soviet Working Class: Tendencies and Problems of Development', *Soviet Sociology*, vol. 19, no. 4 (1981) p. 50.

44 *Vestnik statistiki*, no. 8 (1981), pp. 78–9.

45 For detailed figures see: D. Lane and F. O'Dell, *The Soviet Industrial Worker* (1978), pp. 80–2.

46 Alex Pravda, 'Is There a Soviet Working Class?', p. 5.

47 *Vestnik statistiki*, no. 6 (1983), p. 60.

48 N.P. Konstantinova, O.V. Stakanova and O.I. Shkaratan, 'Changes in the Social Character of Workers under Developed Socialism'. *Soviet Sociology*, vol. 17, no. 4, 1979, pp. 26–7.

49 O.I. Shkaratan, 'Sotsial'naya struktura sovetskogo rabochego klassa', *Voprosy filosofii*, no. 1 (1967), p. 36.

50 'KPSS v tsifrakh', *Partiynaya zhizn'*, no. 15 (August 1983), p. 18.

51 D.S. Lane and F.O. O'Dell, *The Soviet Industrial Worker...* (1978), p. 19.

52 S. White, 'USSR': Autocracy and Industrialism', in A. Brown and J. Gray,

Political Culture and Political Change in Communist States, (1977), p. 43.
53 V.I. Mukhachev and V.S. Borovik, *Rabochi klass i upravenie proizvodstvom* (1975), pp. 33-4.
54 J. Bielasiak, 'Workers and Mass Participation in "Socialist Democracy"', in J.F. Triska and C. Gati, *Blue-Collar Workers in Eastern Europe* (1981), pp. 100-1.
55 R. Blauner, *Alienation and Freedom* (1964).
56 A.G. Zdravomyslov, V.P. Rozhin and V.A. Yadov (eds), *Chelovek i ego rabota* (1967). Translated by S.P. Dunn, *Man and his Work: A Sociological Study* (1970).
57 D. Nelson, 'Romania: Participatory Dynamics in "Developed Socialism"', in Triska and Gati, *Blue Collar Workers in Eastern Europe* (1981) p. 250. Nelson is here generalization about workers' participation.
58 D. Lockwood, 'Sources in Variation in Working Class Images of Society', in M. Blumer (ed.) *Working Class Images of Society* (1975).
59 Ibid., p. 18.
60 A. Nove, 'Is There a Ruling Class in the USSR?', *Soviet Studies*, vol. 27, no. 4, (1975), p. 624.
61 H. Smith, *The Russians* (1976, Sphere Books), p. 312-3.
62 Ibid., pp. 314-7.
63 See Lane and O'Dell, *The Soviet Industrial Worker*, pp. 71-3.
64 M. Rakovski, *Towards an Eastern European Marxism* (1978), p. 47.
65 M. Holubenko, 'The Soviet Working Class', *Critique*, no. 4, 1975, p.8.
66 V. Treml, 'Death from Alcohol Poisoning in the USSR'. *Soviet Studies*, vol. 34, no. 4, (1982), p. 487.
67 W.D. Connor, *Deviance in Soviet Society: Crime, Delinquency and Alcoholism* (1972), p. 39.
68 Yu.N. Tundykov, 'Znanie kak predposylka formirovaniya nravstvennoy lichnosti', *Dukhovnoe razvitie lichnosti* (Sverdlovsk: 1967), p. 47.
69 G.G. Zaigraev, 'O nekotorykh osobennostyakh profilaktiki p'yanstva,' *Sotsiologicheskie issledovaniya*, No. 4, (1983), pp. 97, 102.
On the cultural importance of alcoholic beverages, see B. Kerblay, *Modern Soviet Society*, (1983) pp. 290-1
70 A. Pravda, 'Some Problems of the Soviet Industrial Worker', in Kahan and Ruble, (eds). *Industrial Labour in the USSR*. p. 349.
71 Harbermas, J. *Legitimation Crisis* (1976), p. 77.
72 Lockwood, *'Sources in Variation...'*, p. 19.
73 Ibid., pp. 19-23.
74 M. Holubenko, 'The Soviet Working Class', *Critique* no. 4 (Spring 1975), p. 14.
75 E.C. Brown, *Soviet Trade Unions and Labor Relations* (1966); M. McAuley, *Labour Disputes in Soviet Russia 1957-65* (1969), p. 251; B. Ruble, 'Factory Unions and Workers' Rights', in A. Kahan and B. Ruble, *Industrial Labor in the USSR* (1979); and A. Pravda, 'Spontaneous Workers' Activities in the Soviet Union', in Kahan and Ruble, ibid.
76 McAuley, ibid.

77 See Lane and O'Dell, *Soviet Industrial Workers*, op. cit. and B.G. Madison, 'Trade Unions and Social Welfare', in Kahan and Ruble, *Industrial Labor in the USSR*, pp. 94–6.
78 J.H. Westergaard, 'Radical Class Consciousness: a Comment', in M. Bulmer (ed.), *Working Class Images of Society* (1975), pp. 255–6.
79 *The Russians* (1976), p. 305.
80 W.D. Connor, 'Workers and Power', in Triska and Gati, *Blue-Collar Workers in Eastern Europe* (1981), p. 169.
81 A. Pravda, 'Political Attitudes and Activity' in Triska and Gati, ibid., p. 49.
82 R. McKenzie & A. Silver, *Angels in Marble: Working-Class Conservatives in Urban England* (1968).
83 W. Teckenberg, 'The Social Structures of the Soviet Working Class', *International Journal of Sociology*, vol. XI, no. 4 (1981–82), p. 145.
84 Ibid., p. 140.
85 W.D. Connor, 'Workers, Politics and Class Consciousness', p. 317.
86 See J.B.de Weydenthall, 'Poland: Workers and Politics', in Triska and Gati, *Blue-Collar Workers in Eastern Europe*, pp. 193–4.
87 This is an element in the process of corporatist intermediation, discussed in *State and Politics in the USSR*, Chapter 8.
88 V.I. Staroverov, *Sotsial'naya' struktura sel'skogo naseleniya SSSR na etape razvitogo sotsializma* (1978), p. 7. *Narkhoz 1922–1982*, p. 417.
89 J. Stalin, 'Ekonomicheskie problemy sotsializma' (1952), *Sochineniya*, vol. 16 (1967), p. 205.
90 Basile Kerblay, 'The Russian Peasant', *St. Antony's Papers*, no. 19 (1969), p. 15. Since this piece was written, collective farmers are paid regular wages at the same rates as sovkhozniki.
91 *Narkhoz 1922–82*, p. 230. A. Nove, 'Soviet Agriculture: New Data', *Soviet Studies*, vol. 34, no. 1 (1982), p. 118.
92 For example, P.I. Simush, *Sotsial'ny portret sovetskogo krest'yanstva* (1976).
93 See I. Hill, 'The End of the Russian Peasantry?' *Soviet Studies*, vol. 27 (1975), pp. 109–27.
94 *Sotsial'naya struktura razvitogo sotsialisticheskogo obshchestva v SSSR* (1976), p. 124. See also P.I. Simush, *Sotsial'ny portret sovetskogo krest'yanstva* (1976), pp. 145–6.
95 *Narkhoz 1922–1982*, p. 449.
96 *Sotsial'naya struktura razvitogo sotsialisticheskogo obshchestva v SSSR* (1976), p. 142.
97 I. Hill, 'The End of the Russian Peasantry?', p. 120.
98 *Vestnik statistiki*, no. 6 (1981), p. 79.
99 'KPSS v tsifrakh', *Partiynaya zhizn'*, no. 15 (1983), p. 21.
100 'KPSS v tsifrakh', *Partiynaya zhizn'*, no. 14 (1981), p. 15.
101 K. Marx and F. Engels, *Selected Works*, vol. 2 (1968), p. 510.
102 A. McAuley, *Women's Work and Wages in the Soviet Union* (1981), p. 21.
103 *SSSR v tsifrakh v 1982g* (1983), p. 173.
104 A.E. Kotliar and S. Ya Turchaninova, 'The Educational and Occupational

Skill Level of Industrial Workers', in *Problems of Economics*, vol. 24 (1981), pp. 71–3.
105 *Vestnik statistiki*, no. 1 (1982), p. 72.
106 Kotliar and Turchaninova, 'The Educational and Occupational Skill Level of Industrial Workers'.
107 M. Ya. Sonin, 'Aktualnye sotsialno-ekonomicheskie problemy zanyatosti zhenshchin', in A.Z. Maikov, *Problemy ratsionalnogo izpolzovania trudovykh resursov* (1973), pp. 352–78. Cited in McAuley, *Women's Work and Wages in the Soviet Union*, p. 81.
108 *Vestnik statistiki*, no. 1, (1982) pp. 71, 73.
109 McAuley, *Women's Work and Wages in the Soviet Union*, pp. 87–89, and *Narkhoz 1922–1982*, pp. 317, 319. Calculations added.
110 *Vestnik statistiki*, no. 1 (1982) p. 68. *Pravda*, 7 March 1984
111 S. Firestone, *The Dialectics of Sex* (1972), p. 13.
112 G. Lapidus, *Women in Soviet Society* (1978), p. 335.
113 Ibid., p. 337.
114 Ibid., p. 345.
115 See M. Tumin, 'On Equality', *American Sociological Review*, vol. 28 (1963).
116 In 1982, they came to 27.9 per cent: total (average) income being 246 rubles per month, payments in kind coming to 69 rubles, *SSSR v tsifrakh v 1982g* (1983), p. 181.
117 Data cited in: *Klassy, sotsial'nye sloi i gruppy v SSSR* (1968), p. 53.
118 Data cited in J.G. Chapman 'Recent Trends in the Soviet Industrial Wage Structure', in A.Kahan and B. Ruble, *Industrial Labor in the USSR* (1979), p. 155.
119 J. Chapman, ibid., p. 157.
120 *Problemy raspredeleniya i rost narodnogo blagosostoyaniya* (1979), p. 121, *Vestnik statistiki*, no. 5 (1983), p. 78.
121 J. Chapman, 'Recent Trends ...', p. 175.
122 1982 figure calculated on basis of data in *Vestnik statistiki*, no. 5 (1982), pp. 73, 78.
123 D.W. Bronson and B.S. Severin, 'Soviet Consumer Welfare: The Brezhnev Era', in Joint Economic Committee US Congress, *Soviet Economic Prospects for the Seventies* (1973), p. 379; A. Nove, *The Soviet Economic System* (1977), p. 209.
124 See M. Ellman, 'A Note on the Distribution of Earnings in the USSR under Brezhnev', *Slavic Review*, vol. 39, no. 4 (1980), p. 670.
125 *Vestnik statistiki*, no. 5 (1983), p. 78.
126 M. Matthews, *Privilege in the Soviet Union* (1978).
127 Ibid., Hendrick Smith, *The Russians* (1976), chapter 1.
128 Figures from émigré reports.
129 *Vestnik statistiki*, no. 4 (1983), p. 65.
130 *SSSR v tsifrakh v 1982g*, p. 171.
131 K.E. Wädekin, 'Income Distribution in Soviet Agriculture', *Soviet Studies*, vol. 27, no. 1 (1975), p. 11.

132 Ibid., p. 6.
133 *Narkhoz 1922–82* (1982), pp. 285, 405.
134 Gerhard E. Lenski, *Power and Privilege* (1966), pp. 312–13. 'The Rich'. *New Society*, 6 October, 1983. Konstantin Simis, *USSR: Secrets of a Corrupt Society* (1982) pp. 24–5.
135 P. Wiles and S. Markowski, 'Income Distribution under Communism and Capitalism', *Soviet Studies*, vol. 22 (1971), p. 344. See also A. McAuley, 'The Distribution of Earnings and Incomes in the Soviet Union', *Soviet Studies*, vol. 29 (1977), p. 234.
136 R. Bendix, *Max Weber: An Intellectual Portrait* (1960), pp. 105–6.
137 Soviet data were derived from interviews with émigrés. A. Inkeles and P.H. Rossi, 'National Comparisons of Occupations Prestige', *American Journal of Sociology*, January 1956, no. 61 (4), p. 333.
138 M.Kh. Titma, *Vybor professii kak sotsial'naya problema* (1975), p. 142.
139 *Sotsial'naya struktura razvitogo sotsialisticheskogo obshchestva v SSSR* (1976), p. 159.
140 *Privilege in the Soviet Union* (1978).
141 Ibid., p. 49.
142 Solzhenitsyn, *Cancer Ward*, 1968, pp. 212–3. Internal passports were not then generally issued to peasants; their occupational and geographical mobility was thereby restricted.
143 Inkeles and Rossi, '*National Comparisons . . .* ',p. 339. See also the extension of this work by Robert W. Hodge *et al.*, 'A Comparative Study of Occupational Prestige', in R. Bendix and S.M. Lipset, *Class, Status and Power* (1967), 2nd edn.
144 D.J. Treiman, *Occupational Prestige in Comparative Perspective* (1977).
145 It is relevant here to point out that a study in Poland explicitly using the methods of Inkeles and Rossi shows a positive correlation of the rankings of occupational prestige hierarchies between Warsaw and USA to be 0.884, Warsaw/England 0.862, Warsaw/West Germany 0.879. Adam Sarapata, 'Stratification and Social Mobility', in *Empirical Sociology in Poland* (1966), p. 41. Skilled workers are rated higher and white collar workers lower in Poland than in advanced Western societies (ibid., p. 42).
146 W.D. Connor, *Socialism, Politics and Equality . . .* (1979), p. 90.
147 See V.S. Semenov, 'Ob izmenenii intelligentsii i sluzhashchikh v protesse razvernutogo stroitel'stva kommunizma', *Sotsiologiya v SSSR*, vol. 1, 1965, p. 422. A.G. Rashin, 'Dinamika promyshlennyakh kadrov SSSR za 1917–58 gg', *Izmeneniya v chislennosti i sostave sovetskogo rabochego klassa* (1961), p. 29.
148 A. Inkeles, 'Social Stratification and Mobility in the Soviet Union 1940–1950', *American Sociological Review*, vol. 15 (1950), reprinted in A. Inkeles and K. Geiger, *Soviet Society* (1961), p. 571.
149 *Kul'turnoe stroitel'stvo SSSR* (1940), p. 114. Cited by A. Inkeles, '*Social Stratification and Mobility . . .* ', p. 572.
150 L.A. Margolin, cited by W.D. Connor, *Socialism, Politics and Equality . . .* , p. 188. See also A. Pravda, 'Is There a Soviet Working Class?', *Problems of Communism*, vol. 31, no. 6, Nov.–Dec. 1982, p. 17.

151 A. Pravda, ibid., p. 13.
152 V.N. Shubkin, 'Molodezh' vstupaet v zhizn'; *Voprosy filosofii*, no. 5 (1965), p. 65.
153 *Problemy sotsial'noy struktury rabochego klassa SSSR* (1970), p. 39.
154 'Vertical mobility of employees in an enterprise', in G.V. Osipov, *Industry and Labour in the USSR* (1966), p. 126.
155 E.C. Brown, *Soviet Trade Unions and Labor Relations* (1966), p. 175.
156 D. Treiman, 'Industrialisation and Social Stratification', *Sociological Inquiry*, no. 40 (Spring 1970).
157 Kingsley Davis, *Human Society* (1948), p. 369.
158 My thanks to Christel Lane for critical comments on an early draft of this chapter.

6
NATIONALITIES AND ETHNIC RELATIONS

Social stratification is fundamentally concerned with hierarchy or inequality in society. But it is not the only or necessarily the most important basis for group differentiation. Nationality, ethnicity and religion are forms of group consciousness which may divide a society. They may transcend class and status boundaries, though they may also reinforce them. Nationality is a socio-cultural phenomenon; it involves a sense of social unity being given by a common language, history, and literature. Religion is a system of values in which believers are united in their relationship to, and belief in, something sacred. Ethnicity comprises a wide range of traits including religious and linguistic characteristics, distinctive skin pigmentation and geographical origin of the individual or his forebears.[1] Both nationality and religion are factors in the Soviet social structure. Today, the USSR is made up of over a hundred different national, tribal or linguistic groups. Great Russians constitute over half of the population (see table 6.1).

In general parlance a 'nation' is usually thought to be a large grouping of people united on the basis of a common culture. A nation is not always coterminous with a state or government; the Polish nation, for instance, has in the past been divided between several states. A state or government is a political unit, whereas a nation is a cultural community, having a common language, often a distinct religion, a sense of its own history and the consciousness of a common destiny. The Soviet conception of nationality has been influenced by Stalin's definition of a nation as 'a historically constituted, stable community of people, formed on the basis of a common language, territory, economic life, and psychological make-up manifested in common culture'.[2]

Marxism and the National Question

The notion of nationality does not rest easily with the Marxist concept of class. Under conditions of socialism in which the proletariat is the ruling class and in which class contradictions have been abolished, class and nationality may be congruent: class providing the political basis of rule, and nationality, cultural values. Historically, however, the concept of nationality has developed with the emergence of the bourgeoisie for whom it provided an ideology.

The concept of 'nation' engendered by the French Revolution involved the people or citizens of France as the repository of political power as opposed to the ousted monarchy. In Marxist analysis, the 1789 revolution only ensured the political supremacy of the bourgeoisie, for the workers had no share in the political control of the nation and therefore had no 'nation'. The struggle of the proletariat was not simply a class struggle against the bourgeoisie, but was also a struggle for the rights which the bourgeoisie proclaimed belonged to all. Therefore, a people's national liberation movement against the national bourgeoisie was an important stage in the class struggle.

Though not in substance, yet in form, the struggle of the proletariat with the bourgeoisie is at first a national struggle. The proletariat of each country must...first of all settle matters with its bourgeoisie. The working men have no country. We cannot take from them what they have not got. Since the proletariat must first of all acquire supremacy, must rise to be the leading class of the nation, must constitute itself *the* nation it is, so far, itself national, though not in the bourgeois sense of the word.[3]

As nationalism was dependent on economic formations, it follows that, as economic structures change, so does the nature of national consciousness. Marx observed that, with the growth of the world market and uniform production relations, differences between national cultures would decline.

National differences and antagonisms between peoples are daily more and more vanishing, owing to the development of the bourgeoisie, to freedom of commerce, to the world market, to uniformity in the mode of production and in the conditions of life corresponding thereto...
In proportion, as the exploitation of one individual by another is put to an end, the exploitation of one nation by another will also be put to an end. In proportion, as the antagonism between classes within the nation vanishes, the hostility of one nation to another will come to an end.[4]

Economic development leads to large economic and political units. Therefore the claims for independence of essentially rural national minorities (such as the Danes in Schleswig) were regarded by Engels as reactionary: the German right to the duchies was the 'right of civilisation against barbarism, of progress against stagnation'.[5]

Nationalism of the bourgeois era, therefore, according to the above extract from Marx, would be transformed into the internationalism of the socialist world. However, it is possible to interpret the evolution of society as involving the abolition of national antagonism while encouraging cultural diversity. Marxists have differed in their attitude to national cultural values, some holding that under socialism they would flourish, others believing that, with the development of internationalism, they would die a natural death. In the Soviet Union today a controversy rages between those supporting the assimilation of nations into one Soviet culture and others who stress the enduring nature of national sentiment and champion the cultural and political rights of minority nations.[6]

Nationalism has been an underlying tension, rather than a major political problem internal to Western European states. Ethnic identity has caused friction in Belgium, Britain, the border areas of Germany, Italy and Spain. In Western Europe and North America, generally, the political order (the state) has coincided with national and ethnic boundaries (Canada, Belgium, Switzerland are notable exceptions). In Eastern Europe and especially Russia before 1917, the national question was a major political issue. Nation and state generally did not coincide: Russia itself was made up of many national groups, though dominated by the Russian-speaking, Orthodox Great Russians.

The Bolsheviks on the National Question

The national question raised itself in an acute form over the formation of a Russian social-democratic* political party. Controversy raged over whether, after the bourgeois-democratic revolution, the Russian Empire should be balkanized (i.e. split into national units) or remain a single state. Advocates of the former asserted the rights of minority nationalities to form their own social-democratic parties. Lenin and the Bolsheviks supported the view that the class struggle was indivisible and that, therefore, the proletariat would weaken itself in the class struggle by forming separate national parties. The Bund (the Jewish Social-Democratic Party in Russia and Poland), and socialist parties from the Baltic and Caucasus sought the exclusive right to represent the proletariat from their respective areas. Lenin and the Bolsheviks opposed this.

But Lenin conceded that a nationality should have the right to secede. The party programme adopted in 1903 declared 'the right of self-determination for all nations comprising the state' (Para. 9).[7] Party policy also gave the right to national minorities of education in their own

---

* 'Social-democratic' here is a term referring to Marxist and non-Marxist socialists. There was no differentiation between social democrats and communists until after 1917.

language and put native languages on equal terms with the main government language in all public affairs.

If one distinguishes between the bourgeois and socialist revolutions, some of the confusion over different statements by Lenin will be resolved. National independence had been associated with the bourgeois democratic revolution. Therefore, in support of it, the social democrats had to recognize the right to secede. Otherwise, to deny it might sustain a feudal autocracy against a revolutionary democratic 'national' movement. For example, the fight for Finnish national independence was a struggle by the Finnish bourgeoisie against the Russian autocracy: such a *right* to independence, therefore, should not be opposed.[8]

But a right to secede did not imply favouring a balkanized form of independent states under socialism. For economic and political reasons, large units were preferable to small ones. Lenin likened the case of self-dermination to divorce, which if granted would in some cases (but not necessarily all) strengthen family ties and the position of women. 'To accuse those who support freedom of self-determination, i.e. freedom to secede, of encouraging separatism, is as foolish and hypocritical as accusing those who advocate freedom of divorce of encouraging the destruction of family ties.'[9] Indeed, if secession should be against the interests of the proletariat, then it had to be opposed.

The demand for a 'yes' or 'no' reply to the question of secession in the case of every nation may seem a very 'practical' one. In reality, it is absurd; it is metaphysical in theory, while in practice it leads to subordinating the proletariat to the bourgeoisie's policy. The bourgeoisie always places its national demands in the forefront, and does so in categorical fashion. With the proletariat, however, these demands are subordinated to the interests of the class struggle. Theoretically, you cannot say in advance whether the bourgeois-democratic revolution will end in a given nation seceding from another nation, or in its equality with the latter; *in either case,* the important thing for the proletariat is to ensure the development of its class. For the bourgeoisie it is important to hamper this development by pushing the aims of its 'own' nation before those of proletariat. That is why the proletariat confines itself, so to speak, to the negative demand for recognition of the *right* to self-determination, without giving guarantees to any nation, and without undertaking to give *anything at the expense* of another nation.[10]

The national problem was essentially a short-term one. In the long-run, with the triumph of socialism, national boundaries would be destroyed and people would be united on a class basis. Under socialism, national autonomy would gradually be replaced by a measure of regional autonomy giving to local governments executive control in their area. This is how Stalin put it:

The advantage of regional autonomy consists ... in the fact that it does not deal with a fiction bereft of territory but with a definite population inhabiting a definite territory. Next it does not divide people according to nations, it does not strengthen national barriers; on the contrary, it breaks down these barriers and unites the population in such a manner as to open the way for division of a different kind, division according to classes. Finally it makes it possible to utilise the natural wealth of the region and to develop its productive process in the best possible way without awaiting the decisions of a common centre – functions which are not inherent features of cultural-national autonomy.[11]

National autonomy was necessary because the psychological conscious-ness of national identity would still prevail under socialism. Only in the communist epoch would nations merge. Until that stage was reached, under socialism nationality would persist in a different and even strengthened form:

The fact of the matter is that the elimination of the bourgeois nations signifies the elimination not of nations in general, but only of the bourgeois nations. On the ruins of the old, bourgeois nations, new socialist nations are arising and developing, and they are far more solidly united than any bourgeois nation, because they are exempt from the irreconcilable class contradictions that corrode the bourgeois nations, and are far more representative of the whole people than any bourgeois nation.[12]

The main points in Bolshevik national policy may now be summarized. First, the equality of nations and languages was advocated. Second, a proletarian party divided on national lines was opposed. Third, under certain conditions, the Bolsheviks supported the right of oppressed nations to secede and to form an independent state. Fourth, the granting of secession had to be reconcilable with the interests of the proletariat in the class struggle. Fifth, in a socialist state, recognition would have to be given to national consciousness.

Soviet Nationalities Policy After the Revolution

The Tsarist Empire was multi-national and this pertains to the present day (see table 6.1). The main slavonic groups are located in the Western and Central European parts of the country and eastwards, through emigration, to the Urals and Siberia. In 1979, Russians and Ukrainians accounted for 52 per cent and 16 per cent of the population respectively. Though slavonic, the Poles, Ukrainians and Russians formed distinct national groups with separate cultural identities; the Poles were Catholic by religion, whereas the other slavonic groups were Orthodox. In the Baltic provinces (forming the present Republics of Estonia, Lithuania and

TABLE 6.1: NATIONAL COMPOSITION OF THE POPULATION 1897, 1959, 1979*

	1897 Census Defined by language (Millions)	1959 Census Defined by nationality (Millions)	1979 Census Defined by nationality (Millions)
Total population	125.68	208.82	262.08
Russians	55.6	114.11	137.39
Ukrainians	22.3	37.25	42.34
Byelorussians	5.8	7.91	9.46
Uzbeks	0.71	6.01	12.45
Tats	0.94	—	—
Tatars	3.6	4.96	6.31
Kazakhs	4.0†	3.62	5.55
Azerbaidzhanies	1.47‡	2.93	5.47
Armenians	1.17	2.78	4.15
Georgians	0.81	2.69	3.57
Lithuanians	1.20	2.32	2.85
Jews	4.9	2.26	1.81
Moldavians	1.11	2.21	2.96
Germans	1.78	1.61	1.93
Chuvases	0.84	1.46	1.75
Latvians	1.42	1.39	1.43
Tadzhiks	0.34	1.39	2.89
Poles	7.8	1.38	1.15
Mordvinians	1.01	1.28	1.19
Turkmenians	0.27	1.00	2.02
Bashkirs	1.31	0.989	1.37
Estonians	0.99	0.988	1.01
Kirgiz	4.0†	0.968	1.90
Other nationalities§	—	7.000	3.11

Notes: *The statistics are not strictly comparable because the areas of the countries have changed, and for the 1897 census the basis of classification is language spoken; since the 1959 census the basis is 'nationality'.
  †Kazakhs and Kirgiz undifferentiated in 1897 census.
  ‡ Source: R. Pipes, The Formation of the Soviet Union (1964), p. 12.
  §Most of the 103 other nationalities were less than a quarter of a million.
Sources: Itogi vsesoyuznoy perepisi naseleniya 1959g. SSSR (sovdny tom) (1962), pp. 184–9.
  Pervaya vseobshchaya perepis' naseleniya rossiyskoy imperii 1897g. (Obschi svod), Vol. 2 (Spb. 1905), Vestnik statistiki, No. 7 (1980).

Latvia), Indo-European languages quite different from Russian were and still are spoken.

Each of these societies has a distinct cultural tradition and history. Finland, though part of the Russian Empire, had a special status and was relatively more independent than other provinces having, even before the revolution, its own parliament, official language and currency, and separate army and educational system. In the Caucasus lived the

Armenians, Georgians, Persians and Tatars, the most important and developed nationalities being the first two. In Central Asia and Siberia were a multitude of indigenous peoples, and some nomadic tribes. Colonization and population movement meant that most areas had small Russian minorities. It is important to remember that the workers taking part in the industrialization of the Ukraine were to quite a large extent Great Russians from the central areas. The skilled workers and overseers in the Azerbaidzhan oil industry were also Russians. In fact, excluding the Polish provinces, of the industrial working class, some three-quarters were Russian.

After the revolution the political fate of these national areas depended partly on geography, partly on the popular support enjoyed by the Bolsheviks and partly on the ability of the new Soviet government to enforce its decisions.[13] Poland, Finland, Lithuania, Latvia and Estonia all became established states. They were all (except Finland) under German occupation at the time of the revolution and many expressed anti-Russian sentiments. Their geography allowed for successful intervention by the Western powers in support of their independence. Despite the presence of Russian immigrants in some of the Baltic provinces, grass roots support for unification with Russia was not large. In these countries, national social-democratic parties were strongest and they favoured separation.

In Finland, a capable bourgeoisie and in Poland a powerful landowning class led strong national liberation movements. Lenin's principle of secession was applied to these states. The Baltic states were established in the early 1920s until they were reoccupied by Soviet forces in the early 1940s and subsequently absorbed as national republics into the USSR.

The Ukraine had a more complex national and class structure. The land-owning classes were mainly Polish and Russian, and the petty-trading strata consisted largely of Jews: a Ukrainian national movement could not be led by such alien national strata. The industrial working class was largely Russian by nationality giving the Bolsheviks a social base. National-social stratification, therefore, was very different from that in Poland. The movement for independence was led by the professional middle strata: writers, teachers, lawyers and professors. In November 1917, a nationalist Rada (or Council) proclaimed a Ukrainian People's Republic. It disarmed the Bolshevik Red Guards and gave sustenance to the White Army. The Ukrainan Bolsheviks set up their headquarters in industrial Kharkov and, in December 1917, the All-Ukrainian Congress of Soviets 'assumed full powers in the Ukraine'. Later on, the Bolsheviks incorporated the Ukraine into the Soviet Republic as a separate unit. Ukrainian culture (language, customs) was given official recognition; the socio-economic system, however, became 'socialist in form'; property was nationalized, anti-Bolshevik parties were banned. Bolshevik policy was to promote a 'culture national in form and socialist in content'. Administratively, this involved the setting up of a federal state. The powers of the Union government, as defined by the Constitution of 1924, included the conduct of diplomatic affairs and the signing of treaties, the alteration of external frontiers and borders between republics, the transaction of foreign trade and loans, the determination of internal trade, the direction of the national economy and the organization of the armed forces. To the individual republics (i.e. the equivalent of state governments such as California in the USA) was granted the formal right of secession. They could amend their own constitutions as long as they conformed to the Union Constitution, and the territory of a republic could not be altered without the consent of its government.

Before the revolution in the Caucasus, the ethnic structure was extremely variegated. There were eight indigenous national groups. The Georgians and Armenians, each about two million strong, had an ancient Christian, non-industrial civilization. The remainder were less developed and mainly illiterate peasant or tribal groups. In Georgia there was an established agrarian class and in Armenia a commercial one. But in both provinces no industrial proletariat had been formed. The main centre of industry was in the oil fields of Baku (Azerbaidzhan), where a substantial skilled Russian and unskilled Persian immigrant labour force had been recruited. National animosities were multilateral rather than bilateral and often based on class issues: peasant Georgians being hostile to Armenian traders, Russian industrial managers oppressing Persian immigrant workers.

Between 1917 and 1920 numerous national governments, often with English, German or Turkish support, were founded in the Caucasus. But following a Bolshevik rising in Baku, the Azerbaidzhan Socialist Soviet Republic was founded in January 1920. Then, after Turkish infiltration into Armenia, Soviet forces intervened and constituted the Armenian Socialist Republic in November of the same year. It was not until February 1921 that the popular Georgian Menshevik government was overthrown by the Red Army and the Georgian Socialist Soviet Republic proclaimed.

The populations of the central and eastern areas of Russia were quite different in social composition from those influenced by European civilization in the west and south. The peoples inhabiting the northern Caucasus, Central Asia, the indigenous population of Siberia and the Arctic reaches were non-Christian, often Muslim, Asiatic, agrarian and sometimes tribal in social organization. Before 1917 these areas were sparsely settled by Russian and Ukrainian immigrants who were clustered mainly in the towns. Politically, the situation was rather similar to that of the British colonies in the eighteenth century, save that Russia's eastern territories were joined to the homeland. There were important social differences, however, between the Russian and British colonies: in the 'White Dominions', the native population was small and British stock (in the early decades at least) largely settled in these areas. In other parts of the British Empire, such as India and West and East Africa, the British provided only an elite of administrators and traders.

At first, after the October Revolution, the indigenous national leaders in Asia supported the communists, who seemed more favourably disposed to national self-determination than the provisional government. Indeed, the communists received nationalist support at quite crucial periods of the Civil War.[14] In practice, however, the early policy of the Soviet government (such as nationalization) undermined the economic foundations of the national elites, and Bolshevik rule appeared as distant as that of the Tsars. Consequently, independent national governments were formed among the Kazakhs, Bashkirs and Tatars which asserted autonomy for these peoples and independence from Petrograd.

In 1918, following the pattern of the Ukraine and Caucasus, the Soviet government intervened militarily against the 'bourgeois nationalist' governments to the east. Such nationalist states, it was argued, were inimical to the interests of the proletariat. Pro-Bolshevik governments were set up, ostensibly with the support of 'quasi-proletarian' strata. But the communist rule in these areas was not solely based on force. The central authorities abolished some of the more oppressive features of Tsarist administration and they promised 'national self-determination'. In Central Asia, the Soviet government found support among the Russian settler population. This was not strictly proletarian by class, but it represented for the Bolsheviks a 'higher stage' of civilization than that of the indigenous population.

In Asia, between 1920 and 1923, 17 autonomous republics and regions were created within the Russian Republic (RSFSR). These were administrative units based on the predominant national group in each area. The central government (i.e. the Russian Republic) had control over foreign affairs, economic planning, finance and defence, and the local bodies supervised education, health, social welfare (the old, child care and so on). The units did not have the status of federal governments, but were rather like glorified metropolitan counties in Great Britian. (At present, unlike Union Republics, they do not have the right to secede from the USSR.)

By 1927, the communists had consolidated their rule: they suppressed hostile elements which were a mixture of national and class opponents. A federal state was founded in which, by 1936, were organized Union

Republics, autonomous republics, autonomous regions, and national areas which gave the nationalities a degree of control over their own affairs. As there are more than one hundred nationalities in the USSR, one cannot study the impact the Soviet regime has had on all of them. I shall outline some of the features of the position of the Jews and then focus on some problems of contemporary ethnic divisions. Finally, I shall turn to the current political position of nationalities.[15]

The Jews

The Jews first came into Russia with the partition of Poland in the late eighteenth century.[16] At the census of 1897, Jews constituted about 3.9 per cent (4.9 million) of the total population. They were mainly urban and located in the western and south-western provinces of tsarist Russia. Warsaw, with a Jewish population of 278,000 in 1908, was the largest Jewish community in Europe. Being urban, the Jews had a higher level of education than other national groups and they were prominent in industry, trade, education, the arts and professions. Under the Tsars, the Jews were restricted to particular areas of the country, the Pale – an area in the west and south-west – and their other traditional settlements in the Caucasus and Central Asia. Exceptions to this law were made for merchants of the highest guild and registered prostitutes.

In the countryside of the Polish and Ukrainian provinces, the Jews were often shopkeepers or money collectors, activities which encouraged anti-Jewish feeling and added to Christian-Jewish antagonism. There were restrictions on their owning and farming land. With the industrialization of Russia in the late nineteenth century, the Jews, as entrepreneurs, began to play an important part in the metal industry, the sugar industry, railways, building and transport, oil and finance. In Poland, the Jewish share of commerce ranged from 80 to 95 per cent.[17] A large proportion of the Jewish population was poor, often being unemployed; others were recruited into the growing industrial centres in Poland and the Ukraine, forming a Jewish proletariat and becoming active in revolutionary politics. The social composition of the Jews, therefore, elicited hostility both from those exploited by the Jewish bourgeoisie and from the authorities who held them responsible for public disorder. In 1899, a quarter of those arrested for revolutionary activities were Jews.[18]

Until 1884, when the Jews were brought under the jurisdiction of local courts, the Jewish community enforced its own laws – and in return collected taxes for the government. Social services were provided by Jewish voluntary societies; these provided for the poor and the sick. Jewish schools were also organized by their community and ensured a high standard of literacy and culture among their people. But the communal solidarity of the Jews was being undermined from the late nineteenth century. Greater control of Jewish affairs was being exercised by the Russian government; not only was the legal autonomy of the community destroyed, but state education began to draw pupils from the Jewish to the state schools. The industrialization process disrupted the guilds and also divided the Jewish community on class lines.

Of the political movements among the Jews, the Zionist movement and the Bund were the most important. The Zionists were imbued with Jewish culture; some sought the establishment of Palestine as a national home, others wanted national rights within the framework of the Russian Empire – particularly, the right to found and control institutions for national education, health, welfare, emigration and 'matters of faith'.[19] The Zionists insisted on the right to use the Hebrew language.

The chief socialist movement among the Jews was the Bund, or the Jewish Social-Democratic Party in Russia, Lithuania and Poland. While the Bund adopted a Marxist view of the class struggle and agitated for the improvement of wages and conditions, it insisted on the right of the Bund exclusively to represent Jewish workers; it also advocated national autonomy for the Jews in Russia. The Bund found itself at odds with the Russian Social-Democratic Labour Party which sought a wider union of workers, rather than national workers' groups. To the Russian party belonged many Jewish intellectuals and workers who had to a greater or lesser extent rejected Jewish 'nationality' and religion. Indeed, a higher proportion of Jews was in the RSDLP than in the population as a whole and many of them, such as Trotsky and Martov, held high office. Of the two factions of the party, fewer Jews joined the Bolsheviks, though they figured largely among the Menshevik leaders.[20]

Stalin, as we have seen, defined a nation as 'an historically constituted, stable community of people, formed on the basis of a common language, territory, economic life, and psychological make-up manifested in a common culture'.[21] And this viewpoint was incorporated into the communists' policy after the revolution. The Jews, on the basis of this definition, did *not* constitute a single nation: they were economically disunited, inhabited various territories and spoke different languages. In practice, therefore, after the revolution, though the Jews in some areas were concentrated enough to form local Jewish Soviets, they were not at once constituted into an administrative national area.

Hostility to the Jewish community by the population existed on many grounds. By class position, the relatively high proportion of self-employed craftsmen, entrepreneurs, and financiers among the Jews made some think that the Jews, as such, were of bourgeois class origin, and were therefore opposed to the communist regime. The demands of the Zionists for a national home outside Russia, together with Zionism's international character, led some to doubt their loyalty to the new Soviet state.

In common with the other religious faiths, the religious aspects of Jewish culture were regarded as superstitious and inimical to the Marxist world view. Lenin regarded the demands for Jewish national culture as a 'slogan of rabbis and bourgeois',[22] showing the close links in Bolshevik eyes between Jewish national, religious and class aspirations. Many of the strongest proponents of the government's attack against the Jewish religion and Jewish nationalism were communists of Jewish ethnic stock and upbringing. *Yevsektsii*, or sections composed of Jews, were organized both in the Communist Party and in the League of Militant Godless. Even in the 1970s, Jews 'remain by far the most "party-saturated" nationality, with more than twice the USSR average [membership – 13 per cent of Jewish population]'.[23]

While persecution of Jewish nationalists occurred and hostility to religious sentiment was expressed, a more positive scheme for meeting the aspirations of the Jews was being worked out. A plan for settling the Russian Jews in a special area in the unpopulated Far Eastern territories of Russia had been devised. This had the political advantage that it countered the proposals of the Russian Zionists for a national home and it was practical, as it involved no dislocation of existing peoples, as might have been the case in the European parts of Russia. Another advantage was that it transferred to the east a hard-working people who could ably develop a new region. After a pioneering start in 1928, the Jewish Autonomous Region (Birobidyan) was proclaimed in 1934. Unfortunately, a large number of Jews moved away from the area (about half in the years 1928–1933) and non-Jews emigrated there, giving it, both in 1934 and today, a non-Jewish majority (15,000 Jews out of a population of 170,000). Small migration continued after the Second World War, but by 1959, the population of Jews amounted to only 8.8 per cent.[24]

After the revolution, the traditional bourgeois occupations of the Jews (such as banking, trading, and small-scale business) were gradually abolished. Jewish workers still pursued their traditional trades (such as shoe-repairing, tailoring, printing) and professions (medicine, teaching). Important changes in the occupational structure of the Jews paralleled the process of industrialization. The number of Jews classified as wage-earners and salaried workers increased from 394,000 in 1926 to 1,100,000 in 1935. The number of Jewish miners rose from 0.1 per cent of Jewish workers in 1926 to 3.3 per cent in 1936, metal workers increased from 14.1 per cent to 23.8 per cent.[25] The access of Jews to higher education and therefore to managerial and white-collar jobs was much greater than that of other nationalities. In 1926, Jews composed 1.8 per cent of the population, whereas their share of students (in 1929) was 13.5 per cent; by 1956 their share had fallen to 4.1 per cent and by 1965 to 2.4 per cent. They still have a relatively privileged position, however, for their share of the population in 1970 was only 0.89 per cent, while their percentage of the student population in higher education in the same year was 2.31. The number of Jewish students expressed as a proportion per 10,000 of the Jewish population is 491, whereas the comparative figure for the USSR as a whole is 189 and for Russians it is 271.[26] Jews still have a higher proportion of white-collar workers than the average. While Jews number only 0.89 per cent of the population, they constitute 6.66 per cent of scientific specialists. In 1966, 14.7 per cent of all Soviet doctors were Jewish; figures for writers and journalists were 8.5 per cent, judges and lawyers 10.4 per cent, actors, musicians and artists 7.7 per cent.[27] They are the most urban nationality group in the USSR, with 95.3 per cent of the population living in towns – compared to 57.7 per cent of Russians.[28]

Culturally, the Jews have fared less well than other minor nationalities in the USSR. Up to the mid-1920s, the Yiddish language used in the Soviet Jewish schools still flourished (Hebrew was also taught). In 1927, about 40 per cent of all Jewish pupils went to Yiddish schools.[29] Thereafter, Yiddish schools were progressively incorporated into other local schools, then dropped completely. The language has suffered: in 1979, 14.2 per cent of Jews considered Yiddish or Hebrew to be their first language – compared to 99.8 per cent of Russians, who thought of Russian as their first language.[30]

The size of the Jewish congregation is declining rapidly. In the whole of the USSR in the mid-1960s, there were 100 synagogues and 300 minians (a gathering under 10), compared to 1,034 in 1917. There is no Jewish seminary to train rabbis. Attendance at synagogues is poor and worshippers, like those in the Orthodox Church, are old. The proportion of avowed atheists among the Jewish population is, according to one survey, higher than that among other national groups – 98.5 per cent against an average of 65.1 per cent.[31] Possibly, this high figure was influenced by Jewish respondents being less secure than others and therefore feeling less willing to say they were Jewish. But the conclusion can hardly be escaped that Judaism has suffered the same fate as other religions in the USSR – a serious decline.

All forms of racial and national discrimination are illegal in the USSR, and this applies to the Jews as to other groups. But it is often alleged in the West that anti-Semitism is still practised. Alec Nove has said that Soviet Jews are 'all but barred from foreign trade organisations'.[32] It is often asserted that Jews are not accepted in the Soviet diplomatic service. If true, this is probably due to prejudice about cosmopolitanism and to possible allegiance to Israel. In fact, however, no statistical analysis of the national composition of the diplomatic service has been provided to substantiate these views, though on a *a priori* grounds they seem likely to be true. Other commentators report on anti-Jewish prejudice in Russia.[33] A much larger proportion of Jews are sentenced for 'economic crimes' than is their share of the population as a whole. In the RSFSR Jews constitute 0.7 per cent of the population, whereas of those executed from July 1961 to August 1963, 64 per cent were Jews.[34] As Jews are disproportionately engaged in trade, one might expect a larger proportion to be involved in speculation. Another possible factor is that the law may be more strictly enforced against Jewish subjects than non-Jews, especially in areas with a history of anti-Semitism.

There is little evidence of official Soviet approval of anti-Semitism, as such. Zvi Gitelman, however, has pointed out that anti-Zionism (opposition to the Jewish state of Israel) which is pursued by the Soviet government is a 'new outbreak of anti-Semitism'.[35] Surveys conducted in the West of Jews who emigrated from the USSR shed some light on the extent of anti-Semitism. Gitelman is at pains to point out that émigrés are likely 'to exaggerate or emphasise Soviet anti-Semitism to reassure themselves that they made the right decision in leaving their birthplace, or to convince the interviewer that they were, indeed, victims of persecution'. In four surveys of 3,200 Jewish émigrés, almost three-quarters 'claimed frequent or occasional personal encounters with anti-Semitism in the USSR'.[36]

The geographical dispersion of the Jews in the USSR together with Soviet social policy has tended to assimilate them into other national groups. The absence of family businesses and Jewish schools means that Jews are educated and employed with other nationalities. This encourages mixed marriages. In one Moscow district in one period of 1966, 66 per cent of the marriages involving one or both Jewish partners were mixed. It is also interesting to note a tendency for Jewish men rather than women to marry exogamously – as with other minor nationalities. Even before the waves of emigration to the West in 1971–74, the Jewish population declined from 2.26 million in 1959 to 2.15 million in 1970. In 1979, it had fallen to 1.81 million. In the decade 1970–1980, about 10 per cent of the Soviet Jewish population had emigrated.[37] The main sources of emigration have been the least assimilated Jews – those from the Baltic, Moldavia, Trans-Carpathia, West Ukraine, Georgia and Central Asia, who had preserved their traditional ways of life.[38]

We might try to explain why the Jews seem to have fared less well politically than other national groups in the USSR. First, the Jews in

Tsarist Russia had no definite territory, as did other national groups. They lack a *national* language: in 1979, 83 per cent of Jews in the USSR consider- ed Russian to be their native tongue.[39] Second, many Jews who had rejected the notion of an autonomous Jewish nationality had jointed the Bolsheviks and, to counter Zionist sentiments, they vigorously supported and advocated an assimilationist policy. Whereas other national leaders were able to achieve considerable concessions, communists with a Jewish background were internationalist in outlook. Third, the international role of Zionism, the large number of Jewish relations of Soviet Jews in capitalist states and, since the end of the Second World War, the presence of Israel have led to a policy of assimilation of the Jews for political reasons. This policy has been politically expedient, but it has resulted in the suppression of the cultural identity of the Jews to a much greater extent than in modern Western states. (We should not, however, attribute the assimilation of Jews in the USSR *solely* to Soviet political pressure, as a decline in Jewish religious faith has taken place in Great Britain and the United States, though the Jews here have maintained their identity on a cultural and social basis.) This has led to a feeling of isolation by the Jewish community in the USSR. As a Jewish biologist cited by Hendrick Smith has put it: 'I am a man without a nationality in a very nationalistic country.' A study of 437 Soviet émigrés to Israel in 1972 concluded that the most important aspect of alienation of Jews in the Soviet Union is the 'perceived incompatibility between one's Jewish identity and one's identity as a member of the Soviet society and polity'.[40] Much of the motivation for leaving has been dislike of the Soviet Union and a desire for the higher standards of the West rather than a religious attraction to Israel.[41]

Contemporary Ethnic Divisions

The contemporary federal structure of the USSR has been mentioned above. Here we may analyse the main national groups in Russia. In table 6.1 above we have seen that the USSR, on the basis of the 1979 census, is composed of over 262 million people, of whom the Great Russians make up more than half (137 million). The next largest nationality is the Ukrainians (42 million), followed by Uzbeks (12.45 million) and Byelorussians (9.46 million). Most of the other minor nationalities are under six million strong, the average being about two million. These peoples are still concentrated spatially in their traditional areas. However, it must not be assumed that a national republic (like Kazakhstan) is inhabited solely by people of its titular appellation.

The Russian Federation (Russian Soviet Federative Socialist Republic or RSFSR) stretches the whole width of the country. It is mixed nationally, containing sixteen autonomous republics, five autonomous regions and ten national areas. The peoples inhabiting these national units are defined in table 6.2. In the second and third columns is shown the proportion of Great Russians (in 1970 and 1979) and in the fourth the next two largest national groups. The table shows the wide spread of Russians, and not only in the RSFSR where they account for 82.4 per cent of the population (1979). In other republics, with the exception of Kazakhstan where Russians constitute 40.8 per cent of the people and the Latvian Republic where they make

TABLE 6.2: THE MOST NUMEROUS NATIONALITIES IN THE UNION REPUBLICS (1970, 1979)

	Russians (%)		Other Nationalities (%)		
	1970	1979		1970	1979
RSFSR	82.8	82.4	Tatars	3.7	3.6
			Ukrainians	2.6	2.6
UKRAINIAN SSR	19.4	20.9	Ukrainians	74.9	73.3
BYELORUSSIAN					
(WHITE RUSSIAN) SSR	10.4	11.8	White Russians	81.0	79.3
			Poles	4.3	2.4
UZBEKISTAN SSR	12.5	10.7	Uzbeks	65.6	68.6
			Tatars	4.9	4.1
KAZAKHSTAN SSR	42.4	40.8	Kazakhs	32.6	35.9
			Ukrainians	7.2	6.0
GEORGIAN SSR	8.5	7.4	Georgians	66.8	68.7
			Armenians	9.7	8.9
AZERBAIDZHAN SSR	10.0	8.2	Azerbaidzhanies	73.8	78.0
			Armenians	9.4	7.8
LITHUANIAN SSR	8.6	8.8	Lithuanians	80.1	79.9
			Poles	7.7	7.2
MOLDAVIAN SSR	11.6	12.8	Moldavians	64.6	63.8
			Ukrainians	14.2	14.2
LATVIAN SSR	29.8	32.8	Latvians	56.8	53.7
KIRGIZ SSR	29.2	25.8	Kirgiz	43.8	47.9
			Uzbeks	11.3	12.0
TADZHIK SSR	11.9	10.3	Tadzhik	56.2	58.7
			Uzbeks	23.0	22.9
ARMENIAN SSR	2.7	2.3	Armenians	88.6	89.7
			Azerbaidzhanies	5.9	5.2
TURKMENISTAN SSR	14.5	12.6	Turkmens	56.6	68.4
			Uzbeks	8.3	8.4
ESTONIAN SSR	24.7	27.9	Estonians	68.2	64.7

Source: Itogi vsesoyuznoy perepisi naseleniya 1970g. Vol. 4 (1970). Adapted from Vestnik statistiki (1980). Nos. 5, 8, 9, 10, 11.

up 32.8 per cent, the native inhabitants are preponderant. This is especially so in Lithuania, Armenia and Azerbaidzhan, where those nationalities make up respectively 79.9, 89.7 and 78.0 per cent of the population. The population of the Soviet Union is not static. The rate of population growth in the Central Asian areas of the country has been much greater than in the Russian and European regions. This is illustrated most clearly by data on the number of children born to women of different nationalities (see table 6.3). The most prolific nationalities are Uzbeks, Turkmens, Kirgiz and Tadzhiks, with over 3,000 births per 1,000 women, followed by Kazakhs, Azerbaydzhanies, and Armenians. Nationalities with a less than average reproduction rate are Russians, Ukrainians, Georgians, Lithuanians, Latvians and Estonians. This is reflected in statistics on the natural increase: in the USSR in 1979, the average was 8.1 (per 1000 of the population): in the RSFSR, it came to 5.0, in the Ukraine 3.6, Latvia 1.0, Estonia 2.6; at the other end of the scale it was 21.8 in Kirgizia, 27.4 in Uzbekistan and 30.1 in Tadzhikistan.[42]

These indexes are influenced by the age composition of the population –

TABLE 6.3: DISTRIBUTION OF WOMEN BY NATIONALITY AND SIZE OF FAMILY, 1979
(per 1000 women of the respective nationality aged 15 and over)

| | | | Number of Children | | | | | | |
	None	1	2	3	4	5	6	7 and more	Average Number of Children
All women aged 15 and over	252	229	253	110	55	36	22	43	1963
Russians	239	266	273	104	47	29	15	27	1773
Ukrainians	223	234	298	128	54	29	14	20	1823
Byelorussians	237	190	271	141	70	42	21	28	2006
Uzbeks	326	89	90	83	77	72	67	196	3293
Kazakhs	346	99	106	86	72	68	58	165	2987
Georgians	286	140	250	167	79	38	19	21	1928
Azerbaydzhanies	388	77	92	87	80	72	61	143	2784
Lithuanians	286	196	260	124	60	33	17	24	1795
Moldavians	286	181	199	115	69	49	32	69	2235
Latvians	294	261	264	100	40	20	9	12	1495
Kirgiz	333	88	93	82	72	66	58	208	3363
Tadzhiks	321	78	78	71	70	67	65	250	3700
Armenians	307	119	179	148	95	61	36	55	2277
Turkmens	350	85	84	76	72	66	60	207	3299
Estonians	281	242	271	113	45	24	11	13	1599

Source: Vestnik statistiki No. 1 (1982), p. 66.

particularly by the number of women in the child-bearing age groups. But the implications are clear. In the next twenty or so years, the balance of population growth will shift from the European part of the country to the East. In 1975 it has been estimated that 16.8 per cent of the cohort for military service came from Central Asia (including Kazakhstan). If present projections are continued, by the year 2,000 the share will rise to 22.9 per cent.[43] One must always bear in mind the fact that as urbanization occurs the birth rate tends to fall. The Central Asian Republics have a large rural peasant population (the USSR's population is 37 per cent rural, Uzbekistan's 58 per cent, Kazakhstan's 45 per cent, Kirgiziya's 61 per cent, Tadzhikistan's 66 per cent, Turkmeniya's 52 per cent).[44] The nationalities of the Central Asian Republics account for a much higher proportion of the collective farm (or peasant) population. Table 6.4 shows that in 1979 only six per cent of Russians were collective farmers, the figures rising to 32 per cent for Uzbeks and 45 per cent for Turkmens. It is probable that the Central Asian Republics will follow the course of the more urbanized areas of the USSR and that population growth will peak out around the turn of the century.

TABLE 6.4: SOCIAL COMPOSITION OF NATIONS OF THE USSR, 1970 AND 1979

	1970			1979		
	Manual	Non-Manual	Collective Farmers	Manual	Non-Manual	Collective Farmers
	%	%	%	%	%	%
Russians	63	25	12	63	31	6
Armenians	60	25	15	62	31	7
Kazakhs	65	22	13	64	28	8
Estonians	57	25	18	57	32	11
Latvians	54	23	23	58	28	14
Lithuanians	52	18	30	56	27	17
White Russians (Byelorussians)	53	15	32	59	23	18
Georgians	41	26	33	49	32	19
Azerbaydzhanies	50	21	29	58	23	19
Ukrainians	47	16	37	56	23	21
Kirgiz	41	15	44	56	20	24
Tadzhiks	37	15	48	55	15	30
Moldavians	32	7	61	54	15	31
Uzbeks	39	16	45	50	18	32
Turkmens	32	17	51	39	16	45
On average in USSR	57	23	20	60	25	15

Source: Data cited in Yu. V. Arutyunyan, 'Korennye izmeneniya v sotsial'nom sostave Sovetskikh natsii', *Sotsiologicheskie issledovaniya*, no. 4 (1982), p. 23.

These demographic trends – the falling birth rate of the Russians and the rising numbers of Asians – provide the backdrop to contemporary discussions of nationalities in the USSR.[45]

A Soviet People?

In attempting to provide a unitary and socialist focus to the multi-ethnic Soviet Union, the political leadership in the 1970s began to stress the supra-national identity of the *Sovetski narod*, or Soviet people. With the development of socialism, the awareness of this wider national identity, it is thought, would displace the narrower and traditional ethnic consciousness. The notion of a Soviet people is characterized by five principal features:

a single common territory (USSR), a single ideology and world view (Marxism–Leninism), a common purpose and goal (the building of a communist society), proletarian internationalism and Soviet patriotism, and peaceful and harmonious relations between classes and ethnic groups .... The Soviet people aggregate is said to be characterised by unity of class and ethnic interests, a high and growing degree of socio-economic homogeneity, a single common multi-ethnic culture, common features of spiritual make-up and psychology, bilingualism and widespread, increasing use of Russian as the language of interethnic communication, and the pre-eminence of the working class and its vanguard – the communist party.[46]

One of the most pervasive elements in the creation of a common identity has been the spread of Russians and the influence of Russian culture, particularly language. Russians have emigrated from their traditional areas extending from Leningrad to the Don in the West, to the Urals in the East. In 1897 in Central Asia there were about 700,000 Russians out of a total population of just over ten million, roughly 6.8 per cent. By 1939, this proportion had risen to 27.1 per cent – a total Russian population of four and a half million.[47] With the exception of Kirgizia, where some immigrants were engaged in agriculture, most of the migrants moved to the towns. The peoples of Central Asia were far less developed and, unlike the advanced nations in western Russia, had little consciousness of 'nationality' at the time of the revolution. Following writers such as Gellner,[48] nationalism must be considered a form of consciousness associated with a modern industrial state.

In the western Christian areas of Russia, Christianity in the form of the Orthodox Church provided some political opposition to the Bolsheviks. (See below chapter 7.) The Moslem faith was more at odds with the demands of an urban industrial civilization. Daily prayers and fasting interfered with the rhythm of industrial life. Between 1928 and 1932 the leaders of the Muslim Church were imprisoned or deported, mosques were closed, and the ritual of the pilgrimage to Mecca and the payment of legal charity were forbidden.[49] While Muslim religious ritual seems to have suffered a decline, native customs have continued. Circumcision appears to be 'universally observed'. Ceremonies at births, weddings and burials continue, though in a less formal manner. Arranged marriages, polygamy, infant marriages and the bride price have been made illegal. But restrictions on marriage between members of the same clan persisted at least to the late 1940s, when other social taboos (such as women not pronouncing the names of their husband's relatives) were still observed.[50]

Dunn and Dunn, after a comprehensive study of the anthropological literature concerning Soviet Central Asia and Kazakhstan, conclude that the culture was divided into

two ... separate storeys on which different values obtain and rather different processes of change take place .... On what might be called the lower storey, the traditional values remain relatively intact, and ... much of the ceremonial which expresses and maintains these values continues to be practised. The major difference from the pre-Revolutionary situation lies in the fact that there now exists a means of transit from the lower to the upper storey by way of advanced education ...[51]

Even if, as a critical note following this article has maintained,[52] the Dunns define too sharply a discontinuity between the traditional and modern society, one should accept the fact that cultural traditions may persist quite independently of changes in the economic order. Industrialization involved the immigration of Russian manual and non-manual workers to Central Asia and the growth of an indigenous working class. The trends may be illustrated by study of Kazakhstan. Data from the census of 1939 show that, while the working class (manual and non-manual) of Kazakhstan was more than half of the population (51.2 per cent), of the native population it was only 33.6 per cent. If we distinguish between the number of native workers employed in agriculture and those in branches of industry, the figure cited above for Kazakhstan is seen in a new light. In 1939, 63.8 per cent of Kazakhs in employment came in the former category and only 25.1 per cent from the latter. Hence a very large proportion of manual workers in these areas were in agricultural occupations (say on state farms) and were living in the countryside. While this analysis of the data suggests that the actual occupational changes of the native manual worker population were not as great as they might appear at first sight, one should not minimize the extent of growth of an indigenous working class. In Kazakhstan, the number of native manual workers in industry (excluding agriculture) rose five-fold between 1926 and 1939.[53]

Settlement seems to follow the pattern of immigration to cities in the Western world. The European immigrants have tended to live beside the indigenous population, which continued to live in the Oriental quarter of such cities as Bokhara, and the Russians in separate parts of the towns. With the redevelopment of towns in the 1960s, it is probable that more mixing has taken place. On the other hand, the provision of separate Russian-language and native-language schools tends to promote segregation.

The war saw a movement of many more people to Central Asia and Siberia. Not only were many voluntarily evacuated from western Russia, but the Volga Germans, the Crimean Tatars and the Kalmyks (each having their own Autonomous Republic) were also moved to the east.[54] By the time of the 1979 census, Russians constituted significant minorities in the Republics outside the RSFSR (see table 6.2): in the Ukraine, 20.9 per cent, Kazakhstan 40.8 per cent. The Russian immigrant population in such Republics lives mainly in the towns, particularly the capitals (except in Tbilisi and Erevan).

By the 1980s, the occupational and class distribution of the population has become more homogeneous between the national groups. The proportions of manual workers, non-manual and collective farmers in the different nationalities for the times of the censuses in 1970 and 1979 is shown in table 6.4 above. The trend towards homogenization is apparent when we consider the divergence of each nationality class group from the mean of the USSR. In 1970, Russians had 6 per cent more manual workers than the average – only 3 per cent more in 1979; Kazakhs had 8 per cent more in 1970 and only 4 per cent in 1979; at the other end of the scale Kirgiz were 16 per cent below the average in 1970 but only 4 per cent in 1979.[55] Similarly, the density of collective farmers among the non-Russian, and especially Central Asian, nationalities is falling.

Intermarriage is the chief process by which a minor racial or national group may be absorbed by, or assimilated into, another culturally dominant nationality. Both before the revolution and during the Stalin era, Muslims and Russians did not intermarry very much. Pipes puts this down to cultural differences, sexual customs, the control of Muslim parents over female children, and the problems of a mixed family in a Russian or Muslim community.[56] Those who do break the racial barriers are Russian women who marry Muslim men. In the 1960s, in the towns of Tashkent and Samarkand, 20 per cent of marriages were of mixed ethnic stock. Mixed marriages between the different national groups are frequent and usually take place between Uzbeks on the one hand and Kazakhs and Karakal-paks, on the other.[57] By 1979, the proportion of families of mixed ethnic stock in the USSR as a whole was 149 per thousand families: in the towns it was 181.[58] This tends to encourage the spread of the Russian language and a certain degree of assimilation to Russian nationality.

Russian Influence

In the towns, where the population is mixed, Russian is better known. It is the principal language of instruction in higher education (especially universities) in Central Asia. (This is not the case in the European national areas, where Ukrainian, Latvian and Georgian are the mode in higher education.) Promotion in institutions with an All-Union complexion (such as the party or Supreme Soviet) would seem to depend on ability to speak Russian. This probably accounts for the higher enrolment by non-Russians in Russian-speaking schools. In the Georgian Republic, where Russians constitute 10.8 per cent of the population, 20 per cent of the children are at Russian-language schools; in the Baltic, it should by noted, the differential is much lower – in Estonia, where 21.7 per cent of the population is Russian, only 22 per cent of the schoolchildren are in Russian schools. In Central Asia and the European national republics, while the indigenous languages have persisted, enrolment in Russian-language schools is high.

Between 1970 and 1979, the number of people in the USSR fluently speaking Russian as a second language rose from 17.3 per cent to 23.4 per cent (census data). But the other languages of the peoples of the USSR are vigorous. The censuses of 1970 and 1979 showed the following percentage of people who considered their 'native language' to be the same as that of their national group: Ukrainians 82.8 per cent (85.7 per cent in 1970), Uzbeks 98.5 per cent (98.6 per cent), Byelorussians 74.2 per cent (80.6 per cent), Kazakhs 97.5 per cent (98 per cent), Tatars 85.9 per cent (89.2 per cent), Armenians 90.7 per cent (91.4 per cent), Georgians 98.3 per cent (98.4 per cent), Germans 57 per cent (66.8 per cent), Jews 14.2 per cent (17.7 per cent).[59]

In cultural aspects of life, Russification does not seem to have penetrated very deeply. The native language is still spoken at home. In the eight-year schools, instruction is often given in the vernacular. The changes in material aspects of life (clothing, food and housing) are all influenced by the Russians. But it is incorrect simply to call these changes Russification: they are a synthesis of international features, and are as much related to urbanization as Russification. The impact of the town and urban culture is also felt in the villages where the 'village intelligentsia', having had higher education in the town, in turn influences the villagers. Smirnova observes, on the basis of her research, that in mixed marriages there is a tendency to generate a nationally mixed home culture. Of Cherkesi-Russian marriages, the family ate local and Russian food, the children wore local and Russian clothes, but the home language was Russian and the children went to the Russian-language school.[60]

A study by L.M. Drobizheva, conducted in 1971–76 and 1979–80 in the

RSFSR, Uzbekistan, Georgia, Moldavia and Estonia, concluded that 'national exclusiveness' persisted among some social strata. The bases of such prejudice, she thought, were two-fold – first linked to low cultural levels and lack of experience of a multi-national kind and the retention of traditions, this was the case among some of the older age groups and those from the countryside. The other source was due to the frustration of expectations experienced by some of the nationality groups. For instance, young people in Moldavia and Uzbekistan who failed to achieve admission to higher educational institutions sometimes had a sense of grievance and this was expressed as a form of national prejudice.[61]

The socio-economic homogeneity of the peoples of the USSR may be measured by access to education and the degree of saturation of ethnic groups of people with professional qualifications (in Soviet parlance, 'specialists with higher or specialized secondary education').[62] Silver has argued that the nationalities of the Central Asian Republics are substantially under-represented among the professionals. This is at best a misleading assertion and at worst, erroneous. In calculating the level of representation, Jones and Grupp have adjusted the data for age (i.e. standardizing for the size of the 25-year to 59-year age groups). Column 2 of table 6.5 shows that in 1970 Azerbaydzhanies have a higher saturation of specialists than do Russians, and that Kazakhs are only marginally lower. Uzbeks, Kirgiz and Turkmens better Ukrainians in this respect. Estonians, Georgians and Armenians all have a higher proportion of professionals than do Russians. Subtracting the score in 1959–60 from that in 1970 gives an indication of relative change. Study of column 4 indicates that there has been an equalization of occupational attainment between 1959–60 and 1970. Azerbaydzhanies, Georgians and Armenians worsened their position – but remained above the Russians – while all the other nationalities improved absolutely and relatively to Russians.

In columns 5 and 6 are depicted data on the educational levels of different nationality groups. Column 5 is an index of the ethnic student population expressed as a ratio per 1,000 of the 17 to 29 ethnic age group. In column 6 is displayed the participation rate of ethnic groups aged 16 to 24 at specialized secondary schools expressed as an index per 1,000 of the ethnic population. Study of these columns shows that Russians are by no means the nationality with the largest proportion of people with higher education. They are outstripped more than three times by Jews: their relative advantage continued to 1975, when it fell somewhat to 285 per thousand.[63] Georgians, Armenians, Azerbaydzhanies and Kirgiz all had higher participation ratios in higher education than Russians. It is in the sphere of specialized secondary schools – those training technicians – that Russians do well. They come second to Lithuanians, with an index of 138.4

TABLE: 6.5: NATIONALITY AGE-ADJUSTED INDEXES OF PROFESSIONALIZA-
TION AND ACCESS TO HIGHER EDUCATION

Col. 1	1A	2	3	4	5	5A	6
	Rank by pro-portion of non-collec-tive farm population	Specialists having higher education 1959-60 1970		(Col. 3-2)	In higher education 1970	Rank	In specia-lized second-ary schools 1970
Slavic							
Russians	1	103	103	0	112	5	138.4
Ukrainians	10	78	82	+4	85	13	127.0
Byelorussians	7	73	76	+3	81	14	123.9
Baltic							
Estonians	4	110	121	+11	104	8	128.9
Latvians	5	100	103	+ 3	90	11	124.2
Lithuanians	6	74	89	+15	102	9	168.8
Muslim							
Uzbeks	14	59	85	+26	108	7	84.7
Kazakhs	3	77	101	+24	111	6	98.4
Azerbaydzhanies	9	131	114	−17	132	3	106.7
Kirgiz	11	77	94	+17	128	4	89.6
Tadzhiks	12	61	76	+15	88	12	69.1
Turkmens	15	72	92	+20	96	10	77.0
Tatars	—	—	—	—	83	—	—
Other							
Georgians	8	211	164	− 47	154	1	110.0
Moldavians	13	31	45	+14	62	15	82.7
Armenians	2	181	145	−36	136	2	123.2
Jews	—	—	—	—	355	—	—

Source: Ellen Jones and Fred W. Grupp, 'Measuring Nationality Trends in the Soviet Union: A Research Note', *Slavic Review*, vol. 41, no. 1 (Spring 1982), pp. 117, 119, 121. Rankings added.

per 1000 (168.8 for Lithuanians); other Slavic groups are close behind (Ukrainians 127, Byelorussians 123.9). The Muslim population here fares relatively badly, ranging from 69.1 (Tadzhiks) to 106.7 (Azerbaydzhanies). A peculiarity in these figures is the very low level of participation in specialized technical schools by Muslim girls. If one excludes girls from the statistics, the participation rate for Russian male students falls to 118.3 per thousand; it rises to 138.6 for Azerbaydzhanies, 116.3 for Turkmens, 114.7 for Uzbeks, 111.5 for Tadzhiks, 104.8 for Kazakhs and 95.7 for Kirgiz.[64]

The overall picture we have from these statistics is one of growing homogeneity between ethnic groups. Bearing in mind the backwardness and low starting point of the Muslim population – outlined above – there is now undoubtedly a greater equality between Muslims and the European national groups. It certainly cannot be said that the Russians are superior as far as access to professions and higher education is concerned. One caveat may be in order, however, as far as the quantitative indicators are concerned. They assume that the level of educational institution is the same in different parts of the country. But it seems likely that in practice quality of provision may be better in the European areas of the country.

The standardization of culture which accompanies advanced industrialization is an important ingredient in the socio-economic homogenization of Soviet society. In this respect the cultural identity of the Soviet people shares some features with those of the mass cultures of the capitalist world: mass media, a premium on common consumption goods, wage labour, an urban environment and culture. The 'drawing together' (*sblizhenie*) of ethnic groups in the Soviet Union involves, in my view, the adoption of a modern secularized culture associated with urbanism. Industrial development and population movement make for greater interaction between ethnic groups. It is an open question, however, whether this may lead to heightening of tensions or to 'merging' (*sliyanie*), to the internationalizing of culture. R.A. Lewis has concluded that the process of modernization in the USSR intensifies ethnic identity. 'As groups come into contact and competition with one another, ethnic differences are perceived. That heightens the feeling of ethnic identity of all groups involved and generally results in animosities and tensions.'[65]

The concept of the Soviet people, moreover, is more than a common urban way of life; it embraces a peculiar Marxist–Leninist political culture. This is epitomized in the contemporary slogan: *Partiya i narod ediny* (The Party and Nation are One). Here we see the continuity of a tradition which goes back to Tsarist times with its motif of *Edinenie Naroda i Tsariya* (The Unity of People and Tsar). This notion has raised the ire of the non-Russian *samizdat* writers. They have asserted that the Soviet people concept is a 'myth', a 'fable created by the Kremlin'.[66] The Russians, also, it is alleged, object to the vulgarization of their culture and its diminution when merged into the *Soviet* culture. Vladimir Osipov, a past editor of the *samizdat* paper *Veche*, has argued for the 'strengthening of Russian ethnic culture and traditions in the spirit of the Slavophiles and Dostoevski, and the assertion of Russia's originality and greatness'; for him 'Soviet patriotism alone is "inadequate" for effecting the moral or cultural regeneration of the Russian people.'[67] Soviet writers and some Western commentators, however, conclude to the contrary. They see a qualitative difference in ethnic relations in the USSR from those in Western countries. M. Rywkin writes: '[Muslims] encounter virtually no discrimination in living and housing. They enjoy equal or better opportunities within their own republics and elsewhere in the Soviet Union ... There are no second-class citizens, no man-to-man superiority. Modern Muslim national-religious feelings may conflict with Russian domination, but individual Muslims, including those responsive to such feelings, do not suffer from person-to-person discrimination.'[68]

The growth of a 'Muslim identity' among the native population of Central Asia, Kazakhstan and Azerbaydzhan has been claimed by some Western writers, and notably Hélène d'Encausse.[69] She argues that Islam in the Soviet Union had adapted its teaching and code to Soviet power and thereby has secured a revival. She cites data from the Karakalpak Autonomous Republic (in Uzbekistan) showing that 11.3 per cent of men (11 per cent of women) were 'devout believers', 14 per cent (15 per cent) were 'believers by tradition', 13.3 per cent of men (14.3 per cent of women) were 'waverers', 17.2 per cent (19.3 per cent) were 'non-believers'.[70] (The total of atheists came to 23 per cent of the men and 20 per cent of the women.) d'Encausse asserts that the Muslims regard themselves as being part of a 'community' (the 'Ummah') rather than being members of a religious faith (akin to Christianity). '... Islam in the USSR is undergoing a rebirth amid new conditions ... and this renascence is conscious and desired. It is being aided and guided by the Moslem hierarchy, which is directing its efforts to two particular areas: facilitating the practice of Islam and adapting it to the needs of modern life, and giving it temporal power by uniting it with Soviet ideology.'[71] Soviet Muslims, according to d'Encausse, see a correspondence between Islam and Soviet communism. Unlike capitalism, which is 'built on injustice and exploita-tion', a socialist system is 'based on just laws'.[72] The USSR 'fights for peace, because war is rooted in injustice'; the corresponding Muslim doctrine is that 'Islam also fights for peace and justice.'[73] Soviet socialism is regarded as implementing 'the order of Mohammed'.[74]

It is possible that the development of such a consciousness could be a threat to the unity of Soviet society.[75] It is problematic, however, whether such nationalities will regard themselves as 'belonging first of all to the Muslim nation...'[76] At present such statements are assertions. It clearly is a possible dynamic, but so too is greater identity – a greater Black consciousness in the United States does not necessarily make Blacks less American.

The presence of the Soviet army in Afghanistan has led to some speculation concerning the attitudes of the Central Asian population. Bennigsen[77], on the one hand, writes that 'the Central Asian *masses* are ignorant of the world beyond the Soviet frontiers. Where foreign Islam is concerned, their main feeling is that of a vague religious kinship.'[78] For the Communist Muslim *elites*, however, he argues that they strongly support intervention. The First Secretary of the Communist Party of Azerbaydzhan is reported as saying that Azerbaydzhan could serve as a 'duct for Bolshevik-style revolution into all the states and nationalities professing Islam'.[79] On the other hand, a greater exchange of information derived from greater contact might lead to 'a fundamentalist, conservative religious revival ...'[80] in Soviet Central Asia. Very little hard evidence is available on this score, and such views must be treated with scepticism.

To analyse adequately such a broad and elusive term as the 'Soviet people' would require survey data which are not available. The inclusion of national groups in the political process is one way that we may evaluate the equality of ethnic groupings in the USSR. Here again our measures are indirect; we may only make inferences about participation by people with different ethnic identities occupying various positions.

Political Representation of Nationalities

Brzezinski and Huntington, in comparing American and Soviet political elites, have identified the WASPS (white Anglo-Saxon Protestants) and SRAPPS (Slavic-stock Russian-born apparatchikis) at the apex of each society.[81] While Soviet political leaders had a worker or peasant social background, they appeared to be drawn disproportionately from Slavic, and particularly Great Russian, stock. During the period 1919–62, 75 per cent of the members of the Politbureau (Presidium) and Secretariat of the Party were of Russian nationality, whereas Russians composed only 54.6 per cent of the population. These proportions remained fairly constant in the 1970s. By 1980, Russians occupied 68 per cent of the posts, Ukrainians 7 per cent, a Kazakh, Azerbaydzhani, Georgian, Uzbek and Latvian each 3.5 per cent and two Byelorussians 7 per cent. Comparing ethnic composition over time, the major change is the dramatic disappearance of Jews from the political leadership: in the period 1919–35, 18 per cent were Jews; this figure fell to 4 per cent in 1973 and to zero in 1980. In the Central Committee of the CPSU elected in 1918, 68 per cent of the voting members (319) were Great Russians, 14 per cent were Ukrainians, while Byelorussians and Kazakhs had 2 per cent each (and there was a long 'tail' of single ethnic representatives). One might expect the political leadership to be weighted in favour of the Russians, who not only were among the most culturally advanced peoples of Russia, but also constituted a very large part of the Bolshevik Party before the revolution. Policy has been, and is, to recruit into the party and other political bodies nationalities in similar proportions as they are found in the population as a whole.

At the level of the rank and file and in lower echelons of the political system, the representation of non-Russian nationalities is much higher.

TABLE 6.6: ETHNIC COMPOSITION OF CPSU

	Total Members and Candidates 17 430 413	1981 100	Population of USSR 1981 100	Age-Adjusted Index 1976 per 1,000
Russians	10 457 771	60.0	52.4	111
Ukrainians	2 794 592	16.0	16.1	90
Byelorussians	651 486	3.7	3.6	94
Uzbeks	393 770	2.3	4.7	77
Kazakhs	332 821	1.9	2.5	112
Georgians	290 227	1.7	1.36	127
Azerbaydzhanis	280 498	1.6	2.0	113
Lithuanians	126 704	0.7	1.0	62
Moldavians	89 680	0.5	3.8	42
Latvians	71 911	0.4	0.54	65
Kirgiz	62 694	0.4	0.72	75
Tadzhiks	74 987	0.4	1.1	67
Armenians	261 572	1.5	1.58	115
Turkmens	61 430	0.4	0.77	70
Estonians	55 957	0.3	0.38	71
Other Nationalities	1 424 313	8.2	7.45	—
Average				96

Sources: 'KPSS v tsifrakh,' Partynaya Zhizn', no. 14. (1981), p. 18. Ellen Jones and Fred W. Grupp, 'Measuring Nationality Trends in the Soviet Union; A Research Note', Slavic Review, vol. 41, no. 1 (Spring 1982), pp. 112–22.

Table 6.6 shows the membership of the CPSU in 1981 by nationality. The data illustrate that the Russians are somewhat over-represented and some of the smaller nationalities (Turkmen, Kirgiz) have a lower than proportional share. One must bear in mind, however, that the central Asian nationalities have a skewed age distribution, with many more children in the population. There are also rural/urban and educational disparities, and one would expect the more urban and better educated populations to have a greater participation in politics. Jones and Grupp have carefully analysed participation ratios in terms of appropriate age cohorts (comparing national party membership with the nationality population aged 20 years and over). Their calculations, for 1976, are displayed in the last column of table 6.6; party membership is expressed as an index per 1,000 of the appropriate adult nationality group. The average participation rate for the USSR is 96 per thousand. Russians have a high rating (111), but are not the highest, being bettered by Kazakhs (112), Azerbaydzhanis (113), Georgians (127) and Armenians (115). Low participation is concentrated among Moldavians (42), Lithuanians (62), Latvians (65) and Tadzhiks (67) – all nationalities with a large number of older peasant inhabitants.

Bilinsky provides a good analysis of national representation in the apparatuses of the Union Republics. He shows that the party First Secretary in *all* the republican parties was a national of the indigenous population – e.g. a Moldavian in Moldavia. The party Second Secretary was sometimes of a different nationality: in 1966, six out of fourteen were Russians. The membership of the Republican Politbureaux in 1966 was overwhelmingly made up of nationalities of the titular republic: in the Ukraine, twelve out of fourteen were Ukrainians; in Uzbekistan, seven were Uzbeks, one was a Russian and the nationality of two could not be ascertained; in Moldavia, five were Moldavians, two were Russians and four were of unknown stock; in Latvia, seven were Latvians, one was Ossetian and the nationality of two was not known. Hodnett's analysis of leading posts in Kazakhstan between 1955 and 1972 showed that 47 per cent were occupied by Kazakhs – an *over*-representation, as Kazakhs accounted for less than a quarter of the population of Kazakhstan.[82] In the Council of Ministers of the Republics, the Chairman was without exception a member of the titular nationality, as was the First Deputy Chairman in thirteen out of the fifteen Republics.[83] These findings are confirmed by George Fischer, who shows that executive posts at the USSR level (in 1958 and 1962) had more than an equal share of Russian incumbents, but that the reverse was true for posts below the USSR level.[84] Between 1965 and 1977, the ethnic composition of First Secretaries of Republican and regional party committees remained 'identical': 52 Russians, 8 Ukrainians and 12 other minority nationalities.[85] But below this level, 76 per cent of the members of the Central Committee bureaux and the Republican Presidium of the Council of Ministers were recruited from the indigenous nationalities.[86]

The representation of the various nationalities at the centre varies between different institutions. Russians are *under*-represented in the Supreme Soviet, being 43.4 per cent of deputies in 1974 and 53.5 per cent of the total population. In the Council of Ministers of 1966, the Slavic nationalities constituted 94.2 per cent of the ministers and other functionaries. This figure, however (and this is important), ignores the fifteen chairmen of the Council of Ministers of the Union Republics, who are members of the Council of the USSR, and who are mostly non-Slavs.[87]

The smaller nationalities tend to be under-represented, except in the Supreme Soviet where the federal system assures their representation. Jews come out particularly low: they make up 0.89 per cent of the population, but only 0.39 per cent of the Supreme Soviet (1974), 0.51 per cent of the Central Committee (1966), and their one member of the

Council of Ministers gave them a 1.79 share. Professor Nove has said that this is unique both by comparison with the Russian past when Jews were most active politically and with other countries with a significant Jewish population.[88] But such low participation is accounted for in some respects by the institutional arrangements: as the Jews were not afforded the full status of a nationality and are geographically dispersed, their share of members in the Soviet through the federal system is reduced. The 'quota system' of party membership tends to decrease their share – because of their geographical dispersion. It would be wrong, however, to infer that Jews are *excluded* from Soviet political institutions: in 1974, six were elected to the Supreme Soviet and 4,519 were chosen at all levels of government (3,128 *less* than in 1966). Their numbers are falling, however: in the 1980 elections to the Supreme Soviets of the Union Republics, only 24 were elected out of a total of 6,730.[89]

It is in the Republican and local Soviets that the non-ethnic groups secure their representation. The composition of deputies by nationality in the Republican Supreme Soviets and local Soviets in 1980 is shown in table 6.7. Russians are shown to have a lower participation rate than their

TABLE 6.7: ETHNIC COMPOSITION OF REPUBLICAN SUPREME SOVIETS AND LOCAL SOVIETS IN 1980

Nationality	Per cent of Population 1979	Per cent of Deputies to Republican Supreme Soviets 1980	Per cent of Deputies to Local Soviets 1980
Russians	52.42	27.98	45.34
Ukrainians	16.16	9.82	22.0
Byelorussians	3.61	6.39	3.89
Uzbeks	4.75	6.51	3.8
Kazakhs	2.5	3.77	2.99
Georgians	1.36	5.23	1.74
Azerbaydzhanis	2.09	5.75	2.12
Lithuanians	1.09	4.10	1.09
Moldavians	1.13	3.79	1.32
Latvians	0.55	3.49	0.81
Kirgiz	0.73	3.27	0.84
Tadzhiks	1.11	3.63	0.90
Armenians	1.58	5.44	1.42
Turkmens	0.77	3.49	0.83
Estonians	0.39	3.15	0.44
Other Nationalities	9.75	4.2	10.46

Source: M.I. Kulichenko, *Rastsvet i sblizhenie natsii v SSSR* (1981), p. 276.

numbers in the population as a whole would warrant. The smaller nationalities are 'over-represented' in the Soviets. Brzezinski and Huntington's characterization of a national ethnic elite, therefore, needs some modification. The figures cited above would suggest that, while slavonic stock predominates in All-Union leadership positions, the republican political elites are not so constituted.

Rywkin has suggested that in the Republics of the USSR there is 'reverse discrimination', with non-Russians being given preference over Russians for certain posts. Rywkin turns the accusation of Russian domination in relation to peripheral areas on its head:

Moscow's reservation for Europeans of such positions as republican party second secretaries, heads of special sections, heads of republic security organizations, and directors of 'all-union' importance is a case of ethnic stratification of obvious political importance, but it involves only a few high-level positions. More telling, an even larger number of managerial jobs is reserved exclusively for Muslims (even if they are 'assisted' by Russian seconds.) These include positions of party first secretaries, party secretaries for agitation and propaganda, top positions in the governments and legislatures, in public relations and other highly visible fields; and directorships of most enterprises other than the 'all-union' ones mentioned above.[90]

Bialer, in a study of the ethnic composition of the national republics for 1976, found that in the Party Central Committee bureaux and Presidium of the Council of Ministers of all the national republics, 252 or 75.8 per cent were of the indigenous cadres; in Uzbekistan the figure was 76 per cent, in Latvia 74 per cent and in Georgia 94 per cent.[91] Many *Russian* dissidents (and others even in authority in the USSR) argue that the burden of the non-Russian empire is too heavy. 'The sacrifice at which the empire had been achieved cost the Russian people their freedom, their faith, their culture, and, finally, their personal material welfare.'[92]

Rasma Karklins, in a study of emigrants[93] from the Soviet Union, has shown that there are important regional variations in people's perceptions of the power of various nationalities. In table 6.8 are depicted the responses of ex-inhabitants of various parts of the USSR to the question, 'In your view, is the power of... (local nationality) increasing, or decreasing, or staying the same?' In Kazakhstan (67 per cent) and Central Asia (39 per cent) there were large numbers perceiving an increase in the power of the native population. The majority of the Baltic nationalities thought that their influence was decreasing (59 per cent). Karklins also analysed the reasons why the various nationalities perceived things in the way that they did. The respondents' answers show five underlying features: more natives in higher positions, higher levels of education, more national assertiveness, increase in numbers, 'native culture gains'. The frequency of

TABLE 6.8 PERCEPTIONS OF POWER CHANGES IN NON-RUSSIAN REPUBLICS

Nationality power seen to be	Total	Percentage of Respondents Kazakhstan	Central Asia	Baltic
	(n = 182)	(n = 66)	(n = 36)	(n = 34)
Increasing	40	67	39	6
Decreasing	21	2	11	59
Staying the same	20	15	31	18
Don't know	19	16	19	17
Total	100	100	100	100

Source: R. Karklins, 'Nationality power in Soviet Republics: and Perceptions', *Studies in Comparative Communism*, vol. 14, no. 1 (1981), p. 74.

answers is quantified in table 6.9. The kinds of responses given included the following: 'Now there are more Kazakhs everywhere, frequently one has a Kazakh as the boss and a Russian in the second place; the Kazakhs don't understand as much and then the Russian does his work.'[94] On education, one person pointed out, 'the Kazakhs are getting more and more educated, and when one is educated one understands more and then, at one moment, they say "now listen, this is my country".'[95] Where the population of natives is increasing, this is regarded as giving power: 'Oh yes, their power is larger now, there are three children (per family) in the case of other nationalities, but the Kazakhs have large families,... they have six to seven children, sometimes up to ten.'[96] In Latvia, on the other hand, 'The power of Latvians decreases. Fewer are born, more die...'[97]

TABLE 6.9: ASPECTS OF INCREASING NATIONALITY POWER

	Total	Frequency items mentioned Kazakhstan	Central Asia	Baltic
More native cadre, higher positions	42	26	10	—
More education, development	28	11	9	1
More national pride, assertiveness	22	12	5	—
Increase in numbers	16	10	3	2
Native culture gains	4	2	2	—
Other	10	7	1	—

Source: Karklins, 'Nationality Power in Soviet Republics...', p. 78.

National pride and 'consciousness' was noted to be strengthening. 'Formerly they used to be silent, downtrodden, but now they shout their songs in the streets. Formerly, the Russians were putting the screw on Kazakhs, but now it is the other way round.' In Estonia, however, '[The Estonians] say that they now have to study more Russian, starting even in Kindergarten...I think that everything will be more Russian in time.'[98]

This research shows quite a different perspective on nationality politics in the Baltic states and in Central Asia with a greater dynamic to local national consciousness in the latter reflecting the maturation of the local nationalities. It would a mistake, however, to assume that these groups are likely to advocate 'independence' from the USSR. The political incorporation of the local indigenous elites involves their identification with the Soviet system. While there may be pressures for decentralization and more regional control, local elites have much to lose and little to gain by secession from the USSR. The neighbouring states of Iran, Afghanistan and Pakistan are authoritarian, barbaric and have had little concern for the welfare of the masses: there are very wide differentials of wealth and income and notable deprivation of rights to sections of the population, such as women.

Conclusions

We have seen that considerable changes have taken place in the republics of the USSR. Whether the non-Russian population is now 'worse off' than before, or than they would have been under another non-Bolshevik government, involves not only a comparison of objective indicators but also judgement of value. There seems to be little evidence to sustain the allegation of economic exploitation of non-Slavic areas. Wilber has shown that development in Soviet Central Asia compares most favourably with other underdeveloped countries: 'Central Asia has been transformed from a stagnant, illiterate, disease-ridden, semi-feudal society into a modern, dynamic, progress-oriented society...'[99] It is true that, in the development of the more backward areas, a form of Russification has taken place. While language and culture continue to differentiate the peoples of Soviet Central Asia, there is remarkably little empirical evidence to sustain accusations of manifest ethnic conflict, despite such widespread assumptions in the Western press since the invasion of Afghanistan.[100] Access to occupation and education is comparable to the Russian ethnic population. There is some evidence to suggest the political exclusion of the minor nationalities from the top All-Union political and economic elites, but not at intermediate and lower levels. In the republics the cultural importance of nationality persists; it seems to coexist with industrialization, probably providing a sense of belonging in the growing diversification and anonymity created by an industrial society. In Central Asia such national consciousness is on the increase and becoming more assertive, but in the Baltic regions, the indigenous population feels more under threat.[101]

NOTES

1 M.M. Tumin, 'Ethnic Groups', in J. Gould and W.L. Kolb (eds), *A Dictionary of the Social Sciences* (1964), pp. 243–4.
2 J. Stalin, 'Marxism and the National Question', *Collected Works* (1953), vol. 2.
3 'Communist Manifesto', Marx & Engels, *Selected Works,* vol. 1 (1958), pp. 217, 225.
4 Ibid., p. 225.
5 Engels, cited by E.H. Carr, *The Bolshevik Revolution 1917–1923* (1964) vol. 1, p. 414.
6 These views are discussed by Grey Hodnett, 'What's in a Nation?', *Problems of Communism,* vol. 16, no. 5 (Sept.–Oct. 1967) and 'Introduction', in Edward Allworth (ed.), *Ethnic Russia in the USSR.* (1980).
7 *Vtoroy s"ezd RSDRP: Protokoly.* (1959), p. 421.
8 See V.I. Lenin, 'The Right of Nations to Self-Determination' (1914), *Collected Works,* vol. 20 (1964), pp. 393–451.
9 Ibid., p. 422.
10 Ibid., p. 410.
11 J.V. Stalin, 'Marxism and the National Question', p. 375.
12 J.V. Stalin, 'The Nation Question and Leninism', *Collected Works,* 1954 vol. 11, pp. 355–56.
13 The detailed history of each region may be consulted in E.H. Carr, *The Bolshevik Revolution 1917–1923,* vol. 1.
14 R. Pipes, *The Formation of the Soviet Union* (1964) p. 295. The book deals in detail with the national question 1917–1923.
15 On the impact of revolution in Soviet Central Asia, see D. Lane, *State and Politics in the USSR* chapter 3. The empirical study of the 'national' problem in the USSR is the subject of much research. See, for example, *Sotsiologicheskie issledovaniya,* No. 4 (1982), pp. 8–50; *Aktual'nye problemy natsional'nykh otnosheniy v svete Konstitutssi SSSR* (1981); L.M. Drobizheva, *Dukhovnaya obshchnost' narodov SSSR. Sotsiologicheski ocherk mezhnatsional'nyhk otnosheniy* (1981). Much Western writings is subjective, reflecting the interests of the national minorities. The reader may refer to *Problems of Communism,* vol. 16, no. 5 (Sept.–Oct. 1967), a special issue on nationalities and nationalism; J.R. Azrael (ed.), *Soviet Nationality Policies and Practice* (1978); Z. Katz, *Handbook of Major Soviet Nationalities* (1975); E. Allworth (ed.) *Ethnic Russia in the USSR* (1980); H.C. d'Encausse, *Decline of an Empire: The Soviet Socialist Republics in Revolt.* New York. 1979.
16 For the early history of Russian Jews, see S.W. Baron, *The Russian Jew under Tsars and Soviets* (1964). A useful anthology is Lionel Kochan (ed.), *The Jews in Soviet Russia since 1917* (1978), 3rd edn.

17 Figures for 1914, cited by Baron, *The Russian Jew...*, p. 117.
18 A.C. Abramski, 'The Biro-Bidzhan Project, 1927–1959', in L. Kochan, *The Jews in Soviet Russia...*, p. 65.
19 Baron, *The Russian Jews...*, p. 178.
20 See David Lane, *The Roots of Russian Communism* (1975), Chapter 1.
21 Stalin, 'Marxism and the National Question';
22 Cited by W. Kolarz, *Religion in the Soviet Union* (1962), p. 372.
23 T.H. Rigby, in *Soviet Studies*, vol. 28 (1976), p. 516.
24 For further details, see C. Abramsky, 'The Biro-Bidzhan Project, 1927–1959', in Kochan, *The Jews in Soviet Russia...*, p. 75.
25 Baron, *The Russian Jew...*, pp. 256–7.
26 Figures cited in S. Rabinowich, *Jews in the Soviet Union* (1967), p. 56; V.V. Aspaturian, 'The Non-Russian Nationalities', in A. Kassof, *Prospects for Soviet Society* (1968), p. 177; Katz, *Handbook of Major Soviet Nationalities* (1975), p. 456.
27 For further demographic and occupational data, see Alex Nove and J.A. Newth, 'The Jewish Population: Demographic Trends and Occupational Patterns', in Kochan, *The Jews in Soviet Russia since 1917* (1978).
28 Z. Katz, *Handbook of Major Soviet Nationalities*, pp. 447, 457.
29 Baron, *The Russian Jew...*, p. 271.
30 *Vestnik statistiki* (1980), no. 7, p. 41.
31 Cited by Zvi Gitelman, 'The Jews', *Problems of Communism*, vol. 16, no. 5 (Sept.–Oct. 1967), p. 93.
32 A. Nove, *Soviet Jewry and the Fiftieth Anniversary of the Russian Revolution* (1968), p. 17.
33 Hendrick Smith, *The Russians* (1976), p. 573 ff. Zvi Gitelman, 'Moscow and the Soviet Jews: "A Parting of Ways"', *Problems of Communism*, vol. 29 (1980), pp. 18–34.
34 Figures cited by Gitelman, 'The Jews', p. 96.
35 'Moscow and the Soviet Jews', p. 29.
36 Ibid., p. 30
37 Ibid., p. 34. Between 1945 and 1977, 141,600 Jews left the USSR; 1.6 per cent were refused visas.
38 Ibid.
39 *Naselenie SSSR* (1983), p. 128.
40 Smith, *The Russians*, pp. 581–2; J.A. Ross, 'Alienation of Jewish Emigrants from the Soviet Union', *Studies in Comparative Communism*, vol. 7 (1974), p. 113.
41 In the mid-seventies, according to the *Jerusalem Post*, 50 per cent of Jews arriving in Vienna went to Israel; and the drop-out rate for Jews from the USSR's largest cities was 75 per cent.
42 *Narkhoz v 1979g* (1980), p. 39.
43 M. Feshbach and S. Rapawy, 'Soviet Population ad Manpower Trends and Policies', in Joint Economic Committee US Congress, *Soviet Economy in a New Perspective*, Washington DC (1976), p. 148.
44 Data for 1 Jan. 1981, *Narkhoz v 1980g* (1981), p. 17.

45 For a more detailed account of demographic trends see: Jeff Chinn, *Manipulating Soviet Population Resources* (1977); Ralph S. Clem, *The Soviet West* (1975); H.C. d'Encausse, *Decline of an Empire* (1979).

46 This useful summary is given in Ruslan O. Rasiak, '"The Soviet People": Multiethnic Alternative or Ruse?', in E. Allworth (ed.), *Ethnic Russia in the USSR* (1980), p. 161. Many Soviet sources express similar sentiments: *Razvitie sovetskogo naroda – novoy istoricheskoy obshchnosti* (1980); M.I. Kulichenko, *Rastsvet i sblizhenie natsiy v SSSR* (1981); L.M. Drobizheva, *Dukhovnaya obshchnost' narodov SSSR* (1981). A.G. Zdravomyslov reviews policy and national relations in *Pravda* (27 August 1982); see *CDSP*, vol. 34, no. 34 (22 Sept. 1982), pp. 4–5.

47 Cited by R. Pipes, 'Assimilation and the Muslims' in A. Inkeles and K. Geiger, *Soviet Society* (1961), pp. 588–9.

48 E. Gellner, *Nations and Nationalism* (1983).

49 See A. Bennigsen and C. Lemercier-Quelquejay, *Islam in the Soviet Union* (1967), pp. 149–52, and J. A. Bennigsen and M. Broxup, *The Islamic Threat to the Soviet State* (1983), Chapter 2.

50 T.A. Zhdanko, 'Everyday Life in a Karakalpak Kolkhoz aul', *Sovetskaya Etnografiya* (1949), no. 2. Cited in R. Schlesinger, *The Nationalities Problem and Soviet Administration* (1956), p. 290. Other examples in the Caucasus are given in *Sovremennoe Abkhazskoe selo* (1967), pp. 27–52.

51 S.P. Dunn and E. Dunn, 'Soviet Regime and Native Culture', *Current Anthropology*, vol. 8, no. 3, (June 1967), p. 183.

52 Ibid., p. 190.

53 Data cited by Yu. V. Arutyunyan, 'Izmeneniya sotsial'noy struktury sovetskikh natsiy', *Istoriya SSSR*, no. 4 (1952), p. 8.

54 For a detailed history, see Walter Kolarz, *Russia and Her Colonies* (1952), Chapter 3, and for details of the Islamic peoples, see Shirin Akiner, *Islamic Peoples of the Soviet Union* (1983).

55 Y. V. Arutyunyan, *Sotsiologicheskie issledovaniya*, no. 4 (1982). Abstract in *CDSP*, vol. 34, no. 49 (Jan. 1983), p. 4.

56 Pipes 'Assimilation and the Muslims', p. 601.

57 G.P. Vasil'eva, 'Sovremennye etnicheskie protsessy v Severnom Turkmenistane', *Sovetskaya etnografiya*, no. 1 (1968), p. 13.

58 *Naselenie SSSR* (1983), p. 98.

59 *Naselenie SSSR po dannym vsesoyuznoy perepisi naseleniya 1979g* (1980), pp. 23–4.

60 Ya. S. Smirnova, 'Natsional'no-smeshannye braki u narodov Karachaevo-Cherkesii', *Sovestskaya etnografiya*, no. 4 (1967), p. 141.

61 L. Drobizheva, *Sotsiologicheskie issledovaniya*, no. 4 (1982). Abstract in *CDSP*, vol. 34, no. 49 (January 1983), p. 6.

62 Brian D. Silver, 'Levels of Sociocultural Development Among Soviet Nationalities: A Partial Test of the Equalisation Hypothesis', *American Political Science Review*, vol. 68 (1974), p. 1627.

63 Cited by E. Jones and F. Grupp, 'Measuring Nationality Trends in the Soviet Union: A Research Note', *Slavic Review*, vol. 41. no. 1, (Spring 1982) p. 120.

64 Ibid., p. 121.
65 R.A. Lewis, 'Comment – Intensifying Russian Ethnic Identity by Dispersion', in Allworth (ed.), *Ethnic Russia in the USSR*, p. 306.
66 Maksym Sahaydak (ed.), *Ukrains'kyi visnyk*, VII–VIII (1975), pp. 26, 67. Cited by Rusian O. Rasiak, '"The Soviet People": Multiethnic Alternative or Ruse?', in Allworth, *Ethnic Russia in the USSR*, p. 163.
67 Cited by Rasiak, ibid., p. 164.
68 M. Rywkin, 'Central Asia and Soviet Manpower', *Problems of Communism*, vol. 28, no. 1 (1979), p. 10; R.I. Kosolapov, 'Class and National Relations in the Stage of Developed Socialism', *Sotsiologicheskie issledovaniya*, no. 4 (1982); *CDSP*, vol. 34, no. 49. (Jan. 1983).
69 *Decline of an Empire* (1979), esp. pp. 227–47; A. Bennigsen and M. Broxup, *The Islamic Threat to the Soviet State* (1983), Chapter 4.
70 d'Encausse, *Decline of an Empire*, p. 228.
71 Ibid., p. 231.
72 M. Hazaev, *Azeri dignitary*, cited by d'Encausse, p. 238.
73 *Musulmani Sovetskogo vostoka* (March 1970), p. 35. Cited by d'Encausse, *Decline of an Empire*, p. 238.
74 Hazaev, *Azeri Dignitary*, cited p. 239.
75 See d'Encausse, *Decline of an Empire*, p. 240.
76 Ibid., p. 246.
77 A. Bennigsen, 'Soviet Muslims and the World of Islam', *Problems of Communism*, vol. 29 (1980), pp. 38–51.
78 Ibid., p. 41.
79 This quote is taken from a book written in 1967, cited in ibid., p. 42.
80 Ibid., p. 49.
81 *Political Power: USA/USSR* (1964), pp. 132–3.
82 G. Hodnett, *Leadership in the Soviet National Republics: A Quantitative Study of Recruitment Policy* (1978), p. 40., See also Jones and Grupp, 'Measuring Nationality Trends...', pp. 117–8.
83 See J. Bilinsky, 'The Rulers and the Ruled', *Problems of Communism*, vol. 16 (Sept.–Oct. 1967), p. 19.
84 George Fischer, *The Soviet System and Modern Society* (1968), pp. 74–5.
85 T.H. Rigby, 'The Soviet Regional Leadership', *Slavic Review* (March 1978).
86 S. Bialer, *Stalin's Successors* (1980), p. 214.
87 Based on data cited by Bilinsky, 'The Rulers and the Ruled...', pp. 23–5.
88 A. Nove, *Soviet Jewry...*, p. 17.
89 Itogi vyborov i sostav mestnykh sovetov 1975g (1975), p. 26; *Itogi vyborov i sostav deputatov verkhovnykh sovetov soyuznykh i avtonomnykh respublik 1980g.* (1980), p. 20.
90 M. Rywkin, 'Central Asia and Soviet Manpower.' *Problems of Communism* (Jan.–Feb. 1979), vol. 28, no. 1, p. 10.
91 S. Bialer, *Stalin's Successors* (1980), p. 214.
92 M.A. Meerson, 'The Influence of the Orthodox Church on Russian Ethnic Identity.' in E. Allworth (ed.), *Ethnic Russia....*
93 Oral interviews with two hundred Soviet Germans who emigrated to the West

in 1975. R. Karklins, 'Nationality Power in Soviet Republics: Attitudes and Perceptions', *Studies in Comparative Communism*, vol. 14, no. 1 (1981), pp. 70–93.

94 Ibid., p. 75.
95 Ibid., p. 76.
96 Ibid., p. 77.
97 Ibid., p. 79.
98 Ibid., pp. 77, 80.
99 C.K. Wilber, *The Soviet Model and Underdeveloped Countries* (1969), p. 214.
100 See for example, Bohdan Nahaylo, 'The Muslim Population Problem Raises its Head in Russia', *The Guardian* (London), 23 Dec. 1981.
101 My thanks to Christopher Lane for comments on an earlier version of this chapter.

7

THE CHRISTIAN RELIGION

The Soviet state seeks to inculcate the values, norms and practices of Marxism–Leninism as a world view. In doing so the communist state is confronted by competing conceptions of mankind's place in society. Organized religion is one of the most pervasive and potent ideologies confronting Marxist governments.

A religion has been defined as a system of '*belief, practice*, and *organisation* which shapes an *ethic* manifest in the behaviour of [its] adherents'.[1] Belief involves an interpretation of the universe, usually in supernatural terms. The religious organization defines the membership of the believers and lays down rules of conduct and ritual. The ethic involves interaction of the religious belief with the social environment. The essential characteristic of religion is a belief in the supernatural. Communism itself is said by some to be a religion. Communism, however, is a materialist, atheistic belief system, and while it certainly provides a Utopia in the form of a final state of society, it does not invoke any supernatural authority to do so, and therefore in this book it will not be considered as a religion.[2] One can study a religious institution in terms of its dogma, its membership, the bonds between members, and the effects of an individual's membership of the religious body on relations with other institutions of the society (the economy or the polity). This last aspect is what interests sociologists and political scientists and we shall consider it first, before examining the structure of some religious organizations in Soviet Russia.

Marx on Religion

Marx's analysis of religion follows from his general theoretical outlook. Religious ideas reinforce the class relationships engendered by ownership relations. They reflect, on the one hand, the ideology of the ruling class and thereby act as cement in stabilizing the social order; on the other hand, religion acts as a vent for the misery and degradation of the exploited class.

Marx poignantly summed up his view on religion in a well-known passage: 'Religious belief is at one and the same time an expression of real poverty and a protest against real poverty. Religion is the sigh of an oppressed creature, the heart of a heartless world, just as it is the spirit of a spiritless situation. It is the *opium* of the people.'[3]

Marx here pointed out the more positive role played by religion in being a 'protest against real poverty': the role of religious sects is particularly important in this respect. But the dominant function of religious ideas, especially as expressed through established churches, is that of a soporific or opiate, which deadens the pain of oppression and which at the same time obscures exploitation.

Membership of religious orders and belief in God as salvation are, in a Marxist sense, the 'false consciousness' of the oppressed. That is, the individual attributes his impoverishment to a false cause and religious action can in no way improve his social being. Prayer, belief in God, in the supernatural and in religious salvation can only divert the individual's consciousness from class and revolutionary action.

For Lenin, before the revolution, religion was regarded as an outgrowth of capitalism. 'Religion is the opium of the people ... Religion is a kind of spiritual gin in which the slaves of capital drown their human shape and their claims to any decent life ... All modern religions and Churches, all religious organisations, Marxism always regards as organs of *bourgeois* reaction serving to defend exploitation and to stupefy the working class.'[4]

The Bolsheviks regarded religion as being dependent on class relationships and exploitation. With the abolition of capitalism, they argued, religion would wither away. As an institution, the Bolsheviks opposed the Church, but the struggle against religion was secondary to the class struggle.[5] Religious prejudices, it was thought, would disappear with the introduction of socialist planning and the kind of scientific education that goes with it. This would be the long-term tendency. In the short run after the October Revolution, measures had to be taken to combat the religious beliefs and institutions which flourished in Tsarist Russia.

The Russian Orthodox Church

Under the Tsars the Russian Orthodox Church was the national church of the Empire. As an official church, the Orthodox had special privileges and rights under the Tsars. It was closely linked to the government, it had official representatives in the Council of Ministers, and in the provinces priests might be appointed to meetings of the *zemstva* (local councils).

The Orthodox Church was more than a simple expression of the misery of the poor.[6] It had its own lands and received financial support from the government. The Marxist view of an established religion closely bound to, and representing the interests of, a dominant class fitted well the Russian Orthodox Church of the late nineteenth and early twentieth century. Not only did it have financial support and political privilege, it had also until 1905 a monopoly of religious propaganda; it published its own literature and was able to forbid even other religious propaganda inimical to its interests. It alone gave religious instruction in schools, it had the right to perform missionary work and win converts, and the children of mixed religious marriages had to receive an Orthodox upbringing by law. The Orthodox Church was closely bound to the Tsar: he appointed its Over Procurator and the members of the Supreme governing body (the Synod), and he had power of appointment and dismissal over bishops.

Politically, the Church in the early twentieth century adopted an extreme right-wing position. It opposed atheistic socialist ideas, upheld the Tsarist order and the sanctity of private property. Many of the clergy supported the anti-Semitic *Union of the Russian People*. In the Third and Fourth Dumas (Parliaments) most of the forty or so clergy were extremely conservative. It is true that a minority of priests, such as Father Gapon, took a more liberal view. In general, however, there can be no doubt that the established Russian Orthodox Church was one of the mainstays of Tsarist power.

The belief system of Russian Orthodoxy did not encourage strong evangelical fervour, but stressed liturgy and ritual. It provided little in the form of popular charity. But its influence and ideological grip over the population were on the decline in the late nineteenth century. The intelligentsia generally was hostile to it. The prestige of the priest had fallen and in many villages the clergy were drunken or licentious or both.[7]

The Bolsheviks' Attitude to Religion

After the October Revolution, the Bolsheviks allowed 'freedom of religious and anti-religious propaganda'.[8] This was in line with Stalin's view, expressed before the revolution, that the party should defend the exercise of faiths by various communities, but that it should oppose religion as such as an obstacle to progress. Churches were not closed, and services were allowed to continue. But other measures undermined the Church. The nationalization of land deprived it of its wealth, and in January 1918, Church and state were legally separated. Church schools were taken over by the government. Registration of births, deaths and marriages was made a secular and not a religious affair. Religious instruction of persons under the age of eighteen was prohibited by a decree published in June 1921. As the clergy was regarded as part of the property-owning class – 'servants of the bourgeoisie' – they lost all civil rights under the Bolshevik government. They had no vote, either no ration cards or those of the lowest category, their children were barred from schools above the elementary grade and they had to pay higher rates of taxation.[9]

During the Civil War, the Church generally sided with the White Army and leaders such as Kolchak, Denikin and Wrangel. The Reds were condemned and appeals were made to Christian countries for help. After the Civil War, a period of conflict ensued between Church and state. Resistance to the communists was put up by the Church and disorders occurred, as a result of which many priests and laymen were charged with counter-revolutionary activity and some were consequently executed.

A group of pro-Soviet priests, 'The Initiative Group of the Orthodox Church', was formed which felt that the government was justified in many of its actions during a national emergency. This group, which became known as the 'Living Church', accepted the political power of the Bolsheviks and advised church members to be loyal to the authorities who were 'fighting for the ideals of God's Kingdom'.[10] The Living Church introduced other reforms: services were performed in Russian and not Church Slavonic, married priests were able to become bishops, and the eucharistic ceremony was performed openly, not behind the altar screen. They also envisaged the abolition of the hierarchy of the Church and the introduction of a more participatory structure. The intention of the 'Living Church' was to bring Orthodoxy more into keeping with the times and the new political situation. It was hoped that such reforms and attitudes would behove the Bolsheviks to regard the Church as supporters rather than opponents of the new order. The Living Church was for a while given special privileges by the government: it was allowed a periodical, and it could train priests. It was, however, far too radical for the Orthodox clergy and the mass of believers. From 1923, it gradually petered out.

The more conservative members of the Orthodox Church opposed the new trends, but even here an accommodation with the Bolsheviks was to take place. The first development in this direction was the capitulation of Patriarch Tikhon, who in 1922 gave his loyalty to the government and in 1925, in his will, called churchmen to support Soviet rule. But opposition to the regime continued until 1927 when Tikhon's successor (Metropolitan Sergius) obtained official recognition for his part of the Church. This gave the Orthodoxy headquarters in Moscow and the right to publish the *Journal of the Moscow Patriarchate*. In return the Church was to refrain from politics and be loyal to the regime. This *modus vivendi* has continued to the present day. It did not mean, however, that the Church and church members were to go unpersecuted. One might generalize that until 1929 there was greater tolerance for the Church, but from that time it has been confronted with various degrees of persecution.

Anti-religious newspapers flourished and the *League of Militant Godless* was formed in 1920. Anti-Christmas and anti-Easter campaigns were carried out accompanied by the ceremonial burning of ikons. The League campaigned for the closing of churches and often resorted to harsh measures to get them shut. By 1933, Moscow had only half the number of churches operating as before the revolution. Sometimes, the activity of the League was based on crude materialism: it campaigned for the removal of church bells because ferrous metals were needed by Soviet heavy industry.[11] In the early 1930s, anti-religious evening courses were organized, having an enrolment of some 150,000 students in 1933.[12] The activity of the League was not simply negative: it organized sections concerned with atheistic exhibitions, with artistic forms of atheistic propaganda (the theatre and music), and with the creation of a new way of life. Through these groups it sought to alter the belief systems of the people. Its slogan was: 'the fight for godlessness is a fight for socialism'! The country was flooded with anti-religious posters and leaflets. The League continued until the German invasion, having its main strength in the urban industrial areas, but in the countryside, where religious feeling was strong, it was weakest.

The persecution of the Church stopped during the Second World War. The Great Patriotic War demanded an end to internal dissension. Patriotism – always a strong element in Stalinist ideology – became dominant and the ideological schism between Church and state was ended. The Church actively supported the regime in the war against Hitler. As a result, the Church was given a higher status: it was recognized as a 'juridical person' able to own property and it was acknowledged as the principal religious body in the USSR. Church buildings were repaired. The Church for its part contributed financially to the war effort, condemned collaboration with the Germans and offered prayers for 'our divinely protected land, and for its authorities headed by its God-given leader'.

By the end of the Second World War, in theory the Russian Orthodox Church and the Soviet state each had separate areas of authority. The state was not to interfere with the internal life of the Church. It is still claimed by the Soviet authorities that no persecution of religious faith takes place in the USSR. Freedom of conscience is guaranteed by the Constitution. This view is echoed by many prominent Orthodox churchmen who have officially said that in no country does the Church 'enjoy such favourable conditions of existence as in the USSR'. Sanctions, however, are levied against known religious believers: they are socially stigmatized, the status of religion is officially devalued, believers are excluded from the party and positions of authority, and from some fields of education.[13]

Paradoxically, therefore, one has a situation in which an avowedly communist state provides a framework for the development of a religious institution. It falls to the Communist Party (not the government) to counter religious teaching and the spread of superstition, and in practice, the odds are weighed extremely heavily against the Church.

The Post-war Russian Orthodox Church

From the above we can see that sociologically the Orthodox Church adopted the role of an 'established' church. Its civic ethic, its recommendations for political and social action, coincided with those of Soviet Russia's leaders.

The death of Stalin and the advent of Khrushchev led to a renewed attack on Christianity and the Church. In 1958 under Khrushchev, a propaganda attack was launched, and many churches were closed. It has been estimated that nearly half of the 20,000 Orthodox churches operating in 1960 had been closed by 1965.[14] Closure of a church can be effected if it can be shown that there is no support for it. It is asserted in Western church circles that often such decisions have been taken when a demand does exist.

The leaders of the Orthodox Church, however, have continued their support of the Soviet government. 'At the international level ... representatives of the [Russian Orthodox Church] regularly emphasize the religious tolerance and humanitarianism in general of the Soviet Union.' The Church has supported the Soviet government in its policies for world peace, the abolition of class and ethnic oppression and anti-imperialism; it has endorsed the Soviet intervention in Czechoslovakia, condemned the involvement of the USA in Vietnam, denounced, and dissociated itself from Alexandr Solzhenitsyn.[15]

The social ethic of the Russian Orthodox Church involves aiding the state in the building of a new society. 'Orthodoxy ... sees its basic task in creating a deep unity with the people, in giving support to the people's effort at creating a flourishing and harmoniously developing society ...'[16]

The contemporary Church emphasizes the importance of a collectivist attitude, of support for the revolution, and members of congregations are called to labour. The notion that work is God's punishment for man has been dropped in favour of the maxim that 'he who does not work, neither shall he eat.' 'Soviet Orthodox theologians advocate a "Communist Christianity" or talk about a "theology of revolution" or a "theology of peace". They argue that the atheist Soviet regime, although denying God's will, carries it out in creating a new just society.'[17] The Orthodox Church now functions actively at an international level, and has facilities for the publication of religious literature and for training of clergy. In 1967 Patriarch Alexei was decorated with the prestigious order, Red Banner of Labour.

While the Orthodox Church suffered under Khrushchev, it is notable that there were no arrests of the Orthodox hierarchs, whereas 'over a hundred dissident Baptist leaders went into labour camps during the same period.'[18] When Chalidze campaigned for the cause of re-opening a church, a spokesman for the patriarchate replied: 'If the authorities will not agree to open a church, it means that God does not wish it, so a blessing would be inappropriate.'[19]

The Orthodox Church has suffered a serious decline in personnel and property. The number of bishops has fallen from 163 in 1914 to 63 in 1962, the parochial clergy has declined in the same period from 51,105 to 14,000 and the number of seminaries from 57 to 4.[20] In the early 1970s, there were about 10,000 churches in operation (in 1914 there were 54,174 churches and 23,592 chapels). In addition there were five religious training institutes and between six and ten monasteries.[21]

Russian Orthodox Religiosity

Religiosity is the identification of an individual with any aspect of a religion. Being a 'believer' or a 'Christian' has an extremely wide range of connotations from a vague identification with a church to an intellectual and moral set of convictions concerning the relationship of God to man and the world.

An *intellectual* dimension of religious belief refers to a person's knowledge of the scriptures or dogma of the church; an *ideological* dimension has to do with the believers' acceptance of them. Christel Lane argues that, in terms of the religious beliefs of the Orthodox,

There is a great discrepancy between the tenets of faith propagated by the Church and those held by individual believers. The religiosity of many believers contains a mixture of Christian and pagan magical beliefs; an extremely narrow and eclectic range of beliefs is professed, often only the bare minimum of a belief in a transcendent God ...

The level of knowledge about tenets of Orthodox faith is very low ... Orthodox believers have little interest in the intricacies of dogma, a weak notion of the dogmatic meaning of ritual and of the content of religious literature and do not know the teaching of the Church nor understand the sermons.[22]

It is in the *practice* dimension that Orthodox believers identify with their Church. The practice element is of a ritualistic and cultic character.

Believers perform acts which are 'clearly connected to everyday life, to the family, the community and to social custom ...' Such practices include rites of passage (baptism and funerals) and church holidays (Easter and Christmas): 'attendance at worship ... and participation in confession and communion in particular, have been abandoned to varying degrees by a large proportion of those who call themselves Orthodox.'[23]

Church attendance in the USSR may not give a good indication of religious commitment – unlike in the West where it is accepted as a mark of civic and moral commendation, in the Soviet Union there is social and political pressure against going to church. Distances are great and many churches have been closed. Studies have found that if the church is not too distant Orthodox believers will attend a few times a year. The Orthodox Church is not evangelical, it confines its work to within the walls of the Church. 'We do almost nothing outside the church building. We don't need to because ... for the Orthodox Christian, liturgy is life.'[24]

As to church attendance, the elderly and especially old women predominate at services. This has led to a belief that believers are mainly women. According to Soviet statistics, women constitute more than 70 per cent of all believers – and between 80 and 90 per cent of those in religious sects.[25] Christel Lane has estimated that about 50 per cent of Orthodox believers are aged over 60, and another 'sizeable proportion' is aged between 50 and 60.[26] Kolarz has tried to explain the presence of women in church by arguing that women are not emancipated in the USSR and their family insecurity and the heavy work they perform create a need for religion which nullifies Soviet antireligious arguments.[27] This would only be a partial explanation, for women in other respects – such as access to education and social security benefits – have done well under Soviet rule. Probably a more feasible explanation of female church attendance is the large number of older widows who lack family ties and who were themselves brought up to be religious. In such cases, the Church and its ritual and ceremonies may still provide a heart in a heartless Soviet world.[28] Another explanation of the large number of believers who are over fifty is that old age is synonymous with retirement and also means that such persons are no longer vulnerable to discrimination in their career.

The aesthetic aspects of worship and personal psychological satisfaction derived from the ceremony (incense burning, singing, lit candles, the ornate and splendid architecture and paintings) are also important reasons for church attendance. The presence of icons in homes is not necessarily equated with religious commitment. (Studies have shown that in rural areas as many as 90 per cent of dwellings had icons, in the towns counts range from 14 to 63 per cent – even committed atheists and communists display them.)[29] Studies report a range of between 15 and 30 per cent of homes with icons being a centre of devotional practice.[30] Icons are usually hung as decorations.

Few Orthodox pray at home and of those who do, some 47 per cent prayed for worldly and other-worldly favours. Fasting is no longer practised. Reading the Bible is rare: this is due not only to the absence of Bibles, but also to its low traditional role in the practice of Orthodoxy.

As to the social composition of the Orthodox believers, the overwhelming support comes from the rural areas of Russia; in industrial towns Church membership is low.[31] It has been estimated that between 20 and 25 per cent of the population profess loyalty to the Orthodox Church. As discussed above, the believers are disproportionately old and female and only from two to six per cent of believers are under 25 years of age. Orthodox believers are clustered in the unskilled, low-education social strata. The 'technical intelligentsia' are notably absent from their ranks. In the 1970s and 1980s reports in the West indicate a renewal of interest among the cultural intelligentsia.[32] Many Soviet artists express religious symbolism in their works and the Orthodox Alexandr Solzhenitsyn has many followers among the intelligentsia.

It is the *consequential* dimension of religious belief (the effects on the daily life and consciousness of the individual) that is of concern to Marxists and the Soviet political authorities. Soviet writers argue that there is very little impact of the religious Orthodox ethic on social and political life. Traditionally, in its world ethic, Orthodoxy did not have the same influence as Christianity did in Western Europe. For instance, in its teaching on sexual morality, it was confronted and undermined by a strong pagan tradition manifested in popular orgiasmic rites which were particularly celebrated during holiday festivals.[33] The Ten Commandments 'have become meaningless to many believers who find their content irrelevant to their everyday lives'.[34] The absence of a parish religious community, consequent on the reduction in the number of churches, clergy and parishioners, diminishes the social sanctions on conduct. The Soviet sociologist L.N. Ul'yanov characterizes the consequential dimension of the Orthodox believer: 'For the majority of those who still remain religious, the chief principles in their life and activity have become loyalty to the socialist Motherland, support for the politics of the Communist Party, conscientious work creating spiritual and material benefits for the whole of society.'[35] However, the absence of a link between religiosity and socio-political activity does in itself entail a particular type of social consciousness. The Soviet writer, V.D. Pechnikov, points out that this creates a certain negativity on the part of the believer; it inhibits his or her independent action and the development of a communist social consciousness.[36]

Finally, the *experiential* dimension of faith is concerned with communication with a transcendental force. Orthodox believers experience 'peace of soul, joy, elation, inner liberation'[37] during services. Such diffuse emotionality plays an important part in sustaining the believer's faith; it is congruent with the ritual practice of Orthodoxy and the weakness of its ideological and intellectual dimension.

At the end of this chapter, I shall discuss some of the reasons for the persistence of Christianity. We may conclude here that Orthodoxy lacks vitality both as an ideology – as an interpretation of the world – and as an ethic in providing guiding rules for life. Orthodox religion, therefore, apart from an indirect and negative influence on social consciousness, would not appear to provide any significant challenge to communist ideology.

The Baptists

At the beginning of this chapter, it was pointed out that religion in Marxist theory served both to reinforce the existing relationships of society and to act as a vent for the misery engendered by a social order. 'Established' religions, such as Russian Orthodoxy, largely perform the first function, sectarian religious bodies, the second. Sectarian groups are often distinguished by being composed of lower, more deprived, social strata than those of the more established Church. As Stark has pointed out, religion acts as 'a kind of protest movement, distinguished from other similar movements by the basic fact that it experiences and expresses its dissatisfactions and strivings in religious (rather than in political or economic or generally secular) terms'.[38]

Many small eccentric groups such as the Molokans, Dukhobors, the Sect of the Castrated, the Fyodorist Crusaders, and the Innocents were founded in the Russian Empire.[39] Among the most important Protestant groups are the Evangelical Christians and the Baptists. To illustrate the position of the sects, only these will be commented on here.

Such sects were not regarded by Marxists in the same way as the Orthodox Church. Before the revolution they were as opposed to the autocracy as the Bolsheviks, except that their Utopia was a religious one based on spiritual precepts rather than on political revolution. After the revolution, the Baptists and Evangelical Christians were not regarded by the Bolsheviks as supporters of the *ancien régime*, for they had been persecuted by it. Much of the Bolsheviks' opposition to *established* religion was similar in character to the sects' own position. Thus they were not persecuted or weakened by the new Soviet state for many years. Indeed, for their part many Baptists applauded the social and economic policies of the Bolsheviks.

The forms of communal living practised by many of the sects had none of the social consequences of capitalist competition. Many of their village communities were based on thrift, the abolition of money and the rejection of private property. Their moral code also had similarities to the communist: it strongly disapproved of drinking, debauchery, hooliganism and sexual licence. In the first ten years of Bolshevik rule, the paradoxical position existed that sectarian groups, which had previously opposed and had been alienated from the state, were now given a secure position by Russia's atheistic leaders. The Baptists organized their own collective farms, formed their own youth movement, the *Khristomol,* and were allowed to publish the Bible (25,000 copies were published in 1926).

But with the collectivization campaign and growing centralization of political control from 1928, the attitude of the government to the sects began to change. Politically, they were charged with being connected with, and agents of, religious groups abroad. Economically, they were regarded as *kulak* elements, and were absorbed into collective farms and often deported east of the Urals. Ideologically, however similar some of the sects' moral teaching was to socialism, their religious ideals were at odds with historical materialism, and conflict with the state over education and the upbringing of the young ensued. The sects' position became more akin to what it had been before the revolution. Their periodicals stopped publication and their 'Preachers' School' was closed. To spread the faith they had to rely once more on face to face contact.

After the Second World War, the persecution of sects eased and a formal organization, the 'All-Union Council of Evangelical Christians/ Baptists', was set up. This had the right to represent most of the Protestant sects in the Soviet Union and brought under its wing the western, newly incorporated, areas of the USSR which had relatively large sectarian populations.[40] Thus a number of Christian groups of all opinions were brought under the aegis of the All-Union Council.

The existence of a formal structure did not save the Baptists from the Communist Party's anti-religious propaganda. This, however, did not deplete the numbers or diminish the faith of the Baptist flock until the mid-1950s, when membership figures fell. The following figures are estimates that have to be taken with caution. At the end of 1947, there were 4,000 Baptist communities, 400,000 baptized.[41] By 1954 there were 5,400 communities and 512,000 baptised.[42] Since the 1950s the size of the official Baptist community has declined; in 1966 there were about 2,000 communities with more than 200,000 members.[43] By 1974, membership had recovered: there were estimated to be 550,000 baptized members in that year and also a large number of 'unofficial' Baptists – making this sect the 'largest on Soviet soil and the third largest Baptist group in the world'.[44] The life of the breakaway sects is more dynamic and militant against the Soviet regime than the 'official' body, which has become more like an 'established church'. Illegal schools for the young, the circulation of leaflets, and public meetings have been reported.[45] Baptists are located in both rural and urban areas and about 10 per cent are under 30 years of age. Membership embraces a wide range of occupational groups and includes many skilled workers. As a Russian Orthodox has put it: 'God has raised up the Baptists in this age, so that the Gospel may be heard at the work bench where no Orthodox priest could go.'[46]

The Baptists are particularly strong in the western areas of the USSR in the Baltic, Caucasus and Ukraine, though they also have houses of prayer in the Far East and the European part of Russia.

Baptist Religiosity

Whereas the believers of the Orthodox Church were strong in the 'practice' dimension of their faith (its ritual and cultic aspects) and weak with respect to its ideological and consequential dimensions, the Baptists have quite a different emphasis in their religiosity. The ideological (their beliefs in Christianity) and the consequential (the practice of their faith in their daily life) are well developed, whereas the ritual and the experiential dimensions of religion have little salience. The attempt by the Soviet authorities to isolate and eradicate the Baptist belief and ethic has 'ensured the preservation of deep commitment to religious practice and of thorough knowledge of doctrinal positions, as well as of moral fervour and Christian charity'.[47]

The Orthodox churchgoer has no religious instruction and sermons are devotional rather than didactic. The Baptist is only admitted to the Church on the basis of merit: there is a probationary period and candidates receive religious knowledge from the presbyter. Baptists are regular churchgoers: over eighty per cent, in two areas studied, attended prayer houses at least once a week. Sermons are on biblical themes – and as many as six sermons may be delivered during a service. Baptists own, read and know the Bible. Orthodox believers in general lack a complex and coherent system of beliefs and 'profess only a few amorphous and eclectic elements' of faith. Baptists organize courses for the training of preachers and have a lively and active lay membership – some 30,000 part-time presbyters, deacons and preachers were reported in 1970. The Baptists have successfully maintained their religious exclusiveness against Marxism–Leninism and have resisted the modernization of Western Baptism.

The Baptist ethic pervades the life of the believer. One study showed that, between 1953 and 1963, in one Byelorussian village 42 people were expelled from the Church for drunkenness, theft, malicious gossip and religious passivity. Salvation is universally regarded as being best achieved through Baptism – though a small number do concede the possibility of salvation for other Christians and even atheists. Their religious and life experiences are not compartmentalized.

However, the formation of the All-Union Council (mentioned above) has led to some compromises with the Soviet authorities over socio-political values. Baptist leaders have 'extolled the achievements of the Soviet government, demanded respect for all men in power...'.[48] The Baptist position on war and military service has lapsed among many believers. Many children are not brought up in the spirit of Baptism and often no objection is made if they join communist organizations. Compared to the Orthodox, however, the world ethic of the Baptists is strongly, even exclusively, shaped by their faith. They withdraw from collective societal activities. Some Baptist believers oppose war, including the defence of the Soviet Union. Work is not perceived in communist terms, but as a means to gain salvation. Unlike the Orthodox, the Baptist community is strong and is inclusive of believers' lives. Happiness is conceived of in religious terms.

The 'Unofficial' Baptists: the Initsiativniks

The formation of the All-Union Council and various 'compromises' made by the Baptists who accept its leadership has led to the formation of a breakaway group of Initsiativniks or Reform Baptists. These Baptists hold that the Soviet state through the Council (and acquiescence by its religious members) has caused severe infringement of Baptist principles. In 1960, regulations imposed on the Baptists stipulated that children should not be admitted to services, that preaching and proselytizing by laymen should cease, that baptisms be restricted and that the probationary period be extended to three years.[49]

An opposition group of Baptist leaders and activists was formed who refused to accept the new regulations. The Initsiativniks proclaimed that 'the Word of God is the only fully sufficient and absolutely authoritative guidance for the church.' They claimed the duty and right to preach the gospel, proselytize, and act to fulfil God's will. In doing so they asserted traditional Baptist principles against the Soviet state and 'official' Baptists.

To secure their demands they have agitated publicly, published their own journal and demonstrated in Moscow. For instance, two Baptists wrote to Khrushchev on 13 August 1963 complaining that: 'Today all doubts have been removed that the church, formally separated from the state, is completely under the illegal control of various state organs, for whom both secret and open access to the church has been opened up by the apostate ministers who have entered into illegal deals and collaboration with organs of the government and the KGB.'[50] Many Baptists were arrested and imprisoned and protests were made to the Soviet political leadership. In September 1965, Mikoyan agreed to receive a delegation and in May 1966, 500 delegates from 130 towns descended on Moscow to interview Brezhnev.

Brezhnev at first refused to see them, but after a wait of a day and a half it was agreed to receive a delegation of ten. Bourdeaux and Reddaway point out that later in 1966 further legislation was passed which penalized those organizing or participating in 'group actions which grossly violate public order, involve clear disobedience to the lawful demands of representatives of authority, or entail the disruption of the operation of transport, state and public enterprises or institutions'.[51] This does not seem to have had the effect of stopping illegal Baptist activity and the production and 'mass distribution' of religious literature continued.[52]

In the 1970s and 1980s the arrest and imprisonment of illegal Baptists has continued. The leaders, Georgi Vins and Gennadi Kryuchkov, have been sentenced to long periods of imprisonment for breaking the law. Since 1975, the authorities have relented somewhat. Registration has been allowed to Reform Baptist congregations and the numbers of religious dissenters held in prison has declined. In 1979, Vins was released. In that year the number of Baptists imprisoned fell to a low of 32 and the authorities also have been reported as 'turning a blind eye to many church activities that are technically illegal'.[53] However, in 1980, arrests, according to some accounts, increased, with a total of 84 active Baptists being imprisoned.[54] The major unmet demands of the Baptists are for the rights to organize freely, to teach their religious beliefs to children and to proselytize.

Catholicism

The adherents of Roman Catholicism in Russia and the Soviet Union have been minority nationalist groups. Before the revolution they were concentrated particularly among the Polish, Lithuanian and German ethnic populations. In the contemporary USSR Catholicism is largely found among the Lithuanians. Like the Orthodox Church, the Catholic in Lithuania has suffered a reduction in its facilities since coming under Soviet power in 1940. At that time, there were 708 active churches and 314 chapels. In the 1970s, 628 churches remained.[55] The number of Catholic priests in Lithuania had dropped from 1,451 in 1940 to 772 in 1974.[56]

These are the 'official' numbers and Vardys suggests that many clergy are ordained and practise illegally. (He cites a figure of 1,500 'secret nuns' in 1976.)[57] As to the number of Catholic believers, estimates vary from 47 per cent to 83 per cent of the population of Lithuania.[58] The Catholic Church as a religious force has successfully maintained its presence in Lithuania under Soviet power – more so than Orthodox.

Catholic Religiosity

One lacks detailed and reliable information on the dimensions of Catholic faith. We can say that in general Catholicism has the distinction of being an inclusive religion: it seeks to envelope the whole life of the individual. In Lithuania, its practice, ideological and consequential dimensions would appear to be strong.

In terms of practice, Catholic rites of passage are widely performed: in 1968, according to one Soviet source, 30 per cent of the relevant constituency participated in marriage rites, 51 per cent in baptismal rites and 48 per cent received funeral rites;[59] for 1972, the comparable rates were: 25 per cent, 46 per cent and 51 per cent.[60] On communion and receiving the sacraments, no comparative accurate data are available, though impressions are that numbers are relatively high. Some observers note a weakening of commitment to family evening prayer, to the observance of fasts and to the wearing of crosses.[61]

The ideological content of Lithuanian Catholicism is actively propagated by the priests who 'write and distribute their sermons, memoirs, essays, tracts on theological themes and religious verse'.[62] Catholic priests are more highly educated than Orthodox ones and are better able to combat atheistic arguments and propaganda. Priests have also been vocal in condemnation of government restrictions on their teaching and activity. They have experienced and survived waves of arrests.

The world ethic of Lithuanian Catholicism is not completely incompatible with communism. A study of *samizdat* literature has revealed no serious criticism of the Soviet system. There is respect for public property and conscientious work attitudes. On the other hand, there is a neutrality, even a negative relationship, towards socialism. A study of 300 sermons found only three positive references to socialism or socialist institutions.[63] Perhaps neutrality to the economic and social aspects is more general, with a minority of priests being favourable and some monks and clergy, imbued with the values of an independent Lithuania, even rejecting Soviet values and institutions.

All observers have noted the association of Catholic religion and Lithuanian nationalism. Like Catholicism in Poland, the Church invites identification with the nation – its history, language and culture. As it is not formally a political movement, identity *per se* with the Church is not an expression of political disloyalty to the state, though the Church may covertly oppose the doctrines of the state. Identification with the Church in Lithuania is an expression for many people of a dislike for things Russian and Soviet. It is a link with not only a cultural heritage, but also a capitalist past. During the Second World War the Church did not officially condone partisan activity against the Soviet Union, though many Lithuanian priests approved of the movement as one of independence from the Soviet Union.

The Church identifies itself and is identified with national traditions and customs. As many figures in Lithuanian history were from the Catholic Church, an attack on them or on Catholic religion is interpreted by Lithuanian dissident groups as an attack on Lithuanian culture.[64] Religion may be used as an instrument of ideological protest: claims for the rights of Catholics against the Soviet state are an expression of a philosophy of individualistic rights. Strong nationalist sentiments themselves in turn legitimate the assertion of Catholic interests. Support in defence of the Church has been widespread; and the Catholics in Lithuania have a broad social base. In face of repression, over 17,000 signatures were appended to a protest to the United Nations in defence of the Church in Lithuania.[65] In 1983, the arrest of a priest who was a member of the Catholic Committee for the Defence of Believers' Rights on charges of 'slandering the Soviet state and social system' and for calling for 'resistance against it' led to 35,865 people signing a petition to Andropov calling for his release.[66] In 1972 the self-immolation of a young Catholic led to two days of rioting in Kaunas. (This obviously had political overtones, as the Catholic Church strongly deplores suicide.) As Jancar has put it, the evidence suggests 'an embittered nationalism buttressed by an intense religious faith'.[67]

Explanations of Religion in Soviet Society

Christianity has suffered a serious decline in the USSR, but this should not lead one to under-estimate the persistence of religious belief. With industrialization, a secularization of life has taken place: mass media and entertainment have weakened the appeal of religious ceremony and ritual, the government has taken over the Church's role of provision for the needy and destitute, science has provided an explanation of the physical world. But this does not entail that religion has 'withered away .

Religion has persisted in the USSR. It means different things to different believers and there are many reasons for its survival. There are cultural reasons. Orthodoxy is above all an expression of *Russian* tradition; it has an appeal which enshrines the traditional against the modern, and the

Russian against the Soviet.[68] For the majority of Orthodox believers, however, the ritualistic and cultic phenomena, the haven of emotionality provided by the Church and its services give a psychological satisfaction and social identity lacking in modern life. The mass of Orthodox believers are from the traditional peasant sector of Soviet society and are old and often without family. These are groups outside the thrust of modern Soviet industrial society. For them, Orthodoxy provides religion's traditional role of a 'heart in a heartless world'. It gives identification with the old stable community for individuals striving to grapple with a competitive, rapidly changing, fragmented and differentiated society. Those with no family and the aged are likely to find solace in religion. In Marxism a transcendental dimension is absent; it lacks a psychological support system for those facing death. There is also the cultural appeal of Orthodoxy to quite a different social group. This is composed of young intellectuals from the upper affluent strata of Soviet society. This stratum, experiencing material abundance, seeks a satisfying emotional environment and finds it in the ritual, cultic spiritual and artistic dimension of Orthodoxy. Orthodoxy fills an 'ideological vacuum' left by 'a general disillusionment with Marxism–Leninism',[69] its appeal (analogous to that of Western followers of Hari Krishna) is emotional and is derived from the spirit, not the mind.

Aspects of Lithuanian Catholicism (like the Polish variant) are oppositional. Lithuanian Catholicism is not only a religion but embraces nationalism. This gives the Church an added dimension of vitality and provides a legitimate institution for the expression of political opposition to the dominant Soviet value system. Many (certainly not all) of its adherents identify with 'independent Lithuania' and the external capitalist Baltic states; others see the Church as a supreme manifestation of Lithuanian culture facing eclipse by the numerically and politically superior Russian nation. Neither Orthodoxy nor Catholicism appears to have developed a worldly ethic (the 'consequential' dimension) in opposition to the ways of Soviet communism.

It is the sects, Baptists and particularly the Initsiativniki, who have a type of religiosity in practice, ideology, and world ethic which is opposed to Soviet communism. (The same may be said also for the Jehovah's Witnesses, not discussed here.) They have espoused a form of religious fundamentalism going against the intellectual grounding of Marxism. This is congruent, however, with certain life values of the Soviet order (honesty, even frugality, and hard work), but it is oppositional in terms of its belief in salvation and the individual's right and duty to obey the will of God. The appeal of Baptism is to those who have experienced the violence of Stalin's rule (many communities are located in areas of exile) and are politically hostile to communism. But more important in its social recruitment are those people who have been uprooted in the process of industrialization and urbanization. Baptists are people in urban manual and non-manual occupations; they are, however, located in the newly industrialized areas and have been subjected to rapid urbanization. Baptism provides a moral code and a faith. Marxism, on the other hand, is an objective analysis of social conditioning, it is inadequate in providing emotional satisfaction. If life on earth is unbearable, Marxism is inadequate as a tension-management philosophy for the individual. As a Soviet writer has put it: 'We usually paint young people's future in the rosiest hues, as though there will be nothing but green lights ahead. But this approach only plays into the hands of the churchmen, who are ready with their answers to a troubled young person's every question.'[70]

The welfare and companionship provided by the sects are important ways in which they win support. The commandments for presbyters require them to: 'Know [your sheep's] spiritual situation, their joys and sorrows, their family life. Visit the members of the Church in their homes. Show special love to the weak, the needy, those in sorrow and the sick.'[71] The demonstrations by the Baptists are aimed at securing greater freedom within the framework of Soviet law and greater rights for propaganda and means to spread the word of God.[72] The form of protest is not primarily political, but concerned with securing concessions for the performance of spiritual and religious worship. The relationship between communism and Baptism has been summed up by a young Baptist as follows: 'There are many points in common between the *Komsomol* and the Baptist faith; both aim at the development of the moral virtues in men. But the communists have no fear of God, whereas the Baptists have, and that explains their greater success.'[73] In addition, it should be added that the Baptists provide an alternative *moral* world view to the communists; when sects have adapted to a way of life similar to communism, they have declined.[74] There is then an 'ideological' as well as a cultural, social and psychological component in the persistence of religion. Members of the sects express 'distress at the total domination of Communist ideology ... over personal moral development and the ethics of interpersonal relations'.[75] Ironically, penal sanctions on religious dissenters by the government tend to exacerbate the dissent, not only by making martyrs of them but also by making their dissent the focus of their personal lives.[76]

NOTES

1 N. Birnbaum, 'Religion', in J. Gould and W.L. Kolb, *A Dictionary of the Social Sciences* (1964), p. 588.

2 A belief in communism may provide for some people similar functions to a religious body. In this respect, of course, so do other creeds such as capitalism and libertarianism.

3 'Contribution to "The Critique of Hegel's Philosophy of Law"', K. Marx and F. Engels, *On Religion* (1955), p. 42.

4 V.I. Lenin, cited in R. Conquest, *Religion in the USSR* (1968), p. 7.

5 On Lenin's views, see: 'The Attitude of the Workers' Party to Religion', *Collected Works* (1963), vol. 15.

6 For a detailed description of the Orthodox Church before the revolution, see J.S. Curtiss, *Church and the State in Russia* (1965).

7 J.S. Curtiss, 'Church and State', in Black, *The Transformation of Russian Society,* (1967), pp. 407–8.

8 See Article 13, *Constitution of the RSFSR,* 10 July, 1918.

9 R. Conquest, *Religion in the USSR* (1968), p. 14.

10 W. Kolarz, *Religion in the Soviet Union* (1962), p. 39.

11 For an account, see ibid., p. 6.

12 R. Conquest, *Religion in the USSR,* p. 25.

13 H.L. Biddulph, 'Religious Participation of Youth in the USSR', *Soviet Studies,* vol. 31, no. 3 (July 1979), p. 418.

14 'Russian Churchmen Face New Trials', *The Times,* 3 Jan. 1965.

15 Christel Lane, *Christian Religion in the Soviet Union* (1978), p. 35.

16 *Zhurnal Moskovskoy Patriarkhii,* no. 10 (1966), p. 70. Cited by C. Lane, ibid., p. 36.

17 See Lane, *Christian Religion . . .* , p. 36.

18 Ibid., p. 34.

19 Cited by Christel Lane, ibid., p. 35.

20 N. Struve, *Les Chrétiens en URSS* (1963), p. 341.

21 Lane, *Christian Religion . . .*, pp. 30, 50.

22 The following analysis draws heavily on Christel Lane's book, especially chapter 3. She develops Glock and Stark's theoretical framework.

23 Lane, *Christian Religion . . .* , p. 60

24 Father Mikhail Zernov, cited in M. Bourdeaux, *Opium of the People* (1965), p. 74.

25 *Nauka i religiya* (1957), pp. 61, 411.

26 Lane, *Christian Religion . . .* , p. 224.

27 W. Kolarz, *Religion in the Soviet Union,* pp. 25–6.

28 A good example of this may be seen in M. Bourdeaux, *Opium of the People*, pp. 82–4.

29 See data cited by Lane, *Christian Religion* ... , p. 68.

30 Ibid. See also Yu. V. Arutyunyan, 'Sotsial'naya struktura sel'skogo naseleniya', *Voprosy filosofii*, no. 6 (1966), p. 60.

31 See data in Lane, *Christian Religion* ... , pp. 46–7.

32 A Leningrad survey reported that 50 per cent of the 'cultural intelligentsia regarded the Orthodox Church as having a positive role in the development of Russian art and culture'. See C. Lane, 'The New Religious Life in the Soviet Union', *International Journal of Sociology and Social Policy*, vol. 2, no. 1 (1982), especially p. 48.

33 On sexuality see: I.S. Kon, 'O sotsiologicheskoy interpretatsii seksual'nogo povedeniya', *Sotsiologicheskie issledovaniya*, no. 2 (1982), p. 117. Also discussion in C. Lane, *Christian Religion* ... , pp. 71–5.

34 Lane, Ibid., p. 71.

35 *K obshchestvu svobodnomu ot religii* (1970), p. 166. Cited by Lane, ibid., p. 72.

36 *Vestnik Moskovskogo Universiteta*, no. 4 (1968), pp. 62ff. Cited by Lane, ibid., p. 72.

37 N.P. Andrianov et al., *Osobennosti sovremennogo religioznogo soznaniya*, (1966), p. 204. Cited by Lane, ibid., p. 70.

38 Werner Stark, *The Sociology of Religion* (1967), vol. 2, p. 5.

39 For a detailed description of the Christian sects, see Christel Lane, *Christian Religion in the Soviet Union* (1978).

40 The annexation of the western areas also brought the Jehovah's Witnesses, who now seem particularly strong in the east and north (areas of former deportation to the USSR); C. Lane, ch. 8. The resettlement of Germans in the Perm region brought Baptism there: *Nauka i Religiya*, no. 11 (1966), pp. 32–3.

41 *Bratski Vestnik*, no. 1 (1948), pp. 6–7; S. Bolshakoff, *Russian Non-Conformity* (1950), p. 128, cited by R. Conquest, *Religion in the USSR* (1968), p. 103.

42 *Bratski Vestnik*, nos 3–4 (1954), cited by Conquest, ibid.

43 F. Fedorenko, *Sekty, ikh vera i dela* (1965), p. 166. An estimated 250,000 baptized members according to *Bratski Vestnik*, no. 6 (1966), p. 17, cited by Bourdeaux, *Opium of the People*.

44 Christel Lane, *Christian Religion in the Soviet Union*, p. 140.

45 Yu. Alexandrov, *The Times*, 22 September 1966.

46 Cited by Lane, *Christian Religion* ...

47 Ibid., p. 141. The following section draws from chapter 7 of Christel Lane's book.

48 Ibid., p. 143.

49 *Vestnik Spaseniya* (1964), Vol. 2, no. 6, p. 2. Cited by Lane, ibid., pp. 146–7.

50 Cited by M. Bourdeaux and P. Reddaway, 'Soviet Baptists Today', *Survey* (Jan. 1968), p. 55.

51 Cited by Bourdeaux and Reddaway, ibid., pp. 62–3.

52 Many documents showing the forms of protest are reprinted in *Problems of Communism*, vol. 17, no. 4 (1968). See also 'Appeal of Dissident Baptists',

Religion in Communist Dominated Areas, vol. 9, nos 3–4 (February 1970).

53 W. Sawatsky, 'The Reform Baptists Today', *Religion in Communist Lands*, vol. 8, no. 1 (1980), p. 32.

54 See 'Reform Baptist Group Leader Arrested', RL-101/181 (March 1981), p. 3.

55 V. Stanley Vardys, *The Catholic Church, Dissent and Nationality in Soviet Lithuania* (1978), pp. 196–7. It is not clear whether this latter total includes chapels as well.

56 Ibid., p. 200.

57 Ibid., p. 202.

58 Data cited by Vardys, ibid., pp. 212–13.

59 Data cited in Lane, *Christian Religion* ... , p. 210.

60 Vardys, *The Catholic Church* ... ,

61 Lane, *Christian Religion* ... , p. 211.

62 Ibid., p. 214.

63 Ibid., p. 216.

64 See report by Jonas Papartis in the thirty-fourth issue of the unofficial Lithuanian journal *Auštra*, RL-321/83, Munich (1983), p. 3.

65 See B.W. Jancar, 'Religious Dissent in the USSR', in R. Tökés (ed.), *Dissent in the USSR* (1975), pp. 222–3. See also chapter 11 in Vardys, *The Catholic Church* ...

66 *The Sunday Times*, 18 Sept. 1983.

67 Jancar, 'Religious Dissent in the USSR', p. 223.

68 See E. Allworth, *Ethnic Russia in the USSR* (1980).

69 Christel Lane, 'The New Religious Life in the Soviet Union', *International Journal of Sociology and Social Policy*. vol. 2 no. 1 (1982), p. 49.

70 Cited by Howard L. Biddulph, 'Religious Participation of Youth ... ', p. 419.

71 *Bratski Vestnik*, no. 3 (1946), p. 29. Cited by Kolarz, *Religion in the Soviet Union*, p. 313.

72 M. Bourdeaux and P. Reddaway, 'Soviet Baptists Today', *Survey* (Jan. 1968), especially p. 66.

73 Cited by N. Struve, *Christians in Contemporary Russia* (1967), p. 236.

74 See Christel Lane on The Molokans, *Christian Religion* ... , chapter 5.

75 Christel Lane, 'Some Explanations for the Persistence of Christian Religion in Soviet Society', *Sociology*, vol. 8, no. 2 (May 1974), p. 240.

76 See Chapter 9 of *State and Politics in the USSR* (1984). Many thanks to Christel Lane for comments on an earlier version of the present chapter.

8

THE EDUCATIONAL SYSTEM

The Roles of Education

In distinguishing between the economy and the state, I have pointed out that the former carries out the functions of production and accumulation, whereas the latter includes those institutions which seek to reproduce certain relations to the means of production. In contemporary socialist societies, the state not only *re*produces, but actively seeks to create socialist social relations. Under capitalism, the state is usually regarded by Marxists as an instrumentality; it acts to secure the allegiance of the population to capitalism; it provides cohesion – through coercion and a value and belief system – to the system. Most modern theorists regard the capitalist state as being predicated on the economic structure of society: Ralph Miliband, for example, regards the state as 'primarily and inevitably the guardian and protector of the dominant economic interests'.[1] In the Soviet Union, the state in the form of the political and ideological apparatuses has been a dynamic factor in creating the present form of economy. But one should not make the mistake of assuming a one-way causal influence between state and economy – in capitalism or state socialism. There are important exchanges between state and economy: they shape each other. Various 'interests' become established in the institutions of state and economy. They often act to maximize their sectional interests. Institutions of the state (such as the party, or the police) may become hegemonic, or take a leadership role.

The educational system has a crucial part to play in any society. Under socialism, it has the responsibility for the formal socialization of the 'correct' attitudes in a socialist society; for the creation of a 'communist man'. That is not its only task: as under capitalism, it plays an important role in teaching skills necessary to, and required by, the economy. By virtue of its differential distribution of culture and skills, it effectively allocates its 'products' (pupils and students) to positions in the occupational and status hierarchies. Educational systems also take on a 'life of their own'; educational practitioners are influenced by their own conception of what education should be about. One cannot, therefore, assume, as is often the case, that the educational system merely 'reflects' the directives of a government, however centralized it may be. Government, economy and educational system may not function symmetrically but may conflict over priorities and objectives.

The layman regards 'education' as being largely concerned with schools and the learning of skills. For the sociologist, education has a much wider significance. Durkheim defined it as: 'a methodological socialisation of the young generation'.[2] This definition widens the layman's concept to include all actions performed by the older generation in introducing the young to the moral, social and intellectual tradition of a society. The word 'tradition' implies the inculcation of conservative notions; and educational institutions, therefore, normally stabilize a social order by passing on the values and codes of behaviour of the adult world or, more accurately, of the various social strata making up the adult world. This is an over-simplification, for the adult world is often not consensual itself and sometimes educational institutions may be hotbeds of social change. Learning involves discovering, and in educational institutions research and innovation are also carried out, presenting a dynamic element to the social system and by the same token a challenge to the political elites and ruling classes. In simple, relatively undifferentiated societies, the family is the chief agency for education. In complex ones, it becomes the task of specialized institutions: nurseries, schools, colleges, universities and academies of sciences. These prepare individuals with the necessary skills and attitudes to perform specialized tasks given by the division of labour; the educational system, therefore, inculcates values demanded by the society as a whole and skills demanded by 'the special milieu for which [the individual] is specifically destined'.[3] Due to the tension sometimes created between the 'research' and 'teaching' elements, research or innovation is often organized separately, either in research units in universities or in special research institutes. This, as we shall discover below, is the case in the USSR.

We might define five major functions of educational systems, bearing in mind that they may not be congruent one with another:

1 The transmission of values, and beliefs: religious orientations and secular ethics are examples here. Such dominant values are linked to the interests of the ruling class.
2 The formation of social personalities. An attempt is made to socialize people into an 'ideal' personality: for instance, the ideal of a 'new communist person'. In a more general sense the education system inculcates modes of right behaviour and conduct.

3 Discovery of new knowledge. Modern educational systems are dynamic, they contribute to social change. They have a role in providing new explanations of the social and physical world.
4 Adaptation. The educational system transmits general and special skills and knowledge required by the economy.
5 Integration and tension management. Educational institutions have a political function: they legitimate the political and distributive arrangements. They allocate people to social statuses and validate the process of allotment to jobs and positions.

Whilst most interpretations of Soviet education regard the system as being homogeneous and essentially the handmaiden of the political leadership,[4] the view taken here is that there are serious contradictions or tensions between the various roles defined above.

The importance of research activity and education in modern societies has led some sociologists to give educational institutions a central determining role:

Under conditions of advanced industrialism ... the economy becomes increasingly dominated by the institutions of research and technical innovation, with the result that the differentiation of educational institutions and functions assumes new proportions. So much is this so, that the educational system comes to occupy a strategic place as a central determinant of the economic, political and cultural character of society ...[5]

This statement, however, needs to take into account the demands made by other institutions on the educational system which help shape its character – particularly the requirements of the state for defence and of the economy for skilled manpower. In the USSR, the educational system has also been an agent of the political, and it has played an important role in the inculcation of values. While the political aspect of education is often emphasized by writers on the USSR – especially by those with values opposed to the Soviet system – we should note that all educational systems attempt to inculcate political values. Schools in the United States, it has been said, are expected 'to preserve the capitalist system, to demonstrate that the enemy is always to blame for war, to prevent the intervention of government in business, to maintain permanent patterns of family relations, to teach respect for private property, and to protect the middle class by perpetuating the belief that the poor are inherently lazy "no-count" people for whom nothing can be done'.[6] In Soviet society, the political role of the school is more obvious to Western observers because some values run counter to liberal-democratic ones and because the schools were institutions used by the state to destroy pre-revolutionary values and to inculcate Bolshevik ones.

Throughout this book I have analysed Soviet society in terms of three major components: the Tsarist heritage, Bolshevik ideology and the demands of a modern technological society. These three elements are particularly important in the analysis of Soviet education.

Education Before the Revolution

Before 1917, the first steps had been taken in Russia to introduce an educational system on similar lines to that of Western Europe.[7] Schooling was organized both by the state through local government organs (the Zemstva) and by the church. The church was mainly concerned with primary education and the state with secondary and higher. By the end of the nineteenth century, the census showed that the literacy rate was 24 per cent for the total population (over the age of nine years). Important differences existed between town and country and between sexes: in the town, 52.3 per cent and in the countryside, 19.6 per cent were literate; of the male population 35.8 per cent were literate, but only 12.4 per cent of the female.[8]

Among the young, literacy was much higher than the averages above and witnessed the achievement of the educational policies of the autocracy. A.G. Rashin has shown that, of workers aged 15 to 16 in 1897, 73.3 per cent of the men and 46.8 per cent of the women were literate,[9] and, as shown in the census, 63 per cent of males in the urban areas were literate.

As in other aspects of Russian life, important regional differences existed in educational achievement. In Central Asia under 10 per cent of the male population were literate, the figure rising to an average of only 15 per cent in Siberia. Top of the list were the Baltic provinces (Lithuania, Latvia and Estonia), with male literacy ranging from 65.2 per cent to 79.2 per cent. In the Great Russian areas, these figures were only equalled by St. Petersburg.[10]

In 1914–15, there were nearly ten million pupils in primary and secondary schools of all types. In higher education, at the same time, 105 institutions had been founded, including eight universities with a total attendance of 127,400 students.[11] Institutes of higher education were mainly located in the towns of European Russia. By 1914, a third of the students in higher educational institutions were enrolled in the universities.[12] A study of the social background of students in Russian universities in 1914 shows that 37.6 per cent were of noble and state official background, 7.7 were of the clergy, 11.5 were 'honoured citizens' (i.e. members of the bottom five ranks of the nobility) and merchants; townsmen's and shopkeepers' children accounted for 24.2 per cent, and the children of cossacks and peasants came to 14.6 per cent; this left a residual of 4.4 per cent.[13] The figures show a predominance of the upper social status groups, though the 14.6 per cent from the peasantry and cossacks is surprisingly high; approximately 6.3 per cent of students received grants.[14]

The educational system inherited by the Soviet government was hierarchical in structure and outlook. The universities were designed for the gentry and other upper strata, the commercial and technical schools for the labouring masses: in this respect Tsarist Russia was not unlike Great Britain in the nineteenth century. The educational system, though not as well developed as in Western Europe, was already on the way to providing, at least in the towns, literacy for the masses and the basis of higher education for the ruling classes.

Marxist Views on Education

The Soviet leaders came to power with a Marxist philosophy as a guide to educational policies in the new state. *Soviet* Marxists have regarded education as being a reflection of, or being in correspondence with, the class relations of production. Under capitalism, according to such Marxist theorists, education, like the state, is part of the superstructure of society; control of ideas and knowledge lay with the ruling class. It was pointed out in the Communist Manifesto that 'the ruling ideas of each age have ever been the ideas of its ruling class.'[15] In *The German Ideology*, this view was put in more detail:

The ideas of the ruling class are in every epoch the ruling ideas: i.e. the class which is the ruling material force of society, is at the same time its ruling intellectual force. The class which has the means of material production at its disposal, has control at the same time over the means of mental production, so that thereby, generally speaking, the ideas of those who lack the means of mental production are subject to it. The ruling ideas are nothing more than the ideal expression of the dominant material relationships, the dominant material relationships grasped as ideas ... [They rule] as producers of ideas, and regulate the production and distribution of the ideas of their age, thus their ideas are the ruling ideas.[16]

In capitalist society, education imparts class ideas: it indoctrinates people with the values of 'the system' and prepares them for class rule. From this viewpoint, educational ideas of egalitarianism or individual development are thwarted under capitalism because of the material basis on which social relations rest. But ideas and other sub-systems located in the superstructure also may have an important 'influence upon the course of the historical struggles and in many cases preponderate in determining their form'.[17] Therefore, according to this school of Marxists, significant social change cannot be completed by altering the educational system, because it is organically related to the needs of the economy. But this relationship is not a mechanical one: within the educational system enclaves, as it were, may exist with ideas at variance with the dominant ideology and the ruling class. Contemporary *Western* Marxists tend to stress more the flexibility of institutions such as education under capitalism and have come to regard education as an important lever of social change.

Marx and Engels were less precise about the nature of education under communism. Speaking of the educational policy of the Paris Commune, Marx pointed out that it provided free education for all without ecclesiastical interference and class domination and that there was open access to science and learning.[18] With the abolition of capitalism, society would be free to provide education unfettered by the needs of the ruling classes, based on people's need to develop their potential to the full. But the Bolshevik government had to decide what precisely the needs of the individual were and the ways human potential could be developed.

Officially, in the new Soviet Republic, education was to reflect the dominance of the proletariat and its class aims. After a conference on proletarian culture in 1920, Lenin drafted the following:

1 All educational work in the Soviet Republic of workers and peasants, in the field of political education in general and in the field of art in particular, should be imbued with the spirit of the class struggle being waged by the proletariat for the successful achievement of the aims of its dictatorship, i.e. the overthrow of the bourgeoisie; the abolition of classes, and the elimination of all forms of exploitation of man by man.

2 Hence, the proletariat, both through its vanguard – the Communist Party – and through the many types of proletarian organisations in general, should display the utmost activity and play the leading part in all the work of public education.[19]

Early Soviet Educational Policy

The Commissariat of the Enlightenment (Narkompros) was set up to organize education in its widest sense. Under its first Commissar, Lunacharsky, these revolutionary goals were partly frustrated by the inchoate nature of its organization. In Fitzpatrick's words it was '... rambling, malfunctioning, over-staffed with middle-aged intellectuals and under-staffed with proletarian Communists'.[20] There was, then, not a sharp transition from the traditional system, but a long period of adaptation when new methods and goals came into conflict with traditional ones.

Narkompros had, initially, three major claims to educational innovation.[21] First, like the 'progressive' ideas (of Helen Parkhurst and John Dewey) then current in Britain and the USA, individuality and creativity were encouraged: group work and practical work was favoured;

physical punishment was prohibited; elements of self-government were introduced into the school; physical and craft skills were emphasized. Second, work in science and arts was encouraged with little political persecution – though communist scholars were praised. In this aspect, then, there developed a tension between the more hard-line orthodox Bolsheviks and the liberal practice of Narkompros. Third, the principle of equality of opportunity was pursued. Education was free of charge and based on comprehensive and co-educational principles. Specialization in terms of the old divisions between academic, trade and elementary schools was replaced by general education for all. The new polytechnical schools provided an education in academic subjects, labour skills and physical and aesthetic ones.

However, there was a great deal of disunity and diversity in the educational system and reaction against the new methods. Whether, in fact, the 'progressive' system was adopted in all schools is a moot point; in practice it seems likely that many schools continued to operate in the traditional way, for teachers and lecturers very easily fall into routine ways and resist new ideas and changes. A leading communist in Solzhenitsyn's *Cancer Ward* recalls:

'I could understand it in my day, when I was a school director. All the trained teachers were hostile to our authority, none of them were on our side. The main problem was to keep them in check.'[22]

From the beginning of the 1930s, the libertarian trends of Lunacharsky were reversed in earnest. Complaints were made from two sources: in industry and technology it was said that school leavers were incapable of fulfilling the tasks required of them; law enforcement and child-care institutions were concerned at the lack of discipline and acts of hooliganism of school children and young people. The Soviet system, faced with external hostility and rapid internal social change, became more rigid and authoritarian. Consequently, formal studies based on book learning and assessed by grades (the usual continental five-point scale was used) were re-introduced. Emphasis in the general schools was placed on mathematics, language, geography, physics and chemistry. Polytechnical education in the form of manual activities was curtailed. Authority was restored to heads and to teachers, and other social organizations (such as the party and *Komsomol*) were called on to help assert control. In 1940, fees were introduced for pupils in the last three years of the general secondary schools and in higher education (they were abolished in 1956). In 1943, co-education in urban areas was abandoned and single sex schools were re-established (sex segregation was abolished in 1954). The educational system during the years of Stalin reverted in many of its organizational forms to those characteristic of the Tsars. A major difference, however, was that education was now widespread.

In practical terms, the Bolsheviks defined three main aims for the educational system: first, to inculcate socialist and collectivist attitudes: second, to make literacy universal; third, to increase scientific and technological education.

In an attempt to abolish illiteracy, schools for adults were organized and existing buildings were utilized on a two or three shift basis. In 1930, compulsory attendance was introduced at the four-year school (for children of eight to twelve years of age in the rural areas), and at the seven-year school (eight to fifteen) in the towns. It was not until 1949 that seven-year education was made compulsory in all areas, though it is doubtful whether the provisions in practice were fully enforced. As measured by official statistics, illiteracy, at least among the younger generation, was abolished in the USSR by the end of the 1930s. (In 1939, it was claimed that 81 per cent of the population over nine years of age could read.)

The Cultural Revolution in Central Asia and Kazakhstan

In the eastern areas of the country, the Bolsheviks attempted to carry out a similar educational strategy, though here they were confronted with problems of a qualitatively more difficult kind. A 'cultural revolution' was initiated by the Bolshevik rulers. This had three aims: to overcome the ideology of the previous ruling classes; to bring up the educational level of the backward nations to that of the most advanced; and to create a common Soviet value system.

The first aim of the Bolshevik government was to introduce universal literacy which would reduce the population's dependence on personal traditional communication and would enable directed change to occur through the medium of the printed word. By the end of the 1920s, a wide network of schools, providing rudimentary instruction in reading and arithmetic, had been founded, but by 1935 only three-quarters of the Kazakhs were in such schools. The standards were low: of the teachers, even, some 70 per cent had had only primary education.[23] Nevertheless, significant results were obtained: adult literacy rose from well under 3.6 per cent in 1897 in the present areas of Uzbekistan to 11.6 per cent in 1926 and 78.7 per cent in 1939; for Kazakhstan the comparable figures were: 8.1, 25.1, 83.6.[24]

The inception of full-time education in schools organized on Soviet principles had an important effect on the socialization process, and undoubtedly drew many Kazakhs to the side of the Soviets. One cannot with the sources available know how successful this was. In the early 1920s, many of the school textbooks had 'ideological shortcomings', some 'propagandized nationalist ideology' and others 'idealized feudal culture'.[25] The latinization of script and then the introduction of cyrillic letters was an effective way of limiting the influence of classical eastern literature and breaking links with Islamic countries.

The creation of an intelligentsia recruited from the indigenous peoples was equally as important as the induction of the masses into literacy. In relatively homogeneous societies, one of the specific roles of an intelligentsia is to transmit in an acceptable and understandable form ideas from a ruling elite or class to the masses. Lack of ideological commitment on the part of the intelligentsia to the goals of the revolutionary elite presents a serious problem for the transformation of a society. In Kazakhstan 'only an insignificant part' of the indigenous urban intelligentsia supported the establishment of Soviet power and the majority supported the Cadets.[26] The indigenous urban intelligentsia was politically divided; not only were there very traditional groups supporting Islam and opposing modernization, but also there were more progressive people who welcomed modernization, and among these the communists were able to make some headway.[27] But the main thrust of policy was to form new Soviet cadres from among the young.

From 1933 a comprehensive policy of development of secondary and higher education was introduced. By 1937, 113 specialist secondary schools had been founded from which 22,000 students had graduated.[28] By 1940, 20 higher educational institutions had been set up. The intake of Kazakh students was as follows: in 1937–38, out of 1,453 students, 557 were Kazakhs; in 1938–39, there were 865 out of 2,315; in 1940 out of 2,672 students, 1,025 were Kazakhs.[29] Of course, these figures show that the majority were Russians. Comparing the stock of the educated population for the USSR and Kazakhstan we see that, in 1939, of people of working age in the USSR, 12 per thousand had completed higher education, and 135 had incomplete higher and secondary or incomplete secondary education. In Kazakhstan the comparable figures were 8 per thousand and 100. In the villages of Kazakhstan where the majority of the native population lived, the share of people with post-primary education fell to 5 per thousand (complete higher) and 69 (for the remainder).[30] Despite this considerable imbalance, the direction of educational change was to include the native population into the wider society, and educational advance undoubtedly broke down the walls separating the Kazakhs from the Russians, though by 1939 this process was still incomplete.

The chemistry of the Soviet educational system under Stalin was a compound made up of the practices from pre-revolutionary times (the five-point system, the formalism of the classroom Soviet Russia shared with its continental neighbours), some political values of communism (formal socialization attempted to exhort pupils to adopt a communist spirit and identification with the Soviet motherland – a combination of traditional and communist values), and the economic exigencies of an industrial economy – widespread literacy, discipline, and knowledge of languages and science.

The Modern System of Soviet Education

The present Soviet educational system may be divided into three main parts: preschool, school and higher. This is shown in table 8.1 which is sub-divided horizontally by age and vertically by type of institution.

Preschool education is neither compulsory nor free. Creches (*yasli*) are available for children from three months to three years of age and kindergartens (*detskie sady*) for the three to six year olds. (Full-time education starts at seven years, though this is being reduced to six.) Creches and kindergartens are organized by factories, farms, Soviets and the Ministries of Education. One of the aims of preschool education is to release women for productive work. Though nurseries are cheap (parental fees ranging from 3 to 6 rubles per month), accommodation has until recently, been limited. De Witt has estimated that in 1938–39 only 7 per cent of all children in a given age group could attend a creche.[31] In 1961, just over three-and-a-half million children under seven were in nurseries (roughly 10 per cent of the child population under seven), by 1974, approximately 37 per cent of children under seven years were in preschool establishments[32] and by 1977, 77 per cent of children in urban areas were in regular preschool institutions; in rural areas, however, the proportion was only 23 per cent.[33] Children may stay in kindergartens all day (from 8 a.m. to 6 p.m. or sometimes to 8 p.m.). In certain circumstances, if the need of the parents warrants it, they may stay full-time as boarders (for example, the offspring of university students). Education at this level consists of games, play and story-telling. Through stories about glorious deeds of leaders, children may learn a little about the history of the Soviet state and party. More important, the school routine teaches them ideas of order, neatness and personal relations. (See the Basic Rules for Pupils, Appendix F.) But the significance of preschool education generally as a socializing agency and its effectiveness in weakening the cohesion of the family are less than is sometimes claimed because of inadequate provision. Many young children are brought up in the family (either by the mother or grandmother) or by friends (see above, chapter 4). The influence of family outside of school is also important.

TABLE 8.1. SOVIET EDUCATIONAL STRUCTURE

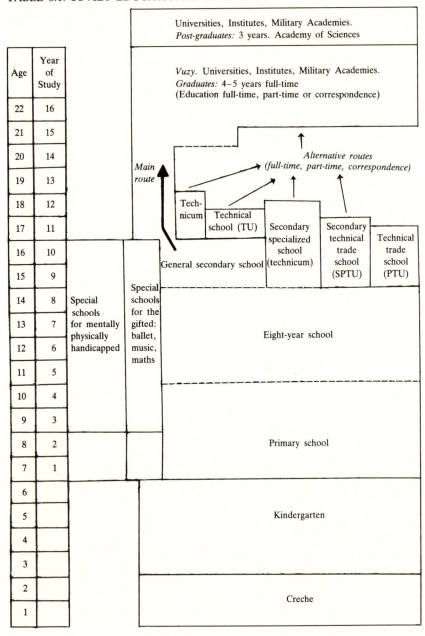

A distinction of the USSR compared to Western societies is that the government has a monopoly over educational provision: there are no private schools, though one can take private lessons. The aim of the first eight years of school education is to give a general education. This, in Soviet educational theory, has five main aspects:

1 *Physical education,* aimed at developing health and physical strength through curricular instruction and extra-curricular participation in sports.
2 *Aesthetic education,* directed at developing appreciation of 'artistic realism' among all students and/or mastery of a 'performing arts skill' by those who are particularly gifted.
3 *Mental education,* intended to develop the mastery of all subjects of instruction, and a conscious scientific and materialistic outlook; the mastery of the dialectical method; and orderly and systematic study and thought habits.
4 *Polytechnical education,* aimed at developing a specific manual skill; detailed familiarity with methods and general knowledge of production techniques and the organization of socialist industry.
5 *Moral education,* directed at creating a 'conscious communist morality', the elements of which are: conscious discipline; Soviet patriotism and proletarian internationalism; dedication to the goals of the community, the state and the Communist Party; dedication to socialist labour; and the acceptance of approved common rules of conduct and etiquette.

These components are said to represent a 'new, superior stage in the development of the theory and practice of education'.[34]

The Soviet regime has put the greatest emphasis on training in science and practical work. The figures in table 8.2 show how the emphasis has changed from 1871 to 1981. The table shows considerable continuity

TABLE 8.2: SOVIET SCHOOL CURRICULUM, 1871, 1915, 1959 AND 1981

		Per cent of time		
	1871*	*1915+*	*1959‡*	*1981***
Humanities	77	43	33	44
Maths and sciences	23	39	32	34
Physical culture, practical work and arts	—	18	35	24

Notes: * Classical *gymnasium* (8 upper years)
+ *Real* school (8 upper years)
‡ Eight-year school
** USSR ten-year general school (excluding optional subjects)
Sources: Nicholas Hans, *The Russian Tradition in Education* (1963), p. 157, 1981 data calculated from *Byulleten' normativnykh aktov Ministerstva prosvesheniya SSSR* (1980) no. 12, pp. 27–30. My thanks to John Dunstan for a copy of this source.

between 1915 and 1981. One must bear in mind that the *real* school had a greater technical basis than the *gymnazium*, where there was little practical work. More activities have been added to the time-table, rather than there being a wholesale change of emphasis.

Before 1970, after the eighth year, compulsory education ceased and students left school and finished education completely, or continued part-time or proceeded to more specialized study for another two years. (Compulsory ten-year education was introduced in 1970.) This was a form of educational differentiation. The children staying on to complete their general education (then about 25 per cent of the total) constituted a high proportion of subsequent applicants to higher educational institutions. Other pupils either left school to go to work, or entered trade schools (PTUs, *professional'no tekhnicheskie uchilishcha*). While such school leavers could study part-time to complete a ten-year education and thereby compete for a place in a higher educational institution, in practice this was a much more difficult process than staying on at school. There is also some evidence that children entering the ninth and tenth classes of the general schools were disproportionately recruited from white collar or professional backgrounds. Osipov has shown that children entering these last two forms tended to come from the upper strata groups.[35]

Polytechnization under Khrushchev

The Soviet educational system has been characterized by a tension between its adaptive function (teaching and training for jobs in the economy) and its integrative and research role. This is manifested in many ways. During the time of Khrushchev concern was expressed that educational institutions were not training pupils for productive work in the economy. Study was too academic and pupils strove for places in higher education – to ensure for themselves the status of a person with superior education. This is a clear example of one of the ways in which the roles expected of the educational system conflict. The participants (or the 'objects' of the system) define the purposes of education to suit their own interests. Khrushchev attempted to bring the school more into line with requirements of practical economic life.

A new wave of 'polytechnization' began from the mid-1950s. There occurred (see below table 8.3) a considerable increase in instruction of practical labour skills. This involved more workshop practicals in agricultural, mechanical and electrical work, and more applied and 'concrete' study of the services (such as household equipment, for example) and visits to, and production practice in, factories and farms. Under Khrushchev, practical training was increased partly to ensure that school students were

TABLE 8.3: CURRICULUM FOR SECONDARY POLYTECHNICAL SCHOOL: PRE-AND POST-1964

No.	Subject	Before the 1964 reform revision — Number of hours per week for grades			After the 1964 reform revision — Number of hours per week for grades		1981/82 — Number of hours per week for grades	
		IX	X	XI	IX	X	IX	X
1	Literature	3	3	3	5/4	4/3	4	3
2	Mathematics	4	4	4	6	6	5	5/4
3	History	2	3	4	3/4	3/4	4	3
4	Social science	—	2	2	—	2	0	2
5	Geography	—	2	2	—	2	2	0
6	Physics	4	4	2	5	5	4	4/5
7	Astronomy	—	1	—	—	1	0	1
8	Chemistry	2	3	2	4	3	3	3
9	Biology	3	—	—	2	—	1	2
10	Drawing (mechanical)	2	—	—	1	—	0	0
11	Foreign language	2	2	3	2	2	1	1
12	Physical training	2	2	2	2	2	2	2
	Total	24	24	24	30	30	26	26
13	Production (theoretical and practical) and military training	12	12	12	12	8	6	6
	Total	36	36	36	42	38	32	32
14	Electives	2	2	2	2	2	4	4

Sources: S.M. Rosen, *Significant Aspects of Soviet Education*, US Department of Health, Education and Welfare (1965), facing p. 22. For post-1964 syllabus, see also, *Uchitel'skaya gazeta*, 20 August 1964. Data for 1981/82 from *Byulleten' normativnykh aktov Ministerstva prosveshcheniya SSSR* (1980) no. 12, pp. 27–30. (See note to table 8.2).

well versed in the affairs and activity of the real world. After eight years' secondary education, another three (not two, as above) were spent in completing the school course. Much of this time was taken up with practical work. By 1955, practical and vocational instruction in the RSFSR took up 15 per cent of school time – compared to only 8 per cent in 1947 when it was restricted to physical and military training, and technical drawing.[36]

However, even at the height of Khrushchev's reforms, school pupils had a very wide range of subjects to study – much more so than in the sixth forms of British schools. In the early 1960s, for example, in the final three years of schooling pupils had per week nine hours of literature, twelve hours of maths, nine of history, two of social science, four of geography, ten of physics, one of astronomy, seven of chemistry, three of biology, two of mechanical drawing, seven of a foreign language, six of physical training and thirty-six of production training. (Data refer to hours per week summed for the three year period. Production training came to 12 hours per week in any given year.) The amount of direct instruction (42 and 38 hours per week) was much greater than in Great Britain and the USA. Homework was (and still is) additional and compulsory. (Under Brezhnev, hours at school were reduced to 36 in the last three school years; see table 8.3.)

The polytechnical secondary schools should not be thought of simply as 'trade schools'. They aim to provide an education relevant to the needs of an industrial order; Soviet polytechnical education 'is based on the notion that labour is a basic form of activity essential not only to man's survival (and therefore undertaken merely as a necessary evil) but also to his satisfaction as a human being'.[37] Khrushchev, particularly, stressed the important fact that academic study and work activity should be united, unlike in practice, where, he asserted, Soviet educational institutions were training students with little knowledge of the practical problems of the world. On more social grounds polytechnical education is sometimes seen as a means by which manual and white collar workers can be drawn together in an educational process.

The scheme described above, introduced under Khrushchev, was not effective and was subject to much internal criticism. By 1961, only half the schools had effectively introduced production training. There were considerable problems connected with the provision of trained staff and of linking school activity with outside industrial work. In 1964 there was a significant change in policy. To achieve the intended levels of practical and vocation training, Khrushchev's reform had extended the period of schooling by one year: i.e. the general compulsory eight-year school was followed by three years' study, not two (a total secondary education of eleven years). The decree of 1964 reverted to the ten-year school. In 1966, under Brezhnev, trade training was no longer obligatory, but was offered when conditions were appropriate. Discussion took place concerning the 'right mix' of education. Sociologist Aitov advocated that after eight years only one-third of pupils should stay for a full secondary education leading to higher education and that the remainder should receive vocational training. Voicing the views of industry and the need to make education more relevant to the needs of the economy, he was opposed by the Education Ministry of the RSFSR and the leadership of the Komsomol. These groups advocated the importance of a full secondary education for all and they pointed to the social divisiveness of such policy, which would involve strengthening the social advantage of the white collar and professional groups.[38]

The difficulty of putting into operation Khrushchev's reforms and modifications taken subsequently illustrate the contradictions in the goals of the educational system. Many teachers (and parents as consumers) regard education as being *personally* instrumental – in giving a status and in transmitting culture. They are loathe to accept the training of (lower-status) vocational skills. (In Britain a similar hostility was encountered by Margaret Thatcher's policy of creating vocational schemes under the finance of Manpower Services – this effectively reduced the power of the Ministry of Education and the local education authorities.) Hence the training of an effective 'economic man or woman' satisfying immediate industrial and commercial needs is difficult to implement even in centrally planned economies. The reason for this is the stress put by teachers and educationalists on the schools' other roles of cultural reproduction and research and the resistance of parents and pupils who regard the system of schooling as a means of status achievement. However, the 'mismatch' between the aspirations of pupils and the needs of the economy became the concern of Brezhnev in the 1970s.

Reform under Brezhnev

In the resolution[39] of the CPSU at its Twenty-Third Congress (1966) it was envisaged that a ten-year or a full secondary education should be obligatory for all; eight-year education had been made compulsory in 1958. By 1970, a ten year education had been decreed, and the numbers of pupils completing ten years rose during the 1970s – though even in the early 1980s nearly 50 per cent of ninth and tenth year pupils were at school in the evenings or taking correspondence courses (see below). To bring education nearer to the demands of the economy, a significant change took place in the *post* eight-year schools. This involved a form of specialization of schools and a similar policy to that advocated by Aitov, discussed above.

Until the end of the eighth year, the general schools provide a common syllabus for all pupils. At the end of each year an assessment is made of the progress of each pupil and those with satisfactory attainment are allowed to proceed to the next grade. Though Soviet teachers and educationalists rightly deny that an undue number of students repeat the year, it is sometimes asserted in the West that this procedure results in ability streaming 'by age'. Khrushchev said that before the 1958 reforms, 20 per cent of children in the seven-year schools repeated so often that they did not complete the course.[40] *Literaturnaya Gazeta* reported that in 1964 approximately four per cent or nearly two million children were repeating a year, but by 1982, 97.6 per cent of pupils completed the eight-year school on time, others having to repeat grades.[41]

In addition to the general schools are a number of educationally stratified schools. At one end are schools for the mentally and physically handicapped, while at the other end are those for the artistically gifted (art, ballet and music schools) and for children with exceptional ability in physics, chemistry and mathematics. In between are schools specializing in teaching foreign languages: in 'English schools', after a certain level has been reached, certain subjects also are taught in English.[42] An informal streaming system between schools is denied by the Soviet authorities, but the possibility nevertheless exists. Within all schools, children with special aptitudes may join voluntary 'circles' in which more advanced work is pursued. In mathematics and physics, outside schools competitions are held and summer courses take place.

After the eight-year school, at the age of fifteen pupils have a number of choices. They may stay on at the general school and receive an education which is appropriate for entry to an institution of higher education (a *vuz*). An alternative is to enter, for a two-year course, a technical school, or technicum (*srednee spetsial'no-uchebnoe zavedenie* – specialized secondary educational establishment). These institutions provide tuition to technician standard. A third possibility, and much favoured under and since Brezhnev, is entry to a secondary technical trade school (*srednee professional'no-tekhnicheskoe uchilishche*, SPTU) for a three-year course, or to a technical trade (or vocational) school (a *professional'noe tekhnichesko-uchilishche* – PTU) for a two-year course.[43] These schools teach trades (rather like the level of the British City and Guilds). An important implication of passing out from the technicums and SPTUs is that the education received is deemed equivalent to that of the general ten-year school, and successful graduates may compete for a place in a *vuz*. In 1981–82 the distribution of pupils at various educational institutions was as follows:[44]

In general secondary schools (ninth and tenth forms)	9,500,000
(of which, evening and correspondence)	4,423,000
Technical trade schools (PTUs)	3,998,000
Secondary technical trade schools (SPTUs)	4,557,000

The large number of pupils (47.3 per cent) in schools with a vocational orientation is remarkable. Rather than there being a break with Khrushchev's policy of polytechnization, this seems to me to be evidence of continuity. The setting up of specialist schools provides for better liaison with industry. The PTUs, it should be noted, come under a State Committee for trade training, not the Ministry of Higher and Specialized Secondary Education. The changing emphasis away from academic subjects to vocational education is brought out by the following extract from a speech by the Soviet Minister of Education (M.A. Prokof'ev) in 1977:

Conditions have been created in which the replenishment of the army of workers will be effected from young people with a full secondary education. Historically, a high level of education predetermined the training of people for the sphere of intellectual labour. Now it is necessary to destroy these notions. In the conditions of compulsory secondary education for all, the school must prepare its pupils in the university, *tekhnikum* and PTU, and for work directly in the factory or on the *kolkhoz*. The range of its activity has broadened. This makes its mark on the process of education.[45]

In 1977, the vocational 'relevance' of education was further strengthened by doubling the amount of time in senior forms for labour training, and the same decree 'demanded more effective links with local industry, and created combined careers guided agencies and job centres'.[46]

Under Andropov and Chernenko the trend towards the greater practical use of education (the strengthening of the links between work and school) has continued. As M. Rutkevich (the head of a department of the USSR Council of Ministers' Academy of the National Economy) has pointed out: 'In the near future, the implementation of universal secondary education is to be combined with the implementation of universal vocational education – i.e. with the training of young men and women for specific types of work ...' Rather like Sir Keith Joseph in Britain in 1984, Rutkevich calls for the restructuring of the educational system as follows: 'In today's conditions, the entire younger generation, on entering the workaday world, should have not only a general secondary education but also a broad vocational education obtained within the walls of a regular educational institution ...'[47] The educational reform enacted in 1984 envisages an eleven year school (children will start at six not seven, years of age); in the final two years of all schools, vocational education is to be introduced. Pupils who do not go on to higher education from the general schools are to receive an extra year's vocational training in the PTU or technicum.[48]

Socialization: Economic and/or Political?

Socialization (as a process by which the values and norms of a society are transmitted from one generation to another) is a function of the educational system. This statement, however, ignores what values and whose values are to prevail. Socialization is a problem, not a self-evident fact. There are three main kinds of values and beliefs that may be transmitted: those concerning interpersonal social relations, those inculcating attitudes to work and leisure, and those that legitimate the existing structures of authority and the process of the political system. Article 19 of the *Fundamentals of Legislation of the USSR and Union Republics on Public Education* (1973) defines the 'main tasks of the secondary educational schools' as follows:

provision of general secondary education for children and youth, conforming to the present requirements of social and scientific and technological progress, furnishing the pupils with profound and substantial knowledge of the fundamentals of science, fostering in them a desire for a continuous improvement of their knowledge and the ability to replenish this knowledge on their own and to apply it practically; development in the younger generation of the Marxist–Leninist world outlook, fostering in them a feeling of socialist internationalism, Soviet patriotism, and a readiness to defend their socialist Homeland;
fostering in the pupils noble moral qualities in the spirit of the requirements of the Moral Code of the Builder of Communism;
provision of an all-round harmonious development of the pupils; of their cultural standards; building their health; provision of aesthetic and physical education; training of the pupils for active labour and public activities; a conscious choice of trade or profession.

Writers who regard social systems as homogeneous and unitary regard these three types of socialization (social, political and economic) to be congruent. The values of the political elites and ruling classes are said to be in correspondence with those of the media, family and educational system. Writers taking a totalitarian approach to Soviet society see the political elites as effectively *controlling* socialization;[49] they are omnicompetent and omnipotent.

In Western societies, where there is a high level of social integration, the 'community of assumptions' shared by members of the community may be maintained by the educational system without any conscious effort. Hence

Western conservatives and liberals regard the schools as being apolitical and inculcating educational values rather than political ones. As noted above (p. 264), the truth is rather that political values, in a general sense, are unconsciously propagated. In Soviet society, the schools have attempted to inculcate loyalty to the communist regime, to the ideals of Marxism–Leninism and to the practices of the ruling Communist Party. The Soviet leadership has been confronted with a peasant culture and with a mass population with a traditional and subject political culture. Also, and as T. Anthony Jones[50] has noted, attempts by the political leadership to use the educational system as a means of social change are limited by the role of the family and the demands of the economy. The centralization of syllabuses and administration is an attempt to ensure control of the content of education.

The content and process of socialization is defined and systematized in Soviet pedagogy. Though the indoctrination of communist political principles is often stressed by Western writers, Soviet schools are charged with much general character training, impressing on the child elementary ideas of good and bad, love of the motherland, industriousness and frugality, truthfulness, honesty, modesty and kindness, friendship and comradeship, discipline, love of studies and conscientiousness, good social conduct – in the school, at home, in the streets and in public places. The systematization of 'right behaviour' and the ideal of a 'communist person' play an important part in school activities. The Code of Moral Education in some respects presents a set of values not unlike that of the 'Protestant ethic': it stresses discipline, industriousness and frugality; honesty and modesty; it seeks to develop attitudes to work based on punctuality and conscientiousness. Of more practical and immediate concern to the school pupils are the school rules (see Basic School Rules, Appendix F, below). These stress in a concrete way the values described.

The political values taught are peculiarly Soviet: loyalty to the theories of Marxism–Leninism, the Communist Party of the Soviet Union, the Soviet government and its people, the Soviet motherland. Teaching inculcates a strong Soviet patriotism. The objective is to foster a conviction of the 'superiority of the Soviet system and the inevitable worldwide victory of communism'.[51] There is explicit sex role socialization with girls being socialized into 'caring' and domestic roles and boys into more competitive and work roles.[52]

Soviet children generally are exposed to more *explicit* political indoctrination than those in Britain and the USA. In addition to the school, other media perform a political socialization role. For instance, a study of the children's monthly magazine *Barvinok* (circulation 145,000) in 1965, shows stories about the Civil War and the great hero fighting for the Bolshevik cause, about the activity of Red Partisans in the Civil War, about the revolutionaries' battles with the Tsar who did 'not want the people to build a new bright happy life for themselves'. Communist political socialization is not pervasive, however, for O'Dell found, in a study of reading themes in secondary schools, that 140 themes were 'socio-political, whereas 220 were concerned with the season, folk-tales and the family.'[53]

Studies conducted in the Soviet Union show that the school is not a very effective means for the transmission of narrowly political information (*politinformatsia*). The press, television and radio make a greater impact, whereas there is apathy to 'politinformatsia' in school. After a review of Soviet studies of the subject, Zajda concludes that 'there is a trend among some Soviet teachers to ignore their ideological role in political education.'[54]

Interpersonal relations play an important part in character formation. Teachers are encouraged to use 'positive' methods: to point out the bad effects of hooliganism and to glorify Soviet achievements. Persuasion and personal example are the chief disciplinary methods advocated. Corporal punishment is illegal and, by all accounts, resorted to very rarely. Oral reprimands, being kept behind at school, a bad mark in the pupil's record book, pressure on parents and, in the last resort, expulsion are the sanctions open to the head teacher. Responsibility for behaviour and discipline is shared more widely in Soviet schools than in the West. The pupils' organization, *The Pioneers*, will attempt to bring bad boys and girls to heel – by offering advice, by socially isolating the individuals or by public ridicule. Other organizations, such as the Communist Party, parents' committees and trade union branches, may help or publicly condemn the parents of badly behaved children.

Parents' committees have been strengthened in the 1970s; they have a statute defining their procedures and duties. They are required to meet at least four times per year; on points of disagreement with the school head, they have the right to appeal to the local office of education. Their duties include promoting good attendance, helping with extra-curricular supervision, supporting social and cultural activities and assisting with school maintenance.[55] The boundaries between the school and other institutions are not as closely defined or maintained as in the West: the school is integrated with, and responsible to, the Soviet state and other groups. This closer link reflects the greater fusion of state and society in the USSR than in liberal societies.

The effectiveness of socialization is difficult for the Western observer to determine. An important work by Bronfenbrenner, based on individual observation and systematic investigations, concludes that socialization in the USSR is effective in producing a child 'who conforms to adult standards of "good conduct" '. His research confirmed the conclusions of a report made at the International Congress of Psychology in 1963. This said:

In their external actions, [Soviet children] are well-mannered, attentive and industrious. In informal conversations, they reveal a strong motivation to learn, a readiness to serve their society, and – in general – ironically enough for a culture committeed to a materialistic philosophy, what can only be described as an idealistic attitude toward life. In keeping with this general orientation, relationships with parents, teachers and upbringers are those of respectful but affectionate friendship. The discipline of the collective is accepted and regarded as justified, even severe as judged by Western standards. On the basis not only of personal observations and reports from Soviet educators, but also from entries in the minutes of the Pioneer and Komsomol meetings which I had an opportunity to examine, it is apparent that instances of aggressiveness, violation of rules, or other anti-social behaviour are genuinely rare.[56]

Bronfenbrenner attempted to compare systematically the behaviour of Soviet schoolchildren with those in the USA, England and Western Germany. The results indicated that 'Soviet children are much less willing to engage in anti-social behaviour than their age-mates in [these] countries ... The effect of the peer group was quite different in the Soviet Union and the United States. When told that their classmates would know of their actions, American children were even more inclined to take part in misconduct. Soviet youngsters showed just the opposite tendency. In fact, their classmates were about as effective as parents and teachers in decreasing misbehaviour.' Soviet schoolchildren also showed more initiative in correcting the behaviour of friends and classmates. Peer group behaviour not only supports the values of the adult world, but also succeeds in creating a sense of responsibility for developing that behaviour. '... Soviet children, in the process of growing up, are confronted with fewer divergent views both within and outside the family and, in consequence, conform more completely to a more homogeneous set of standards.'[57]

A later Soviet study attempting to compare the effects of a new syllabus in moral education with a class that did not pursue it, found that it had positive results. At the beginning of the school year it was found that about half the children would not help a classmate against their own interests. Dunstan reports that by the end of the school year, this fell to 17 per cent in the class following the syllabus, but rose to 62 per cent in the control class.[58]

In this area of Soviet life we in the West have to rely on visitors' impressions. While noting himself that many deficiencies exist, Dunstan has remarked that 'visitors to the USSR usually comment very favourably on the outgoing self-confidence, camaraderie and general behaviour of young Soviet citizens and on the virtual absence of vandalism. In terms of the system's own goals, they appear to have been well socialized into the values of adult society.'[59]

Contradictory Elements in the Socialization Process

The stress put on the homogeneity of Soviet society – whether it be organic, as held by Soviet Marxists, or forced, as believed by some Western writers – ignores important areas of duality or even incompatibility between different kinds of values. This is particularly the case, I believe, between the political ideals of a communist society and the pragmatic requirements of the economy. These different claims are advocated by various groups located in the state and economy – within the ideological apparatus of the party, on the one hand, and by the producers of commodities in the industrial ministries, on the other. The educational system has to mediate these various demands.

Study of the media – of the textbooks of pupils and the educational books of teachers – points to four specific values which the educational system attempts to inculcate.[60] These are:

1 Discipline is necessary for efficient work;
2 Work is a basic fulfilment of man's life;
3 All jobs are worthy of respect;
4 The better one works and the more one studies, the greater one contributes to the Soviet motherland.

To some extent these various goals conflict and I would draw attention to a possible cleavage between the ideal goals of social relations in a communist society and those which are more instrumental in meeting the demands of the present Soviet economy and are not unlike those of the ethic of capitalism. This may be illustrated by examining the last two of the above points. That 'All jobs are worthy of respect' stems from the Marxist notion that all labour is interdependent and gives manual labour an important status as a creater of value. In Soviet ideology a comparison is made between capitalism based on exploiters and exploited groups and socialism where all labour contributes to the social good. 'To each according to his work and the more one studies the more one contributes to the Soviet motherland' emphasizes the *unequal* social and economic effects of *different kinds* of study and labour. As noted above in chapter 5, the distribution of rewards is unequal under Soviet socialism.

Since Stalin's ascendancy, wage rates have been determined by levels of skill, which in turn are measured by qualifications and education. The implication here is that manual unskilled labour is less valuable than work requiring skill or training. This principle has been promulgated by the *industrial* elites, because it stimulates ambition and legitimates unequal rewards for different kinds of work. This was perhaps necessary in the early rapid industrialization of the Soviet Union which was set in a traditional peasant society. Then the need was to postpone gratification and to encourage study for qualifications.

How are these values put across, and which has most salience for the young worker, or prospective worker? My conclusion is that the pragmatic achievement-oriented principle has been promoted and internalized at the expense of the principle which asserts the equality of all labour. Since the 1970s and into the 1980s, changes are taking place to move in the opposite direction. This may be illustrated by a consideration of the ways in which socialization is carried out, and by looking at the effects of socialization, by examining the aspirations of school leavers and young workers.

One can find many examples of attempts to inculcate attitudes involving the equality of *all work* and the dignity of the working class. In my view, in the past, these have been put across in a contrived fashion and are indirect. In socialist realism, for instance, the working class is given a primary moral role and has a symbolic place of honour. This can be effected by portraying workers in stories as heroes. In a symbolic fashion, workers or the workers' collective have their pictures prominently shown on the front page of *Pravda*. There are many orders and nation-wide slogans which glorify the worker: for example, 'Glory to Labour', 'Preserve and Multiply the Traditions of the Factory Collective'. Attempts are made to heighten the status of being a worker: a formal ceremony is conducted initiating the worker into the working class.[61] But these are largely moralistic imperatives. They are indirect and in fact have not been very effective.

They may be contrasted with the methods of promotion of study and the award of qualification. These are much more direct and have been effective. Reading books emphasize that the pupil has to study continuously. Not only are there incantations to 'Study, study and study like Lenin did', but also, achievement is linked directly to praise and rewards in the form of prizes, books, excursions and posts of responsibility. Hence students have higher grants if they perform very well. More importantly, perhaps, in the work situation, pay scales have been and are systematically arranged to reward those with higher qualifications, and also those who produce more. It is not so much the absence of socialist values, but the fact that they have been less tangible, which is important. The effects of socialization may be examined by studying the kinds of aspirations for different types of work.

Aspirations for Work and Qualifications

Many studies show that there are very high levels of aspirations of school leavers to achieve higher educational qualifications. There has been a very low desire for manual work or skilled manual trades. A Soviet writer on education in 1971 pointed out:

Unfortunately there still occur instances of a petty bourgeois, haughty attitude towards the working man and workers' jobs. Some pupils do not want to go into productive work, considering it to be almost an insult. Sometimes the young person finds himself in a false position because of the lordly, disdainful attitude to labour which still exists in some families. If he studies badly he is threatened by his parents with: 'If you don't get into a *vuz* (institution of higher education) you'll end up in a factory as an ordinary worker.'[62]

This attitude of belittling the importance of manual work is a traditional one among some strata in the USSR. Vera Dunham cites a teacher recalling the Leningrad seige:

'Industrial School No 5 is open for admission. A worker's ration card is guaranteed to students.' I read all this, go home, and say: 'Mama, mama, listen to this announcement ...' She listens to me ... and suddenly says: 'What's the matter? Have you gone mad? ...' She started to cry terribly. 'Where are you going? They are artisans, aren't they? What will become of you?'[63]

Soviet writers on vocational education point to an imbalance or even a contradiction between the 'pyramid of preferences' of pupils and the 'pyramid of demands' of the economy. The first Secretary of the Central Committee of the Komsomol has complained:

School children have at times a most confused impression of many jobs and have not understood the significance of such indispensable and important trades as those of the turner, the milling-machine operator, the metal-worker and the polisher, etc.[64]

This is borne out by a number of pieces of research which have shown that many more Soviet schoolchildren aspire to higher education than can actually receive it. In 1975, to fill the numbers of jobs available, about 50 per cent of all school leavers should have entered directly into the labour force. It has been calculated by one study that in 1968 7 per cent of potential school leavers polled in Leningrad, Sverdlovsk, Khabarovsk, Irkutsk, Uta and Novgorod intended to go to work.[65] Comparatively a study of school leavers in Essex found that 59 per cent of boys and 43 per cent of girls intended to take up semi-skilled jobs. If one included clerical and skilled manual jobs, then the numbers rose to 96 per cent of the boys and 100 per cent of the girls. Another Soviet survey in 1972 showed that 92 per cent of leavers wanted to enter higher educational institutions. (The

English source found that 26 per cent of the boys and 13 per cent of the girls had any desire for further study).[66] Pointing to the same conclusions are various studies which show that the prestige of particular jobs among contemporary Soviet young people depends more or less directly on the amount of training required for a job (see above chapter 5).

During the 1960s and early 1970s there was an imbalance between aspirations for occupational role (and all that goes with it) and the structurally determined supply of status positions to fulfil such aspirations.[67] The slowing down of the rate of growth of the economy, together with the large quantitative base of children with a ten-year education, resulted in, first, a fall in the rate of increase of jobs of a non-manual kind, second, an increase in the number of potential non-manual workers, and third, a rise in the numbers of those with minimum levels of qualifications for higher education. A major problem for the authorities became the creation of demand for, and satisfaction with, skilled and unskilled manual work. Having 'raised the level of expectations' during the early years at school, there was a need to 'cool out levels of ambition' at around the school leaving age and later.

The high levels of ambition can be attributed, I think, to the egalitarian educational system created by the state. As noted above, the Soviet educational system is largely an egalitarian/contest one (i.e. the conditions of learning are similar for all students who compete for higher education). For the first eight years it is comprehensive with non-streaming and a common syllabus for all children. For higher and specialized education it is selective on the basis of competitive examinations. This has the effect of heightening ambition and ensures that talent is not wasted.

Educational institutions in the USSR become of even greater importance in placing people in the occupational and stratification structure than in capitalist countries. This is because the absence of private wealth reduces the role of ascribing a place in the occupational hierarchy. 'Achievement' through educational success is the hall-mark of allocation to a job or profession. There are high levels of aspirations of school leavers for higher education and for non-manual jobs. Fulfilment of these expectations is linked to social background. There are greater 'class chances' for non-manuals to enter higher education than manuals. (Empirical data on access to education has been discussed above, chapter 5.)

'Cooling-Out' Ambition

How then do students readjust their levels of expectations in line with what are for them 'objective realities'? In the educational contest, do they concede victory to those who 'won the race', or do they become frustrated dissidents? I think that the 'cooling-out' procedure is relatively effective and has become more so. There are five major ways that 'cooling-out' takes place.

First, there is the legitimation of the selection procedure. The system is regarded as egalitarian in the sense that all follow the same syllabus in a common eight-year school. People come to believe that the school provides as equal a chance as is possible. Though there are objectively many inequalities of provision, no ideology articulating an alternative strategy of selection or occupational placement is politically possible. Hence, people come to believe that failure in educational competition is due to individual inadequacy rather than system inequality.

Second, there is a well-developed number of 'alternative routes'. The educational system is designed to encourage switching tracks. This has increased in recent years. A pupil now entering a three-year secondary technical trade school is now technically qualified on graduation to enter a higher educational institution (providing the competitive examination is passed). There is an extensive network of part-time and correspondence education, enabling gaps in secondary education to be made up and also giving the possibility of part-time higher education. There are preparatory courses at all major universities for underprivileged school leavers. The party itself has its own system of schools and colleges providing yet another stream of higher education. Such institutions provide opportunities for people who have an interest in political advancement and may not be able to compete successfully in the formal educational system.[68]

Third, cooling-out may be more effective through a movement towards greater recruitment within social strata – i.e. to 'a greater crystallisation of the social structure'. The formally comprehensive school nevertheless has a differential process of education within it. A major development is the use of informal methods of channelling ambition through vocational guidance in schools. Various institutions for vocational guidance have been set up with the explicit aim of making 'the mass of working occupations more attractive and to instil in the younger generation a greater respect for labour' (*Izvestiya* 22 September 1974). The Moscow Scientific Research Institute of Labour Education and Vocational Studies recommends that schools be guided by the following programme:[69]

Classes 1–4: acquainting pupils with the basic types of work and jobs available;

Classes 5–8: further study to ascertain and develop pupils' abilities and interests; and

Classes 9–10: broadening of pupils' knowledge about jobs and developing a firm interest in their chosen spheres of labour activity.

These processes may well involve the informal 'cooling-out' and channelling of ambition on the part of many schoolchildren: i.e.by 'ascertaining and developing pupils' interests and abilities' and by 'developing a firm interest in their chosen spheres of labour activity'.

The developments described above are a tendency towards the school system itself becoming more differentiated. The group of 'foreign language schools' and the greater specialization after the general eight-year school is a process by which the school population is sorted into various occupational streams: the ten-year, preparing students for higher education; specialized secondary schools, giving a technological qualification; and the technical trade schools providing training for craftsmen. It seems probable that in the general eight-year school are subtle forms of encouragement for certain kinds of jobs and tempering of ambition for some within the unstreamed secondary school. The informal role of teachers is most important here. At 15, there is an informal allocation process at work and one reads complaints in the Soviet press that teachers decide which children should go to the general secondary school and which to the trade schools (*Izvestia* 26 May 1974). The numbers of places available in different types of schools are planned in relation to economic needs.

There is also some evidence to suggest that differential socialization is occurring within the population. In large industrial towns the working class provides recruits for vocational trade schools. In one study it was shown that, of pupils wishing to enter a PTU, 87.3 per cent of boys and 95.8 per cent of girls were from manual families.[70] Schools try to recruit from families of workers. Open days are organized and pupils are encouraged to bring their friends. An attempt is made to glorify 'workers' dynasties' at factories, to encourage children to follow in their parents' footsteps. These ceremonies and traditions no doubt help to heighten the solidarity of the working class and also tend to promote internal stratum recruitment.

Further evidence concerning the aspirations of school leavers in the 1970s confirms this tendency. Compared to the some 90 per cent of leavers with desires for higher education in the 1960s noted above, the figure fell dramatically to 46 per cent in 1976 – the remainder wanting to go to work. These pupils were *not* drawn from the special language schools, where 95 to 98 per cent of the eighth-formers entered the ninth form and 70 per cent of the tenth-formers went into higher education.[71] These empirical data confirm the argument advanced here.

Fourth, Soviet Marxism–Leninism provides values which 'compensate' for failure in the educational contest system. Marxism–Leninism provides an alternative belief system to competitive individualism. For those who drop out of the competition for higher education and the more creative non-manual jobs that go with it, the idea that 'all jobs are equal', which has a central place in the ideology, provides a safety net. It gives a different basis for the evaluation of the contribution to society from that connected to educational success. It seems likely that there will be a greater stress on this 'ideological' value of Marxism–Leninism than on the other more 'pragmatic' ones mentioned earlier. It involves a greater stress on loyalty, on serving the nation, on the 'equality of all labour' and on the 'dignity of manual work'. This is reflected also in the greater role being given to the Communist Party, and to the strengthening of manual workers within it. Of new entrants to the party, in recent years 57 per cent are manual workers; in some parts of the country, nearly three-quarters are manual workers.[72]

Finally, another important change which is taking place is in the structure of incomes. The Soviet Union has followed the trend of other industrial societies in both the rising level of real income and in the greater equalization of income over time.[73] As noted above (chapter 5) there has been a considerable equalization of earnings in the USSR and the differential between manuals and non-manuals has been falling. The explanation of these changes lies in the effects of demand and supply of labour. Higher grade labour has become less scarce due to a fall in the rate of creation of non-manual jobs. Low grade jobs are not wanted as the educational levels of the population rise. To ensure greater labour stability and commitment to work, wages have increased; hence Khrushchev's and Brezhnev's egalitarianism was firmly rooted in economic needs.

On the basis of this analysis we may come to some general conclusions concerning the role of state and economy operating through the educational system. The ideological role of the state seems to be strengthening and the raised levels of ambition previously required for the operation of the economy are less necessary. As far as the working class is concerned, the political leadership is putting greater stress on certain aspects of Marxism–Leninism. There is a greater emphasis on the egalitarian aspects of work and a heightening of the importance and status of manual work. But this leads to greater stratum renewal, to the creation of 'workers' dynasties', and has a braking effect on upward mobility through the school system.

There are limitations to the influence of the educational system in creating an egalitarian society. Where there is a division of labour, in an economic sense, the educational system should not only provide basic and appropriate levels of skill, but must also engender the right patterns of motivation for different kinds of jobs. The Soviet general polytechnical school system has succeeded in raising levels of expectations. These were congruent with the demands of an economy undergoing a rapid rate of growth in the pre-Khrushchev era and in a society with a relatively unambitious and lowly educated peasant population. Greater levels of ambition and striving were necessary for the efficient and effective operation of the economy. In the post-Khrushchev period, the supply of higher level jobs has fallen short of the demand for them. The problem now is one of managing ambition and of inculcating a state of satisfaction or at least resignation with manual work. What seems to be taking place is a form of stratification within the formally unstreamed comprehensive school, resulting in the social stratification of opportunities. While the system is 'open' in relation to educational opportunity, the tendency seems to be towards greater stratum recruitment. One reason for the development of the stratification of educational opportunity and occupational placement lies in the fact that the school system operates in the context of socially structured families. The family exerts different types of influence on the educational aspirations and performances of children depending on their social background.

Furthermore, the ideal goals of the party and the more pragmatic ones of the economy do not always coincide. In the past, pragmatic, instrumental goals reflecting the needs of the economy were uppermost: there was a premium on striving for qualifications reflected in wide income differentials. In the 1980s this is changing: the present need is to 'cool-out' ambition. The party is becoming more important: and normative goals are receiving emphasis in labour education. The Educational Reform of 1984 seeks to provide vocational training for all. Wage differentials between manuals and non-manuals are falling. In addition 'alternatives routes' for the ambitious manual worker are being increased. This strengthens the incorporation of the working class into society and prevents the development of political dissent. The emphasis on the normative aspects of Marxism–Leninism (the importance of manual work) does not disturb the differential access of non-manual workers' children to non-manual jobs. Rather paradoxically for a socialist society, it legitimates the tendency of the stratification system to become more self-recruiting. These developments in turn have led to other demands. Some have sought the widening of differentials to provide stimulus for achievement and to increase productivity. Others have emphasized the importance of greater educational opportunity for collective farmers and manual workers. These counterclaims will be discussed further below.

HIGHER EDUCATION

Higher educational institutions, like secondary ones, have the tasks of socializing students; reproducing knowledge and culture; placing the graduate in an occupation and in the status order; and in addition they pursue research – the creation of new knowledge. Article 41 of the *Fundamentals of Legislation of the USSR and the Union Republics on*

Public Education (1973) defines the 'main tasks of higher educational establishments' as follows:

training of highly skilled specialists having a knowledge of Marxist–Leninist theory, profound theoretical knowledge and practical habits of work in their line and experience in organizing mass-political and educational work;

fostering in students noble moral qualities, communist consciousness, culture, socialist internationalism, Soviet patriotism, readiness to defend the socialist Homeland, physical training of students;

constant perfection of the quality of training specialists, with due account to the demands of modern production, science, engineering and culture and the prospects of their development;

doing research work which helps the level of training of specialists and promotes social, scientific and technological progress;

preparation of textbooks and study aids;

training of cadres and instructors;

raising the qualification of the faculty staff of higher and specialized secondary educational establishments, and also specialists with a higher education employed in the corresponding sectors of the national economy.

It is fairly straightforward to describe the kinds of institutions and changes in the stock of students; it is problematic to analyse the success of the various objectives of higher learning. Some of the major problems are to do with the roles of teaching and research (between replicating existing knowledge and creating new ideas), with the 'fit' between the needs of the economy and the aspirations of those in the educational system; finally, there is a conflict between the more ideological goals of using the educational system to create more equality of opportunity for all underprivileged social strata and the tendency of the educational system to differentiate on the basis of given intellectual attainment.

The Structure of Higher Education

Higher education (including research) is carried out at three separate types of institutions: the Academies of Sciences, the Higher Educational Institutions (*vuzy*), and the Higher Party Schools (see table 8.1).

The Academies of Sciences are responsible for the conduct of research in the sciences and arts. There are a number of different institutions. The most prestigious is the Academy of Sciences of the USSR. This is directly subordinate to the Council of Ministers of the USSR. With the exception of the Russian Republic (RSFSR), all the Union Republics have their own

Academy of Sciences, subordinate to their own Republican Council of Ministers. A 'co-ordinating council' is charged with general oversight of all the Academies. In addition, there are four other separate Academies of the USSR concerned with Art, Agriculture, Medicine and Pedagogy. In 1981, the Academy of Sciences of the USSR employed 49,000 scientists, the next largest was the All-Union Academy of Sciences of Agriculture with 19,850, then the Ukrainian Academy of Sciences with 13,600, followed by the Academy of Medical Sciences of the USSR with 6,775 scientific employees.[74] Elections to the Academies are made by their own scientific members and are conducted by secret ballot; party nominations for election have been rejected. Apart from teaching postgraduate students, members of Academies are freed from teaching responsibilities and are concerned solely with research.

The main training ground for undergraduates in sciences and arts are the higher educational establishments or *vuzy (vysshye uchebnye zavedeniya)*. *Vuzy* are of two kinds: universities and institutes or polytechnics. Generally, though not universally, universities have higher status than institutes. The former have a greater theoretical component in their subjects: they include arts and the pure sciences, and they cover a range of disciplines. Institutes (some of which do have high status) concentrate on applied and more vocationally oriented subjects and cater for a limited range of specialist subjects. For instance, Moscow University has a comprehensive range of faculties and disciplines; languages taught would be on a more humanistic literature base, whereas the Maurice Thorez Institute of Foreign Languages is more specialized, being required to train teachers, translators and interpreters. The *vuzy* also pursue research and the training of postgraduate students. However, undergraduate training is their main activity. The *vuzy* are administered by various ministries, the most important being the Ministry of Higher and Specialized Secondary Education, which has 351 institutions (including all universities) under its purview. The more vocational educational institutions are directly subordinate to production ministries. Their subordination is shown in table 8.4. Some (e.g. Health) are subordinate to the Council of Ministers of the USSR and to Union Republican Councils of Ministers. This list is not complete; in addition are military academies and institutions for diplomats and the security services.

Of less importance, at least in a quantitative sense, are the Communist Party's own educational establishments. These provide a higher education mainly in the social sciences – economics, law, international affairs, sociology and foreign languages. The party schools are not merely 'schools of propaganda', but provide high level study facilities and supervision of postgraduate work in the social sciences. Research is also geared to the

TABLE 8.4: ADMINISTRATIVE SUBORDINATION OF HIGHER EDUCATIONAL INSTITUTIONS

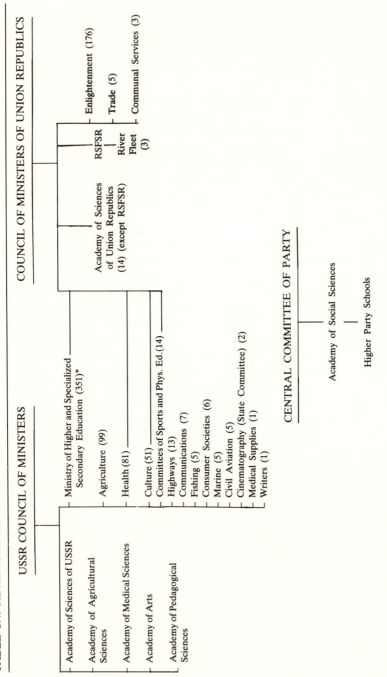

USSR COUNCIL OF MINISTERS

Academy of Sciences of USSR
Academy of Agricultural Sciences
Academy of Medical Sciences
Academy of Arts
Academy of Pedagogical Sciences

Ministry of Higher and Specialized Secondary Education (351)*
Agriculture (99)
Health (81)
Culture (51)
Committees of Sports and Phys. Ed.(14)
Highways (13)
Communications (7)
Fishing (5)
Consumer Societies (6)
Marine (5)
Civil Aviation (5)
Cinematography (State Committee) (2)
Medical Supplies (1)
Writers (1)

COUNCIL OF MINISTERS OF UNION REPUBLICS

Academy of Sciences of Union Republics (14) (except RSFSR)

RSFSR
River Fleet (3)

Enlightenment (176)
Trade (5)
Communal Services (3)

CENTRAL COMMITTEE OF PARTY

Academy of Social Sciences

Higher Party Schools

Note: * Numbers in brackets denote number of institutions.
Source: Data on ministries cited by M. Matthews, *Education in the Soviet Union* (1982), p. 110.

party's own political programmes. The party's institutions are subordinate to the Central Committee of the CPSU.

All Western commentators on Soviet education point to the massive growth of higher education under Soviet power. The rise in the numbers of students is shown in tables 8.5 and 8.6.

The emphasis in Soviet education is on applied sciences, and on vocational use of higher education. The large numbers in *prosveshcheniy* (enlightenment) are mainly destined for school teaching. Compared with Western capitalist countries, a striking difference is the lack of liberal arts education as a form of consumption – rather than as an instrumentality to teach others. This may not be a cause for rejoicing, since many of the expensively trained engineers end up performing tasks of a kind not requiring such training. Engineers, however, might argue that engineering is a form of *general* education.

A second difference from the West is the higher proportion of students having part-time or correspondence tuition. Of the 5,284,000 higher

TABLE 8.5: POSTGRADUATE (ASPIRANTOV) STUDENTS (TOTAL NUMBERS AT END OF YEAR)

	1940	1965	1975	1981
Total	16,863	90,294	95,675	97,860
In *vuzy*	13,169	53,412	55,706	58,663
In other institutions of higher learning (including Academies of Science)	3,694	36,882	39,969	39,197

Source: Narkhoz 1922–1982 (1982), p. 127.

TABLE 8.6: STUDENTS IN HIGHER EDUCATION BY SPECIALITY (TOTAL NUMBERS AT BEGINNING OF YEAR, 000's)

	1940	1965	1975	1982
Total number of students	812	3,860	4,854	5,315
industry and building	168	1,528	1,950	2,108
transport and communication	36	221	278	300
agriculture	52	377	460	550
economics and law	36	264	354	384
health, physical culture and sport	110	239	352	389
culture and education (*prosveshcheniya*)	339	1,199	1,415	1,532
art and cinematography	10	32	45	122

Source: Narkhoz v 1982g (1983), p. 465.

education students in 1981–82, 56.9 per cent were full-time, 12.2 per cent were evening (or part-time) and 30.7 per cent were taking correspondence courses.[75] (The proportions for 1959 were: full-time 55 per cent, evening 7 per cent, correspondence 38 per cent.) Correspondence students are attached to institutes or university departments and are required to attend for 'consultation' with their supervisors; short courses at the institution are also arranged. Part-time and correspondence students share scarce buildings and teachers, they require less subsidy by the state and, by continuing with their work, they also contribute to production.

These figures show the intensive use made of facilities and indicate the way education costs have been kept down while the number of students has been increased. The direct yearly cost of educating a student in the early 1970s was 920 rubles per full-time student, 268 rs and 107 rs respectively for evening and correspondence ones.[76] Soviet expenditure on education and science was estimated at 13.4 per cent of the state budget in 1981.[77] However, while part-time and correspondence education are useful alternatives for students who do not manage to compete successfully for full-time places, it must be pointed out that the quality of education is often said to be less good on these courses than on full-time ones. The drop-out rate is also relatively high. The usual period of full-time higher education is from four to five-and-a-half years; medicine takes five-and-a-half; engineering five; law, history, journalism and art four years; agriculture, four-and-a-half. Though Soviet education involves specialized study, it also calls for considerable effort on subjects outside the speciality. Excluding courses on civics (party history, economics, dialectical and historical materialism), which comprise 10 to 12 per cent of contact hours, other subjects constitute from 10 to 16 per cent of the total time; a foreign language 3.0 per cent and physical education 3.0 per cent. Soviet university education is more specialized than the American and is much wider than the British – at both upper school and university.

At the undergraduate level, students have to carry out a piece of research work which forms part of their diploma examination. But the chief research role of the university lies with the training of postgraduates. Students register for the Candidate of Science degree (*Kandidat nauk*) which is roughly equivalent to an American PhD; it involves course work, examinations and the submission of a dissertation.

The standard of diplomas (awarded to successful undergraduates) of Soviet higher educational institutions is roughly equal to the level of British university degrees.[78] According to Zajda, Soviet higher education is geared to knowledge and comprehension, rather than to analysis and evaluation.[79] The 1975 examination in the History of the USSR and Social Studies, for instance, contained the following topics:

TABLE 8.7: TOTAL NUMBER OF STUDENTS RECEIVING FULL-TIME HIGHER
EDUCATION IN SELECTED COUNTRIES

	Year	Per 10,000 population
Great Britain	1978–79	98
Canada	1976–77	140
France	1977–78	165
USA	1978–79	261
USSR	1981–82	197

Source: Narkhoz 1922–82 (1982), p. 116.

1   Lenin's struggle in founding the Marxist proletarian party in Russia
     between 1900 and 1903. The Second Congress of the RSDRP and its
     historical significance.
2   Labour relations under socialism.[80]

Soviet educational achievement, in quantitative terms, in the last half
century, is remarkable and is illustrated by table 8.7. The numbers of
students in higher education as a proportion of the population surpass
those of advanced European countries, even though much of the education
may be more equivalent to the higher levels of school in the advanced
Western European countries.

Interests within Higher Education

The discussion above has perhaps laboured the point that Soviet higher
education has provided facilities for the enhancement of the general
cultural level of the population and has provided cadres with a high level of
technical knowledge for the operation of a modern economy. Higher
education, however, is concerned not only with the provision of trained
personnel for industry, but also with research and innovation. The latter
function requires independence from detailed control and it implies a
certain autonomy for intellectual effort and also the preservation of the
institutional identity of particular interest groups. This criterion comes into
conflict with the need to 'bring education into close contact with life'.

The identification of interests and discussion of conflict is not widely
publicly practised in the Soviet Union. It is only when a group is
significantly threatened by the political leadership that interests become
explicit. Such a case occurred in connection with Khrushchev's proposals
to bring research more into correspondence with the realities of industrial
life. He suggested that research work be co-ordinated to prevent

duplication and that the more applied aspects of research be the responsibility of industrial enterprises.

... Let us set up laboratories at plants and factories, establish scientific institutes and other scientific centres under the economic councils, and assign more young people to them, along with experienced and well-known scientists. Think over this problem, comrades, and make suggestions on it. I think the policy will prove correct ... We shall ask the USSR Academy of Sciences, its Presidium, to draft proposals for further improving the activity of the Academy.[81]

This suggestion led to the emergence of two opposed groups in the Academy. On the one hand, pure scientists tended to support applied work being carried out in industry and saw science as an autonomous institution generating its own laws and processes. On the other hand, applied scientists tended to emphasize the unity of theory and practice – and opposed any movement of engineering away from the Academy.

The pure scientists, led by a chemist, Nikolay Semenov, proposed that the Academy be re-shaped, in practice to resemble its non-Soviet predecessor in Tsarist Russia. Semenov's proposals included removal of the narrow engineering institutes, concentration on fundamental research by the Academy, reduction in the size of the Presidium of the Academy, the abolition of planning of theoretical research and the right of the Academy to retain the top ten to fifteen per cent of its postgraduates.[82]

Semenov's views were opposed by the engineers who, led by Ivan Bardin, argued that science and technology could not be divorced. Engels, it was pointed out, had noted that: 'Technology depends to a considerable extent on the state of science, science depends to a far greater degree on the state and requirements of technology'.[83]

The issue of reform of the Academy was not restricted to conflict between engineers and scientists. The members of the Academy of the Republican institutes also feared that their independence would be undermined by greater 'co-ordination'. A spokesman of the regions said: 'We must reject the idea that a central organ can plan and co-ordinate all the scientific work being conducted in the various institutes, laboratories, and higher educational institutions in the Soviet Union.'[84] Scientific councils or co-ordinating councils, organized on a subject, rather than a geographical, principle were advocated to co-ordinate research.

Yet another group interest voiced its disapproval of Semenov's and, indirectly, Khrushchev's proposals. This was composed of the university teachers. Here the status of the Academy was resented and its control over research opposed. Professor Kurosh wrote:

Academician N. Semenov's suggestion that the universities ... should regard their main scientific activity as being the development of already extant branches of science gives rise to serious objections ... It is precisely the universities that are best adapted to the establishment and development of fundamentally new trends in theoretical mathematics ... since it is there that the opportunity exists to draw into research young students who are just taking their first steps in science and are therefore better able to grasp new ideas.[85]

The universities were regarded, by the university teachers, as being more virile institutions, more associated with 'life' and its pressures, whereas the Academy was 'academic', an ivory tower, aloof, and not able to play such a positive role as the universities.

The configuration of interests in the reorganization of the Academy then appears as Khrushchev and the pure scientists against the applied scientists, the universities and regional Academicians.

The reforms carried out since 1960 have tended to be along the lines advocated by Semenov. The narrow engineering institutes have been removed from the Academy, though engineers concerned with advanced engineering research have remained in it. The State Committee of the Council of Ministers of the USSR for the Co-ordination of Scientific Research[86] has been set up to co-ordinate all scientific work. In 1963 the co-ordinating role of the USSR Academy in the activities of Republican Academies and the higher education sector was re-emphasized.

This example illustrates the articulation of interests of those in institutions closely intertwined with the bureaucratic apparatus. As Graham concludes:

The reforms of the Academy illustrate that the leaders of the Communist Party of the Soviet Union rely on the expert opinion of specialists making decisions related to specific sectors of cultural and economic activity ... Within the framework of strict political control by the party, the Soviet Union has devised a workable, but constantly evolving system for the inclusion of scientific advice in the process of making governmental decisions.[87]

Again, we can see from this that higher education generates groups that conceive of their own interests and attempt to define a role for higher learning in educational (rather than political or economic) terms. The educational system then, while not being an 'autonomous' social institution, cannot be conceived of as merely an instrumentality of the ruling political elites. Another area in which a conflict of political values and educational ones has taken place is that of the selection of students for higher education.

Selection for Higher Education

The process of educational selection is instrumental in assigning to individuals their occupation in society and the roles and status that go with it. Selection for higher education, therefore, is a crucial social and political process. From a political point of view, Soviet Marxists emphasize the rights of all persons, particularly manual workers and peasants, to education. Many teachers in higher education, however, tend to emphasize the intellectual potential of the student independently of social background. In practice, given competition for places in higher education, the higher social strata perform better in educational tests, as already discussed. Therefore, a 'contest' educational system tends to be elitist and excludes students from lower educational backgrounds.

In the 1920s and early 1930s selection was strongly politically biased: priority was given to applicants of proletarian origin and restrictions were placed on groups of other social origins, such as the aristocracy or bourgeoisie. But according to data summarized by DeWitt, the intake of higher education students between 1927 and 1938 included only 39.7 per cent of worker origin; 19.3 per cent of peasant and 41.0 per cent of 'other' origin (white collar and intelligentsia).[88] Jews (largely of the intelligentsia and non-manual groups) accounted for 12.4 per cent of the students between 1929 and 1935 compared with their 1.8 per cent share of the population.[89] These figures suggest that the 'proletarianization' of higher educational institutions was only partially successful. Inkeles and Bauer's survey of post-1945 Russian émigrés found that, of those aged between 21 and 35 in 1940:

... the great majority of the children of the intelligentsia got to college. Most of the rest got at least to high school and very few 'disgraced' their families by failing to get past the primary school. By contrast the overwhelming majority of the peasants got just this minimum although about one in ten did attain the exalted college level. Between these poles the proportion with only elementary schooling falls and with college training rises as one ascends the occupational ladder. The sharpest point of division comes, however, when we pass over the line from manual labour to white-collar jobs. The poor showing of the peasants cannot be attributed to the high proportion of the dekulakised [i.e. previously 'rich peasants'] among them, since they fared about as well as those not discriminated against by the government.[90]

At present, merit is the main official criterion for admission to higher educational institutions in the Soviet Union. Rules are laid down by decree of the Ministry of Higher Education. Selection is on the basis of competitive examination conducted by the institute or university. Examinations, both oral and written, take place in the student's speciality, together with Russian and a foreign language. Differences in the standards required exist between institutions. The older or better-known urban centres, such as Moscow and Leningrad, attract more better-qualified applicants and, therefore, higher marks may be necessary. Specialist courses, for instance on computer technology, are also in great demand. No centralized 'clearing house' system has been organized. Should students fail in their initial application, they may persuade some other institutions to take them (they receive their entrance examination marks), otherwise they have either to start work or wait to compete again the next year. For those who are admitted, education is provided free and a system of grants is operated to help students meet their living expenses. Grants are awarded on the criteria of parental income, year of study (senior students get more than junior), field of study (scientists receive more than those in humanities), and performance (good students get more than bad ones). In the 1970s, about three-quarters of students received maintenance grants; the maximum grant is 40 rubles per month, about a quarter of the average wage (though less than the minimum wage of 70 rs).

Academic standards are not the only criteria for admission to higher education. Students have to produce a reference from their place of work or from party or *Komsomol* organization. Much is made of this condition by Western writers, but no comprehensive statistics of exclusion on political grounds are available. It seems likely that in some cases party activists may be favoured and known Christians excluded, although much may depend on the subject and institution; political considerations are more important in history or philosophy than in physics or ballet. The main criterion for admission is academic achievement.

As noted above, 'academic achievement' is likely to be correlated with social background. This is not only due to performance but also to family influence: '.... a person is admitted to a higher educational establishment not because he is well prepared, but because he has an influential papa and mama who can help to get him in.'[91] Again, in September 1958, Khrushchev said, '... frequently, it is not enough to pass the examinations to enter college. Great influence of the parents also plays a part here. With good reason, one rather widely hears youths entering college saying that after they themselves pass the contest, a contest among the parents begins – and it often decides the whole matter.'[92] It is doubtful, however, whether such practices are wide-spread: examination committees are frequently changed and examinees must submit written scripts under pseudonym. In some cases selection boards may be swayed by parents' pressures.[93] Probably more important is the greater 'know-how' of executives and professional workers, who are more able to place their children for admission to higher education.

The proportion of students from peasant and lower working strata has nowhere been comprehensively and accurately detailed (see also chapter 5 above). Khrushchev said that only 30 to 40 per cent of all students at Moscow higher educational establishments were of worker or peasant origin, and in Latvia in 1970 the comparable figures were 39.9 per cent for workers and 11.5 per cent for collective farmers.[94]

Performance at school is clearly linked to social background of parents. One Soviet study showed that, of schoolchildren required to repeat a year because of poor performance, only 3 per cent of children of parents with higher education had to do so, compared with 16 per cent of those whose parents had four years or less. At the other end of the scale, 51 per cent of children of parents with higher education received 'excellent' and 'good' marks, compared with only 18 per cent of those whose parents had only four years education or less. In terms of the occupation of parents, of students entering the ninth year of the general school, 'The share of professionals' children grew by 46 per cent ... The proportion coming from skilled manual workers' families declined by 10 per cent, while the share of children of semi-skilled and non-manual personnel fell by 54 per cent.' Another survey of candidates for admission to the physics faculty at Novosibirsk University in 1968 found that children from specialists' families comprised 28 per cent of the applicants, 35 per cent of successful applicants and 46 per cent of those getting top grades.[95] Matthews has calculated that the 'social access ratios' to full-time *vuzy* in 1973 were 1.93 for non-manuals, 0.78 for manual workers and 0.64 for collective farmers; by 1977, the ratio had fallen to 1.69 for non-manuals and risen to 0.8 for manual workers and collective farmers combined.[96]

The existence of greater opportunity for non-manual groups, as shown above, is inconsistent with an egalitarian political policy. Criticisms on these grounds have come from the political party elites, particularly Khrushchev. It is instructive to study Khrushchev's educational policy, for he attempted to reverse such forms of discrimination: but he was baulked by the educational (and possibly industrial) elites.

Khrushchev attempted to strengthen the access to higher educational institutions by manuals and collective farmers; he gave more prominence to part-time and correspondence tuition and deemed that all school leavers should spend two years 'in production' before starting higher education. Though this was modified after pressure from the universities and some 20 per cent of the intake were allowed in straight from school, Khrushchev's reforms did have some positive results. This may be illustrated by a study of students to the Urals Polytechnic. In the period 1962–63, 61.6 per cent of the intake hailed from manual worker and collective farmer background, while only 19.1 per cent were recruited from school. In 1967–68, though the proportion of school leavers rose to 67.8 per cent, the number of students of working class and peasant background fell to 43.7 per cent.[97]

These developments were attacked in the Soviet educational press. In what Matthews calls 'an unusually poignant article', part-time education was deplored and shown to lead to poor results and many drop-outs. Higher education as a whole declined in standards, it was argued, because of the poorer motivation and preparation of students and the greater difficulty in teaching students 'from production'. Consequently positive discrimination for such students was opposed. Khrushchev's reforms 'from the academic point of view' had been 'a disaster'.[98] From 1966, the reforms were officially modified and from 1964 the qualifications for selection to higher education were not dependent on formal work experience. By 1970, 80 per cent of Moscow University students were from non-manual backgrounds.[99] Here again we witness the difficulty of the political elite in putting into effect its ideological values and the success of the educational system in maintaining its own priorities.

This, however, is not the end of the story, for in 1969 Preparatory Divisions were set up at universities. These were to recruit deserving manual workers for a school year's intensive course prior to entry to a higher educational institution. (Such students on passing the course would be guaranteed a place without passing the entrance examination.)[100] The initiative for these institutions came from outside the Ministry of Higher and Specialized Education, and was put into effect in the Urals with support from the local party and Komsomol activists. It appears that legislation was prepared and thrust upon an unwilling ministry. Since the introduction of such courses, some 100,000 students (about 16 per cent of intake to full-time *vuz* courses) have been admitted. In the 1969–70 intake, 67 per cent of students in Preparatory Divisions were industrial workers, 7.4 per cent state farmers, 14 per cent collective farmers, 11 per cent ex-servicemen; by 1975–76 ex-servicemen came to 33.6 per cent, collective farmers 11.4 per cent, state farmers 8.9 per cent, and industrial workers 46 per cent. This development has not been without adverse criticism: many studies have shown a higher drop-out rate and a diminution of academic standards as a consequence of the mediocre quality of the Preparatory Divisions' graduates. Complaints have been voiced about the abuse of privilege and have seen the process as a form of patronage.[101] The fact that the Divisions have continued despite the charges of academics points not only to the seriousness with which some Soviet ideologists take the issue of educational equality, but also to the ways that the political elites are able to exert power over the educational ministries.

Our study of Soviet education confirms Durkheim's view that education is a 'methodological socialisation of the young'. It not only transmits the culture of a society to the young, but inculcates values and attitudes usually determined by the society's political leadership. In the USSR, the educational system has been an agency for the indoctrination of Bolshevik social and political norms. As in other advanced industrial societies, the teaching of skills has become institutionalized in schools and higher education establishments. These have become important levers in economic change; Soviet technological development has depended on the supply of trained manpower from the educational sector. Education has become universal, ensuring widespread literacy, and the Soviet system has emphasized technological competence. In all societies, education is a major determinant of the individual's life chances. This is particularly so in the USSR, where the family has no legal rights over property. The educational system allocates (directly and indirectly) people to different occupational roles and status positions. People know this and seek to use the educational system to their own advantage. Measures which reduce the 'class chances' of established groups are resisted. Access to higher education has been determined by a combination of merit and ascription. In the early days of Bolshevik power, the previously deprived proletarian and peasant strata were given priority, though other social factors, particularly the higher 'educability' of the professional and white collar strata, gave some weight to 'merit'. While Soviet education has attempted to bring down the barriers which barred deprived social and national groups from higher education, the cultural forces generated by family and parental occupation have reasserted themselves. As in Western societies, though perhaps to a lesser extent, professional strata pass on the advantages of their own education to their children. Khrushchev's attempts to mitigate this tendency by stipulating recruitment from the bench rather than from the school desk were egalitarian. They were short-lived but appeared in another form in the Preparatory Divisions. In addition to the economic and political roles of the educational system – in its functions 'on behalf of' the economy and the polity – educational institutions themselves have been seen to be partially successful in perpetuating their own conceptions of the social good. If they are unable to resist control by the political leadership they are capable of vetoing it.[102].

NOTES

1 Ralph Miliband, *The State in Capitalist Society* (1969), p. 123.
2 E. Durkheim, *Education and Society* (1956), p. 71.
3 Ibid.
4 See, for example, M. Matthews, *Education in the Soviet Union* (1982).
5 Jean Floud and A.H. Halsey, 'The Sociology of Education', *Current Sociology*, vol. 7, no. 3 (1958), pp. 169–70.
6 W.B. Brookover and D. Gottlieb, *A Sociology of Education* (1964), p. 74, cited by O. Banks, *The Sociology of Education* (1968), p. 201.
7 Two interesting tables showing the growth in educational provision between 1801 and 1825, and the similarity of syllabuses in the Russian gymnasia and in the French *Écoles Centrales* are shown in N. Hans, *The Russian Tradition in Education* (1963), pp. 21–2.
8 *Narodnoe obrazovanie v SSSR* (1957), p. 733.
9 A.G. Rashin, *Formirovanie rabochego klassa* (1958), p. 584.
10 Pervaya vseobschaya perepis' (1905), vol. 1, pp. 42–3.
11 *SSSR v tsifrakh v 1963g* (1964), pp. 155–7.
12 B.M. Remenikov and G.I. Ushakov, *Universitetskoe obrazovanie v SSSR* (1960), p. 18.
13 Ibid., p. 8.
14 Ibid., p. 19.
15 K. Marx and F. Engels, *Selected Works*, vol. 1 (1958), p. 225.
16 K. Marx and F. Engels, *The German Ideology* (1965), p. 61.
17 F. Engels, 'Letter to J. Bloch', September 21 1890, in *Karl Marx and Frederick Engels, Selected Works*, vol. 2 (1951), p. 433.
18 'The Civil War in France, Address of the General Council of the International Workingmen's Association' (n.d.), p. 44. Cited by M. Shore, *Soviet Education* (1947), p. 59. Shore considers Marx's views on education at some length.
19 V.I. Lenin, 'On Proletarian Culture', *Collected Works*, vol. 31 (1966), p. 316.
20 S. Fitzpatrick, *The Commissariat of Enlightenment* (1970), p. xiv.
21 The following is based on Fitzpatrick, ibid. See also S. Fitzpatrick, *Education and Social Mobility in the Soviet Union 1921–1934* (1979), esp. chapter 7.
22 *Cancer Ward* (1968), p. 209.
23 M.S. Dzhunusov, *O zakonomernostyakh perekhoda narodov ranee otstalykh stran k sotsializma* (1961), pp. 152–3.
24 Census data, cited in *Itogi vsesoyuznoy perepisi naseleniya SSSR, 1959g* (1962), pp. 88–9.

25 Dzhunusov, *O zakonomernostyakh perekhoda narodov...*, p. 156.
26 Ibid., p. 164.
27 R. Vaidynath, *The Formation of the Soviet Central Asian Republics* (1967), p. 53.
28 *Istoriya Kazakhskoy SSR* (1963), p. 525.
29 Ibid., p. 529.
30 *Itogi vsesoyuznoy perepisi naseleniya SSSR, 1959g* (1962), p. 81; and *Itogi... Kazakhskoy SSR* (1962), p. 50.
31 N. DeWitt, *Education and Professional Employment in the USSR* (1961), p. 73.
32 *Zhenshchiny i deti v SSSR* (1963), p. 133; *50 let Sovetskogo zdravookhraneniya* (1967), p. 116; *Zhenshchiny SSSR* (1975), p. 103.
33 F.R. Filippov, 'Deti v strane razvitogo sotsializma', *Sotsiologicheskie issledovaniya* no. 4 (1979), p. 56. In 1975, 11.5 million children were in preschool institutions; by 1981 the total was 14.8 million.
34 N.K. Goncharov, 'Sovetskaya pedagogicheskaya nauka', *Narodnoe obrazovanie*, no. 11 (Nov. 1957), p. 70, cited by N. DeWitt, *Education and Professional Employment in the USSR*, p. 78.
35 G. Osipov, *Rabochi klass i tekhnicheski progress* (1965).
36 M. Matthews, *Education in the Soviet Union* (1982), pp. 21–3.
37 Kenneth Charlton, 'Polytechnical Education', *International Review of Education*, vol. 14 no. 1, (1968), p. 45. See also John Dunstan, 'Curriculum Change and the Soviet School', *Curriculum Studies* vol. 9 no. 2, (1977), pp. 111–23.
38 M. Yanowitch, *Social and Economic Inequality in the USSR* (1977), pp. 74–6.
39 For a discussion of developments leading to this resolution, see J. Dunstan, 'Curriculum Change and the Soviet School', *Curriculum Studies*, vol. 9, no. 2 (1977), pp. 112–18.
40 Cited by N. Grant, *Soviet Education* (1964), p. 44.
41 'Eto kasaetsya vsekh', *Literaturnaya gazeta*, 24 April 1965. *Byulleten' normativnykh aktov Ministerstva prosveshcheniya SSSR* (1983), no. 3, p. 3. (My thanks to John Dunstan for this reference.)
42 For further details see John Dunstan, *Paths to Excellence and the Soviet School* (1978).
43 There are also trade schools organized at factories, commercial schools for sales personnel, and courses for hairdressers. These provide short courses of a specific 'trade training' kind.
44 *Narkhoz 1922–1982* (1982), pp. 499–500.
45 M.A. Prokof'ev, 'Novy uchebny god', *Narodnoe obrazovanie*, no. 9 (1977), 8–31, pp. 10–11. Cited by J. Dunstan, 'Developments in Soviet Education, 1975–79', *Journal of Russian Studies*, no. 39 (1980), p. 35.
46 J. Dunstan, ibid., p. 36.
47 M. Rutkevich, 'Put Labour into the Secondary School Graduation Certificate – A Sociologist's Opinion', *Sovetskaya Rossiya* (21 Sept 1983). Abstract in *CDSP*, vol. 35, no. 40 1983, pp. 1–2.

48 'Basic Guidelines for the School Reform,' *CDSP*, vol. 36, no. 18, 1984.
49 Matthews' book is an example of the (implicit) view of the absolute and comprehensive control of the government over the process of socialization.
50 T. Anthony Jones, 'Modernisation and Education in the USSR', *Social Forces*, vol. 57, no. 2 (1978), pp. 522–46.
51 See John Dunstan, 'Soviet Moral Education in Theory and Practice', *Journal of Moral Education*, vol. 10, no. 3 (1981), pp. 192–202, esp. p. 195.
52 See F. O'Dell, *Socialization Through Children's Literature* (1978), p. 81. See also above, chapter 4.
53 Ibid.
54 J.I. Zajda, *Education in the USSR* (1980), p. 123.
55 M. Matthews, *Education in the Soviet Union*, pp. 50–51.
56 Urie Bronfenbrenner, *Two Worlds of Childhood* (1971), pp. 76, 77.
57 Ibid., pp. 78, 81.
58 J. Dunstan, 'Soviet Moral Education...', p. 198.
59 Ibid.
60 These points are dealt with in more detail in D. Lane and F. O'Dell, *The Soviet Industrial Worker* (1978), chapters 4, 5, and 6.
61 For details, see Christel Lane, *The Rites of Rulers* (1981), chapter 7.
62 N.N. D'yachenko, *Professional'naya orientatsiya i vovlochenie molodezhi v sistemu professional'no-tekhnicheskogo obrazovaniya* (1971), p. 117.
63 V.S. Dunham, *In Stalin's Time* (1976), p. 93.
64 E.M. Tyazel'nikov, 'Sovetskaya molodezh' i tekhnickeski progress', *Kommunist*, 16 (1971), p. 45.
65 *Komsomol'skaya pravda* (27 January 1968), and quoted in *CDSP*, vol. 1, no. 2, 1968 p. 10.
66 V.I. Shirinski, 'O gotovnosti vypushnikov shkoly k trudu v sfere promyshlennogo proizvodstva' in R.G. Gurova (ed.), *Sotsiologicheskie problemy obrazovaniya i vospitaniya* (1973), p. 129; Y.P. Gupta, 'The Educational and Vocational Aspirations of Asian Immigrants and English School Leavers – A Comparative Study.' *British Journal of Sociology*, vol. 28, no. 2 (June 1977).
67 See particularly, V.N. Shubkin, 'Molodezh' vstupaet v zhizn', *Voprosy filosofii*, no. 5 (1965).
68 For a detailed study, see E. Mickiewicz, *Soviet Political Schools*, (1967).
69 B.L. Omel'yanenko, *Tekhnicheski progress i sovremennye trebovaniya k urovnya kvalifikatsii i podgotovka rabochikh kadrov* (1973), p. 119.
70 Yu. Petrov and F.R. Filippov, *Kak stanovyatsya rabochimi* (1973), p. 37. F.R. Filippov, *Sotsiologiya obrazovaniya* (1980) pp. 57–8.
71 V.I. Sidorov, 'Komsomol i nastavnichestvo', *Sovetskaya pedagogika*, no. 10 (1977), p. 27. Cited by J. Dunstan, 'Developments in Soviet Education...', pp. 36 and 37.
72 See D. Lane, *State and Politics in the USSR* (1984) chapter 5.
73 D. Treiman, 'Industrialisation and Social Stratification', *Sociological Inquiry*, no. 40 (Spring 1970), p. 217.

74 *Narodnoe khozyaystvo SSSR, 1922–1982* (1982), p. 125.
75 *Narodnoe khozyaystvo SSSR, 1922–1982* (1982), p. 506.
76 Data cited by Matthews, *Education in the Soviet Union*, p. 104.
77 *Narkhoz 1922–82*, p. 562.
78 M. Matthews qualifies this somewhat, see *Education in the Soviet Union*, p. 107.
79 J.I. Zajda, *Education in the USSR* (1980), p. 105.
80 Ibid.
81 *Pravda* (2 July 1959). Cited by L. R. Graham, 'Reorganisation of the USSR Academy of Sciences', in P.H Juviler and H.W. Morton, *Soviet Policy-Making* (1967), p. 139.
82 Graham, ibid., p. 141.
83 Cited by Graham, ibid., p. 144.
84 A. Kirillin, 'Nauka i zhizn', *Pravda*, 13 March 1959. Cited by Graham, ibid., p. 145.
85 A. Kurosh, 'Dorogu smelym ideyam', *Izvestiya*, 18 Aug. 1959. Cited by Graham ibid., p. 146.
86 Re-named State Committee for Science and Technology in 1965.
87 Graham, 'Reorganisation of the USSR Academy of Sciences', pp. 155–9.
88 N. DeWitt, *Education and Professional Employment in the USSR* (1961), Table IV-A-6, p. 655.
89 Ibid., Table IV-A-7, p. 656.
90 Alex Inkeles and Raymond A. Bauer, *The Soviet Citizen* (1959), p. 141.
91 N. Khrushchev, *Pravda*, 19 April 1958, cited by DeWitt, *Education and Professional Employment ...*, p. 247.
92 N.S. Khrushchev, 'Ob ukreplenii svyazi zhiznyu i o dalneyshem razvitii sistemy narodnogo obrazovaniya v strane,' *Pravda*, 21 September 1958, cited in G.F.Z. Bereday, W.W. Brickman and G.H. Read, *The Changing Soviet School* (1961), p. 427.
93 Examples are known of parents bribing lecturers to secure their children's admission. See account in *The Times*, 23 Sept. 1969. Hendrick Smith, *The Russians* (1976), pp. 67 ff.
94 M.E. Ashmane, *Sotsial'nye aspekty obrazovaniya* (1972), p. 17.
95 R.B. Dobson, 'Social Status and Inequality of Access to Higher Education in the USSR', in J. Karabel and A.H. Halsey, *Power and Ideology in Education* (1977), pp. 260, 271. See also D. Lane and F. O'Dell, *The Soviet Industrial Worker* (1978), chapter 7.
96 A ratio of 1 indicates that the proportion of students of a given group is equal to their weight in the population as a whole: M. Matthews, *Education in the Soviet Union*, p. 159. For further discussion see ibid., pp. 158–61.
97 *Klassy, sotsial'nye sloi i gruppy v SSSR* (1968), p. 158.
98 See discussion in M. Matthews, *Education in the Soviet Union*, pp. 139–40.
99 Dissertation, cited by Zajda, *Education in the USSR*, p. 98.
100 For a detailed description of these courses, see George Avis, 'Preparatory

Divisions in Soviet Higher Education Establishments 1969–79', *Soviet Studies*, vol. 35, no. 1 (Jan. 1983).

101 Ibid., pp. 14, 17–18, 25 and 30.
102 I am indebted to John Dunstan for many comments on an earlier draft of this chapter and to Felicity O'Dell for advice on some points.

BIBLIOGRAPHY TO PART II: SOCIAL RELATIONS

This bibliography does not include all references cited in the text. It is intended to assist the reader who wishes to pursue further study. Under 'Introductory' are listed works dealing with general themes; under 'Basic' are articles and books that are reliable guides to particular topics; 'Specialized' includes literature involving a more detailed treatment and which might be consulted by the specialist.

Introductory

Atkinson, D., A. Dallin and G.W. Lapidus. *Women in Russia*. Stanford: Stanford University Press 1977.

Azrael, J.R. (ed.). *Soviet Nationality Policies and Practice*. New York: Praeger, 1978.

Bennigsen, A. 'Soviet Muslims and the World of Islam', *Problems of Communism*, vol. 29, 1980, pp. 38–51.

Bereday, G.Z.F., W.W. Brickman and G.H. Read (eds.) *The Changing Soviet School, The Comparative Education Society Field Study in the USSR*. London: Constable, 1961.

Brine, J. et al. *Home, School and Leisure in the Soviet Union*, London: Allen and Unwin, 1980.

Bronfenbrenner, U. *Two Worlds of Childhood: USA and USSR*. London: Allen and Unwin, 1971.

Churchward, Lloyd. *The Soviet Intelligentsia*. London: Routledge and Kegan Paul, 1973.

Grant, N. *Soviet Education*. London: Penguin, 1979.

Jancar, B.W. *Women under Communism*. Baltimore: Johns Hopkins University Press, 1978.

Kahan, A. and B. Ruble (eds.). *Industrial Labor in the USSR*. New York: Pergamon Press, 1979.

Kerblay, B. *Modern Soviet Society*. London: Methuen, 1983.

Kharchev, A. *Marriage and Family Relations in the USSR*. Moscow: 1965.

Kochan, L. (ed.) *The Jews in Russia Since 1917*. Oxford: Oxford University Press, 1978.

Kuzin, N.P. et al. *Education in the USSR*. Moscow: 1972.

Lane, Christel. *Christian Religion in the Soviet Union. A Sociological Study*. London: Allen and Unwin, 1978.

Lane, David. *The Socialist Industrial State*. London: Allen and Unwin, 1976.

Lapidus, G.W. *Women in Soviet Society*. Berkeley: University of California Press, 1978.

Littlejohn, Gary. *A Sociology of the Soviet Union*. London: Macmillan, 1984.

Matthews, M. *Class and Society in Soviet Russia*. London: Allen Lane, 1972.

Matthews, M. *Education in the Soviet Union*, London: Allen and Unwin, 1982.

Pravda, Alex. 'Is There a Soviet Working Class?' *Problems of Communism*, vol. 31, no. 6 (Nov – Dec. 1982), pp. 1 – 24.

Sacks, Michael Paul. *Women's Work in Soviet Russia*. New York: Praeger, 1976.

Smith, Hendrick. *The Russians*. London: Sphere Books, 1976.

Wesolowski, W. *Classes, Strata and Power*. London: Routledge and Kegan Paul, 1979.

Wilber, Charles K. *The Soviet Model and Underdeveloped Countries*. Chapel Hill: University of North Carolina Press, 1969.

Zajda, J.I. *Education in the USSR*. Oxford: Pergamon, 1980.

Basic

Allworth, E. *Ethnic Russia in the USSR. The Dilemma of Dominance*. New York: Pergamon, 1980.

'Basic Guidelines for the School Reform', *CDSP*, vol. 36, no. 18, 30 May 1984.

Besemeres, J.F. *Socialist Population Politics*. New York: M.E. Sharpe, 1980.

Bialer, S. *Stalin's Successors: Leadership, Stability and Change in the Soviet Union*. Cambridge: Cambridge University Press, 1980.

Bourdeaux, M. *Patriarch and Prophets*. London: Mowbrays, 1975.

Bronson, D.W. and B.S. Severin, 'Soviet Consumer Welfare: the Brezhnev Era'. Joint Economic Committee of the US Congress, *Soviet Economic Prospects for the Seventies*. Washington: Government Printing Office, 1973.

Chinn, J. *Manipulating Soviet Population Resources*. London: Macmillan, 1977.

Connor, W.D. *Socialism, Politics and Equality, Hierarchy and Change in Eastern Europe and the USSR*. New York: Columbia University Press, 1979.

DeWitt, N. *Education and Professional Employment in the USSR*. Washington: National Science Foundation, 1961.

Dobson, R.B. 'Social Status and Inequality of Access to Higher Education in the USSR'. In J. Karabel and A.H. Halsey, *Power and Ideology in Education*. New York: Oxford University Press, 1977.

Dodge, Norton. *Women in the Soviet Economy*. Baltimore: Johns Hopkins University Press, 1966.

Dunstan, J. *Paths to Excellence and the Soviet School*, Windsor: National Foundation for Educational Research, 1978.

d'Encausse, H.C. *Decline of an Empire: The Soviet Socialist Republics in Revolt*. New York: Newsweek, 1979.

Fitzpatrick, S. *Education and Social Mobility in the Soviet Union, 1921–1934*. Cambridge: Cambridge University Press, 1979.

Geiger, K. *The Family in Soviet Russia*. Cambridge, Mass.: Harvard University Press, 1968.

George, V. and N. Manning. *Socialism, Social Welfare and the Soviet Union*. London: Routledge and Kegan Paul, 1980.

Gordon, L.A. and A.K. Nazimova. 'The Productive Potential of the Soviet

Working Class: Tendencies and Problems of Development', *Soviet Sociology*, vol. 19, no. 4, 1981.

Hill, Ian. 'The End of the Soviet Peasantry?' *Soviet Studies*, vol. 27, 1975, pp. 109–127.

Inkeles, A. and R.A. Bauer. *The Soviet Citizen*. Cambridge, Mass.: Harvard University Press, 1959.

Jancar, Barbara W. 'Religious Dissent in the Soviet Union', in Rudolph Tökés (ed.). *Dissent in the USSR*. Baltimore: Johns Hopkins University Press, 1975, pp. 191–23.

Jones, E. and F.W. Grupp, 'Measuring Nationality Trends in the Soviet Union', *Slavic Review*, vol. 41, no. 1, Spring 1982, pp. 112–22.

Kahan, A. and B. Ruble, *Industrial Labor in the USSR*, New York: Pergamon Press, 1979.

Katz, Zev (ed.) *Handbook of Major Soviet Nationalities*. New York: The Free Press, 1975.

Kharchev, A.G. *Brak i sem'ya v SSSR*. Moscow, 1964 (1st edn.), 1979 (2nd edn.).

Kharchev, A.G. and M.S. Matskovski. *Sovremennaya sem'ya*, Moscow, 1978.

Lane, Christel, 'Some Explanations for the Persistence of Christian Religion in the Soviet Union', *Sociology*, vol. 8, 1974.

Lane, David and F. O'Dell. *Soviet Industrial Workers: Social Class, Education and Control*. Oxford: Martin Robertson, 1978.

McCagg, W.O. and B.D. Silver, *Soviet Asian Ethnic Frontiers*. Oxford: Pergamon Press, 1979.

Matthews, Mervyn. *Privilege in the Soviet Union*. London: Allen and Unwin, 1978.

Narodnoe khozyaystvo v SSSR za 60 let. Moscow, 1977.

Naselenie SSSR. Moscow, 1983.

Nove, A. and J.A. Newth. *The Soviet Middle East. A Model for Development*. London, Allen and Unwin, 1967.

Schroeder, G.E. and B. Severin. 'Soviet Consumption and Income Policies in Comparative Perspective'. Joint Economic Committee of the US Congress, *Soviet Economy in a New Perspective*, Washington: Government Printing Office, 1976, pp. 620–660.

Stalin, J.V. 'Marxism and the National Question', in *Collected Works*, vol. 2, Moscow, 1953.

Wiles, Peter, 'Recent Data on Soviet Income Distribution', *Survey* , 1975, no. 3, pp. 28–41.

Yanowitch, Murray and W.A. Fisher (eds.). *Social Stratification and Mobility in the USSR*. New York: International Arts and Sciences Press, 1973.

Yanowitch, Murray. *Social and Economic Inequality in the Soviet Union*. Oxford: Martin Robertson, 1977.

Zdravomyslov, A.G., V.P. Rozhin and A. Iadov. *Man and His Work: A Sociological Study*. New York: International Arts and Sciences Press, 1970.

Specialized

Arutyunyan, Yu. V. 'Sotsial'naya struktura sel'skogo naseleniya', *Voprosy filosofii*, no. 5, 1966, pp. 51–61.

Arutyunyan, Yu. V. 'Izmeneniya sotsial'noy struktury sovetskikh natsiy', *Istoriya SSSR*, no. 4 (1972).

Avis, George, 'Preparatory Divisions in Soviet Higher Education Establishments 1969–79', *Soviet Studies*, vol. 35, no. 1, 1983.

Bennigsen, A. and C. Lemercier-Quelquejay. *Islam in the Soviet Union*. London: Pall Mall, 1967.

Bennigsen, A. and M. Broxup, *The Islamic Threat to the Soviet State*, London: Croom Helm, 1983.

Bociurkiw, B.R. and J.W. Strong (eds.). *Religion and Atheism in the USSR and Eastern Europe*. London: Macmillan, 1975.

Bourdeaux, M. and P. Reddaway. 'Soviet Baptists Today', in *Survey*, no. 66.

Butler, W.E., *Studies on the Socialist Legal System* (vol. 2). New York: Oceana, 1981.

Cary, Charles D. 'Peer Groups in the Political Socialisation of Soviet Schoolchildren', *Social Science Quarterly*, September, 1974.

Chapman, J. 'Recent Trends in the Soviet Industrial Wage Structure', in Kahan and Ruble, *Industrial Labour in the USSR*, New York: Pergamon Press, 1979.

Chauncey, Henry (ed.). *Soviet Preschool Education*. 2 vols. New York: Holt, Rinehart and Winston, 1969.

Clem, R.S. *The Soviet West*. New York: Praeger, 1975.

Davis, C. and M. Feshback. *Rising Mortality in the USSR in the 1970s*. Washington: U.S. Bureau of the Census, 1980.

Dunstan, J. 'Developments in Soviet Education, 1975–79', *Journal of Russian Studies*, No. 39, 1980.

Dunstan, J. 'Soviet Boarding Education', in J. Brine et al. *Home, School and Leisure in the Soviet Union*. London: Allen and Unwin, 1980.

Dunstan, J. 'Soviet Moral Education in Theory and Practice', *Journal of Moral Education*, vol. 10, no. 3.

Feshback, M. and S. Rapawy, 'Soviet Population and Manpower Trends and Policies', *Soviet Economy in a New Perspective*, Washington: U.S. Congress, Joint Economic Committee, 1976.

Filippov, F.R. 'Deti v strane razvitogo sotsializma' *Sotsiologicheskie issledovaniya*, no. 4, 1979.

Graham, L.R. 'Reorganisation of the USSR Academy of Sciences', in P.H. Juviler and H.W. Morton, *Soviet Policy-Making*, London: Pall Mall, 1967.

Hodnett, G., *Leadership in the Soviet National Republics*: A Quantitative Study of Recruitment Policy. Ontario: Mosaic Press 1978, p. 40.

Holland, B. ' "A Woman's Right to Choose" in the Soviet Union', in J. Brine et al. *Home, School and Leisure in the Soviet Union*, London: Allen and Unwin, 1980.

Holubenko, M. 'The Soviet Working Class', *Critique* (Glasgow), no. 4, 1975.

Jones, E. and F. Grupp. 'Infant Mortality Trends in the Soviet Union', *Population and Development Review*, vol. 19, no. 2, 1983.

Jones, T.A. 'Modernisation and Education in the USSR', *Social Forces*, No. 2, 1978.

Kollontay, A. *Communism and the Family*. London: Workers' Socialist Federation, 1920.

Kon, I. 'Studying Sexual Behaviour in the USSR' (*Voprosy filosofii*, No. 10, 1981) in *CDSP*, vol. 33, 1981, no. 50.

Kon, I.S.'O sotsiologicheskoy interpretatsii seksual'nogo povedeniya', *Sotsiologicheskie issledovaniya*, no. 2, 1982.

Kosolapov, R.I., 'Class and National Relations in the Stage of Developed Socialism'. (*Sotsiologicheskie issledovaniya*, no. 4, 1982.) CDSP. vol. 34, no. 49 (Jan. 1983).

Kotliar, A.E. and S. Ya Turchaninova, 'The Educational and Occupational Skill Level of Industrial Workers', in *Problems of Economics*, 1981, vol. 24.

Lane, Christel. *The Rites of Rulers*. Cambridge: Cambridge University Press, 1981.

Lane, Christel. 'Russian Piety: Religious Commitment among Contemporary Russian Orthodox', *Journal for the Scientific Study of Religion*, vol. 14, 1975

Lane, David. 'Ethnic and Class Stratification in Soviet Kazakhstan, 1917–39', *Comparative Studies in Society and History*, vol. 17, no. 2, 1975, pp. 165–89.

Lenkii, G.E. *Power and Privilege. A Theory of Social Stratification*. New York: McGraw-Hill, 1966.

Lipset, S.M. and R.B. Dobson. 'Social Stratification and Sociology in the Soviet Union', *Survey*, vol. 19, Summer 1973.

'Love, Sex, Marriage: Changing Times', *Current Digest of the Soviet Press*, vol. 28, no. 15, 12 May 1976.

McAuley, Alastair. *Economic Welfare in the Soviet Union*. London: Allen and Unwin, 1979.

Mickiewicz, E. *Soviet Political Schools*. New Haven: Yale University Press, 1967.

Mukhachev, V.I. and V.S. Borovik, *Rabochi klass i upravlenie proizvodstvom*. Moscow: 1975.

Novikova, E.E., U.S. Iazykova and Z.A. Iankova. 'Women's Work and the Family', in *Problems of Economics*, vol. 24, 1981.

O'Dell, F. *Socialization Though Children's Literature*. Cambridge: Cambridge University Press, 1978.

Osipov, G. *Rabochi klass i tekhnicheski progress*. Moscow: 1965.

Pennar, Jaan, I.I. Bakalo, G.Z.F. Bereday, *Modernisation and Diversity in Soviet Education*. New York: Praeger, 1971.

Perevedentsev, V.I. 'Population Reproduction and the Family'. Abstract in *CDSP*, vol. 34, no. 19.

Pravda, A. 'Spontaneous Workers' Activities in the Soviet Union', in A. Kahan and B. Ruble, *Industrial Labor in the USSR*, New York: Pergamon Press, 1979.

Rabkina. N.E. and I.M. Rimashhevskaya. *Osnovy differentssiya zarabotnoy platy i dokhodov naseleniya*. Moscow. 1972.

Rigby, T.H. 'The Soviet Regional Leadership: The Brezhnev Generation', *Slavic Review*, March 1978.

Rywkin, M. 'Central Asia and Soviet Manpower'. *Problems of Communism*. Vol. 28, 1979.

Sedugin, P. *New Soviet Legislation on Marriage and the Family*. Moscow: Progress, 1973.

Shkaratan, O.I. *Problemy sotsial'noy struktury rabochego klassa SSSR*. Moscow: 1970.

Shubkin, V.N. 'Molodezh' vstupaet v zhizn'', *Voprosy filosofii*, no. 5, May 1965, pp. 57–70.

Shubkin, V.N. 'Social Mobility and Choice of Occupation', in G.V. Osipov (ed.) *Industry and Labour in the USSR*. London: Tavistock, 1966, pp. 86–98.

Silver, Brian D., 'Levels of Sociocultural Development among Soviet Nationalities: A Partial Test of the Equalisation Hypothesis', *American Political Science Review*, vol. 68 (1974).

Soper, J. 'Unofficial Islam: A Muslim Minority in the USSR. *Religion in Communist Lands*, vol. 4, 1979.

Sotsial'naya struktura razvitogo sotsialisticheskogo obshchestva v SSSR (Moscow, 1976).

Sotsiologiya v SSSR, vols. 1 and 2. Moscow, 1982.

'Soviet Feminism – What Future for Marxism?' *Women in Eastern Europe*, no. 4, 1981.

Sysenko, V.A. 'Razvody: dinamika, motivy, posledstviya', *Sotsiologicheskie issledovaniya*, no. 2, 1982.

Teckenberg, W. 'The Social Structure of the Working Class'. *International Journal of Sociology*, vol. XI, no. 4, 1981–82.

Titma, M.Kh., *Vybor professii kak sotsial'naya problema*. Moscow: 1975.

Trud v SSSR. Statisticheski sbornik. Moscow: 1968.

Tsentral'noe statisticheskoe upravlenie.

> *Itogi vsesoyuznoy perepisi naseleniya 1959g. SSSR* (svodny tom). Moscow, 1962.

> *Itogi vsesoyuznoy perepisi naseleniya 1970g.* (Vols. 2 and 7). Moscow, 1972.

> *Narodnoe khozyaystvo SSSR za 60 let*. Moscow, 1977.

> *Narodnoe khozyaystvo SSSR 1922–1982*, Moscow, 1982.

> *Zhenshchiny i deti v SSSR*. Moscow, 1969.

> 'Zhenshchiny v SSSR', *Vestnik statistiki*, no. 1, 1981.

> *Zhenshchiny v SSSR*. Moscow, 1983.

Vasil'eva, E.K. *The Young People of Leningrad*. New York: IASP, 1975.

Vysshee obrazovanie v SSSR. Moscow, 1961.

'Why Small Families are Proliferating'. *CDSP*, vol. 33, no. 9, 1981.

Wiles, P. and S. Markowski. 'Income Distribution under Communism and Capitalism', *Soviet Studies*, vol. 22, 1971.

Zhdanko, T.A. 'Sedentarisation of the Nomads of Central Asia, including Kazakhstan, under the Soviet Regime', in *International Labour Review*, no. 93, 1966, pp. 601–20.

Zhdanko, T.A. 'Everyday Life in a Karakalpak Kolkhoz aul', *Sovetskaya Etnografiya*, no. 2, 1949, in R. Schlesinger, *The Nationalities Problem and Soviet Administration*. London: Routledge and Kegan Paul, 1956, pp. 280–94.

APPENDIX A

The Soviet Government
USSR Council of Ministers

PRESIDIUM OF THE USSR COUNCIL OF MINISTERS

CHAIRMAN OF THE USSR COUNCIL OF MINISTERS (1)

FIRST DEPUTY CHAIRMEN (3)

DEPUTY CHAIRMEN (11)

Including: Chairman, USSR State Planning Committee (Gosplan)

USSR Representative, Council for Mutual Economic Assistance (Comecon)

Chairman, USSR State Committee for Science and Technology

Chairman, USSR State Committee for Material and Technical Supply

Chairman, USSR State Committee for Construction Affairs

Chairman, Commission for Presidium of USSR Council of Ministers for Foreign Economic Questions

Chairman, Military-Industrial Commission of Presidium of USSR Council of Ministers

OTHER MEMBERS OF THE COUNCIL OF MINISTERS

(U) = Union Republic Organizations* (A) = All-Union Organizations

Minister of Agriculture (U)
Minister of Automotive Industry(A)
Minister of the Aviation Industry (A)
Minister of the Chemical Industry (A)
Minister of Chemical and Petroleum Machine Building (A)
Minister of Civil Aviation (A)

* The All-Union Ministries govern the branch of state administration entrusted to them throughout the territory of the USSR either directly or through bodies appointed by them. According to Article 76 of the USSR Constitution, the Union Republic Ministries, as a rule, direct the branches of state administration entrusted to them through the relevant Ministries of the Union Republics; they administer directly only a certain limited number of enterprises according to a list approved by the Presidium of the Supreme Soviet of the USSR.

Minister of the Coal Industry (U)
Minister of Communications (U)
Minister of the Communications Equipment Industry (A)
Minister of Construction (U)
Minister of Construction of Heavy Industry Enterprises (U)
Minister of the Construction Materials Industry (U)
Minister of Construction of Petroleum and Gas Industry Enterprises (A)
Minister of Construction, Road, and Municipal Machine Building (A)
Minister of Culture (U)
Minister of Defence (U)
Minister of the Defence Industry (A)
Minister of Education (U)
Minister of the Electrical Equipment Industry (A)
Minister of the Electronics Industry (A)
Minister of Ferrous Metallurgy (U)
Minister of Finance (U)
Minister of the Fish Industry (U)
Minister of the Food Industry (U)
Minister of Foreign Affairs (U)
Minister of Foreign Trade (A)
Minister of the Gas Industry (A)
Minister of General Machine Building (A)
Minister of Geology (U)
Minister of Health (U)
Minister of Heavy and Transport Machine Building (A)
Minister of Higher and Secondary Specialized Education (U)
Minister of Industrial Construction (U)
Minister of Installation and Special Construction Work (U)
Minister of Instrument-making, Automation Equipment, and Control Systems (A)
Minister of Internal Affairs (U)
Minister of Justice (U)
Minister of Land Reclamation and Water Resources (U)
Minister of Light Industry (U)
Minister of Machine Building (A)
Minister of Machine Building for Cattle Raising and Fodder Production (A)
Minister of Machine Building for Light and Food Industry and Household
    Appliances (A)
Minister of the Machine Tool and Tool Building Industry (A)
Minister of the Maritime Fleet (A)
Minister of the Meat and Dairy Industry (U)
Minister of the Medical Industry (A)
Minister of Medium Machine Building (A)
Minister of Nonferrous Metallurgy (U)
Minister of the Petroleum Industry (A)
Minister of the Petroleum Refining and Petrochemical Industry (U)
Minister of Power and Electrification (U)

Minister of Power Machine Building (A)
Minister of Procurement (U)
Minister of the Pulp and Paper Industry (A)
Minister of the Radio Industry (A)
Minister of Railways (A)
Minister of Rural Construction (U)
Minister of the Shipbuilding Industry (A)
Minister of the Timber and Wood Processing Industry (U)
Minister of Tractor and Agricultural Machine Building (A)
Minister of Trade (U)
Minister of Transport Construction (A)
Chairman, State Committee for Cinematography (Goskino USSR) (U)
Chairman, State Committee for Construction Affairs (Gosstroi USSR) (U)
Chairman, State Committee for Foreign Economic Relations (GKES) (A)
Chairman, State Committee for Forestry (Gosleskhoz USSR) (U)
Chairman, State Committee for Inventions and Discoveries (A)
Chairman, State Committee for Labour and Social Questions (Goskomtrud USSR) (U)
Chairman, State Committee for Material and Technical Supply (Gossnab USSR) (U)
Chairman, State Planning Committee (Gosplan USSR) (U)
Chairman, State Committee for Prices (Goskomtsen USSR) (U)
Chairman, State Committee for Publishing Houses, Printing Plants, and the Book Trade (Goskomizdat USSR) (U)
Chairman, State Committee for Science and Technology (GKNT) (A)
Chairman, State Committee for Standards (Gosstandard USSR) (A)
Chairman, State Committee for Television and Radio Broadcasting (Gosteleradio USSR) (U)
Chairman, State Committee for Vocational and Technical Education (U)
Chairman, Committee for People's Control (U)
Chairman, Committee for State Security (KGB) (U)
Chief, Central Statistical Administration (TsSU USSR) (U)
Chairman, *Soyuzsel'khoztekhnika* (U) (Association for the Sale of Agricultural Equipment and the Organization of Machinery Repairs and Utilization)
Chairman of Board, USSR State Bank (Gosbank USSR)
Chairman, Armenian SSR Council of Ministers*
Chairman, Azerbaijan SSR Council of Ministers
Chairman, Byelorussian SSR Council of Ministers
Chairman, Estonian SSR Council of Ministers
Chairman, Georgian SSR Council of Ministers
Chairman, Kazak SSR Council of Ministers
Chairman, Kirghiz SSR Council of Ministers
Chairman, Latvian SSR Council of Ministers

* According to Article 128 of the 1977 USSR Constitution, the Council of Ministers of the USSR includes the Chairmen of the Councils of Ministers of the Union Republics ex-officio.

Chairman, Lithuanian SSR Council of Ministers
Chairman, Moldavian SSR Council of Ministers
Chairman, RSFSR Council of Ministers
Chairman, Tajik SSR Council of Ministers
Chairman, Turkmen SSR Council of Ministers
Chairman, Ukrainian SSR Council of Ministers
Chairman, Uzbek SSR Council of Ministers

HEADS OF ORGANS OF THE USSR COUNCIL OF MINISTERS NOT HAVING MINISTERIAL STATUS

Administrator, Administration of Affairs of the Council of Ministers
Chief Arbiter, State Board of Arbitration (Gosarbitrazh) (U)
Chief, Main Archives Administration (GAU)
Chairman, State Committee for Utilization of Atomic Energy
Board Chairman, All-Union Bank for Financing Capital Investments (Stroibank)
Chairman, Higher Certification Commission (VAK) (A)
Chief, Main Administration of Geodesy and Cartography (GUGK)
Chief, Main Administration of Hydrometerological Service (Glavgidrometsluzhba USSR)
Chief, Main Administration of the Microbiological Industry
Chairman, Commission for the Establishment of Personal Pensions
Chairman, Committee for Physical Culture and Sports (U)
Chairman, Committee for Lenin Prizes and State Prizes in Literature, Art, and Architecture
Chairman, Committee for Lenin Prizes and State Prizes in Science and Technology
Chairman, Council for Religious Affairs
Chief, Main Administration of State Material Reserves (GUGMR)
Chief, Main Administration for Safeguarding State Secrets in the Press (Glavlit) (U)
Chairman, State Commission for Stockpiling Useful Minerals (GKZ) (A)
Chairman, State Committee for Supervision of Safe Working Practices in Industry and for Mine Supervision (Gosgortekhnadzor) (U)
Director General, Telegraph Agency of the Soviet Union (TASS) (U)
Chief, Main Administration for Foreign Tourism (Glavinturist USSR) (U)

HEADS OF OTHER ORGANS

Chairman, Main Committee for Exhibition of Achievements of the National Economy (VDNKh) (headed by a Deputy Chairman of the USSR Council of Ministers)
Chairman, State Committee for Civil Construction and Architecture (Gosgrazhdanstroi) (A) (subordinate to State Committee for Construction Affairs above)
Source: Based on *Radio Liberty* research. RL 95/77.
For a list of those elected in April 1984, sec. *Current Digest of The Soviet Press*, vol. 36, no. 15, pp. 15–16.

APPENDIX B

Population Statistics

Basic Population Data of USSR

Total Population

	Total (Mills)	Urban (Mills)	Rural (Mills)	Percentage of total Urban %	Percentage of total Rural %
1897	124.6	18.4	106.2	15	85
1913	159.2	28.5	130.7	18	82
*1926	147.0	26.3	120.7	18	82
*1929	153.0	28.7	124.7	19	81
1940	194.1	63.1	131.0	33	67
1950	178.5	69.4	109.1	39	61
1960	212.3	103.8	108.5	49	51
1971	243.5	139.1	104.8	57	43
1980	264.5	166.2	98.3	63	37
1981	266.6	168.8	97.8	63	37
1983	271.2	174.6	96.6	64	36

* Figures for 1926 and 1929 refer to borders of USSR before 17 September 1939. All other dates refer to area encompassed by present borders.

Changes in the Sex Ratio in the USSR

	Total (Mills)	Male (Mills)	Female (Mills)	Percentage of total Male %	Percentage of total Female %
1926	147.0	71.0	76.0	48.3	51.7
1939	170.6	81.7	88.9	47.9	52.1
1959	208.8	94.0	114.8	45.0	55.0
1970	241.7	111.4	130.3	46.1	53.9
1980	264.5	123.4	141.1	46.7	53.3
1983	271.2	126.9	144.3	46.8	53.2

Birth and Death Rates and Natural Increase in Population of the USSR

Year	Per 1,000 of the Population			No. of deaths, per 1,000 of population, of children under 1 year
	No. born	No. of deaths	Natural Increase	
1913 (within frontiers of USSR up to 17/9/39) (within	47.0	30.2	16.8	273
contemporary frontiers of USSR)	45.5	29.1	16.4	269
1926	44.0	20.3	23.7	174
1928	44.3	23.3	21.0	182
1938	37.5	17.5	20.0	161
1940	31.2	18.0	13.2	182
1950	26.7	9.7	17.0	81
1960	24.9	7.1	17.8	35
1970	17.4	8.2	9.2	25
1980	18.3	10.3	8.0	27.9*
1982	19.0	10.1	8.9	—

* Figure for 1974.

Population Distribution in the Republics of the USSR (thousands)

	1913	1940 (1 Jan)	1959 (1 Jan)	1976 (1 Jan)	1983 (1 Jan)
USSR (Total)	159,153	194,077	208,827	255,524	271,203
RSFSR (Russian Federation)	89,902	110,098	117,534	134,650	140,952
Ukraine	35,210	41,340	41,869	49,075	50,456
Byelorussia	6,899	9,046	8,055	9,371	9,806
Uzbekistan	4,366	6,645	8,261	14,079	17,044
Kazakhstan	5,565	6,054	9,154	14,337	15,470
Georgia	2,601	3,612	4,044	4,954	5,137
Azerbaidzhan	2,339	3,274	3,698	5,689	6,400
Lithuania	2,828	2,925	2,711	3,315	3,504
Moldavia	2,056	2,468	2,885	3,850	4,053
Latvia	2,473	1,886	2,093	2,497	2,568
Kirghizistan	864	1,528	2,066	3,368	3,803
Tadzhikistan	1,034	1,525	1,981	3,486	4,236
Armenia	1,000	1,320	1,763	2,834	3,222
Turkmenia	1,042	1,302	1,516	2,581	3,045
Estonia	954	1,054	1,197	1,438	1,507

APPENDIX C

The Soviet National Anthem (1977)

Linked up eternally, Republics standing free,
Surviving for ever, great USSR.
Children of Russ-i-a, strong in adversity
Born of a people entrenched near and far.

CHORUS
Fame's flame long burning, sustaining our Motherland,
Friend to all the nations, strong bulwark of right;
Forceful and fearless in the spirit of Lenin,
Speeding the victory of Communist might.
Freedom's sun never dimmed, while we survive ever on
Led through the tempest time by Lenin the Great;
Rousing up nations, making the blindest see,
Marking the open path to freedom's broad gate.
All clear, far ahead, see our fortune and future
Unperished and safe in our Communist hands,
Faithful and steadfast, through pain and endurance,
Behind the Red Banner as proudly it stands.

APPENDIX D

Statute Concerning Artisan Trades of Individual Citizens

1. An artisan trade (*kustarno-remeslennyi promysel*) of individual citizens is the activity of making articles for sale to the population, as well as the furnishing of consumer (*bytovye*) services for payment.

The conduct of any trade with the use of hired labor is prohibited.

2. All artisan trades may be conducted on the territory of the USSR, except those that are prohibited by this Statute or by other laws of the USSR or the union republics.

3. Throughout the USSR, citizens are forbidden to conduct the following kinds of artisan trades:

(a) the processing of agricultural or other food products, whether purchased or customer furnished, including the preparation of any food articles and any beverages (whether in finished or semifinished form);

(b) the making or repair of any kind of weapon, the making of ammunition, explosives, or pyrotechnical articles;

(c) the making of duplicating or copying devices, any kinds of seals, [rubber] stamps, or type, [and] the duplication of any kind of printed or photographed matter, phonograph records, cinematographic films, and magnetic recordings;

(d) the making of plates or dies for medals or tokens;

(e) the making of chemical, toiletry, and cosmetic articles;

(f) the making of poisonous articles and narcotics, and of any medicines or medical devices;

(g) the processing and dyeing of leather, hide, and fur materials, and the making of articles from the skins of valuable fur-bearing animals, which carry no government brand (stamp) and therefore are liable for compulsory delivery to the state in accordance with legislation of union republics;

(h) the carrying of passengers and freight by any means of transport (except [small] boats, horses, and other animals, if so permitted by local government authority);

(i) the operation of boarding houses, bathhouses, gambling establishments, any kind of amusements, and the organization of shows;

(j) the making of articles from precious or nonferrous metals, precious stones, or amber, and of articles using such materials, and the repair or rebuilding of said articles using own precious or nonferrous metals, precious stones, or amber; and

(k) the making of candles, icons, and ecclesiastical articles. In addition, Councils of Ministers of union republics may prohibit the conduct of other artisan trades by citizens, if the development of such trades may harm the interests of society.

From *Sobranie postanovelenii pravitel'stva SSSR*, 1976,: 7, No. 39.

*   *   *   *   *   *   *   *

The following extract names some of those artisan trades which are allowed, and those for which no license is required.

Among permitted trades are, for instance, the blacksmith's trade, engraving, barber's and manicurist's trade, photography and making of photo-portraits, repair of automobiles, motorcycles, motor scooters, motor buggies, mopeds, bicycles, television sets, loudspeakers, clocks and watches, fountain pens, etc. ...Citizens desiring to pursue artisan trades must obtain...special licenses. ...No licenses are required for the sale of articles made from the agricultural produce of one's own subsidiary garden, or the sale of articles of artisan trades produced under contract with state and cooperative enterprises, institutions, and organizations. Also, no license is required for the rendering of services of a household nature (sawing and chopping firewood, washing of clothes in the home without installation of any special laundering facilities, the washing of floors and windows, etc.).

From *Izvestiia*, 6 August 1977, p. 2.

Source: Soviet Economy in a Time of Change. (Vol. 1.) Joint Economic Committee, US Congress, Washington DC (1979), pp. 854–5.

APPENDIX E

Tax Rates on Income of Manual and Non-manual Workers

Tax on Income of Blue- and White-collar Workers at their Main Place of Employment

Monthly income	Tax payable	Monthly income	Tax Payable
up to 70 rubles	none	84 rubles	4.77 rubles
71 rubles	0.25 rubles	85 rubles	5.11 rubles
72 rubles	0.59 rubles	86 rubles	5.45 rubles
73 rubles	0.93 rubles	87 rubles	5.79 rubles
74 rubles	1.30 rubles	88 rubles	6.13 rubles
75 rubles	1.65 rubles	89 rubles	6.47 rubles
76 rubles	2.00 rubles	90 rubles	6.81 rubles
77 rubles	2.39 rubles	91 rubles	7.12 rubles
78 rubles	2.73 rubles	92–100 rubles	7.12 rubles + 12% of income above 91 rubles
89 rubles	3.07 rubles		
80 rubles	3.41 rubles		
81 rubles	3.75 rubles	101 rubles and more	8.20 rubles + 13% of income above 100 rubles.
82 rubles	4.09 rubles		
83 rubles	4.43 rubles		

Source: Vedomosti Verkhovnogo Soveta SSSR, no. 43 (1983). Cited in RL (Munich 1982) 452/82

APPENDIX F

'Basic School Rules for Pupils'

First to Third Classes

1 Study diligently. Listen attentively to the teacher's explanations and try hard independently to do all the tasks she sets you. Behave well in class. Don't be late for lessons.
2 Participate in physical work and the business of your class. Help your comrades to study and work better.
3 Respect school and other public property, your own things and those of your comrades. Protect plants and animals.
4 Do your gymnastic exercises every day. Always be clean and neat.
5 Read a lot. Participate in clubs.
6 Observe a daily routine. Use your leisure time to advantage.
7 Be an example to others in school, at home, on the street. When you meet teachers, other school workers, acquaintances and friends, greet them politely. Give way to older people and give up your seat to them. Observe the Highway Code.
8 Listen to your parents and the older members of the family, help them at home. Be friendly to your comrades and look after small children.
9 Do what your teachers and the duty monitors request.

Fourth to Eighth Classes

1 Master your schoolwork with determination. Study and work hard. Be attentive and active at lessons.
2 Work for the good of the community in school and at home. When carrying out physical work, carefully observe the safety rules.
3 Take an active part in the social work of the class and the school.
4 Take care of national property. Look after things, protect nature, keep the country clean.
5 Do exercises and sport. Observe the rules of personal hygiene.
6 In your free time, do useful things – read, be creative technically and artistically, play sensible games.
7 Respect your own and other people's time. Be punctual. Follow an established daily routine.

8 Behave in an exemplary way. Be modest, polite, attentive, neatly dressed. Strictly observe the Highway Code.

9 Respect your parents. Help them at home.

10 Conscientiously carry out the instruction of your teachers, other school workers and also carry out the decisions of the pupil self-government committees.

Ninth to Tenth (Eleventh) Classes

1 Master the foundations of science and the skills of self-education with determination and perseverance.

2 Take an active part in socially useful labour. Prepare yourself for the conscious choice of a job. In doing labour tasks, strictly observe safety rules.

3 Take an active part in the social and cultural life of your school, town, village and the work of the pupil self-government committees.

4 Concern yourself with the protection and growth of the national wealth, the riches of nature.

5 Systematically practise physical culture and sport. Strengthen yourself. Prepare yourself for the defence of the Soviet Motherland.

6 Master modern culture and technology. Develop your skills in different fields of activity.

7 Plan and use your time sensibly. Be punctual. Learn how to organize your work correctly.

8 Live according to the norms of a socialist community. Be a worthy example of good behaviour to your younger comrades. Be intolerant towards amoral and anti-social activities.

9 Help to strengthen the school collective, preserve and develop its useful traditions. Be a principled and honourable comrade.

10 Respect your parents. Show a constant regard for all members of the family. Help with the housework.

11 Respect your teachers' work. Carry out and actively support the teachers' requests and the decisions of the organs of pupil self-government.

Source: Spavochnik klassnogo rukovoditelya (1979), pp. 100 – 102. My thanks to Felicity O'Dell for this translation.

GLOSSARY

Anti-Party Group	Applied to those who, in 1957, tried to unseat Khrushchev. Molotov, Kaganovich, Malenkov, and Shepilov are among the best known individuals identified with it.
Apparat	Apparatus, staff. The top officials of the CPSU or of the government.
Apparatchik	A member of the apparatus: a Party functionary.
ASSR	Autonomous Soviet Socialist Republic.
AUCCTU	All-Union Central Committee of Trade Unions.
AUCECB	All-Union Council of the Evangelical Christians and Baptists.
Bolsheviks	Faction of Russian Social-Democratic Labour Party led by Lenin. In 1918 formed into Communist Party (Bolsheviks).
CCTU	Central Council of Trade Unions.
CDSP	Current Digest of the Soviet Press, Published weekly.
COMECON	Council of Economic Mutual Assistance. Formed in 1949 with the purpose of improving socialist economic co-operation. Membership includes the USSR, the socialist states of East Europe and Mongolia.
Cominform	Communist Information Bureau. Established September 1947, abolished April 1956.
Comintern	Communist International. 1919–43.
CPSU	Communist Party of the Soviet Union (in Russian, KPSS).
Desyatina	Measure of area: one desyatina equals 2.7 acres.
Duma	Name of advisory assembly in Tsarist Russia. There were Town Dumas and the State Duma.
Edinonachalie	One-man management.

Gorispolkom	Executive Committee of a City (Town) Soviet.
Gorkom	City Party Committee.
Gosbank	State Bank.
Gosplan	State Planning Committee (Commission).
Hectare	Area equal to 10,000 square metres or 2.471 acres.
Ispolkom	Executive Committee.
KGB	Committee of State Security.
Kolkhoz	Collective Farm. Co-operative form of agricultural production.
Komsomol	YCL. Young Communist League. (Full title – All-Union Communist League of Youth).
Kray	Territory. A large sparsely populated, administrative region.
Kraykom	Territorial Party Committee.
Kremlinology	A process of forecasting based on indexes of Soviet protocol (e.g. order of appearance of names).
Kulak	Rich peasant.
Mensheviks	Non-Leninist faction of Russian Socialist Democratic Labour Party. Favoured trade union type and decentralized form of party.
Mestnichestvo	Localism, regionalism. Pursuit of local interests at the expense of national interests.
Mir	See Obshchina
MTS	Machine-Tractor Station. Until 1958 the government owned and operated MTS's which supplied the collectives with agricultural equipment.
MVD	Ministry of Internal Affairs.
Narkhoz SSSR	*Narodnoe khozyastvo SSSR*. The Statistical Handbook of the USSR, published annually.
Narodniki	Populists. Nineteenth – century revolutionaries.
NEP	New Economic Policy. Practised by Bolsheviks between 1921 and 1928. Allowed limited private enterprise and trade.
NKGB	People's Commissariat of State Security.
NKVD	People's Commissariat of Internal Affairs.
Nomenklatura	Appointment list controlled directly or indirectly by the Party.
NTO	Scientific Organization of Labour.
Oblast	Province, region.
Oblispolkom	Executive Committee of Province Soviet.
Obkom	Region or Province Party Committee.
Obshchenarodnoe	State of the whole people. (Official description of

gosudarstvo	the Soviet State since 1961).
Obshchina	A village community, a commune (in Tsarist Russia).
Okrug	Area, district.
Politbureau	Supreme body of CPSU. Called Presidium between 1952 and 1966.
Partiynost	Party allegiance; party spirit.
Plenum	Full assembly of all members (e.g. of the Central Committee of the Communist Party).
Provisional Government	Established after abdication of Nicholas II in February 1917. Overthrown by Bolsheviks in October 1917.
Rayon	District; an administrative division of a region, territory, republic, or large city.
Rayispolkom	Executive Committee of District Soviet.
Raykom	District Party Committee.
RSFSR	Russian Soviet Federative Socialist Republic.
RTS	Tractor Repair Station.
Samizdat	Illegal 'do it yourself' publications.
Sovkhoz	State Farm. Organized on same principles as industrial enterprise.
Sovnarkom	Council of People's Commissars.
Sovnarkhoz	Council of National Economy. Established on a regional basis in May 1957.
USSR	Union of Soviet Socialist Republics.
USSR Council of Ministers	Highest executive and administrative branch in the Soviet Union. Has power to issue decrees and is subject to ratification by the Supreme Soviet.
USSR Presidium of the Supreme Soviet	Elected by the Supreme Soviet, the Presidium of the Supreme Soviet is in full power while the Supreme Soviet is not in session.
USSR Supreme Soviet	The highest legislative body in the USSR. It consists of two Houses, the Council (or Soviet) of the Union and the Council (or Soviet) of Nationalities.
VOIR	All-Union Society of Inventors and Rationalizers.
VSNKH (Vesenkha)	Supreme Economic Council.

INDEX